The
Wildest
Dream

The Biography of
George
Mallory

Peter & Leni Gillman

THE
MOUNTAINEERS

Published by
The Mountaineers Books
1001 SW Klickitat Way, Suite 201
Seattle, WA 98134

First North American Edition, 2000

Manufactured in the United States of America

Project Editor: Kathleen Cubley
Design and typography by Amy Winchester
Cover design by Helen Cherullo
Maps by ML Design

Cover photograph: George Mallory, 1911. (Photo by Duncan Grant © Henrietta Garnett/ Tate Gallery)

Library of Congress Cataloging-in-Publication Data on file

♻ Printed on recycled paper

To Blake, Ben, and Orla

⚭

Contents

Acknowledgments

George Mallory's life covered a canvas whose breadth we had scarcely imagined when we started our research. We gratefully acknowledge the help of a wide range of people who assisted us with great goodwill and generosity. We wish to make clear that the conclusions we reached are, of course, our own.

Our greatest thanks go to the family and descendants of George Mallory for their help and their hospitality, and for drawing on their individual and collective memories of family history, buttressed by a range of documents. In particular we thank: Clare Millikan and her sons George and Rick Millikan; John Mallory, his daughter and son-in-law, Virginia and Frank Arnott, and his son George Mallory II; George Mallory's niece Mollie and her daughter Sally Dalglish; his son-in-law David Robertson and his wife, Harriet; his nephew Ben, Ben's wife, Stella, and their son, Mike Longridge. We were especially saddened that Ben Longridge died before we had completed our book.

We owe particular thanks to other writers in our field. We have already mentioned David Robertson, George Mallory's son-in-law and the author of the 1969 biography, and thank him and his wife, Harriet, again. John Cleare, mountaineering photographer, writer, and sage provided copious detailed information and advice. Audrey Salkeld, co-author of *The Mystery of Mallory and Irvine* and *Last Climb*, and the most assiduous Everest researcher of all, once again shared her knowledge and expertise. We also received generous help from Tristam and Bill Pye, sons of the first Mallory biographer, David Pye; Walt Unsworth, author of the definitive history, *Everest*; Tom Holzel, coauthor of *The Mystery of Mallory and Irvine*; Jochen Hemmleb, coauthor of *Ghosts of Everest*; Dudley Green, author of the 1990 illustrated biography; and Jim Smith, author of *Everest, the Man and the Mountain*.

We should also like to thank the following people for their generous assistance in key areas of our research.

At Mobberley, Rick and Alex Ellison were most hospitable in allowing us to visit Newton Hall and immensely helpful in the further research they conducted into the history of the Leigh-Mallory and Jebb families. We were helped in respect of St. Wilfrid's church by Canon Howard Randle, Anne Davidson, and Tim Hall.

For information about Winchester College, we were helped by Dr. James Sabben-Clare, Dr. James Webster, and Mark Feltham.

At Magdalene College, Cambridge, librarians Dr. Richard Luckett, Aude Fitzsimons, and Bridget Alexander gave us their unstinting help. We thank the Master and Fellows of Magdalene College for giving permission to quote from the voluminous letters written by George and Ruth Mallory held in the library, and from the diaries of A. C. Benson. Dr. Elizabeth Leedham-Green, archivist at Cambridge University Library, and Michael Richardson of the Board of Continuing Education provided details of Mallory's employment by the Cambridge University Examination and Lectures Syndicate. Professor Richard Eden of Clare Hall and Malcolm Underwood, archivist of St. John's College, helped us with information about Herschel House and Mallory's lecturing work, and Mike Petty provided further assistance.

Marcia Newbolt gave us assistance and information about her father, Geoffrey Winthrop Young, and most generously gave us permission to quote from his published and private writings.

At the Alpine Club, we thank the librarian, Margaret Ecclestone, for her patient and tireless help, together with club secretary Sheila Harrison and archivists Bob Lawford and Livia Gollancz. The *Alpine Journal* offers an unparalleled record of mountaineering events that was of enormous benefit to us. For further climbing information we were greatly assisted by Ray Wood and the article by Martin Crook published in *High* magazine in December 1999. Derek Walker helped to identify the Birkenhead quarry where George Mallory fractured his ankle in 1909.

For the Bloomsbury period, Richard Shone, writer on the Bloomsbury group and curator of the Tate's 1999 Bloomsbury exhibition, provided invaluable help and advice, particularly in respect of Duncan Grant. Henrietta Garnett, granddaughter of Duncan Grant, generously gave access to her archive and permission to quote from Duncan Grant's letters. We thank the Society of Authors for giving us permission on behalf of the Strachey Trust to quote from the writings of James and Lytton Strachey; and the Provost and Scholars of King's College, Cambridge, for permission to quote from the letters of Maynard Keynes. For further help we also thank Michael Holroyd, biographer of Lytton Strachey; Frances Spurling, biographer of Duncan Grant; Nigel Jones, biographer of Rupert Brooke; and Keith Hale, editor of the Rupert Brooke-James Strachey correspondence. Sara Walden and Sue Bastable conducted invaluable research in Provence.

Acknowledgments

Joanna Gordon, executor of Mary Anne O'Malley's estate, and Benita Stoney, her biographer, provided generous access to her diaries and other writings and Joanna Gordon has kindly allowed us to quote from these.

At Godalming, we were helped by Bill and Mary Brister and by Hilda Haig Brown, the granddaughter of a former Charterhouse headmaster, who assisted with historical background and memories. At Charterhouse, historians and archivists Shirley Corke, Sue Cole, and Margaret Mardall provided details of George Mallory's career at the school. Marianne Nevel kindly showed us her archives and photographs concerning her late husband Franz Nevel and the Mallorys. Ruth Brown was most hospitable in allowing us to visit Westbrook. For further information we thank Lucy Grindley, who lent us her thesis "The Life and Work of Thackeray Turner," written for an AA Diploma in Conservation in Historic Buildings, and Jeremy Musson of *Country Life*. We thank Paul Morgan, Ruth Mallory's nephew and the son of "Auntie Mill," for kindly allowing us to reproduce one of his mother's watercolors.

At the Royal Geographical Society we were helped by Huw Thomas and Joanna Scadden, the picture librarian. We gratefully acknowledge permission from the society to quote from letters and other documents in its extensive Everest archives.

Sandra Mail, daughter of John Noel, supplied both information and photographs taken by her father. Peter Odell, grandson of Noel Odell, and David Somervell, son of Howard Somervell, were also most helpful.

Blyth Wright of the Sportscotland Avalanche Information Service and Alan Dennis, former coordinator of the Canadian Avalanche Center, provided their expert appraisal of the 1922 avalanche on the North Col. Andy Heald conducted research on our behalf in the archives of the Climbers Club in Caernarvon. Roger Croston, who found a Mallory letter on the day his body was reported to have been discovered, provided invaluable information about Mallory and the Union of the League of Nations. Michael Papworth of Hunter and Krageloh provided useful research help as well as supplying books. Tom Barron conducted research in the New York Public Library. Patrick Deale and Marie Tieche of the National Motor Museum at Beaulieu supplied helpful information, as did Roly Smith.

Julie Summers, great-niece of Sandy Irvine, generously provided information and photographs and helped us to a fuller understanding of his character. We are pleased to acknowledge the work of the Sandy Irvine Trust, a nonprofit organization dedicated to preserving his name and establishing the Sandy Irvine archive. At Merton College, Oxford, librarians Dr. Sarah Bendall and Fiona Wilkes gave their help. We thank both the Sandy Irvine Trust and the Warden and Fellows of Merton College for permission to quote from Sandy Irvine's diary.

For information about Stella Cobden-Sanderson, we thank Marianne Tidcombe, biographer of Thomas Cobden-Sanderson, and Judy Faraday, archivist at the John Lewis Partnership archive collection.

For practical help, we thank Louise Falp of American Airlines. For further help, advice, and support we thank Seth Gillman, Danny Gillman, and Rose Croxford.

At The Mountaineers Books, custodians of the highest publishing standards, we thank Kathleen Cubley, Alison Koop, and Mary Metz.

Prologue

The great enemy, George Mallory told his wife, Ruth, was the wind. The men of the 1921 Everest expedition had met it as soon as they reached the great Tibetan plateau, a desolate and barren place, bordered by rolling hills, with snow peaks towering on the distant horizon. Usually at daybreak, as they struck camp and prepared to move off on their ponies and mules, the air was blessedly still. But the wind would soon build up, gathering strength in the hills, scything across the gray plain: a dry, incessant wind, George wrote, cutting through their clothes, driving sand and dust into their eyes and noses. Each evening they would hasten to pitch their tents to provide shelter. Even so, the nights were bitterly cold, bringing fifteen degrees of frost, the streams frozen hard by morning. And still Everest was at least a month's march away.

George had already been traveling for two months. He had sailed from England on April 8, 1921, arriving in Calcutta five weeks later, followed by a twenty-four-hour train ride to Darjeeling. There he and his eight colleagues—four climbers, three surveyors, and a doctor—had embarked on their trek to Everest. With them were forty porters, cooks, and interpreters, together with a hundred mules to carry their six tons of equipment and supplies. Ahead lay a 250-mile trek that would take them in a great arc through Sikkim and Tibet, crossing the plain to the north of Everest and then striking south towards the mountain from there. At first they would follow the road to Lhasa but would then head into unmapped territory, intersected by wild mountain ranges and turbulent river gorges, where no Europeans had ever been. Not until the end of June would they be able to begin their task of finding a route onto, perhaps even to the top of, the highest mountain in the world.

They met problems from the start. There were not enough mules in Darjeeling to carry all their equipment and so they were compelled to leave half of it behind in the hope of sending for it later. The mules they did hire were unfit for the task, some collapsing and dying on the trail. The humidity in Sikkim was intense, and torrential rain reduced long stretches of the mountain paths to mud. Leeches were a constant menace, dropping onto both men and mules from the shrubs beside the path. When they crossed the 14,000-foot Jelep Pass into Tibet they suffered from pounding headaches and nausea, the symptoms of high-altitude sickness caused by their exertions in the oxygen-depleted air.

Once in Tibet they passed through lush valleys with white clematis and roses, purple irises, great white and yellow rhododendrons, and groves of juniper, birch, and mountain ash. At times George went on foot, at times he rode on a mule that seemed dwarfed by his powerful, muscular frame, his legs reaching almost to the ground. In the space of a few hours, as the great line of men and animals climbed up to the Tibetan plateau, everything changed. George called it a new world. Beside the vastness of the landscape, and the relentless wind, there was the sun, scorching their skin, and clouds of midges that forced their way into noses and ears. There was trouble with the porters: their leader, the sirdar, was found to be embezzling the expedition's supplies, and the cooks were often drunk. The food was abysmal—"nasty, dirty messes that are most unappetising," George wrote—and every member of the expedition bar him succumbed to diarrhea.

Throughout the journey he compiled an account of the expedition's progress, which was contained in a series of letters that he sent home to Ruth. They had always written to each other when they were apart, particularly during the war, when he was an artillery officer on the western front, and they exchanged affectionate and intimate accounts of the passage of events and their own hopes and fears. They carried photographs of each other, including one for which they had posed together in the war. George, staring intently at the camera, wore his officer's uniform, with a wisp of mustache and a severe hairstyle, which he grew long as soon as he left the army; Ruth sat beside him, the wistful look on her gentle Pre-Raphaelite face framed by her fine center-parted hair.

Now, writing in ink, in an elegant semi-italic script, on notepaper headed "Mount Everest Expedition," he would compose his letters when and wherever he could. On the SS *Sardinia*, when he had time on his hands, he described his fellow passengers, the heat of the Red Sea, the great swells of the Indian Ocean, his determination to stay fit by running around the deck (thirteen circuits equaled a mile). During the trek through Tibet he would grab a few moments to write before setting off on the day's march and would complete his letter in the evening. Once, at the Tibetan village of Phari, he told Ruth that he was writing from the middle of a dusty plain with the giant peak of Chomulhari towering above him—as isolated and dominant, he said, as the Matterhorn at Zermatt.

George was quick to form instinctive judgments of the people he met, although he often revised his views once he knew them better. He provided Ruth with pen sketches of his companions. There was the surveyor Henry Morshead, strong and energetic, "an attractive man." A second surveyor, Edward Wheeler, was "a bore in the colonial fashion." "Kellas I love already," he said of the Scottish climber Alexander Kellas, who was "full of humor." By contrast the senior climber, Harold Raeburn, had "a total lack of calm or sense of humor." George reserved his most critical remarks for the expedition leader, Lt. Col. Charles Howard-Bury: "He is well-informed and opinionated and doesn't at all like anyone else to know things he doesn't know." He was particularly irked by Howard-Bury's political views. He was "too much the landlord," and displayed "not only tory prejudice but a very highly developed sense of hate and contempt for other sorts of people than his own."

Through all the difficulties, George conveyed his excitement at the great adventure he had undertaken. "Oh Ruth," he declared, "this is a thrilling business." At the age of thirty-four he had not lost his sense of wonder or his determination to live new experiences to the full. He described the villages he passed through, the people he encountered, the strange flowers he could not identify, the landscape that he came to savor despite the hardships it imposed. In the evening, he told Ruth, "the harshness becomes subdued, there is a blending of lines and folds until the last light so that one comes to bless the absolute bareness, feeling that here is a pure beauty of form, a kind of ultimate harmony."

His letters, carried by runner to the nearest mailing post, took up to four weeks to reach Ruth at their home at Godalming in the Surrey hills, thirty miles south of London. She would sit and read them in their loggia, a covered terrace opening on to the lawn and overlooking a steep wooded bank. She replied, in her careful handwriting, on notepaper headed with the name of their house, the Holt. She told him about their garden, difficulties with the servants, the shortage of coal due to the miners' strike, and most of all about their three children, Clare, Beridge, and John. George sympathized with her problems, passed on suggestions about the garden or the servants, mailed her a flower resembling a valerian that he had worn in his button hole, hoping its scent would last until it reached her, and sent lace and a necklace for the two girls, then aged five and three, and kisses for them all, including John, who was not yet one. He yearned to bridge the distance between them: if only he could talk to Ruth, rather than write. "You are very often in my thoughts and do seem at times very near," he told her, "but so very much too far." "Lord," he ended another letter, "how I have wanted you to see all this with me."

On June 6 George had more bad news to relate. The expedition had just reached Kampa Dzong, the fortress town that was the first staging point after leaving the Lhasa road. Kellas, who was fifty-three, had been weakened by dysentery to the point where his porters were carrying him on a stretcher. The previous day, just after they had crossed a 17,000-foot pass, Kellas had died, probably from heart failure brought about by his weakness and high-altitude sickness. He had been buried that morning at Kampa Dzong. It was, said George, a "tragic and distressing" business.

Then came another disaster. Harold Raeburn, at fifty-six the oldest man in the team, had also been stricken with dysentery and had returned to Sikkim. At a stroke the expedition had lost its only two climbers with Himalayan experience and, in Kellas, its expert on the problems of climbing at high altitude. As the senior mountaineer, George was appointed the new climbing leader. Their prospect of success, he told Ruth, seemed slim. "I suppose no one who could judge us fairly as a party would give much for our chances of getting up Mount Everest."

As the expedition struggled to recover from these setbacks, there was a new preoccupation. Where was Everest? They had glimpsed it from Kampa Dzong as a snowy crest, towering above its neighbors some ninety miles to the southwest. Since then it had been obscured by clouds. George felt they still had a great barrier to surmount, a screen of mountains running from north to south, before they could come to grips with the mountain. His unease was compounded by his awareness, as he put it, that they were about to walk off the map. They had already gone beyond the furthest point reached by the Younghusband mission in 1904, when the British had sent a military force to secure Tibet's allegiance in their fight for territorial supremacy with Russia and China. Such charts as the expedition possessed were misleading or simply wrong: rivers flowed in the wrong direction, mountains appeared where none were marked.

On June 11 George resolved to obtain a view of Everest. He was traveling with Guy Bullock, his only previous friend on the expedition. They had been at school together at Winchester and had climbed in the Alps: George called Bullock his "stable-companion," a workhorse, solid and dependable. That morning, as the expedition traveled west along the valley of the Yaru River, he and Bullock climbed to a vantage point on the mountainside above. By the time they reached it they were nauseous with fatigue, only to find Everest still shrouded in cloud.

Two days later they tried again. George and Bullock went ahead of their colleagues and followed the Yaru through a gorge and out on to a broad alluvial plain. George had a sudden presentiment, a feeling that he and Bullock were "penetrating a secret," like travelers passing a watershed both in the landscape and in their fortunes. They left their ponies to graze and set off to climb the cliffs at the exit from the gorge. After an hour they reached the crest of a stony peak where they lay down and peered through their field glasses in the direction of Everest. At first they could see nothing but the usual clouds; then they caught a glint of snow. Over the next hour, they watched transfixed as the clouds gradually lifted, revealing fragments of mountainsides and glaciers and ridges, then its snow-covered east face, and finally the triangle of rock and ice that was the summit. It was far higher than they had imagined, George told Ruth. But they were certain that it was Everest, not only because they had calculated its distance and height, but also because, in its grandeur, there was no other mountain it could be.

George and Bullock watched for another hour, taking photographs of Everest and trying to identify its individual features, even working out possible lines of ascent. Far below they saw the rest of the expedition strung out across the plain like a desert caravan and knew it was time to descend. They caught up with their colleagues at a campsite beside a spring near a tiny settlement called Shiling. The wind was as relentless as ever, sweeping over the sand, George wrote, so that it rippled like a sea of watered silk. As usual the climbers took refuge in their tents but as dusk approached the wind dropped. George led his colleagues to a mound beside the Yaru where they could see Everest rising "absolutely clear and glorious" beyond the river to the southwest. George took another photograph with a telephoto lens showing the mountain in all its distant splendor. Later he gave a large print of the photograph to the Alpine Club. Captioned "Everest—the first sight," it has hung in the club to this day.

For George, the vision from the mountaintop remained a transcendental moment. He described it in a letter to Ruth dated June 15, then reworked his account for the official book about the expedition. He held strong views about mountaineering writing, which he thought should convey the emotional truth of climbing, and was determined to capture the significance of his first full sight of Everest. "Mountain shapes are often fantastic seen through a mist," he wrote; "these were like the wildest creation of a dream." He told again how the rocky shapes, the mountain crests, the glaciers, and the ridges, came together to form a whole. "We were able to piece together the fragments, to interpret the dream."

The image of the dream recurs throughout George's writing. Some of his critics have used it against him, suggesting that he was an impractical person, a fantasist unable to put his dreams into effect. The image is in fact a key to understanding George, for his dreams represented ideals that he was determined to meet. That day, he told Ruth, had been a great landmark. Everest had become "more than a fantastic vision; one began to know it as a peak with its individual form; the problem of that great ridge and glacier began to take shape, and to haunt the mind." Now he and his colleagues understood Everest and had "one whole clear meaning" with which they could plan their ascent. Although it would be several more weeks before they could come to grips with Everest, the hardships and disappointments were beginning to recede. "My job begins to show like a flower bud soon to open out," he told Ruth. He could hardly wait for a closer view of Everest, enabling them to "unveil a little more of the great mystery" and resolve how to fulfill their dream.

✧

Almost three years to the day after George's vision of Everest, the clouds closed around him and his young partner Sandy Irvine as they made their final summit bid. It was George's third visit to Everest, and the highest he ever went on the mountain, leaving a mystery that endured for the next seventy-five years. In that time he and Irvine attained the status of legends, two men of inspirational courage and determination who had gone forward together to meet their destiny. What had happened to them? Could they have reached the summit? How and where did they die?

In the pre-monsoon Himalayan season of 1999, a U.S. expedition at last found some of the answers. On May 1, during a spell when the north face of Everest was unusually free of snow, an American climber, Conrad Anker, caught a glimpse of something white lying among the rubble and scree at 26,760 feet on the mountain's north face. As he approached he found it was a body, its clothes in tatters, its skin bleached like a marble statue, its arms extended above its head, one leg clearly fractured, a single boot lying nearby. The Americans had been convinced that if they found anyone it would be Irvine, and it was hard for them to break that preconception. When Anker and his colleagues uncovered a laundry label bearing the name G. Mallory, alongside the address of a clothing store in Godalming High Street, they wondered why Irvine would be wearing Mallory's shirt.

Then the Americans, and soon the world, realized that George had been found at last. With the body was a collection of personal items that enhanced the poignancy of the discovery. They included a box of matches, a pair of nail scissors, a pencil, a wristwatch minus its hands, lists of stores and supplies, and three letters George had received shortly before setting off on his attempt. The find was followed by a flood of speculation over one principal issue: was it now possible to decide whether George and Sandy had reached the top? The issue was minutely debated, encompassing such matters as precisely where they had been last seen in 1924, their respective climbing abilities, the routes they might have followed, the flow rates of the oxygen cylinders they were carrying, and the interpretation of some notes about oxygen supplies that George had made on one of the envelopes in his pocket.

As the debate raged, we began to feel that the personality and character of the man himself was being overlooked. The Mallory legend was becoming a cipher, a focus for theories and arguments that were becoming as desiccated as George's body. There was so much more we wanted to know. Since George was thirty-seven when he died, and Everest had occupied only the last four years of his life, we wanted to know about the other thirty-three years. What were his hopes and fears, his goals and aspirations, his friendships and his loves? And how had they shaped the ambitions of a man willing to stake his life on an attempt to climb the world's highest mountain?

As we began our search, we felt to some extent on familiar ground. George had been part of our lives ever since we knew about mountaineering, which began with the headlines about the ascent of Everest—"Everest: the Crowning

Glory," "All this and Everest too"—which appeared in the British newspapers on Coronation Day, June 1953. Later that year we were in the lines of school-children taken to see *The Conquest of Everest*, transfixed by cameraman Tom Stobart's endless panning shot from the glacier floor to the corniced crest of the summit ridge. Our parents told us of the prewar efforts to climb the mountain, made during their own lifetimes, which had helped to motivate the 1953 attempt. We learned that Ed Hillary had been inspired by George, who epitomized all that was most valiant about the 1920s expeditions, and remained for Hillary the most heroic figure in the mountain's history. Later we went to Cambridge to interview Noel Odell, the last person to see George and Irvine before they disappeared into the clouds. We visited John Noel at his home in Kent, marveling at the photographs he took on the 1922 and 1924 expeditions, wondering at his tales of developing his pictures in his improvised darkroom at the foot of the Rongbuk Glacier.

We felt we knew George's landscapes too. It was more than thirty years since we first went climbing in Snowdonia, scrambling over the same ridges he had followed, fingering the granite he had grasped as he helped push rock climbing to new standards not so long after the sport was born. We knew his haunts: the Pen y Gwryd Hotel, the Snowdon Ranger, and the Gorphwysfa Inn at Pen y Pass (the latter two now youth hostels). We climbed in the Lake District, and on the Cuillin Ridge in Skye. We went to Tibet, traversing that same barren gray landscape, staying in towns used as stopping places by the 1921 expedition, witnessing Everest rising from the plain, the historic landmarks of the northeast ridge sharp and clear.

We also knew his England: the home counties, public school (which are really private schools*), Oxbridge, the army, and the Alpine Club, where relics and photographs from his days are on display, and whose ambiance still has echoes of the Mallory era. As we continued our researches, and were received with unfailing kindness and hospitality by his descendants and relatives, we sensed traces of his world. These included the welcoming of strangers into their homes; the mealtime etiquette; the deep knowledge of plants and flowers; and the unmistakable tones of those, like him, who were educated at public school—the "upper-crust" accent, as one niece put it, in which George himself spoke.

---

*In Britain, the term "public school" refers to schools whose students to pay for their tuition, as opposed to state schools, funded by the national government and local councils, where there is no direct charge for tuition. The public schools are also known as "private schools," which is in fact a more accurate description. Their role has generally been to provide a privileged education for an elite of the British middle and upper classes, and they have usually had far more money to spend on their students than the hard-pressed state schools.

We knew the previous biographies, of course, of which the most important were David Pye's, published in 1927, David Robertson's, published in 1969, and the writings of the tireless Everest researcher, Audrey Salkeld. While all contained invaluable material, we felt that none presented a full perspective on Mallory's life or motivations. We also wanted to address some surprisingly strong criticism of George made during the postdiscovery debate. It was alleged that he was a poor climber, unintelligent, given to rash decisions, obsessed with Everest, and irresponsible in taking Irvine on a near-suicidal dash for the summit. Some of these criticisms echoed the arguments of the Everest historian Walt Unsworth, who wrote that George was "a drifter, uncommitted and indecisive," a second-rate climber who had even drifted into attempting Everest.

Certainly we became aware of George's flaws: he was forgetful, sometimes impractical, and could be strident and dogmatic, particularly as a young man. But writers who described these faults often ignored his counterbalancing virtues, which were revealed to us as our research progressed. He was as courageous in his political and social ideas as much as in his climbing, an idealist who maintained his integrity and his belief in honesty and emotional truth. Ironically, that handed his critics a weapon, for in his writing he admitted to his inner struggles, and his attempts to reconcile his personal objectives with those of his expeditions, the conflict between selfishness and altruism that all of us know.

The greatest conflict of George's life concerned Ruth. They were passionately in love when they married in July 1914, on the eve of the First World War. During the war, when he spent sixteen months on the western front, Ruth gave birth to their two daughters, and their son was born shortly after the war. Ruth had spent much of the war trying to contain her anxiety over his safety and her longing for his return: feelings that were replicated during his three expeditions to Everest. Yet George too had to contend with his own feelings of separation and loss, and his knowledge of the pain he was causing Ruth. As we became aware of this ourselves, we sensed more and more strongly that the most significant questions about George's life and death did not concern whether he reached the summit of Everest. Far more important, we felt, was to understand what had led him to make the two most momentous decisions of his life. Why did he depart for Everest for the third time in 1924? And why, when the expedition was in desperate straits from illness and exhaustion, its supply lines dangerously extended, did George and Irvine make their final attempt?

The answers are to be found in a life as rich, diverse, and exciting as any this century. The quest starts in the village of Mobberley in Cheshire, where Mallory was born in 1886: an unimaginable world away from the barren plateau of Tibet.

CHAPTER ONE

A Taste for Risk
1886–1905

George Mallory's first climbing ground was the roof of his father's church in the Cheshire village of Mobberley. An austere, thirteenth-century building, St. Wilfrid's has a square stone tower that is visible, like a distant mountain crag, across the surrounding fields. For an imaginative boy of seven, who apparently knew no fear, there were many ways to reach the angled slate roof. A drainpipe led to a lower roof, which you traversed to the far end; climb another drainpipe, bracing your feet against the right-angled roof of an adjoining chapel; grasp the coping stone to heave yourself up, and you were there.

Mobberley, in the early 1890s, had other lures for George. "He climbed everything that it was at all possible to climb," his sister Avie said. These included the walls dividing the farmers' fields and the drainpipes of Hobcroft House, a rambling building half a mile from the church, where the Mallory family lived. Once George led his younger brother Trafford on to the roof and, while George knew how to get down, Trafford had to be rescued with a ladder. During a family seaside holiday at St. Bees in Cumberland when he was eight, he stood on a rock to see what would happen when he was cut off by the tide. The boatman who rescued him said that George had seemed quite unconcerned by the danger he was in.

It may seem incongruous that the elder son of the local rector should behave in so wayward a manner. Mobberley was a prosperous parish, with a number of mansions belonging to the merchants and industrialists of Manchester, a dozen miles away. Most of the villagers worked on the neighboring farms, or in the crepe mill by Mobberley Brook. Herbert Leigh Mallory was a devout and conventional man who frowned on radical or nonconformist views. He and his wife, Annie, were the epitome of respectability as they rode to St. Wilfrid's through Mobberley's stony lanes in their pony and trap. In his services he stressed the ritualistic and sacramental side of worship and communion, although he delivered more populist sermons after the local Methodists began attracting worshippers to their chapel near Mobberley Brook at the southern edge of the village. He was generous to the parish, helping to fund restoration work at St. Wilfrid's soon after he became rector in 1885, and paying for new oak choir stalls.

Annie was different. Certainly she was well-meaning, doing her best to fulfill her role as the rector's wife. During the services, she would occupy one of the front pews alongside her four children and make suggestions in a stage whisper to Herbert as he read out the church notices. She felt obliged to lead the singing but had more enthusiasm than a musical ear, for she was often several bars ahead of the rest of the congregation and would swoop down on her notes from higher up the scale. Similar disharmony marked her life at Hobcroft House. She was chaotic and disorganized, moving perpetually from crisis to crisis. She found it impossible to keep servants as she changed her mind frequently and exasperated them by ringing all the bells simultaneously to bring them scurrying from all parts of the house. She was a hypochondriac who was constantly anxious about her health and took herself off for cures at spas—Bath in southwest England and Aix-les-Bains in France were her favorites. Today she would be called a drama queen.

As a mother, her children observed, she was more noticed for her absences than the attention she gave them. As a result, Avie remarked, "We were exceptionally unruly children." The children were closer to each other than to Annie, although George's two sisters, Avie and Mary, vied for his affections. They came to resent their mother's interference and when she did intervene she usually provoked another dispute. "Why is it," George once asked, "that whenever mother comes in a row starts?" There were rows when she wanted them to learn the piano, and on one occasion Mary slammed down the piano lid and marched out. Herbert's habit, when he heard storms such as this brewing up, was to quietly withdraw.

Annie's most positive effect as a mother was to encourage her children to acquire a spirit of adventure. Sometimes she led them on walks through the fields, ignoring the farmers and other landowners whose walls they climbed. It was thus not surprising that George should acquire a taste for risk. "It was always fun doing things with him," Avie said. "He had the knack of making things exciting and often rather dangerous." She learned never to suggest that there might be anything that was impossible to climb, as that only spurred him on. Once he talked of lying between the railway tracks and letting a train pass over him. "I kept very quiet," Avie said. "I was afraid he would do it."

∽

As the engraved marble plaques and gold-inscribed wooden panels at St. Wilfrid's testify, there have been Mallorys at Mobberley for centuries. The first is Thomas Mallory, appointed rector in 1621. There is a second Thomas Mallory in 1684, a third in 1770. The year 1795 brings a John Holdsworth Mallory, whose occupancy is commemorated with an intriguing verse from the book of Matthew: "When thou does thine alms, let not thy left hand know what thy right hand doeth." In 1832 this Mallory was succeeded by George Mallory, the father of Herbert Leigh Mallory. Finally there was Herbert Leigh Mallory himself in 1885.

Although Herbert was the last of the Mallorys to be Mobberley's rector, there is another memorial to the Mallory family. In a wall on the left-hand side of the church, close to the pulpit, is a stained-glass triptych depicting three heroic figures from English mythology, King Arthur, Saint George, and Sir Galahad. It commemorates Herbert Mallory and his two sons, Trafford and George. Trafford became head of the Royal Air Force's Fighter Command and died in a plane crash in 1944. There is an inscription to George that reads: "All his life he sought after whatsoever things are pure and high and eternal." At last in the flower of his perfect manhood he was lost to human sight between earth and heaven on the topmost peak of Mount Everest." The window is most moving when the light from outside bathes the flagstones of the floor with patterns of red and blue.

There is one curiosity about the memorial, for the name of George Mallory is shown as George Herbert Leigh Leigh-Mallory. How George Mallory came to acquire such a convoluted name is part of a family history that is not quite as straightforward as the roster of names at St. Wilfrid's appears to suggest. The story is one of interlopers, disputed wills, premature deaths, and a concern for status and appearances, which left its mark on the memorial to George Mallory himself.

Thomas Mallory, the first of the Mobberley Mallorys, was a seventeenth-century carpetbagger. He was already the Dean of Chester when he came to Mobberley in 1619 and purchased the living of St. Wilfrid's church. A year or so later he bought the nearby Manor House, which made him the squire of Mobberley. He had the right to appoint the village rector and so he chose himself.

MALLORY FAMILY TREE

GEORGE MALLORY'S 19TH-CENTURY FOREBEARS

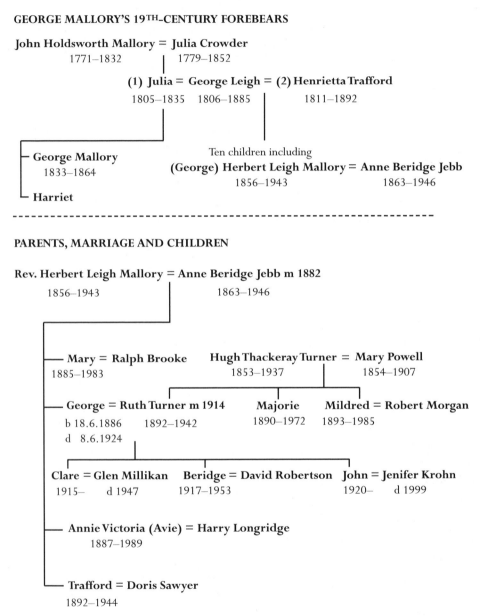

John Holdsworth Mallory = Julia Crowder
1771–1832   1779–1852

(1) Julia = George Leigh = (2) Henrietta Trafford
1805–1835   1806–1885   1811–1892

George Mallory
1833–1864

Harriet

Ten children including
(George) Herbert Leigh Mallory = Anne Beridge Jebb
1856–1943   1863–1946

PARENTS, MARRIAGE AND CHILDREN

Rev. Herbert Leigh Mallory = Anne Beridge Jebb m 1882
1856–1943   1863–1946

Mary = Ralph Brooke   Hugh Thackeray Turner = Mary Powell
1885–1983   1853–1937   1854–1907

George = Ruth Turner m 1914   Majorie   Mildred = Robert Morgan
b 18.6.1886   1892–1942   1890–1972   1893–1985
d 8.6.1924

Clare = Glen Millikan   Beridge = David Robertson   John = Jenifer Krohn
1915–   d 1947   1917–1953   1920–   d 1999

Annie Victoria (Avie) = Harry Longridge
1887–1989

Trafford = Doris Sawyer
1892–1944

The first tree shows the two marriages of George Leigh, George Mallory's grandfather.
When Leigh married Julia Mallory, he took the Mallory name. When he married for a second
time, he restored "Leigh" to his surname (see pages 23 and 26).

His descendants inherited the same rights and sometimes appointed outsiders as rectors, sometimes themselves, as the names recorded at St. Wilfrid's shows. However, the George Mallory—father of Herbert Mallory, grandfather of George Mallory the mountaineer—who became rector in 1832, was not a Mallory at all, but an interloper. His real name was George Leigh, a curate from Liverpool. In 1831 he came to Mobberley and asked the incumbent rector, John Holdsworth Mallory, for permission to marry his daughter, Julia. John Holdsworth Mallory had no sons, and no better prospect for a husband for his daughter either. He was also seriously ill. He agreed to Leigh's request on one condition. When Leigh married Julia he should forsake his own surname and take hers, thus ensuring the survival of the Mallory name and line.

The couple were married at St. Wilfrid's in 1832, becoming George and Julia Mallory. Julia's father, John Holdsworth Mallory, died three months later. George and Julia had two children: a son, also called George Mallory, and a daughter, Harriet. Julia died in March 1835, when she was just twenty-nine. Barely a year or so after that the widowed George Mallory married again. His new wife was a cousin, Henrietta Trafford from Outrington in Cheshire, and they had ten children. Now that he was free of the oversight of his first wife and her father, George Mallory reinstated his old name. He did so by adding Leigh to his own and his children's names, giving the impression that it formed part of their surnames. When his seventh son and tenth child was born in 1856, he was christened Herbert Leigh Mallory.

George Leigh Mallory also managed to acquire the Mallory family estate. John Holdsworth Mallory had bequeathed the Manor House and some nearby cottages to his grandson, Julia's son George, hoping to ensure that it remained within the Mallory family. But when grandson George became an adult he incurred debts that he could only discharge by selling the Manor House and the nearby cottages. They were purchased by his father, George Leigh Mallory, who thus completed his takeover of both the family name and its estate.

Of the original George Mallory's seven sons, it was Herbert who was selected to follow his father into the church. He was sent to boarding school at King William's College on the Isle of Man, progressing from there to Trinity College, Cambridge. He left with a B.A. in 1878 and began his ecclesiastical apprenticeship in a succession of junior posts: assistant curate at St. Andrew the Less in Cambridge; curate "in sole charge" of the Abbey Church, Cambridge. It was during this time that he met the young Annie Jebb.

The Jebbs were a prosperous church family from Derbyshire. Annie's father was the Rev. John Beridge Jebb, named after a relative, the great eighteenth-century evangelist John Berridge (it should be noted that alternative spellings of the name, Berridge and Beridge, appear in family records). John Jebb owned a splendid mansion, Walton Lodge, with forty-one acres of grounds, and was minister at the nearby church of St. Thomas. Like Herbert Mallory's father George, he too married twice. His first wife, Charlotte, came from Devonshire, and they had a son, John Beridge Gladwyn Jebb, who became an adventurer in the finest Victorian tradition. But Charlotte died in 1859 and in 1861 John Jebb married Mary Frances Jenkinson, a vicar's daughter from Kensington. Mary became pregnant but John Jebb died shortly before she gave birth to their first daughter, Anne Beridge, who was born on April 16, 1863.

Mary Jebb was thus left to bring up Annie alone. She found ample consolation in her husband's will. John Jebb had left his son by his first marriage a meager inheritance consisting of his gold watch and the furniture that had belonged to his first wife. Everything else went to Mary and her daughter. Mary acquired railway company shares worth £6000 ($46,000)*, while Walton Lodge and its forty-one acres were left in trust to her daughter Annie. The family of John's first wife were outraged and wanted to challenge the will, but there was nothing they could do, and Mary and her daughter Annie continued to live at Walton Lodge. There Annie, as she was known, had an unfettered upbringing. Her mother was preoccupied for much of her life with good works, setting up a canteen for the mill girls of Derby, running a scripture class for local policemen, opening a hospital, and becoming its matron. During her mother's absences, Annie was taught by governesses and was often lodged with her mother's friends. She acquired a taste for the freedom of the countryside, riding out on to the moors on her pony, walking and scrambling in the hills when she was taken on holiday to Wales.

Meanwhile her mother, anxious to have her daughter safely married, resolved to find her a husband at an early age. According to family legend, she effectively brought about a shotgun wedding. Annie met Herbert Mallory when she was still a teenager and he was completing his theological studies. When Herbert showed a tentative interest in Annie, her mother accused him of trifling with her daughter's affections and demanded that he marry her. Herbert's family was incensed, telling him that the accusation was preposterous. But Mary persisted in her accusation and Herbert, who said he did not want to hurt Annie's feelings, complied. He was twenty-five, she was nineteen, when they were married in Kensington in June 1882. They spent their honeymoon in the Lake District, eating copiously and working off the excess through hill walking.

By then Herbert was a curate at the Abbey Church in Cambridge. He next moved to the parish of Harborough Magna near Rugby, then became assistant

---

*All U.K. Sterling figures have been converted to U.S. dollars at the rate prevailing at the time. In 1863, £1 was $7.67.

curate at Great Haseley in Oxford. In 1884 he moved back to Mobberley. His elderly father was ill, and the moment when Herbert would succeed him was nearing. Annie was pregnant, and so rather than move into the Manor House, where his parents lived with two of his unmarried sisters, Herbert looked for somewhere else to live. A mile or so from St. Wilfrid's he found a grand Elizabethan house called Newton Hall, which he rented from a prosperous Birkenhead publican named Thomas Adkinson. With its white-painted facade and three steep gables, it seemed an appropriate home for the prospective rector of Mobberley and his wife.

On February 3, 1885, Annie gave birth to their first child, Mary. Just four days later, and in preparation for the family succession, Herbert became the curate of Mobberley. His father, George Leigh Mallory, died on July 26, and on September 23 Herbert became the rector of Mobberley. In theory he should have moved back to the Manor House, which was still occupied by his mother and two sisters, but on March 18, 1886, the church authorities in Chester gave him and Annie permission to remain at Newton Hall. It was there on June 18 that their second child and first son was born. His father—a "Clerk in Holy Orders"—registered the birth, recording his name as George Herbert Leigh Mallory. He was baptized at St. Wilfrid's seven weeks later.

Herbert and Annie had a third child, Annie Victoria—known throughout her life as Avie—at Newton Hall on November 19, 1887. By now the Mallorys were planning a home of their own, and in 1890 construction of Hobcroft House began in Hobcroft Lane on the far side of St. Wilfrid's from Newton Hall. The family left Newton Hall and moved into Hobcroft House around the end of 1891. Annie's mother Mary joined them soon afterwards, living with them until her death in 1906. The Mallorys' fourth and last child, Trafford Leigh Mallory, was born at Hobcroft House on July 11, 1892.

The family lived in Hobcroft House until 1904, and it is from these twelve years that their children's principal memories of life in Mobberley emanated. These accounts were passed down to their children, who amplified them with their own recollections of Herbert and Annie. They remembered how Herbert called the servants to attend when he said grace before meals, and how he would read aloud from the bible when the family was seated around the dining table. They also recalled how Herbert acquired a diplomatic deafness as his strategy for coping with Annie's excesses and then, after they had left Mobberley, would retreat to his study with the family chauffeur and wait there until the latest crisis had passed.

Strongest of all were the memories of Herbert's and Annie's extravagance. Although photographs show that Annie had a reasonably trim figure, she was a compulsive eater who observed a succession of mealtimes: breakfast, the mid-morning snack known as elevenses, lunch, a mid-afternoon snack, high tea, dinner, and supper. There was always far more food provided than anyone could consume, from the mammoth breakfasts when the sideboard was weighed down with eggs, ham, bacon, kippers, and kedgeree, to the enormous joints of beef or mutton that were served for dinner and remained half-eaten in the larder for days. The Mallorys bought every new household gadget on offer, from carpet-sweepers to ice cream–makers. They had a cavalier attitude towards their debts, and children or grandchildren who went to visit them would search the house for bills from local tradesmen that were long overdue and had to be paid.

Such profligacy may help to explain one of the family mysteries. The Mallorys should have been more than comfortably off. Soon after moving into Hobcroft House, Herbert had acquired the Manor House, left to him when his mother died. Annie should also have benefited from the inheritance settled on her by her grandfather. Yet by the time Herbert and Annie died in the 1940s, the family fortune had gone. "They were as poor as church mice," their grandson John Mallory observed.

All of this left its mark on the young George. He too had an inconsistent attitude towards money, sometimes parsimonious, sometimes extravagant. Money became an issue in his marriage and was a constant irritant in his dealings with the Mount Everest Committee. He worked hard to improve his practical skills but never overcame his endemic forgetfulness, to the delight and despair of his friends. But his upbringing also helped frame his character as adventurer, experimenter, risk-taker; someone who delighted in new experiences, determined to push them to the limits.

But what of the name, George Herbert Leigh Leigh-Mallory, which is recorded on the memorial at St. Wilfrid's? One of the Leighs resulted from the determination of his grandfather, George Leigh, to restore his own surname. The second stemmed from his father's concern for propriety and status. In 1914 Herbert Leigh Mallory decided to apply for a family coat of arms. But when the officials at the College of Arms delved into his family history, they found a curious anomaly. It appeared that when George Leigh assumed the name Mallory in 1832, the change applied only to his first marriage, and not to his second. This news was broken to a shocked Herbert Leigh Mallory in March 1914 by the Garter King of Arms, Sir Arthur Gatty, who told him that as a consequence he was "in the almost unique position" of having no surname at all.

All of this was related by Herbert in a letter to his son George on March 30, 1914. Herbert asked his son not to tell anyone else: "It seems so silly," he confessed. But there was good news too, for Sir Arthur had found a solution. The best way out of the impasse, he suggested, would be for Herbert to apply for a new surname, Leigh-Mallory. Herbert agreed that this was the most convenient solution, particularly as he had been signing himself "Leigh Mallory" anyway. So it was that the boy who had been christened George Herbert Leigh Mallory officially became George Herbert Leigh Leigh-Mallory. George never used his full name, although he once wrote to the Mount Everest Committee to insist that his rightful name was George Leigh Mallory. But his father's social aspirations went unsatisfied as his request for a coat of arms was turned down.

∝

When George was nine, he was sent away from home. After a brief spell at a preparatory school at West Kirby, near Birkenhead, which was abruptly closed down when its headmaster died, he moved to Glengorse, a preparatory school in Eastbourne. It had fifty-four pupils and George shared a dormitory with five other boys. "My dear Mater," he wrote to his mother on February 14, 1896, "I had my first experience of football on Friday. It was a very nice experience. The first damage I did was to charge two boys over on their faces, the second was to kick the ball into a boy's nose, and the third damage was to charge a boy over on his ribs."

Much later, George was to challenge the practice of separating children from their parents by dispatching them to boarding school, particularly at so young an age. He felt that it produced people who were "superficial and self-satisfied" and "disastrously ill-equipped for making the best of life." It was a remarkable indictment, stemming from his experiences as both pupil and teacher. But at Glengorse he showed nothing but enthusiasm for his new life, even if his spelling required attention. "There is only one boy in the school who is atal nasty," he told his mother, adding that this recalcitrant pupil was the matron's son. His biggest shock came when one of his friends decided to run away from Glengorse. Although George had no wish to leave Glengorse he agreed to keep him company, and brought along his geometry books wrapped in a brown paper parcel. The two runaways were tracked down by a teacher who promised that if they returned to Glengorse at once they would not be punished. George agreed but as soon as they had arrived they were soundly beaten. When George told the story in later life, he made clear his outrage that the teacher should have tricked him into going back by telling a lie.

George's strongest school subject was math, and in 1900, when he was thirteen, he entered for a math scholarship to Winchester College. Winchester had a high academic reputation among the English public schools and George faced stiff competition. He won the scholarship, saving his father all but £30 ($144.00) of the customary annual fees of around £200 ($960.00). When he started at Winchester in September he was placed in College House, the preserve of the brightest pupils, and allocated rooms in the main quadrangle, known as Chamber

Court. There he was given one of the studies, known as the toys, in a communal living room, or chamber, and slept in a dormitory on an upper floor with up to ten other boys.

Even more than at Glengorse, George immersed himself in the spirit of the place. He rapidly adopted its private argot (known as the "notions") and within days of arriving wrote to his mother. "I like being here very much—ever so much better than Glengorse, and I like the *men* better too. (Instead of chaps, we always say men): We have plenty of work to do, and I'm afraid I'm running you up a heavy book bill; we shan't begin playing footer—the Winchester game—for some time yet; we get up at 6.15 and begin work—morning lines it's called—at 7.00." A month later he told her he was enjoying Winchester immensely. "It's simply lovely being here; life is like a dream."

One of the characteristics that marked out George from his contemporaries, both at Winchester and later at Cambridge, was his versatility. Many of the scholarship boys concentrated on their academic studies, but George excelled at sports too. He took up Winchester's idiosyncratic version of soccer, which took place on a long, fenced-off pitch with anything from six to fifteen a side, and played in the technically demanding "kick" position in the college team. He became the best gymnast in the school, the only one who could perform a complete circle with his arms and body held straight on a horizontal bar. In 1904 he was a member of the eight-strong shooting team that competed for the Ashburton Shield against the other public schools at the annual Bisley contest. The team won with a bull's eye on its very last shot and George relished every moment of the triumph. "It was simply glorious," he wrote to Avie. "We won the Public School Racquets last holidays, we badly beat Eton at cricket, and now we have won the Public Schools Shooting, which is really the best of the lot, because every decent school goes in for it, and it comes into public notice much more than anything else." The entire school turned out to greet the team at Winchester station, cheering them and carrying them shoulder-high into college. "It is simply ripping," George said.

While George's account of the contest showed that, in sport at least, he was absorbing the public school ethos, he also challenged some of its excesses. At the end of the autumn term ("Short Half") in 1903, his chamber prefect—an older boy who supervised his chamber—recorded notes of George's progress. George was "a mathematical-minded, smooth-chinned, pre-Raphaelite looking young man" and had insisted on complaining about a prefect in another chamber who was notorious for his bullying. By the following term ("Common Time") the problem seemed to have been dealt with, and he was described as a "kindly individual character" and a "sweet young fellow."

George was now at a critical point in his school career. He had been studying math and chemistry, subjects that would equip him for the army, and he was entered for exams that would qualify him for the officer training school at Woolwich. George had no wish to become a soldier and told his sister Mary that he hoped to fail. As a letter to his mother suggests, he duly ensured that he did. "The mathematical papers were so absurdly easy that it was quite impossible to score on them, especially as I always do easy papers badly," he told her. Besides, leaving Winchester would have been "perfectly awful."

Certainly George was enjoying life at Winchester, and he was about to explore a new activity, which would bring even greater pleasure and rewards. He did so through the intervention of the senior master ("College Tutor") in his house, Graham Irving, a member of the Alpine Club and later a prolific writer about mountaineering. As Irving told it, he was looking for new climbing companions after his own partner had keen killed in an accident. He discovered that one of his pupils, Harry Gibson, a keen photographer, had been on several trips to the Alps with his father. From Gibson, he learned about George, and his habit of climbing on buildings.

Later, when writing his obituary for the *Alpine Journal*, Irving recalled his first impressions of George. "He had a strikingly beautiful face. Its shape, its delicately cut features, especially the rather large, heavily lashed, thoughtful eyes, were extraordinarily suggestive of a Botticelli Madonna, even when he had ceased to be a boy—though any suspicion of effeminacy was completely banished by obvious proofs of physical energy and strength." It was an early example of the impact George could have on those meeting him and of the important relationships this could lead to. At that time, George had done no serious mountaineering at all. Although his forays on drainpipes and roofs had continued at Winchester, he had shown little curiosity about the wider mountaineering world, and had read none of the mountaineering books in the college library. Irving—who at twenty-seven was just ten years older than George—nonetheless proposed that he and Gibson should go to the Alps with him that summer. Both were delighted at the prospect, and their parents gave their consent.

The three took the night ferry from Southampton to le Havre on August 2, reaching Bourg St. Pierre in the French Alps on August 4. Over the next three weeks Irving provided a dramatic introduction to alpine climbing, with all its hazards and rewards. The days were long and demanding, often lasting from dawn to dusk or beyond, as they tramped over glaciers, crossed high mountain passes, and tackled several major peaks, including Mont Blanc, highest mountain in the Alps. They had to contend with altitude sickness, rockfall, storms, and bitter cold. George devoured it all, writing long, detailed letters to his mother and contributing to a diary of the trip, describing the overnight stops in primitive mountain huts, the rudimentary food, and the characters they met, like the hut guardian who had climbed with the great Italian mountaineer and photographer, Vittorio Sella.

Their first climb, on a snow peak named Mont Velan, brought a spectacular view of sunrise on Mont Blanc. "The first few hundred feet of the climb were in moonlight, and the dawn afterwards was glorious," George wrote. Then the sun rose on Mont Blanc, "which was a perfectly delightful pink; and we watched it spread over a range of peaks with infinite delight." Sadly, the attempt ended in failure when both George and Gibson were hit by altitude sickness. George vomited a dozen times and they turned back 600 feet from the summit. Their next attempt was on the Grand Combin, a complex mountain peak with a long approach: they climbed the 1800-foot west ridge and then started across a vast snowfield leading to the summit. After "a rest and some grub," George wrote, "[we] went up the last 700 feet in fine form in half an hour. The Grand Combin is 14,100 feet and of course the view from the top was simply ripping." Irving later wrote of "the blessed certainty in all of us that we had spent the best day of our lives."

While Gibson had to go home after a week, George and Irving spent seventeen of the next eighteen days on the move, traversing peaks and cols as they crossed between France, Switzerland, and Italy. There were several troubling moments: while descending from the Col de l'Evêque, Irving fell into a hidden crevasse, George helping to haul him out on their rope; later they lost their way and lost two hours crossing the wrong col. Most dangerously of all, they were assailed by rockfall as they were returning to France via the Col du Chardonnet. George dived for shelter but Irving was almost hit by a boulder. "The cannonade probably continued for about half a minute and seemed, both from the noise, which occurred in three main waves, and from the debris, to be fairly extensive," George related. "Altogether it was a very interesting and somewhat exciting incident." There was bad weather during their final week, and they were driven back by a storm as they attempted Mont Blanc via the Dôme Glacier and the Bionnassay Arête. After sheltering in the Dome hut overnight they tried again the next day, climbing the final stretch in a bitter wind that pierced their clothing and threatened to tear them from their holds. Having come through such a severe test, Irving wrote, they had a "thrill in their hearts . . . It is impossible to make any who have never experienced it realise what that thrill means. It proceeds partly from a legitimate joy and pride in life."

While George found the gamut of mountain experiences utterly exhilarating, Irving's actions were to lead him into a bitter controversy. Even the most

experienced alpinists were unsure whether it was safe to climb without professional guides; and yet Irving continued to take boys from Winchester, most of
them novices, to the Alps for the next four years. In December 1908 he read a
paper to the Alpine Club entitled "Five Years with Recruits." He described how
he had enlisted George and Gibson and justified the practice as "fitting the recruits for service in the great and growing army of mountaineers." It was a somewhat truculent defense for, after admitting that he had expected to be attacked for
"corrupting youth," he accused his critics of taking more risks during their climbing careers than he had, adding that he would not have wanted to climb with some
of them himself. It was a provocative onslaught on some of the most distinguished
names in British alpinism, among them Tom Longstaff, Walter Haskett Smith,
Douglas Freshfield, and Geoffrey Winthrop Young, who sent a collective letter to
the *Alpine Journal* to dissociate themselves from Irving's beliefs. Willfully or otherwise, Irving was missing the point, as there was a world of difference between
taking chances for oneself and putting other people, particularly young people, at
risk. Irving could claim, as he did, that he had got away with it, but the odds
eventually turned against him, for in 1930 he was leading a party of young climbers
on l'Evêque at Arolla when two of them slipped and fell to their deaths.

❧

Four days after reaching Chamonix, George was back in Britain. Home was no
longer Mobberley, however. During his absence the family had been preparing
to leave rural Cheshire for a far less attractive neighborhood: an industrial parish adjoining the docklands on the Mersey at Birkenhead. Instead of trees and
fields, there would be rows of terraced houses clustered around the church of St.
John, a mid-Victorian building with a tall spire set among the homes of
Birkenhead's dockyard workers. The precise reasons for the move have remained
a mystery; but several explanations have circulated both in the family and in
Mobberley, together with some convenient glosses that almost certainly concealed the truth.

The parish register for Mobberley in the summer of 1904 gives little away. It
reveals only that Herbert proceeded with his parochial business, helping to organize the usual summer fruit, flower, and vegetable show. Then came reports that he
had decided to leave Mobberley, the villagers presenting him with an illuminated
vellum address and some items of furniture—a dressing case and bookcase—to
mark his departure.

Other documents contain some clues. The records of the Chester diocese reveal
the details of a suspiciously neat transaction involving the Rev. Herbert Leigh Mallory,

31

rector of the parish church of Mobberley, and the Rev. Gerald Campbell Dicker of the vicarage and benefice of St. John, Birkenhead. On the same day, July 27, 1904, both men tendered their resignations to the Bishop of Chester. They were then installed in each other's former parish, Herbert Mallory taking over at St. John's, Birkenhead, Dicker replacing him at St. Wilfrid's in Mobberley. The switch, so smooth and convenient, looked, in short, like an ecclesiastical fix.

Since then, several possible explanations have emerged. One version, apparently retailed by the Mallorys' daughter Mary and passed on to her daughter Barbara, asserted that her mother Annie had become excessively friendly with a local man, although how far this excess of friendship went remained unclear. A second version, which reached some of Avie's descendants, related that it was not Annie but Mary herself who had implicated her family in scandal. There was a third version that placed Herbert at the center of the episode. Herbert, who had business connections in Liverpool and Birkenhead, had incurred a debt with the Rev. Gerald Dicker, which was settled when he exchanged his Mobberley parish for the bleaker environs of Birkenhead.

Then there was version four, which also featured Herbert: it was neither his wife nor his daughter who became entangled with a parishioner, but Herbert himself. This version, which was still being recounted by older Mobberley residents ninety years later, held that Herbert had been "involved" with several other parishioners, namely the young serving women who came and went from the Mallory household so frequently. The story goes that when Annie learned about Herbert's transgressions she at first refused to go to Birkenhead with him, only changing her mind when she realized that this would create an even greater public scandal.

The evidence to decide which of these accounts could be true is scanty. But there is one further clue. In the spring of 1904 there was an air of crisis in the Mallory family, for Annie had suffered a nervous breakdown. Avie accompanied her to Boscombe, a town near Bournemouth on the south coast, where she was to convalesce. George visited her there and took her on a tour of Winchester. The timing is suggestive, for other evidence shows that Herbert was preparing his family for the move to Birkenhead at about this time, and long ahead of the maneuvers in the bishop's office in Chester. On May 18 George wrote to Avie from Winchester to inform her he had received a letter from their father telling him "a lot more about Birkenhead." His father had told him it was "an exceedingly important parish, so that father is jolly lucky to get the chance of it, and I think he is quite right in accepting." Herbert appeared to be anticipating doubts about the move: while admitting it would be a "wrench" to leave Mobberley, "he seems to think that it won't be at all a bad place to live." George remained puzzled, particularly when he learned that church politics were involved. In a letter to his mother on August 23, in which he supposed she was "fearfully busy getting things ready to move," he added the intriguing remark: "I can't understand the connection of Archdeacon Barber."

From this fragmentary evidence, it is clear that none of the Mallorys' children was told the whole truth. Our best guess—and it remains a guess—is that some kind of impropriety, possibly sexual, was overlain by some equally murky church politics. We could find nothing in the diocesan records held in Chester to enable it to be resolved, and it remains a tantalizing episode in the backplot of the Mallory family history.

The Mallorys' new home was St. John's Rectory, a somber mid-Victorian building with a large garden on the edge of industrial Birkenhead. Herbert pursued his new duties with his customary commitment, moving a vote of thanks at the next church meeting to the lady parishioners who had decorated the church so magnificently at Easter. Annie engaged a new raft of servants, whose terms in office proved to be shorter, if anything, than those of their counterparts in Mobberley.

George, now seventeen, returned to Winchester in September for the start of his final year. In a bold move, he decided that he wanted to study a subject that concerned the real world, and switched from math to history. Irving was impressed with his progress and recommended that he sit for a history scholarship to Cambridge. His father had been at Trinity College but Irving suggested he try for Magdalene, a smaller and more intimate place. When George sat the exams he was awarded a scholarship known as a sizarship, an achievement all the more notable since he had taken up his new subject at such a late stage.

As the summer approached, so did a second visit to the Alps. Climbing had gripped George's imagination, and he had been practicing his techniques on the Winchester architecture, attracting a rapt crowd when he bridged his way up between a chimney and the brickwork of a gate tower fifty feet above Chamber Court. Irving meanwhile had been on the lookout for more recruits. In January he formed the Winchester Ice Club—he was the president—and held its inaugural meet in Snowdonia in January, staying at the Pen y Gwryd Hotel. George could not be there but Harry Gibson attended, plus two of the new recruits, Harry Tyndale and Guy Bullock—the same Bullock who was George's companion when he obtained his first visionary sighting of Everest in 1921.

The Ice Club returned to the Alps in August 1905, with Tyndale and Bullock—but not Gibson—joining Irving and George. It was more of a sociable affair than the previous year, for Irving had invited his sister as well as Tyndale's mother and his two sisters. The climbing proceeded at a relatively easy pace, concentrating on the straightforward peaks around the Val d'Arolla high in the Pennine Alps above Sion in Switzerland, with glistening sunrises, glowing sunsets, views of the peaks under fresh snow, and hearty evening meals in mountain inns. While it was a far less strenuous trip than in 1904, it helped George consolidate his skills, learn about safeguarding less experienced climbers, and appreciate just what he had achieved the previous year. He also became acquainted with the frustrations of sitting out bad weather, for there were several blank days due to storms.

On August 21, Irving, George, and Bullock left the novices behind to attempt the Dent Blanche, a fang-like 14,000-foot peak at the heart of the Pennine Alps. It had a daunting reputation, as the Welsh pioneer Owen Glynne Jones had fallen to his death from its west ridge in 1899, but Irving was undeterred. They left the Bertol hut at 3:15 A.M., crossing a huge snowfield by moonlight, "on the most delightful hard crisp snow," George wrote, then as dawn broke, embarked on a scramble over easy rocks which took them on to the long, exposed south ridge—a serious alpine undertaking even today. As they climbed, George related, "peak after peak was touched with the pink glow of the first sun, which slowly spread until the whole top was a flaming fire—and that against a sky with varied tints of leaden blue." They reached the summit before midday, and duly celebrated, for as George told his mother, the Dent Blanche was "the one peak we had set our hearts upon doing."

The rest of the stay was blighted by bad weather, but George was content. He left the Alps on the last day of August, returning to Birkenhead on September 2. In less than a month he would be starting at Cambridge: another new world to enjoy and explore.

CHAPTER TWO

The Charming Mallory
1905–1908

A day or so before the start of the Michaelmas term in 1905, George attended the early-morning service at King's College Chapel, a few minutes' walk from Magdalene College. There was only a scattering of people among the pews and few of them seemed familiar with the order of service, unsure precisely when they should be standing, sitting, or kneeling. When the service ended and George got up to leave, he glanced at a bulky middle-aged man, with center-parted hair and a bushy mustache, who had been sitting behind him. Although George did not know it then, the man had been looking at him throughout the service, anxious for a sight of his face.

A few days later, George paid his first visit to his college tutor, Arthur Benson, who was to guide his history studies during his three years at Cambridge. When he arrived at Benson's rooms, in a converted granary a short distance from Magdalene, he discovered that it was Benson who had been sitting behind him in the chapel at King's. Benson, by the same token, was delighted to learn that the "fine looking boy, evidently a freshman" he had watched was to be one of his pupils. As George turned to leave at the end of the service, Benson had been struck by the "extraordinary and delicate beauty of his face." Now, as they talked about his studies for the coming term, George showed his enthusiasm for his subject, and said he was keen to develop his essay-writing techniques. Benson was further drawn to George, who seemed "full of admiration for all good things," but with no touch of priggishness.

"A simpler, more ingenuous, more unaffected, more genuinely interested boy I never saw. He is to be under me, and I rejoice in the thought."

The first encounter between George and his college tutor provides a further example of the magnetic effect he could inspire. To say that someone has an aura is to describe how they are perceived by their beholders; George certainly seemed to have a poise and stillness, suggesting an inner confidence and certainty which, combined with his looks and physique, served to prompt such a response. It equally reflected the reserve he maintained while evaluating new characters or situations before committing himself to his response. Later, his confidence showed itself in less agreeable ways, his Cambridge colleagues discovering that he could be tendentious, combative, and dogmatic when expounding and defending his views, before these traits eventually softened.

For George, the meeting with Benson also served as his introduction to the notable assembly of characters he was to encounter during his four years at Cambridge. His friends included Rupert Brooke, James Strachey, and Maynard and Geoffrey Keynes, and he met other luminaries such as H. G. Wells and Henry James. This was a time of social and political ferment, as radical ideas in politics, literature, and the arts gained ground. Socialism was in the air, the fight for women's rights was intensifying, and there was a new iconoclasm in the arts. In personal areas too, the new Cambridge generation was questioning Victorian taboos and exploring the diverse nature of both friendship and sexuality. For a time climbing remained in abeyance but then George's interest was rekindled as a further outcome of his Cambridge friendships.

Benson, as George found, was a somewhat nervous figure, who sat twisting a cigarette between his fingers as he conducted his tutorials. In his forties, he had been appointed history supervisor at Magdalene the year before George arrived. He was a prodigious writer and biographer, his magnum opus being a massive two-volume account of the life of his father, the late Archbishop of Canterbury. He had previously taught at Eton, where he held views that were decidedly radical for their time. He disagreed with traditional teaching methods, from flogging to learning by rote, arguing for a more considerate and sympathetic approach. At Magdalene, he took an expansive view of the requirements of the history curriculum, and encouraged George to read as widely as possible. "The best rule," he told George succinctly, "is to read what interests one." To help George develop as a writer, Benson recommended Boswell's *Life of Johnson* and Trevelyan's *Life and Letters of Lord Macaulay*. Benson praised George for the broad scope of his work, although he rebuked him when he delivered an essay late. George looked crestfallen but Benson forgave him when he explained that he had worked on it through the night.

While George enjoyed Benson's praise as his tutor, he did not understand, at least at first, that Benson had a more personal agenda. As an extension of his educational theories Benson believed in friendships "across the generations," which brought together "youth and age." He went further, referring to "romantic attachments," which were to be conducted with "seemliness and decorum." He was, in truth, attracted to young men, particularly if they possessed George's combination of apparent innocence and a striking physique. He was what would be called today a celibate gay, for he did not pursue physical relationships with the objects of his affection but instead conducted emotional courtships in which he probed their innermost thoughts and feelings as if to penetrate to the core of their psyche.

The outcome, for Benson, was to suffer the pangs of unrequited love, wooing his students to the very edge of propriety, yet always unable to express his love for them in words, let alone venture into what he called the "dark places," a coded term for sex. Benson confided much of this in voluminous secret diaries, amounting to four million words, most of which he ordered should be kept sealed until fifty years after his death. When they were finally opened in 1975 they revealed the extent of his torment, with George the focus of his most fevered adoration.

There was much in Benson's background to account for his tribulations. His father was a guilt-laden, puritanical man who before becoming Archbishop of Canterbury had ruthlessly flogged his pupils at Wellington, where he was headmaster. He treated his wife Mary as a chattel, even though she provided him with six children in eleven years, and she had a mental breakdown and temporarily fled from home. When he died, Mary took as her companion a friend, Lucy Tait, the daughter of the previous Archbishop of Canterbury, and shared her marital bed with her for the rest of her life. Of Mary's six children, none ever formed a satisfactory relationship with the opposite sex and several had mental breakdowns. The most accomplished was Benson's brother Fred, who—as E. F. Benson—wrote novels about the manners and morals of English society, which became regarded as masterpieces of high camp.

George's relationship with Benson set him a difficult test. Benson can be seen as another of the older figures who served as his mentor through successive phases of his life. George undoubtedly found it flattering that a respected older figure should award him such personal attention. Benson's gradual exploration of his emotions, encouraging him to express himself openly, was an important benefit for someone who had been brought up in a semidysfunctional family and had passed through the repressive public school system with its emphasis on the traditional stiff upper lip. But George was also having to deal with someone who was not merely probing his emotions but seeking to manipulate them as he sought to secure his affection and love. Gradually he divined Benson's motives but decided to continue with the relationship for the benefits it would bring; in this, as with climbing, he judged that the risks, which he felt he could manage, were outweighed by the potential rewards. In the end it was George who gained control of the relationship and Benson, not he, who was its casualty.

Before long Benson was extending invitations to George to take tea at his rooms in the converted granary. "The charming Mallory came, and we were all very serious together," Benson wrote. In due course, George returned the compliment. "By invitation to tea with the charming Mallory in his rooms at the corner of the court. We talked like old friends." When George confided that he found Cambridge "shallow" in comparison with Winchester, Benson agreed that it must have been a wrench to leave Winchester, but advised: "You must find room for Magdalene by-and-by."

George soon immersed himself in Cambridge life. As a scholar he was unusual in showing a keen interest in sport, for the intellectuals and the "bloods," as the sportsmen were known, normally had little to do with each other. Although he had not rowed before, his gymnastics at Winchester had given him an oarsman's physique and he joined the Magdalene rowing club. He made his first forays into politics, joining the university Fabian Society, and becoming Magdalene's representative on the committee of the university's Women's Suffrage Association. When news of George's political conversion reached Birkenhead, his father was shocked, but George took care to conceal an even more momentous shift. Although he would still say he was a Christian, he was questioning the trappings of religion, treading a path that would lead him to become an agnostic.

He also became more assertive. At first he had seemed diffident and cautious, as if weighing up the new world he found himself in. Now he let his hair grow and wore black flannel shirts and bright-colored ties. When a fellow student, David Pye, accused him of dressing in "peculiar" clothes for effect, George said it was a natural form of self-expression. Pye, a brilliant scientist who was to become one of the most steadfast of George's friends, also felt that George was unduly aggressive and dogmatic in political discussions and debates, sometimes becoming so excitable that he spoke far too fast and cut off the endings of his words. George justified himself to Pye by saying that debates were like "intellectual fisticuffs in which you hit out as shrewdly as you could and did not resent your adversary doing the same." Some of his opponents were unforgiving, accusing him of intellectual arrogance, but Pye accepted his explanation. He also saw the gentler side of George's personality when the two men explored the countryside around Cambridge during the summer term. They searched for prehistoric earthworks near Newmarket, and traced the route of the Via Devana, a stretch of Roman road south of Cambridge which crosses the gentle mounds known as the Gog Magog hills. Once they went rowing on the Ouse at St. Ives. They followed a reed-covered channel to Houghton where, Pye wrote, they watched the dripping wheel of a water mill, "with the sweet scent of the fresh river water all about it."

Benson, meanwhile, was continuing his courtship. Just before the term ended he invited George for dinner in his rooms. He wrote in his diary that George was "gentle, considerate, grateful" and "more than beautiful." Yet George was clearly holding back: "I think he is unsympathetic, hard and self-absorbed," Benson later wrote. Although he felt that George liked him—"and I certainly like him"—something seemed to be missing. "I don't feel in contact with him."

At the start of George's second academic year in October, he was elected secretary of the Magdalene boat club, a token of his popularity among his sporting colleagues. Academically, his goal was to prepare for part one of the history tripos, his first university exams, which took place in June. Benson continued in his dual role of tutor and suitor, inviting him to tea and taking him to a Greek play for which, as he proudly recorded, he had secured the best seats. At the end of term, Benson invited George to stay with him at Hinton Hall, a mansion he had leased in the fens at Haddenham, ten miles north of Cambridge. Benson confided in his diary that he still hoped to pierce George's reserve and explore his true feelings on topics such as religion and the vexed subject of "relationships." When George arrived they went for a cycle ride in drizzling rain. Benson asked George about his family and George told him that his father was the vicar of Birkenhead. When Benson appeared surprised, George related the story of his father's self-sacrifice in moving to Birkenhead. "He deliberately exchanged his own rich and comfortable living for this ghastly work at the age of forty-five, feeling he was growing too comfortable," Benson recorded.

Each night Benson wrote of his increasing affection for George. He was "one of the most ingenuous and purest-minded creatures I know . . . very beautiful, too, to look at, and finely proportioned, so that it is a pleasure to me to see him move, or do anything." Benson was clearly relishing the air of danger, for one evening he compiled his diary while George sat nearby reading *Dr. Jekyll and Mr. Hyde*, which Benson had lent him. "He sits behind me ensconced in a chair," Benson wrote, "in absolute silence except for his breathing and a turned page."

When Benson asked George about his spiritual beliefs George evidently revealed some of his doubts, for the discussion turned to "religious difficulties, miracles etc." On December 14, the day George left, the two men posed for a photograph in the doorway of Hinton Hall. George, who was wearing a belted tweed jacket, faced the camera confidently, while Benson looked at him rather coyly from one side. Benson thought the photograph was "somewhat grotesque—he appears impish, I like an old bear." Benson nevertheless felt he had achieved the long-awaited breakthrough he had sought. "This boy has grown much with my heart—he is so simple, ingenuous, affectionate and grateful . . . a little barrier seems to have melted between us."

⚭

In the new term Benson gave George his reward. It was as if George were a debutante and Benson his chaperone, as George was introduced to the higher echelons of Cambridge life. On February 7, 1907, Benson took him to dinner at Christ's College, where the guests included Charles Darwin, grandson of the author of *The Origin of Species*; Benson's brother Hugh, who had achieved the notoriety, as the son of the Archbishop of Canterbury, of converting to Catholicism; and Charles Sayle, an under-librarian at the university library. The most significant of these, in terms of George's Cambridge career, was Sayle. He was one of the patrons of Cambridge's intellectual social life, holding salons at his rooms at 8 Trumpington Street, effecting introductions to Cambridge's overlapping and interlocking social cliques.

Like Benson, Sayle was gay, but whereas Benson remained discreet and chaste, Sayle was more liberated. He was attracted to the poet Rupert Brooke, who had arrived at Cambridge the year after George, and was "great in his ideals, great in his imagination, great in his charm." Sayle also developed a close relationship with Geoffrey Keynes, a scientist and future surgeon, and the brother of the eminent economist, Maynard Keynes. Much later Benson judged that Sayle had been one of the emblematic figures of Cambridge in the years before the First World War, when it was a place "of books, music and beautiful young men." Sayle termed the young men who congregated at Trumpington Street his "swans," although a more cynical observer described them as "Sayle's menagerie."

Within days, Sayle invited George to tea. Sayle too kept a diary, though far less intimate than Benson's, in which he recorded every coming and going at Trumpington Street. His first tea alone with George swiftly appeared, followed by their first dinner alone, and before long Sayle was accounting George one of his swans. The attraction for George was the select company Sayle kept, and he soon met Brooke, Geoffrey Keynes, Cosmo Gordon—a fellow member of the Women's Suffrage Association—and others. This brought George entrée to other Cambridge circles and took him to the fringe of the most celebrated network of all, the Apostles, the secretive, self-selecting intellectual elite, with a strong gay component, which provided many future leaders of the British political and artistic classes. The main purpose of the Apostles was intellectual debate, and each apostle in turn was obliged to prepare and lead a debate that would be contested by the others: failure in readiness to speak was punished by expulsion. Although George was not in the end invited to join he found himself on the guest list for lectures by H. G. Wells (on socialism) and Hilaire Belloc (the Appreciation of History) and for private soirees with distinguished guests of the status of Henry James. He was enlisted into the Marlowe Society, which Sayle had just set up and which was due to stage its first production, *Dr. Faustus*, in November. Rupert Brooke would play Mephistopheles, Justin Brooke (no relation) Faustus, Geoffrey Keynes the Evil Angel, Gordon a magician, and George the Pope.

Another of the activities presided over by Sayle at Trumpington Street was a continuing series of discussions about the psychology and morality of human relationships. To some extent they paralleled the innovative theories emanating from Vienna, where Freud had published his pioneering psychoanalytical work, *The Interpretation of Dreams*, in 1899, and were matched by the development of corresponding themes in literature and the arts at the turn of the century. There was further impetus from the work of the Cambridge moral philosopher G. E. Moore, who declared in 1904 that since there was no objective basis for moral conventions, they should be based on notions of friendship and loyalty. E. M. Forster, who was at Cambridge shortly before George, took up the issues in his early novels, which asserted that the greatest happiness came from being true to your feelings.

These ideas underpinned the debates at Trumpington Street, which ranged across the wellsprings of thought and feelings, the mechanisms of relationships, and the need to express both emotion and affection. These themes became important in George's life, in his writing and his relationships, and he was among the most determined of Sayle's swans to explore them. He was much taken by Forster's novels, in particular *A Room with a View*, which was published in 1908. Forster drew some of his characters from life in Cambridge, and the novel contains some beguiling echoes: Forster's hero is named George, he is healthy and muscular, is compared to a figure by Michelangelo, is a Fabian, and has a taste for the open air. Coincidence or otherwise, the novel held strong resonances for George, as he gave a copy to his sister Avie.

In April, to his intense chagrin, George contracted jaundice, which ruled him out of the intercollege rowing races held in May. Both Sayle and Benson visited him in his room, Benson recording that a delivery boy arrived with a bunch of lilies of the valley, together with a note, written in capitals, "from a fair unknown." When George asked who had sent the flowers, the boy told him that "a gentleman" had paid for them without leaving his name. The episode clearly disconcerted Benson. As soon as George had recovered from jaundice, and they resumed their walks along the Cam or into the countryside, Benson began probing what he called George's "romantic attachments." Benson was particularly keen to hear about his "attachment" to a sixteen-year-old woman named Olive Blood, a doctor's daughter whom George knew in Birkenhead. George did not seem especially committed to the relationship, telling Benson he hadn't even mentioned it to his parents, but Benson brought up the subject time and again. "I don't wonder at a girl falling in love with him," Benson concluded; he was after all fine, thoughtful, and independent; his face was pensive, innocent, displaying a curious melancholy. "Why should I pretend that I do not love this young friend, and take deep pleasure in his company and his toleration for myself?"

On May 26, George sat the first of his Cambridge exams, part one of the history tripos. George seemed unworried, telling Benson the previous day: "I am always happiest on the eve of the fray—it is a stimulus which suits me," a remark revealing his love of excitement, the adrenalin rush, that preceded difficult or dangerous tasks, of which mountaineering was the paradigm. George's optimism proved misplaced, for when the results were published three weeks later, he was disappointed to learn that he had been awarded a third class. It was not as bad as it sounded, for most Cambridge undergraduates sat for the lesser-status pass degree, only a quarter aiming like George for an honors degree. But George berated himself for "a worthless performance," though he consoled himself that he had been awarded high marks for his essay. Benson shouldered some of the blame, telling George he had encouraged him to read too widely and should have insisted on more disciplined essay preparation.

A few days later, as the academic year ended, Benson's relationship with George moved to its climactic phase. Confessing in his diary to the "haunting wish" to establish some "permanent tie" between them, Benson again invited George to stay with him at Hinton Hall. He did so against a background of fresh disasters in his family. His sister Maggie, who was living at the family home at Tremans, a country house near Horsted Keynes in Sussex, had become insatiably jealous of her mother's friendship with Lucy Tait. When Tait and her mother prepared to depart on holiday to Venice, Maggie suffered a spectacular mental breakdown, locking herself in her room for two days and flagellating herself with a whip. Benson dashed to Tremans, where he signed a committal order confining his sister to a nearby convent. He was distraught at witnessing her distress, while also fearing that he would succumb to the same affliction. "The shadow waits," he wrote.

When George arrived at Hinton Hall, Benson was clearly on edge, wondering how it would all be resolved: "I am alone in my own comfortable house with a boy to whom I am greatly attached, who is attached to me, and whose company I love." Benson had just bought a car, and his chauffeur took them for drives across the fens, to Peterborough, Huntingdon, the Hemingfords, and St. Ives. Benson found George "more and more congenial, caring about all the things I care about, a love of poetry and beauty," and recorded his "exclamations of pleasure which break from him spontaneously at the beauties of the place, and his vehement laughter and rippling smiles if he is amused."

George's reports home gave no hint of the undercurrents at Hinton Hall. It was, he observed mildly, "a jolly place to stay." He described the excursions into the countryside, adding: "One generally arrives back in time for a late tea, after which A.C.B. produces gems of literature and we both read till dinner at 8.15." After dinner Benson would play the organ, George a pianola—"though not at the same time." The joy of the place, he added, was that "one can do exactly as one likes, and everything is so peaceful and quiet and comfortable."

On June 30, the last day of George's stay, Benson steeled himself to broach the most intimate subject: could he tell George he loved him, would George reciprocate? He asked George what he thought about "the expression of sentiment." Benson thought he saw in George "a great and deep penetration of emotion—I felt scorched, as by a fire." He tried to encourage George by saying that you could reveal your deepest emotions to a trustworthy friend. But George rebuffed him, replying that such things "should never be expressed." That afternoon they went for a walk and Benson tried again. A thunderstorm broke and as they took shelter under a bridge Benson raised the topic of "Magdalene and Cambridge." When George agreed that there was "much romantic friendship in the air," Benson became bolder, talking of "a darker moral region, the shadow that lies behind such friendships"—a coded reference to physical sex. Once again George gave him no encouragement. After tea George left Hinton Hall and returned to Birkenhead. So the moment passed and Benson had not declared his love for George: yet he still described it as a "day in a thousand," adding that listening to George made him feel "young and rash." Benson never came near to raising the subject again, for the next time they met was on an entirely different footing.

⁂

That summer George rediscovered climbing. He did so as a result of Sayle's assiduous networking, for Sayle was a founder member of the Climbers' Club, set up in 1898 to foster British climbing, as opposed to the older Alpine Club whose focus was abroad. It was almost certainly Sayle who pointed out to George that, having had two seasons in the Alps, it was time he discovered what the British mountains had to offer. George set about organizing a trip to North Wales with three of his fellow swans: Geoffrey Keynes, Rupert Brooke, and Hugh Wilson, whose father was the Canon of Worcester. In the end Brooke dropped out, sending George a note of regret from Brussels, written on a postcard of Rodin's *Penseur*: "My soul yearns for mountains, which I adore from the bottom. But the pale gods have forbidden it."

Before he could go to Wales, George had an engagement to fulfill in Scotland. He had agreed to act as personal tutor to a boy from a wealthy family who lived in a castle at Udny near Aberdeen. Although he was well paid, George disliked the work, telling his sister Mary that the family were "too rich and tradesy." He arrived in Wales on September 13, staying with Wilson and Keynes at a farm named Gwern-y-Gof-Isaf in the Ogwen Valley. Among their ropes, boots, rucksacks, and other climbing paraphernalia, their single most important item of equipment was a book entitled *Rock Climbing in North Wales*, which had appeared the previous year. Written and published by George and Ashley Abraham, two brothers from Keswick, it provided an introduction to the mountains and climbs of Snowdonia, describing the crags where the young sport of rock climbing was developing, the now-classic venues such as Tryfan, Lliwedd, Glyder Fawr, Crib Goch, and Craig yr Ysfa.

The earliest climbers had followed the gullies that cleaved their way to the top of these cliffs but these had nearly all been ascended and now climbers were turning their attentions to the cliffs' ridges and faces, making ascents that required new balancing techniques and a trust in smaller hand- and footholds. In comparison with modern guidebooks, *Rock Climbing in North Wales* provided few technical details to the new routes, consisting mostly of personal reminiscences and anecdotes, enriched by the Abrahams' superb pioneering photography. Even so, it was not entirely welcomed by the Welsh climbing world, for the Abraham brothers came from rival territory, the English Lake District. Although much of their information had been provided by O. G. Jones, the Welshman who died in the Alps in 1899, some Welsh climbers regarded them as interlopers who wanted to pirate the Welsh routes. The Abrahams were also considered tainted by commercialism for publishing their book; and in any case, some in the Wales camp still believed that climbers should not use guidebooks at all but should rediscover the routes for themselves.

Since George was still outside the higher councils of British climbing, it is unlikely that he was aware of the ideological debate the Abrahams' book had sparked. In other respects, too, he and his two companions were naively unaware of what they were about to undertake. This was a time when climbers' equipment and safety techniques were in their infancy, and the simplest mistakes could prove fatal. The most common footwear consisted of heavy hobnailed boots whose grip could be improved by fastening soft iron clinker-nails around the edge, leaving a trail of scratches on the rocks that are visible today. Their ropes were made of natural fiber such as hemp, with a far lower breaking point than the nylon ropes introduced in the 1950s.

Most crucial of all, the methods that have made rock climbing a comparatively safe sport had hardly been thought of. Modern climbing leaders deploy a range of techniques to limit the length of a possible fall. They use their rope, in conjunction with equipment such as slings, carabiners, and jamming devices, to install what are known as running belays. If they should slip, they fall only as far as the running belay, and then the same distance again, before they are held on the rope. In George's time no such protection existed. The best that climbers could do to limit a fall was to pass their rope around a spike of rock or thread it through a hole. But most often they would climb fifty or sixty feet above their partner with no protection at all, meaning that a fall would usually prove fatal.

It was against this background that George, Keynes, and Wilson contemplated the routes in the Abrahams' book. They chose a representative sample on the principal crags then being climbed, from the slanting slabs and ribs of Lliwedd on the Snowdon massif, to the isolated cliffs of Craig yr Ysfa, hidden away deep in the Carneddau range—so remote that it was said to have been first spotted by telescope from the summit of Scafell in the Lake District. George's first two British rock climbs, which he accomplished on August 14, were on Tryfan, the slender crenellated peak close to their lodgings in the Ogwen Valley. North Gully, which leads to the gap between Tryfan's main and north summits, was described by the Abrahams as "one of the most popular courses in Snowdonia," although also requiring "a confident leader." North Buttress—"exceptionally suitable for parties that have passed through the novitiate stages"—gave several rewarding pitches of exposed climbing with magnificent views and a long drop.

On Craig yr Ysfa, they climbed Great Gully, described by the Abrahams as "a lengthy expedition of exceptional severity," containing the notorious eighty-foot cave pitch. It was the hardest of their climbs, and they were soaked by the waterfall that often surges down the cave pitch. Then they climbed Amphitheatre Buttress, a magnificent 900-foot rib of rock, narrowing in places to a knife-edge, which the Abrahams called "one of the finest in Wales." On September 18 they established an historical landmark of their own, although not quite as they would have intended. They were climbing the Central Route on Lliwedd's East Buttress—

suitable, the Abrahams said, only for "thoroughly expert parties"—when one of them dislodged a stone. It crashed down the cliff, narrowly missing one of the most illustrious figures of Welsh climbing, Archer Thomson, then making the first ascent of a new route. Thomson delivered a stern reprimand, but named his new route Avalanche.

The climbing diary celebrates another of the pleasures to be derived from the mountains. On September 19, George wrote, the three men rounded off their day on Craig yr Ysfa with a swim in Ffynnon Llugwy, the lake they passed on their return to Ogwen, Wilson making "the hills resound with a magnificent belly-flopper." That George should record this detail was no accident, for he was a devoted swimmer himself. He did so in unabashed style for, as a range of photographs taken in locations from Cornwall to Everest testifies, it was his invariable practice to strip off. Skinny-dipping has always been a pleasurable accompaniment to climbing, although most practitioners prefer the summer, when to soothe your limbs in the rock-pools of a tumbling Scottish burn, or the deeps of a river winding through a glen, is the perfect finish to a hard-won day.

It was certainly the style of George's day too but he took it to extremes, plunging into glacier lakes in the Alps or into British llyns and tarns even if it meant pushing the ice aside first. He also did so one evening in Cambridge, when he was boating with some friends on the Cam. His companions rowed away with his clothes, leaving George to climb out of the river, creep down the street still naked, and hammer on the door of Magdalene to be let in. A policeman threatened to arrest him, and the college porter only defused the situation by promising to report George to the college authorities. But in Snowdonia that September, swimming added to the luster of the experience. The three men doused themselves in a stream beside the farmhouse each morning and plunged into the nearest llyn during the return from their climb. "Such bathes!" Wilson wrote. In now familiar judgments, he wondered whether he could ever repeat such a time, while Geoffrey Keynes described these as the best days of his life.

⚬

George returned to Magdalene for the start of his third and final year as if renourished. He was elected captain of the boat club, and he resolved to improve on his third class in part one of his degree. He was also eager to show his talents in *Dr. Faustus*, the maiden production of the Marlowe Society, when it was staged at the university theater in Jesus Lane in November. There was a distinguished first-night audience, headed by Prince Leopold of the Belgians and his entourage, and George's sister Avie was there too. The production was somewhat austere, for there was no music, footlights, or scenery, and it proved that acting was not among George's talents. Rupert Brooke had already taken a dim view of his acting during rehearsals, and his performance as the Pope was hardly noticed.

His fortunes as an oarsman brought him better cheer, for his spell as captain of the Magdalene boat, according to the club's official history, threw all others "into the shade." With George rowing at number 7, the college boat moved up four places in the Lent semester bumps, as the intercollege races are known, and five places in May. George launched an appeal for the £130 ($624.00) the crew needed to take part in the Henley Regatta in July. The appeal was successful and the crew performed creditably enough. Academically, his hard work paid off, for he improved on his result of the previous year, being awarded a class two degree. After the exams he made a return to the stage, in Milton's masque *Comus*. This time Rupert Brooke was in full charge, stage-managing the production and reserving one of the leading parts for himself. George was relegated to a minor role as a member of a troupe of Morris dancers. A distinguished audience attended the opening performance on July 10, among them Thomas Hardy, Robert Bridges, Edmund Gosse, and Alfred Austin, the poet laureate.

On the day of the second and final performance of *Comus*, George had new dramas to face. The previous autumn, Arthur Benson had succumbed to his long-feared breakdown. George's visit to Hinton Hall had accentuated the conflicts of his emotional life, and his moods fluctuated alarmingly. His depression deepened when he visited his sister in Sussex, for he felt that the convent she was staying at was a place of "torture and living death," and her paranoia seemed to give real form to his own fears. He saw George just once more, meeting him by chance at Bletchley railway station and having a "scrappy, bawled sort of talk" as their train clattered its way to Cambridge. At the end of October 1908, after "fighting hour by hour against acute and perfectly mechanical depression," he yielded.

Benson's family doctor, Ross Todd, dispatched him to a nursing home in Mayfair, where he felt shrouded in "ultimate and inexorable darkness." In December he was sent to Italy in the hope that a tour of familiar Renaissance landmarks in Rome and Florence would have a beneficial effect, but to no avail. He was shunted between friends and nursing homes, made several brief and disastrous returns to Cambridge, and, after his sister had been moved to a priory in Northampton, found the greatest comfort at Tremans, the family home in Sussex. One of Benson's first public outings in 1908 was to attend the production of *Comus* in Cambridge. He had not seen Rupert Brooke before, and noted his "beautiful arms and radiant figure." But during his return journey to Horsted Keynes he was on the verge of suicide. "I prayed to have courage to end my life—it seemed so easy to lean out and let myself be struck senseless by some bridge or signal post."

It was George who came to Benson's rescue. Having learned of his distress, he dashed to Cambridge station after the closing performance of *Comus* on July 11, arriving at Horsted Keynes that evening still in his makeup. Benson was delighted to see him: "He was very charming," Benson wrote, "and very tired." George stayed for several days, conversing with him and taking him for walks, and talking and playing cards with members of Benson's family. Benson wrote that George was "very intelligent, clear-headed" and by the time he left, Benson felt "much less depressed." Benson's depression continued over the next two years and in that time George was one of the few friends who stayed loyal to him, visiting him, accompanying him on walks, and even joining him on holidays. Benson was moved by George's selflessness, particularly as he knew himself to be tetchy and difficult, and prone to jealousy when he learned of George's other friends. Although at times Benson felt "so old, so disenchanted with life," he remained deeply grateful to George. "It is a very charming thing to lend a hand."

✂

Equipped with his degree, George now had to consider a career. His firmest idea was to become a teacher and he looked into the possibility of doing so at Winchester. But when he consulted the deputy headmaster, Howard Rendall, whom he had known as a pupil, he was given a stern rebuff. "He says that as I have nothing to teach and would probably teach it badly, there is not the least chance of ever getting to Winchester," George told Benson. George did his best to absorb Rendall's criticism stoically, even though he had suggested that George should go into the church, and should look for "a good country parson" who needed a curate. At first George told Benson he was ready to consider "parish work of some kind," since it did at least fit his idea of undertaking social work, and he sensed that it would please his father. Then his doubts resurfaced, for he admitted he disliked almost every parson he had met. "They're excessively good, most of them, much better than I can ever hope to be, but their sense of goodness seems sometimes to displace their reason." Since his own father was a parson, it was a telling judgment.

Benson had an alternative suggestion, which suited Benson too: why not stay at Cambridge for another year? George could take his exams again in the hope of improving his degree; and he could try for a literary prize, for there was one on offer for the best essay on James Boswell, the biographer of Dr. Johnson, whose writing Benson had commended to George during their first tutorials. In the end it was an easy choice: there was little to compare between an apprenticeship to an "excessively good" parson in a remote country parish and the heady attractions of Cambridge. Benson was delighted by George's decision and so was Sayle, who helped him find rooms in Pythagoras House, a venerable building close to the northern reaches of the Backs.

In August George paid his second visit to Snowdonia in the company of his brother Trafford, who was then sixteen and attending Haileybury, a public school in Hertfordshire. As the youngest of the children, Trafford had grown up somewhat detached from his three older siblings, but his elder brother was clearly a hero figure. George had refused Trafford's entreaties to take him climbing with Keynes and Wilson the previous summer, but now resolved to make it up to him. With their bikes laden with equipment and climbing ropes coiled around their shoulders, they cycled the forty miles from Birkenhead to Snowdonia. They camped in a cowshed beside the Llugwy River at Capel Curig, where there was a pool deep enough to swim. They made a mattress from hay, but slept outside when the night was clear.

Although some days were lost to rain, George led Trafford up the Central Buttress on Tryfan, following a route put up by Archer Thomson in 1894, later called Second Pinnacle Ridge. They also visited Lliwedd, where an ascent by George gave rise to one of the founding myths of British climbing, as well as to a small controversy. George, it is told, left a pipe on a ledge known as the Bowling Green on Lliwedd's East Buttress. That evening, in the fading light, he climbed back up to retrieve it via a 230-foot line of rock ribs now known as Mallory's Slab Climb. The Abrahams were to describe it as "an exceedingly steep ascent of the face . . . there is quite 180 feet of difficult work, the lower half of which is most trying."

The controversy arises from the fact that George climbed the route alone. At that time solo climbing was considered an unjustifiable practice, since anyone who fell would almost certainly be killed. Some climbers did it but kept their ascents secret. Later guidebook editors dismissed the story of George's ascent as apocryphal and refused to include it in their lists, but his biographer David Robertson, who assessed the evidence carefully, concluded that it was true. In retrospect it is most likely that George's description of the ascent was accurate but the pipe story was not. It may well have been that George had gone with Trafford to sniff around Lliwedd for fresh routes. Having set off up the line of Slab Climb, he found that Trafford was unable to follow, and so completed the route himself. Because solo climbing was considered such anathema, George may have invented the story of the pipe to justify what he had done.

After climbing with Trafford, George undertook another session of private tutoring, at Dunrobin Castle in Sutherland. There was a disconcerting end, as his pupil stole some money and accused George of being the thief. His parents absolved George and administered their son a beating. Then came another climbing trip, this time to the Lake District with Geoffrey Keynes. The plan almost came to grief, for Keynes had helped to organize a Fabian summer school in Wales, with lectures on topics as diverse as Tolstoy, Shaw, and the Poor Law, and rambles and dances as well. Rupert Brooke, James Strachey, the younger brother of Lytton Strachey, and Hugh Dalton, later to become a minister in the postwar Attlee government, had all agreed to go, and Keynes pressed George to join them. But although George considered himself a "keen socialist," he sent Keynes a curiously sour reply. "If any of your Fabian friends should again mention my name, you might tell them what an enthusiast I am, and how I go about converting business men in Birkenhead, if not to be socialists, at all events to think seriously about the Fabian propositions."

The climbing arrangement somehow survived this contretemps, and George and Keynes met at the Wastwater Hotel on September 15. They were joined for a time by Harry Gibson, his fellow founder member of the Winchester Ice Club, and Harold Porter, a friend from Birkenhead. It was George's first visit to the cradle of English rock climbing, and they used another of the Abrahams' guidebooks, *Rock Climbing in the English Lake District*, to start with two of its set-piece climbs. The first was Kern Knotts Crack, consisting mostly of a seventy-five-foot pitch, which the Abrahams described as "for an expert, and none other should attempt the course," although George and his companions may have used a toprope, secured at the top of the crag, for protection. The Abrahams also gave it a technical grading, rating it as "Exceptionally Severe," the toughest standard of the time—it is graded today as "Medium Very Severe" (see Appendix 3).

The next day they climbed Napes Needle, the legendary rock spire on Great Gable whose ascent by Walter Haskett Smith in 1886 is considered the first great milestone in English rock climbing. Over the next week they climbed on Green Gable, Scafell Pinnacle, Great Gable, and Gable Crag, testing themselves against the local climbers' standards, then searching for new routes of their own. On the Napes they climbed Eagle's Nest Arête Direct, the best route of the cliff, another Exceptionally Severe, also rated today as Medium Very Severe. On Gable Crag they found some virgin rock on the far left-hand side of the cliff. They put up two new routes, Left-Hand Route and Right-Hand Route, the latter rated now as a "strenuous" Very Severe. George was pleased with his accomplishments, which set the pattern for both his climbing and his life: assess the territory, find your level, then push ahead.

CHAPTER THREE

L'Affaire George
1908–1909

When George returned to Cambridge for the 1908 Michaelmas term he visited Benson at Hinton Hall. Benson, who was feeling "so old, so disenchanted with life, so broken-winged," recorded his pleasure when George accompanied him on a walk: they talked "of many things, socialism, friendship"; George was "full of interests and enthusiasms."

Despite his cheerful appearance, George appeared to have been touched by Benson's air of gloom, for as winter approached he succumbed to feelings of introspection and ennui, even wondering whether he should have returned to Cambridge at all. On November 18, 1908, he wrote to his sister Avie on the occasion of her twenty-first birthday. "I wonder if you are feeling as sad as I did on my twenty-firster," he asked. "It is after all very natural, when one has enjoyed youth as much as you and I have, to hate the thought of leaving it behind, and to think that one is never going to enjoy oneself quite so much as one gets older." He did find one note of consolation: "I for one can honestly say that life is more worth living now than it was two years ago—not because there is less pain and evil—there is more, but for some reason I know a little more of the Good in this world and can appreciate and enjoy it the better." Later that month, normally so determined to present himself to his parents in a positive light, he confessed to his mother that he was bored.

George's listlessness proved to be temporary, for he was soon to be caught up in a bewildering series of events that tested his relish for new experiences to the utmost. The climate was partly set by the evolving nature of the discussions among the swans at Trumpington Street, which had resumed with new intensity and had even been accorded a title, the Cambridge School of Friendship. Benson had invoked the notion of friendship to try to lead George into the taboo "dark places," which George resisted. The use of the word friendship provides an important clue to what was about to ensue, for it has been suggested that it held several meanings, including a coded reference to homosexuality. Several books containing homosexual subtexts and the word friendship in the title were published in the 1900s, including *Ioläus: An Anthology of Friendship*, edited by Edward Carpenter, and *The Hill: A Romance of Friendship*, a public school novel by Horace Vachell. It has also been argued that the term embraced relationships across the sexual spectrum, and that the distinction between gender was fundamentally unimportant—indeed the very word homosexuality was not even coined until 1897, and was certainly not in widespread use.

Whatever the truth, and whatever term was used, there was no doubt that in Cambridge in 1908 "friendship" was an increasingly frequent topic of conversation. That summer Geoffrey Keynes's brother Maynard, who had spent two years working in India, returned to Cambridge to take up a fellowship at King's. On July 28 he wrote to his friend, the Bloomsbury artist Duncan Grant, to tell him: "The thing has grown with leaps and bounds in my two years of absence and practically everybody in Cambridge, except me, is an open and avowed sodomite." In November Rupert Brooke wrote in similar terms to his cousin Erica Cotterill. "Do you understand about loving people of the same sex?" he asked her. "It is the question people here discuss most, in all its aspects. And of course most of the sensible people would permit it."

This moment presents George's biographers with potentially the most sensitive phase of his life. The notion that George might at any stage have had homosexual tendencies, to use that time-honored phrase, is one that disturbs some members of his family. Others who find it less troubling still do not believe it happened. His daughter Clare said: "My father didn't mind what his gay friends did with one another. He wasn't gay, and he just didn't want to do it himself."

It should not be surprising that anyone might acquire homosexual leanings at Cambridge. The university remained a predominantly male institution that had long resisted the incursion of women. Far more than Oxford, it had developed a heavily homoerotic ambiance, to be detected, inter alia, in an obsessional interest in Greek art and statuary and in devotion to the poetry of A. E. Housman and Gerard Manley Hopkins, whose despair at the conflict between his faith and his sexuality was even more tormented than Benson's. There were homosexual undertones in Forster's writing and in 1913, encouraged by Edward Carpenter, he wrote *Maurice*, his clandestine novel about Cambridge homosexuality which was not published until 1971. Even so, Mallory biographers face a conundrum at this point. Previous mountaineering writers have tended to skirt the issue of whether there were homosexual episodes in his life. Some have raised it in order to deny it; others have mentioned it in passing. One recent book stated: "There is little evidence that Mallory was bisexual" and then cited two contradictory items of testimony. The first was an imaginatively phrased denial that George was homosexual, which supposedly emanated from the painter Duncan Grant; the second was the assertion that "James Strachey, George's Cambridge class-mate, testified in the affirmative." Biographers from the non-mountaineering world, by contrast, have shown few inhibitions, stating as a fact that George had at least one homosexual affair.

Although we were aware of the difficulties and the sensitivities involved, we felt that it was impossible to understand this phase of George's life unless we addressed the issue. After reading a file of his letters which are held at the British Library, we concluded that there could be no doubt that he had what was termed an "affair" with another man. What constituted an "affair" at that time remains a moot point, and one which was minutely debated in the Cambridge School of Friendship. Although it did not necessarily entail any sexual acts, they were certainly not ruled out, and among the more committed homosexuals they were almost de rigueur. In George's case there is pertinent evidence, which we have set out. The episode is interwoven with George's other activities for, while strug-gling with the emotional turmoil the affair induced, George climbed at a far more demanding level than before. He did so with another key figure whom he met through Sayle's menagerie and who was to be the dominant influence on his mountaineering career.

The story of George's affair features a colorful cast of characters. Among them are the Strachey brothers, Lytton and James. Lytton, who left Cambridge the year before George arrived, became the brilliant writer and man of letters, whose iconoclastic book *Eminent Victorians*, published in 1918, redefined the nature of biography. He was waspish, bitchy, and amusing, a lover of gossip and intrigue, and delighted in discussing the minutiae of romantic affairs, usually between men, and not least when he was one of those involved. His volumi-nous letters to friends, relatives, and lovers were written in an arch, sometimes sarcastic style and are perhaps better appreciated by imagining them spoken in his near-falsetto voice.

Lytton's brother James, seven years younger, had arrived at Cambridge in 1906, and shared Lytton's irreverent beliefs. Later he was a dedicated Fabian, an opponent of the First World War, an ardent campaigner for women's suffrage, and a distinguished psychoanalyst who translated the key works of Freud into English. While at Cambridge he exchanged gossip with Lytton regularly, James writing from King's College, Lytton from his home in London's Belsize Park Gardens. Virginia Woolf took against them at first, describing them as "cold and nasty," and they certainly made a formidable pair, displaying an air of snobbish superiority and taking delight in manipulating the affairs of lesser mortals, as George was most painfully to find out.

Then there was Maynard Keynes, brother of George's climbing partner Geoffrey, who arrived at Cambridge in 1902, becoming president of the Union and later one of the most influential economic theorists of the century. Lytton Strachey remarked that his intellect was so intimidating that it was "enough to freeze a volcano," although he was another inveterate gossip and manipulator, who, Lytton added, sat "like a decayed and amorous spider in King's, weaving purely imaginary webs, noticing everything that happens and doesn't happen, and writing to me every other post." James Strachey was even more forthright, calling him "the iron copulating machine."

The fourth figure in the imbroglio was the painter Duncan Grant, a cousin of the Stracheys and one of the central figures in the emerging Bloomsbury group, whose members, even more than the Cambridge friends, believed in the utmost openness and honesty in human affairs. Nothing was too private or intimate to feature in their discussions, which were sometimes so devastating in their effect that they were termed "bloodbaths." After training as an artist in Paris, Grant returned to London in 1908, gradually working his way through an eclectic succession of styles which were condemned by the less generous critics as opportunist and derivative. In contrast to the sophisticated Cambridge intellectuals, he had an intuitive, ingenuous, and more gentle approach to relationships, even if it was one which led him into spectacular confusions.

Among and beyond these four characters was a jigsaw of interlocking relationships and infatuations, some unrequited. Lytton was an Apostle who recruited his brother James for the group. James and Lytton then contrived to secure membership for Rupert Brooke. James fell passionately in love with Brooke, writing him a series of indiscreet and revealing letters until shortly before Brooke died in 1915. Lytton, who tended to fall in love with every handsome young man he met, was successively in love with Grant and Brooke, while Grant transferred his affections to Maynard Keynes. Although Grant's relationship with Keynes was deep and long-lasting, his later life became the most convoluted of all. For a time he and Keynes lived with Adrian Stephen and his sister Virginia (the future Virginia Woolf) at their home in Brunswick Square. Later Grant formed a ménage à trois with the painters Clive and Vanessa Bell. Vanessa had children by both of them: two sons by her husband Clive, and a daughter, named Angelica, by Grant. Angelica grew up believing that Clive was her father, learning only in adulthood that it was Grant. To complete the circle she later married one of her father's former lovers, David Garnett.

While the complications of Grant's life reached a state of such spectacular excess, it had one thing in common with many of his gay contemporaries, for a high proportion went on to marriage or other heterosexual relationships. As well as suggesting that human sexuality is more inclined to adapt to changing circumstances than many people are willing to believe, this shows George's behavior not as an aberration but as a norm. The story can be told in detail because those involved wrote to each other frequently, recycling the latest news and gossip. The overwhelming impression they convey is that while George had resolved to explore this aspect of his sexuality, he was also an innocent abroad, unaware of the amusement his tribulations were causing, as conveyed by the recurring epithet: "Poor George."

The instigator of these events was Maynard Keynes, who had just taken up his fellowship at King's. On learning that George and James Strachey had never met, he contrived for them to be invited to a lunch in Cambridge on February 7, 1909. As he told Grant the following day, the result was a resounding hit. "James and George Mallory fell into an intimate conversation and almost one another's arms!"

It is clear that something important had occurred in George's life. Benson, who went for a walk with him a day or so later, observed that his ennui had been replaced by a far more positive mood. "The blessed child tried to convert me to an optimistic view of life and the educational view of sorrow—all out of his own deep experience . . . I thought that perhaps today God had sent his angel, to walk lightly and cheerfully beside me and comfort me by affection and helpfulness." George wrote in equally uplifting vein to an old Winchester friend, Eddie Morgan, then at Oxford University and preparing to enter the church. He told Morgan he had just read a paper about St. Francis to the college literary society. "I feel quite certain that no better Christian has ever lived . . . I believe it at all events to be a sign of grace that I feel so much joy in the world."

The next day George wrote to Strachey from Pythagoras House asking if they could meet. "Will you come here on Thursday either to tea or sometime in the evening? I feel that we broke off in the middle of a discussion—which oughtn't to be: if you are willing I should like to resume it. I can't guarantee another batch of optimism for you. Yours sincerely, George H. L. Mallory."

News of the encounter was circulating fast. On February 11 Keynes updated

Grant on what was already being called "l'Affaire George." Strachey had shown George's letter to Keynes, who helpfully paraphrased several key passages for Grant's benefit: "We broke off, I feel, in the middle of a discussion. I am willing to continue it—if you are." Strachey reported that Rupert Brooke was passing on the gossip too: according to Brooke, George was unsure whether he liked James or loved him, and had referred to James as a "beautiful languishing flower, and so forth."

George and Strachey in fact met again that very day. Strachey had visited George in a mood of high expectation—"agog for a proposal" was how Keynes put it—but for the moment, George did not oblige. Even so, the two had talked of "nothing but love." But although George had been at his most alluring, "infinitely incredibly bright . . . charming and impulsive and in beautiful good looks," Strachey was vacillating, as he was far more interested in Brooke. After two hours, Strachey made his excuses and left. Although Strachey invited George to tea the following Monday he was still in two minds. "James declares that he doesn't in the world know what line he is to take," Keynes reported.

With the incipient affair thus delicately poised, George prepared for another important social event. The next day, February 12, he attended a dinner at the University Arms Hotel which had been organized by Charles Sayle in honor of the writer and critic Charles Lamb. It was a high-powered occasion, with senior Cambridge academics and writers in attendance, as well as Rupert Brooke and Maynard Keynes. There was a further guest, known to Sayle from the climbing world: Geoffrey Winthrop Young, who was placed on the same table as George, Brooke, and Keynes. "What could be more perfect?" Keynes asked.

Young came to Cambridge in high renown, at least in the mountaineering world. Aged thirty-three, dashingly handsome, and invariably colorfully dressed, he was the leading British mountaineer then active in the Alps, where he had first climbed in 1897. Between 1905 and 1908, mostly in partnership with the Swiss guide Josef Knubel, he made a series of audacious first ascents in the Pennine Alps, the main mountain chain astride the border of Switzerland and Italy, including the southwest face of the Täschhorn, still considered fifty years later one of the most testing routes in the Alps. He was one of mountaineering's movers and shakers, an impresario who liked to make things happen around him, a prospector and collector of promising young talent. He was an accomplished and prolific writer, describing his climbing in numerous articles and books. In Britain his most prominent role was as organizer of the celebrated Pen y Pass parties, gatherings of leading climbers in Snowdonia that usually produced a rash of new routes.

Young became the next of the older figures George was drawn to as he explored the ways of another new world. There are parallels between Benson and Young, as both had taught at Eton, where Young's pupils included Maynard Keynes, and both rejected traditional autocratic educational methods, preferring instead to build on relationships based on individual respect and trust. They both left Eton prematurely after clashing with their superiors. But Young did so under a cloud, for, according to his biographer, Alan Hankinson, he was suspected of having becoming sexually involved with one or more of his pupils. Hankinson also relates how, like Benson, Young struggled to come to terms with his homosexuality. In Young's case this consisted of couplings with "boxers and low-life characters," known otherwise as rough trade. As Young had become a government school inspector after leaving Eton he faced the danger of blackmail, which he reduced by traveling abroad to visit the notorious gay clubs of Paris and Berlin. Yet Young followed many of his peers into marriage. In 1918 he married Eleanor Slingsby, the beautiful daughter of a fellow climber. Although Young continued to have the occasional homosexual tryst, they had two children and remained together until Young's death in 1958.

At the Charles Lamb dinner, Keynes for one was impressed by Young, his former teacher, finding him "as charming as ever." Yet again, Keynes took a hand. Knowing full well that George had so far not secured Strachey's affections, Keynes endeavored to divert him into a relationship with Young. "I tried to get up an affair between him and George Mallory with the greatest possible success," Keynes wrote. "They'd never met before, but George Mallory asked Geoffrey Young to breakfast next morning."

Young was yet another to be struck by George's charisma. George, he wrote in a private diary, presented "six feet of deer-like power concordant with the perfect oval of his face, the classic profile and long, oval, violet eyes," and had a "gravely beautiful tenor voice." For the moment, as others had felt, George seemed to be holding back, but Young was sufficiently intrigued to invite him to the next Pen y Pass party that Easter. George accepted at once. Although he told Young he was looking forward to the trip "with unmixed delight," he also displayed his customary diffidence, warning Young not to expect too much of his climbing. "I don't expect to fulfill your sanguine anticipations! If by chance we may prove that one of the more terrifying places is less difficult than it looks I shall jump for joy."

L'Affaire George, meanwhile, was continuing apace, with James Strachey responding more readily to George. "James and George," Keynes told Grant on February 28, in his latest report from the front, "now stroke one another's faces in public." At this point matters became even more complicated as a new player entered the lists. News of George had reached Strachey's brother Lytton at his home in Belsize Park Gardens, and Lytton was clearly excited by what he had heard. "Please tell George Mallory that he's making a great mistake," he implored James on March 3. "It's James's brother who's the really fascinating person."

James endeavored to reassure Lytton. "I've not even copulated with George. I don't much want to. In fact nowadays I see him so much that he bores me incredibly." The notion of boredom occurs frequently in the writings of the time, and appears to imply a feeling of being unable to cope, rather than mere ennui. Even so, James asked George to go to Paris with him at Easter. He was too late, as George had already committed himself to Wales and Young.

⁂

Young was clearly keen to get to know George, for he invited him to Pen y Pass a week ahead of the main party. The Gorphwysfa Hotel, where the climbers stayed, occupied a dramatic vantage point set among tumbled boulders on the crest of the Llanberis Pass, looking towards the steeply rising north and east ridges of Snowdon itself. For the first week Young and George stayed in a corrugated-iron outbuilding known as the shanty, as Young's terse account records. "Alone with him for a week; had the shanty. At first bitter blizzard, and driven off Parson's Nose. Then perfect weather. Explored Craig-yr-Ysfa, 3 new climbs, swimming each time on way back. Then did his Slab climb on East Buttress. The hardest rocks I have done."

All the elements were there. The two men had shared the extremes of the mountain experience, from the snowstorm which drove them off Parson's Nose, a buttress on Clogwyn y Person, a cliff a mile or so down Llanberis Pass, to the glorious days, cold and clear, when they found virgin rock on Craig yr Ysfa and— even though it was April—plunged into Ffynnon Llugwy afterwards. Most significant was Young's rating—"the hardest rocks"—which placed George in the top rank of British rock climbers.

When the rest of the climbers arrived, the Pen y Pass party assumed its full, expansive nature. Young was now in his element as ringmaster of the climbing world. He had organized the first party in 1905, when climbing, Young wrote, "had the freshness of a dawn," and the parties had initially been climbers' occasions, rallying calls for the elite figures prospecting for new routes in Snowdonia: men such as Archer Thomson, who had berated George and his partners on Lliwedd the previous year, and Oscar Eckenstein, the English-born son of a German refugee, who had climbed as far afield as the Himalaya.

Gradually the parties developed into more sociable affairs, novices joining the experts, women attending and then children, with up to fifty people at a time squeezing into the hotel and its overflow shanty and bunkhouse. In the evenings weary climbers could take baths in tin tubs beside a roaring fire, and afterwards take part in reading and study groups and in intellectual or political debates on the subjects of the day. These could be heated, as they covered the political gamut, and there were strong radical views among the participants, who included socialists, pacifists, and Irish republicans. There was music too: recitals of folk songs and classical Lieder, while the high point was Young's rendition of the climbing songs he was writing and collecting, enshrining the tales of skill and daring already forming the mythology of the sport. Young kept a record of the proceedings in a photographic album which he called the Pen y Pass diary, whose entries have assumed the luster of a lost epoch. In the 1920s, in the aftermath of the First World War, Young wrote a final entry: "The party flashed into being in full bright plumage; ran for a few days like the Golden Age, and melted as silently and suddenly."

When the main group arrived at Easter 1909, George adopted an unassuming role: he tended to become nervous and withdrawn in large groups, and wanted in any case to evaluate his new companions before asserting himself. One of the new arrivals was none other than Archer Thomson, but he appeared to bear no grudge for the near miss on Lliwedd, and Young was soon telling him about George's talent and promise. George put up one more new route, with an Irish climber, Edward Evans, which led to another of Lliwedd's intriguing names. George had intended to climb Thomson's Great Chimney, put up in 1907, but it was misty and so he and Evans missed the starting point, climbing a different line which they named Wrong Chimney. At the end of the stay Young, though troubled by premature thoughts of middle age, felt that he had climbed well. But he considered George, "wonderfully supple," to be the better man.

Before returning to Cambridge, George visited Benson, who was then in Derbyshire. Benson had suffered a relapse and was staying at a hotel in Ashbourne, and George hoped that he could bring some therapeutic benefit. Benson was in the company of another visitor, Hugh Dalton, one of his Cambridge students. Dalton—president of the university Fabian Society—had a strained and sometimes turbulent relationship with Benson, and when George arrived Benson immediately assumed that the two young men were competing with each other for his affections. The next day he decided that they were more interested in each other. "I suddenly became aware that I was the amiable middle-aged man who was only just a figure in their dreams."

⚬

As soon as George returned to Cambridge after Easter, he was immersed once again in l'Affaire. When he wrote to James on April 25, hoping to see him again soon, his diffidence was clear. "If I had wanted to see you last Friday evening, and I believe you had no reason to suppose that I wished otherwise, I might have been disappointed. It is possible that you will come here tomorrow evening; it is also possible that you will not come; the latter contingency is perhaps more probable as you will feel, under the circumstances, rather uncertain of finding me at home: the same reasoning will convince you of the futility of informing me of your purposes. Yours, George H. L. Mallory."

The contorted linguistic style of George's letter was one he adopted when writing to James and his colleagues. In this case it betrayed more anxiety than irony, and a few days later he summoned his resolve and adopted a more direct approach. He invited James to supper on Sunday, May 9, although confessing that he felt "sick with fear at the thought of our next meeting—what a gamble it is." He signed himself: "Ever thine, George H. L. Mallory."

Strachey was still vacillating, perhaps unsure how far he wanted to become involved, perhaps also enjoying the power he held over George. He agreed to have supper on May 9, when he found George apprehensive and depressed. Strachey put on what he termed "a spurious show of affection," which George accepted as real for, so Strachey told Maynard Keynes, George "offered to copulate."

In George's biography it is an extraordinary moment. Taken at face value, it can be seen as a declaration by George that, in trying to woo Strachey, he was prepared, in modern terms, "to go all the way." The phrase is appropriate, fitting George's determination to make the most of new experiences and explore them to the fullest extent. From his previous transactions, George also must have known he was putting himself at risk, in this case of rejection and wounded amour-propre. And so it proved. By Keynes' account, even this startling offer did not "melt James's stoniness," for he turned George down. But James, rather mischievously, made an alternative suggestion. His brother Lytton, who had arrived in Cambridge for a two-week stay, was still entreating him for an introduction to George. James invited George to have tea with them both, and George accepted.

Lytton's first encounter with George left him ecstatic. So many of the men in his world were lean, pale figures, looking as though they were undernourished or rarely saw the light. Here was a man who was both a history scholar and a super-athlete, his body honed through his sporting pursuits, his muscles developed and hard: a suitable model, in short, for the Greek sculptors who had the same passion for the physical ideal. "Mon Dieu! George Mallory!" Lytton declared in a celebrated letter to Clive and Vanessa Bell on May 21. "When that's been written, what more need be said? My hand trembles, my heart palpitates, my whole being swoons away at the words—oh heavens, heavens! I found of course that he'd been absurdly maligned—he's six foot high, with the body of an athlete by

Praxiteles, and a face—oh incredible—the mystery of Botticelli, the refinement and delicacy of a Chinese print, the youth and piquancy of an imaginable English boy. I rave, but when you see him, as you must, you will admit all—all!"

Lytton added that he had heard of George's "passion for James" and the fact that James had rejected George's proposition twelve days before. "Poor George! I met him for the first time immediately after this occurrence, and saw in my first glance the very bottom of his astounding soul." Lytton declared that he had become "a convert to the divinity of virginity, and spend hours every day lost in a trance of adoration, innocence and bliss." And so the complications were multiplying. In a chain of unrequited love, Lytton desired George, but George desired his brother James. And James desired not George but Rupert Brooke.

Meanwhile Geoffrey Young was pressing himself on George. After Pen y Pass, he invited George to spend a week in Venice in the spring and to go climbing with him in the Alps in the summer. George stalled on Venice, telling Young that he was still working on his Boswell essay, which was "swelling into a good sized book," and he was having "awful qualms as to when I shall be able to get away." As for the Alps, George said it would be difficult as he was short of money. Young offered to meet his costs and George agreed. Young had also proposed George for membership of the Climbers' Club, and although George had irreverently included a walk along the Malvern Hills near Worcester among his qualifications— he justified himself by claiming "an expedition of that sort is only undertaken by people who care about the mountains"—he was accepted on May 21.

⁂

In June, his relationship with James Strachey as yet unresolved, George had to address the vexed question of his career. He was still attracted by teaching and had heard that the headmaster at Winchester, Dr. Hubert Burge, was looking for someone who could take French, German, and math. Despite his brusque rejection at the hands of Burge's deputy, Howard Rendall, George traveled to Winchester and stayed for a few days. He told Burge that although he would have preferred to teach history, he was confident he could bring his French and German up to scratch; his math was strong and he also believed he could teach boys how to write good essays. Burge was evidently encouraging, for George told his family that the job was as good as his. He received a clutch of congratulatory letters in response: Mary told him they were delighted at his "most exciting and joyful news," and his father wrote: "I cannot tell you with what feelings of delight we read your letter, and I do congratulate you with all my heart on the prospect of a mastership at Winchester." To George's surprise and disappointment,

Burge turned him down. The post, he explained, was "too mathematical" for George's qualifications. "There is a chance I shall be wanted there at some time," George wrote to Geoffrey Keynes, adding: "I want to be wanted."

George's poignant postscript was appropriate in more ways than one. Back in Cambridge the plot was thickening, the gossip intensifying. He and James were still seeing each other, although George confided that he thought that Lytton was now in love with him. On June 9, Keynes told Grant that George "moves in a cloud of intrigue," adding: "Where he'll find himself next, heaven knows . . . .Poor George lives in a world to which he really has no clue whatever." Meanwhile George renewed his invitations to James, telling him one morning that since he was not rowing until 6 P.M., they could meet at 2:30. "Possibly I shall be able to persuade you to take tea with me later. Please don't be angry. George H. L. Mallory."

By now George can only have been bewildered as he tried to make sense of James's unpredictable behavior, blowing hot and cold by the moment even though his true interest was in Rupert Brooke. Next it was Lytton's turn to stir the pot. George was due to stay with Lytton and James in Belsize Park on June 18, and Lytton had evidently proposed that George should "rape" James. James admitted he was feeling nervous: "I feel that I ought to enjoy it. Shall I?" In fact nothing of the kind occurred. Instead, George and the two brothers paid a sedate visit to Hampton Court, where Lytton told George how pleasant it was "to find oneself with someone who really likes things."

Still George persisted. On July 7, he sent James not one but two invitations. The first consisted of a note, on the back of a King's College memorandum headed "Arrangements for Hall," in which he asked Strachey: "Will you, damn you, come to lunch tomorrow?" The second was a letter in which he proposed calling on Strachey around 10 P.M. the following Saturday, after he had dined with Sayle: "My pleasure, if I should find you there, could hardly be increased."

As James told it, he capitulated at last. His account is in a letter to Rupert Brooke from Stockholm on September 13, in which he described what happened shortly before George left for the Alps. He and George had borrowed the rooms of Goldsworthy Lowes Dickinson, an Apostle and tutor in political philosophy, who had taught E. M. Forster and was a lover, among others, of the artist and writer Roger Fry. There, as James told it, "he insisted, before we parted, on copulating." James claimed that he did his best to dissuade George: "I didn't in the least lead him on. In fact, I was very chilling." But eventually James gave way. "He seemed so very anxious, and as I couldn't pretend to have all virgin horror, I submitted."

James confessed that he had not found it pleasurable. "We went through with it," he said. "I didn't enjoy it much—I was rather bored." For George, according to James, the experience was worse than boring. "He, I think, was shocked. At any rate he shewed no desire to repeat the business." In a closing homily, Strachey observed: "Really, you know, it's only in the most special circumstances that copulation's tolerable."

There are no confirmatory details from George. But from his subsequent letters it is clear that, far from securing James's affections, whatever occurred proved disastrously counterproductive, leaving him in emotional turmoil, while James appeared to be more cold and distant than before. It also apparently left George determined—in James's phrase—not to "repeat the business." Although George maintained relationships with homosexuals or bisexuals such as Lytton Strachey and Duncan Grant up to and beyond his marriage, this remains the only reported account of any "copulation" with a man. Taken as such, it appears a one-time experiment, a rite of passage that others of his peers conducted, and one which hardly classifies him as homosexual by any reasonable definition of the word. A month or so later Rupert Brooke followed suit with a long-standing friend he had known at school at Rugby. He wrote: "I wanted to have some fun, & still more to see what is was like, and to do away with the shame (as I thought it was) of being a virgin." Despite the rumors and gossip surrounding Brooke's flamboyant life, it too remains the only such documented episode. And like George, it left him bemused and with no apparent wish to repeat it either.

As his time at Cambridge drew to a close, George engaged in a flurry of activity. He wrote to Duncan Grant, telling him how much he had liked his sketches for a decoration on the theme of the Queen of Sheba, which had been commissioned by Newnham College. Benson wrote a farewell letter, saying he was glad George had enjoyed his extra year: "It is a great thing to have eaten one's cake without too many crumbs." Benson also thanked George for visiting him so often, "and cheering me up." Rupert Brooke invited him to stay with his family during their summer holiday in Somerset, but George had to decline in view of his impending trip to the Alps with Young. Avie came to stay for a few days, and George invited Sayle to meet her and his Easter climbing partner, Edward Evans, over tea at Pythagoras House.

A day or so later, by delicious irony, George found that the customary roles between himself and Sayle had been reversed. Whereas Sayle had acted the elder counselor, George now took that part. For two years Sayle had nurtured a passion for Geoffrey Keynes, who had evidently reciprocated. But their relationship had hit a crisis, for on July 25 Sayle wrote to Keynes to cancel their long-standing arrangement to have supper on Sundays. "My letter to Geoffrey pointed out that I was no longer able to return his affections," Sayle noted. The next day Sayle unburdened himself to George, who had been "much distressed" to hear his news. They met twice the following day: "We talked for an hour about the Geoffrey episode as I am very much upset." George had clearly been able to console Sayle who described how they said good-bye, then added: "We have been friends now for two and a quarter years and my regard and affection for him is deeper than ever."

Geoffrey Keynes also bade George farewell: "That's that, and the end of you, from a Cambridge point of view—not a very pleasant reflection. Do you realize that you've gone down?" On July 29 George and Young set off for the Alps. Since George had no career in prospect, he had no idea what he would do when he returned. For the gossip machine, that could have been a moot point. "George I hear is climbing with Geoffrey Young in the Alps," Maynard Keynes wrote to Grant. "Will he come back alive?"

George Mallory with his mother Annie and sisters Avie (left) and Mary. The photograph was probably taken in 1889, when George was three and the family was living at Newton Hall, Mobberley, where George was born.

George and the family dog Springer at Hobcroft House around 1894, when George was eight. The Mallory family lived at the house from 1892 to 1904, when they moved from Mobberley to Birkenhead.

The College,
Winchester,
Sept. 22/o

My dear Mother,

I'm sorry I didn't write to you before. I came here all right on Wednesday, alright, although by the 11 o'clock train instead of the 5.10, as otherwise I should have to have waited an hour at Waterloo which I didn't exactly relish. I found Mr Rendall, who took

George at the end of his first year at Winchester in 1901, when he was fifteen, together with his first letter home, written in September 1900.

(Above) George was an accomplished all-around sportsman. He was the best gymnast at Winchester (he is top center in the group). (Below) He took up rowing at Cambridge. Seated second from left, he captained the Magdalene College eight in its triumphant 1908 season.

Family reunion for the silver wedding anniversary of George's parents, Herbert and Annie, in June 1907. George is in the back row with Mary (left) and Avie. Annie is seated in the center, with Herbert to the left and her mother—"Grandma Jebb"—to the right, flanked by two aunts. Trafford is sitting with Springer.

Avie's wedding, at St. John's, Birkenhead, in 1910, when she married Harry Longridge. Left to right: Mary Longridge, George, George's sister Mary, Robert Longridge, Barbara Blood from the Birkenhead doctor's family, Trafford.

George, aged twenty, with Arthur Benson outside Hinton Hall, Benson's home near Cambridge, in December 1906. Benson considered the photograph grotesque—he said that George appeared "impish," and that he was "like an old bear."

(Below) George with Avie in his study at Pythagoras House, his lodgings during his fourth and final Cambridge year, 1908–09.

The halcyon years at Pen y Pass. George, right, with Cottie Sanders—later Mary Anne O'Malley—and her brother Jack.

George and Siegfried Herford in December 1913, with Snowdon's Crib Goch ridge behind. Geoffrey Winthrop Young took the photograph after the three had spent a magical day on Lliwedd. Both Herford and Jack Sanders were killed at Ypres.

The dashing Geoffrey Winthrop Young, who dubbed George "Galahad" and acted as his mentor, guide, and sponsor in the mountaineering world

Young took the only known photograph of George climbing in the Alps as they descended the Moine Ridge of Mont Blanc on August 10, 1909.

The Bloomsbury entanglements and l'Affaire George of 1909. (Above left) James Strachey, standing, with his brother Lytton. (Above right) The artist, Duncan Grant, left, with Maynard Keynes

In 1911, George posed for a series of nude photographs taken by Grant at his studio in Brunswick Square. George told Grant: "I am profoundly interested in the nude me."

CHAPTER FOUR

Fresh Pleasures
1909–1910

"My dear James," George wrote on August 7, 1909, "I wonder if you have ever felt the joy of a completely log-like existence. No I know you haven't. Just to lie here in the sun with great white peaks all around me and the biggest glacier in Europe at my feet, to eat from time to time, to sleep a little and dream a great deal—it is a heavenly existence."

George addressed his letter from: "Concordia Hut, Aletsch Glacier." The hut, one of the oldest in the Alps, was, as George described it, "a sort of small hotel perched upon the rocks; one has food cooked for one by two invaluable caretakers." A hut stands in the same place today, overlooking Europe's largest glacier, a gleaming river of ice up to a mile wide, running more than fifteen miles through the heart of the Bernese Alps in Switzerland. George's letter indicates that, whatever had happened in Lowes Dickinson's room the previous month, he was clinging to the hope that his relationship with James could be prolonged. At the same time his choice of imagery illuminated the contrast between the fevered atmosphere of Cambridge and the feelings of tranquillity and escape to be found in the mountains where other problems dissipate and you can concentrate on the task in hand. Climbing, searching for holds, stretching yourself physically and mentally, probing at your limits; all in an outrageously beautiful environment, the experience deepened for being shared with friends. "To see the Alps again!" George had exulted in a letter to his mother, shortly before departing. "How glorious it will be, after dreaming of them for four years!"

George and Young had arrived in the Bernese Alps, traveling by train via Paris, Berne, and Interlaken, on July 31. This was Young's territory, the scene of some of his most notable pioneering ascents. By then the major summits had been climbed by the most obvious routes, and Young was foremost among the British climbers prospecting for lines on the more difficult ridges and faces, deploying the rock- climbing skills they were acquiring at home. Since Young usually climbed with Josef Knubel, the professional Swiss guide, news would have spread fast that he had selected the promising young amateur climber, George Mallory, to be his latest partner.

From the town of Brig in the Rhône Valley, Young and George toiled up to Bel Alp, a tiny mountain community with a few scattered chalets, a chapel, and an inn, close to the snout of the great Aletsch Glacier. They began by climbing the Unterbächhorn via the Enkel ridge which reminded them of Lliwedd, swimming during their descent in a lake fed by the icy waters from the Unterbächhorn's glacier. They were joined the next day by Donald Robertson, a high-ranking civil servant who had been at Trinity College. A gentle, scholarly man of thirty, Young described him as "tall, powerful, blond with round face and a jutting nose," and a "passionate mountaineer." Young reckoned that while he himself would provide the team's experience, Robertson would bring the strength, George "the brilliance."

On August 4, after a day lost to bad weather, they attempted the first ascent of the southeast ridge of the Nesthorn, a fearsomely jagged peak rising from one of the tributaries of the Aletsch Glacier. Young had failed on three previous bids and it remained a formidable challenge, entailing a lengthy climb along a ridge from the Unterbächhorn before embarking on the southeast ridge itself. It was a typical Young route, with a long approach through demanding territory and the toughest problems arising when they were most extended. The safety factors paralleled those current in British climbing: primitive equipment and techniques, long run-outs of the rope without belays, the likelihood that the simplest mistake would be severely punished. They left Bel Alp in wind and snow well before dawn, but around seven o'clock they came out above the clouds, the peaks around resembling islands "emerging from a desert of sea." By nine they were on the summit of the Unterbächhorn, the ridge stretching ahead to the foot of the Nesthorn. "Think of it!" Young wrote. "Two and something miles of selected ridge climbing: pinnacle and tower and wind-balanced knife-edge, notch and comb and up-ended slab."

They spent the next three hours working their way along the ridge to a col where the ascent of the southeast ridge began. After passing a series of steps and towers they reached the final obstacle, a giant overhanging pinnacle with sheer walls of rock dropping away on either side. It was now that the single most danger-ous moment of George's pre-Everest climbing career occurred. Taking over the lead, he worked his way across the base of the pinnacle in search of a line past the overhangs. He disappeared from view and then reappeared at a higher level, moving back across the face on a tenuous line of fingerholds. Then he struck upwards towards the overhang. So far as Young could see, there were no real footholds at all. "But he fought his way up magnificently, until all that remained below the rock cornice, which cut off everything else above from my sight, were his two boots."

George was now some twenty feet above Young, who was paying out the rope so that it passed behind a flake of rock. As Young well knew, the penalties of a fall could be immense. If George came off, he would fall a total of forty feet, placing so much strain on the rope that it was likely to break. In a final surge of energy, George launched himself upwards and outwards in a bid to find a hold above the overhang. Young saw his feet scrabbling for holds. Then "a gray streak flickered downward, and past me, and out of sight." As Young clung to the rope it sprang "like an elastic band, cracking under my chest and hands on the rock." But it held. Only later did George and Young discover that the type of rope, "a rather popular Austrian woven" model, was notorious for its low breaking strain.

George was still in an alarming predicament, out of Young's sight, dangling at the end of the rope which was liable to suffocate him through the pressure on his ribs and chest. He called to Young to lower the rope so that he could reach a line of holds. He used his ice ax to pull himself in to the cliff and climbed back to the ledge where Young was standing. Young was astonished that George appeared "entirely undisturbed" by the fall, and had even kept hold of his ax throughout. Young found a way past the overhang and then handed the lead back to George. They reached the summit at 7 P.M. to witness a sunset which, George told his mother, "was the most wonderful I have ever seen." They had a demanding descent to Bel Alp, which they reached after midnight. "We were out twenty-one hours and were altogether rather pleased with ourselves," George wrote.

It was two days later that they climbed to the Concordia hut. After George had written his holding note to James Strachey, they set off for their next objective, the southeast ridge of the Finsteraarhorn, at 14,022 feet the highest peak in the Bernese Alps. It was one of those cold, scintillating days, when the ice confections fashioned by the wind glinted in the sun. "Every notch was snow-crested or corniced," Young wrote, "and every pinnacle so deeply flounced with ice and snow-frond that we had to smash a way into it with arm or leg." It was bitterly cold when they reached the summit and they did not pause for long. Then came an incident which illustrates how a moment's carelessness can dangerously tip the odds on which mountain safety depends. George was chipping footholds down a frozen slab when Young noticed he had not retied his climbing rope properly. He called out to George to wait until Robertson could reach him to secure the rope but then Robertson slipped a short distance before managing to regain his hold. George heard the scrape of Robertson's boots and turned in his tiny foothold to see what was wrong. For a moment, Young was convinced that George was going to fall. Although he reassured himself afterwards that George was "as sure-footed and as agile as the proverbial chamois," it served as a salutary warning that accidents are most likely to occur when climbers are tired or relax their guard.

On August 10 George wrote to his mother from Bel Alp, describing some of his climbs and telling her they were planning to move on to Chamonix. He made no mention of his fall on the Nesthorn, nor the moment of danger on the Finsteraarhorn. But it was clear that the risks, and penalties, of mountaineering were on his mind, for he did report the deaths of two Swiss climbers on the Jungfrau—"a most grisly affair"—and that of a teacher from Eton, a friend of Benson, who had been killed in a fall while climbing alone above Chamonix. Three days later Young hired Josef Knubel to accompany them in a traverse of the Aiguille Verte, one of the largest of the jagged peaks fringing Mont Blanc, first climbed by Edward Whymper. During their descent via the Moine Ridge Young took the only known photograph of George climbing in the Alps. The picture shows him with his back to the camera as he balances half on rock, half on snow. He is wearing a belted climbing jacket, breeches, puttees, and nailed boots. His head is turned to the left, so that he is looking away from the rock face towards the Glacier du Géant, with a line of peaks rising behind: Mont Mallet, the Dent du Géant, the Grand Flambeau, the Aiguille Noire de Peuterey. Young said it was his favorite photograph of George: the image depicts a figure poised confidently on the cusp of danger, contemplating the peaks he might one day climb.

Bad weather blighted the rest of the trip. With Knubel they attempted a first ascent to the Col des Nantillons, a narrow gash in the main crest of the Chamonix Aiguilles, deemed "impossible" by a previous party. They camped for three nights on the moraine above the Mer de Glace as they waited for the weather to clear and then climbed a formidable 100-foot crack before a hailstorm forced them to make a difficult retreat. On August 20 they made a traverse of the Aiguille du Chardonnet, ascending by the classic Forbes Ridge, descending via the Col du Passon, which overlooks the Argentière Glacier. It was another of those transcendent days, captured in their memories, Young wrote, by the marching army of shadows cast by the Aiguilles across the glacier in the evening sun.

With the end of August approaching, Robertson had to return to London. Young had arranged to make an attempt on the north face of the Weisshorn with an American climber, Oliver Perry Smith. He and George took the train to Zermatt, booking into the Monte Rosa, the hotel where Whymper, hero and villain of British alpinism, used to hold court. While Young busied himself with his attempt, George was content to read, enjoying the chance to relax at last. In so doing he made a new friend, another of those to be struck by his alluring combination of innocence and composure.

On August 31 a vivacious young woman named Cottie Sanders was among the crowd of climbers sitting at the iron tables and chairs outside the Monte Rosa. The hotel was pulsing, she recorded, with "the whole va-et-vient of a summer's day in Zermatt," as the climbers exchanged gossip and planned routes with their guides. Among them she observed a young man, "picturesque and untidy, in loose grey flannels with a bright handkerchief around his neck." He was reading "in a sort of oblivion, never looking up," although occasionally reaching up to push a shock of brown hair from his head. It was George, and the book he was reading was the latest novel by John Galsworthy, *The Country House*.

A second man, who turned out to be Young, came out of the hotel and introduced George to some friends. George, Cottie observed, showed his reserved, diffident side: "a sort of restive shyness, carefully controlled," returning to his book as soon as he decently could. These two men, as Cottie knew, were climbing luminaries—"Rumour had preceded them, and comment flowed about them"—and she engineered an introduction to George. She was struck by his melodious voice, his modesty, and his "very careful choice of words." He talked about his climbs with "real flame and passion," so different from the normal attitude of the Monte Rosa crowd. All of this Cottie recorded in a journal which she kept for the next two years; after George died, she used her notes to compose a memoir which was incorporated into the biography published in the name of George's Cambridge friend, David Pye.

The next time they met, George persuaded Cottie to try one of his black French cigarettes—something of a trial for Cottie, although she did manage to inhale. He offered her practical advice, recommending that she toughen the skin of her feet with a cream made by a Cambridge chemist (Peck's Hardening Lotion). He talked warmly about the delights of climbing in Wales, leaving Cottie unclear whether he was suggesting they should meet there. "Does he always go, I wonder?"

When George and Young left Zermatt on September 3, Cottie rode with them in the train to Visp. She gave him a packet of sweets, for which he insisted on paying her, and then asked: "You will remember about Wales in September?"

"It seems a most excellent idea," she replied. "And I am certain of going next Easter."

Young cut in, telling her about the Pen y Pass parties, and then George asked: "Shall you be coming here next year?"

George, Cottie wrote in her journal that evening, "did not say he hoped he should meet me—us—but I think that is what he meant."

From the Alps, George returned to Birkenhead. His most urgent task was to finish his essay on Boswell. As his interest in his subject grew, he found that it was becoming a full-length book. He empathized with a figure who had been accused of self-indulgence and egotism and yet had managed to write an acclaimed biography. He was intrigued by the dynamics of Boswell's relationship with Johnson—of the kind "that parents would wish to exist between father and son"—and was curious about Boswell's technique as writer and reporter. Did Boswell make contemporaneous notes of Johnson's conversations and bons mots? Or did he reconstruct them later? George's overall judgment was in Boswell's favor: although he displayed insufficient intellectual rigor, Boswell wanted to understand and be true to his emotions.

George was just completing the essay when he sustained an injury that was to have extended consequences. While at Birkenhead he went climbing at a nearby sandstone quarry, one of several that provided material for Liverpool building projects, including the city cathedral. (Local cognoscenti have identified two possible quarries, at Irby and Thurstaston Hill.) His sisters Mary and Avie were there, together with several friends, including Harold Porter. After several climbs, George said he had spotted a possible new route. As he related, "one of the other people who had never climbed before that day jeered greatly; so of course I was obliged to make the attempt at once."

The holds looked thin but George reassured himself that, if necessary, he would be able to grab a rope which he had secured from the top of the cliff. "I deceived myself, of course." A hold broke and George fell, landing heavily. He fractured a bone in his right ankle, although this was not diagnosed at the time, and he was reduced to hobbling for months afterwards. All climbing was ruled out and George's self-esteem was injured too: he dismissed the injury as a sprained ankle but admitted to Young that the accident had been caused by his reluctance to back down from the challenge thrown at him. "The whole affair is almost too disgusting to think of."

✿

George had other wounds to dress. Two months on he was still in turmoil over James Strachey, smarting from the debacle the relationship had become. Having sent James his note from the Concordia hut, he had written again to let him know he was back from the Alps. James did not appear to care. He wrote to Rupert Brooke, relegating the news of George's return to the penultimate paragraph, along with his account of the incident in Lowes Dickinson's bed. Lytton Strachey, by contrast, was still in pursuit of George, hoping that he would weaken. It was hard to make any plans, Lytton told Duncan Grant, because "at the back of every expectation, there's always George." George was still in turmoil over James—was their relationship on or off?—and bemused by Lytton's continuing attentions.

Out of this, a plan emerged. In October George met Simon and Dorothy

Bussy: Simon, who was French, was a painter; his wife Dorothy was the sister of James and Lytton Strachey. They had married in 1903 and gone to live in Roquebrune, a hillside village near Monte Carlo. Dorothy's family had opposed the match at first: Bussy, a shoemaker's son from the Jura, had no money, no reputation, and could not speak English. But then they relented while Bussy's painting, carried out in a disarmingly simple figurative style with Impressionist touches, gained in renown. He was lionized further when it became known that he was a friend of Matisse and had been praised by Degas, Rodin, and Picasso.

The Bussys paid regular visits to Britain and first met George at Maynard Keynes's rooms in Cambridge in the spring of 1909. They liked him, particularly because he talked to Simon in French. In a jaded note, Keynes complained to Duncan Grant that the Bussys "were allowed to see no one but George who had lunch and tea with them and talked broken French to Simon—'Avez-vous been to Wales?' says George. 'Ah Chiswick,' says Simon and what it's all about no one knows. 'C'est un beau garçon' was Simon's final summary." Bussy, Keynes added, was "entranced" with George.

When they met again in October, Simon Bussy invited George to spend the winter with them at their villa in Roquebrune. The ostensible reason was to enable him to convalesce from his ankle injury; but George also saw that a spell in the south of France, away from James and Lytton and their friends, could give him the space to come to terms with the outcome of l'Affaire George and recover his self-esteem. He had just come into a small family legacy which would enable him to pay the Bussys' modest rent. There were other possible benefits: he could improve his French, bone up on French literature, and perhaps earn some money as a travel writer, following the example of Lytton Strachey, who was contributing to the *Spectator* and *New Quarterly*. To round off the arrangement, Lytton—who while still interested in George, was now pursuing Rupert Brooke, then living in Grantchester—arranged to take over his old rooms in Pythagoras House.

George left London by train at the end of the first week of November. He stopped in Paris en route and called at the Sorbonne to inquire about teaching work for the following year. The first official he met, a Monsieur Hovelaque, was encouraging, but his colleague Monsieur Legouis thought George looked far too young. They suggested that George look for a job in a lycée but he turned that idea down. Once in Provence, he found Roquebrune to be an appealing village, with white houses and narrow streets, set among olive groves in the foothills of the Maritime Alps. But when he arrived at the Bussys' villa, named La Souca, he was taken aback to discover just how small it was. "My bedroom," he told his sister Avie, "is about the size of a grand piano." Also in residence, as well as the Bussys' three-year-old daughter Jane, was a young Frenchman who appeared to be another lodger: "it is a curious menage," George wrote. The Bussys were "pleasant people to live with, very cultivated and clever, but quite unaffected, simple, domestic and sympathetic." The main living space was a balcony between the front door and the garden, covered by an awning and decorated with one of Bussy's frescoes. George supposed this form of existence was "common enough . . . but it is new to me and I find it charming."

George spent much of his time in solitary mode, reading, and swimming, and working on his French. He had hoped to explore the hills above Roquebrune but he still found it painful to walk more than a few hundred yards. His bruised psyche received a further blow when he heard that he had come second in the Boswell essay prize. The judges awarded him a proxime accessit, which meant he had only narrowly lost, but it was scant consolation. He was clearly struggling to contain his disappointment when he told Avie: "Luckily a few hours suffice to bring forgetfulness, or at least indifference, and there are too many other things to think about for it to matter much." In his letters, he seemed to relish a sense of exile and retreat. In early December he wrote to Avie, touching on the family traumas that Christmas tends to induce and declaring that he did not regret "having exchanged the scene of horror which precedes it in England for the reposeful indifference of this domicile." He did not intend to send any Christmas presents, and did not expect to receive any either.

A few days before Christmas, George reached a watershed in his life. For two months he had succumbed to a passivity and despair that bordered on self pity. Now, he knew, it was time to reassert himself, to call on the resilience and inner strength that were among his greatest assets. It was time, too, to break the hold James Strachey had over him and retake control of his life. On December 20 he wrote a letter to James that, while having the courage to reveal the depths of his confusion and hurt, also looked ahead to a time when their friendship, and George's mental state, recovered their equilibrium. The best parallel for the letter is one of George's climbs, requiring an intensity of commitment from which there could be no turning back.

> *My dear James, Write to you I will at last. What do you think of me? That I'm proud? that I'm injured? that I'm angry? that I've forgotten? It is six weeks yesterday since I said goodbye to you at Hampstead and I haven't sent you a word. I who love you! Probably you know the reason for my silence as well as I do. There has never really been anything to say since the day when I told you I loved you. Am I to repeat continually the wearisome news that I want to kiss you. It is about all that I am capable of. And it is all too much for both of us.*

In short, George wanted to call the whole thing off. He told Strachey: "You had better forget that I was ever your lover," although he hoped that Strachey would treat him, in the time-honored phrase, "as an ordinary friend . . . Do you think James, that that would be possible? You're much cleverer than I am I know, but I can understand a good deal of you, and I could understand more if you'd let me. And you understand a good deal of me—but not all yet."

George wondered if it had been foolish to write as he did. "One can't arrange one's feelings. It might have been better to go on saying nothing—but I couldn't. You will see that I am unhappy which I believe will be unpleasant for you. But isn't there something also rather comforting about being loved? Or does it just make you feel you would like to kill yourself? You needn't at all events feel like that for me. I'm not always as I am tonight. And if it is quite certain that I love you, yet I don't love you really as much as loving goes. Now Good Night—and please my sweet James send me a line sometimes."

Strachey did not reply. Even so, George's letters to other people were suffused with a sense of release. "I find myself in a very pleasant land of sunshine," he told Young on December 30. "The Maritime Alps are only about 20 miles away and they must be the most enchanting peaks." He told Young about the upper balcony at La Souca. "I retire to this when I wish to be solitary and look out over the sea to Monte Carlo, which looks well enough in the hollow under a bold headland." As the New Year arrived, George felt more at ease. His ankle was improving—"it makes a great difference being able to walk further"—and he climbed some of the nearby hills. "Mountains I should rather call them for they are real mountain shapes with fine precipices and as high as Ben Nevis. They look better from below when one knows the summits." George's mood was captured in a portrait by Simon Bussy, painted at around this time; now in London's National Portrait Gallery, it shows George's blue eyes picked out by the green background, his long dark hair falling to the right in a shock over his forehead, and captures a look that is both melancholic and expectant.

On January 28, 1910, George wrote to Duncan Grant. They had first met through the Stracheys—Grant's cousins—in 1909 and had exchanged notes and occasional visits since. Later they were to develop a friendship which although intermittent would prove far more satisfying to George than his fevered relationships with the Stracheys. Grant had met George for lunch in London on the eve of his departure for France, and George confessed that he had begun a letter to him shortly before Christmas but had been unable to summon the energy to compile more than the opening lines. Now, he told Grant, he was in a more positive mood, and beginning to make plans. He would be moving on from Roquebrune before long, and was intending to spend time in Paris; would Grant like to meet him there? Two details in the letter were particularly illuminating. The first revealed that George was almost broke again, as he had just received £8 ($38.90), as the final payment of his legacy, rather than the £45 ($218.70) he had expected. The second confirmed that James Strachey had not replied to his letter of December 20, for George, referring to "the matter of correspondence," talked of "the infernal laziness of your Strachey relations."

By the end of February, George knew it was time to leave. Despite James's silence George wrote to him again, making clear that he had broken James's hold. "I'm feeling rather better," he told Strachey, "and have some vague hope of wounding you by the 'coals of fire' method." He referred to his "recovered sanity" and then joked: "I can't see why one should ever be sane—it may be something to do with the idea of leaving here." His greeting emphasized the contrast with his last letter. He began "Dear James" (last time it had been "My dear James") and, instead of "Good night, sweet James," he signed off: "Yours George."

From Roquebrune, George first treated himself to an excursion into Italy, admitting—since he had so little money—it was "rather a wicked expedition, under the circumstances." He visited Milan, Genoa, Pisa, and Florence, telling Geoffrey Keynes: "I have really seen them at last." He then headed for Paris, calling in en route on two Cambridge friends, both former swans. One was Hugh Wilson, who was learning German in Basel; the second was Jacques Raverat, a Frenchman who had studied math at Cambridge and had since became a painter, living in a village near Auxerre. George told Keynes that seeing Raverat had "done me good—mentally I mean—for I now face Paris with a proud and cheerful heart."

When George reached Paris he rented a room at 52 Rue Gay Lussac near the Jardin du Luxembourg. Duncan Grant had turned down his invitation to join him, and so did Lytton Strachey. George had sent Lytton a postcard from Venice, asking him to come to Paris, but Lytton—who by then had returned to live in Belsize Park—had already arranged to stay with Rupert Brooke in Dorset: "A letter has come from darling George begging me to join him in Paris," Lytton lamented to Grant. "It's impossible now I think of it." Strachey sent his regrets, but suggested that George should watch the Comédie Française performing "something infinitely classical," which would help to improve his French.

George stayed in Paris for a month. It is significant that in deciding to do so he missed the Easter Pen y Pass party, thus breaking his undertaking to join Cottie Sanders there. His letters from Paris suggest that he did not yet feel strong enough to meet her and the Pen y Pass crowd or face their questions about what he had been doing in France. They also show that he was enjoying his growing self-sufficiency, the feeling that he could manage his life without recourse to others for guidance and support. There were still solitary notes in his letters, references to his "poky little room" in Rue Gay Lussac, and "lonely strolls in the Tuileries or the Jardin du Luxembourg." But as always he lived his days as fully as he could, working on his French, reading, attending lectures at the Sorbonne, visiting the theater and music hall, forming impromptu friendships among the people he met who were attracted by this tall, engaging Englishman with his excellent command of French. He found an unlikely companion in a poet and critic who recommended to George the paintings he should inspect in the Louvre. "Unfortunately," George added, "my friend is blind."

ℭ

It was perhaps just as well that George missed the Easter gathering at Pen y Pass. Cottie Sanders was there, disappointed at not seeing him, but a far greater tragedy than that occurred, and one which was a defining moment in the sport. Among the group was Donald Robertson, George's partner with Young in the Alps the previous summer, who arrived on the overnight train from London on Good Friday morning. He set out after breakfast intending to lead East Gully, a classic gully climb on Glyder Fach that was one of the early Archer Thomson routes. It should have been well within Robertson's capabilities but it was his first climb in months and his fingers came loose from a hold halfway up the first pitch. He lost his grip and fell thirty-five feet, suffering severe head injuries. A rescue party led by Geoffrey Young got him to Bangor Hospital but he died that night.

Young was devastated by Robertson's death, calling him "all but my closest friend . . . a giant in stature and intellect, irreplaceable in the public service and among his friends." He also felt that Robertson's death "darkened the hills with clouds that never again quite dispersed." After the accident the remaining climbers went home, and Young's comments convey the shock that compounded their grief. It was the first death to befall any of the Pen y Pass parties, and the contrast between the gaiety of the first assemblies and the despair that enveloped the climbers that Easter suggests that many had not addressed the risks of their sport. True, there had been fatalities in the Alps, but somehow they seemed remote from homely Wales. Robertson's death also demonstrated the penalties of a simple slip in that era: today's climbers, who would have placed a running belay and worn a helmet, would almost certainly have survived. Young later admitted that until then they had climbed in "an atmosphere of unreality, like the danger of a dream from which we feel we shall wake." George himself was shaken by the news, telling Young, who had written a tribute to Robertson in the *Alpine Journal*, that he was "very much touched."

At the end of April, George returned to Cambridge. A moment had come that he could no longer avoid: how should he make a living? He had told his father about his ambition of becoming a writer but he had produced nothing from his trip to France and Italy and his father told him it was far too erratic and uncertain a profession. In short, as parents are likely to insist, it was time to settle down and get a job. His best option remained teaching, and he spent two weeks filling a temporary post at the Royal Naval College in Dartmouth. He enjoyed the experience, even though he had to get up at 6:15 each morning, and was sorry to leave. "This charming experiment is to end in a day or two," he wrote on May 20. "Lord! how pleasant it has been!" Then an opening arose at Haileybury, his brother's school. He stayed with Trafford overnight and watched him playing cricket. But he was turned down for the job and his enthusiasm began to wane. His friends began to wonder if his notorious penchant for speaking his mind was harming his cause. Hugh Wilson, who thought he should be aiming for a job as a university lecturer, suggested that George might be his own worst enemy. "What cynicism he has to arm him does not seem to help him in his direct relations with unsympathetic men," Wilson wrote to Charles Sayle.

Arthur Benson took a hand. George visited him at Cambridge and walked with him beside the Cam. Benson was still acutely depressed and was surprised that George treated some of his observations with "ill-disguised contempt," while a friend who met George found him "arrogant and even offensive." Benson wrote George a tactful letter advising him to moderate his behavior. "I have often found your directness and frankness a real compliment, as proving that I was not getting so elderly and portentous as I sometimes fear." But he told George he could be prickly and combative, and too ready to show his adversaries "a kind of rhetorical contempt."

Benson's advice was well-timed. George's next job opportunity came at Charterhouse, a public school in Godalming, Surrey. The headmaster, Gerald Rendall—a cousin of the Winchester Rendall—was looking for someone to teach history, math, French, and Latin. George's qualifications were ideal and he got on well with Rendall, who wrote on July 5 to offer him a job on a probationary basis with a salary of £270 ($1312.20) a year. As a further enticement, Rendall said he hoped that George would be able to teach history to candidates for scholarships to Oxford and Cambridge. George needed no prompting to accept.

The news delighted George's family too. He spent time with them at the end of June 1910 on the occasion of the wedding of his sister Avie, the first of the four siblings to marry. Avie was George's favorite, even though both sisters were devoted to him, competing for his attentions whenever he returned to the family fold. As for his mother, she had taken to writing him querulous letters about her health, her plans for holidays, and trips to the seaside. They usually contained a note of recrimination: why hadn't he written, she had to make plans, she couldn't wait any longer to hear from him, it was all most vexing and troublesome. George usually ignored her attempts to lay her problems on him, displaying an amused tolerance in letters to his brother and sisters that confirms that they had come to a similar view. When he learned that Avie was engaged, he wrote in joking terms to her and her fiancé Harry Longridge, a businessman who had been at Trinity, the same

Cambridge college as George's father. George told them that "to steal my sister was a grievous offence" but quickly added that Harry was forgiven. "How could it be otherwise when my sister's so happy?" It was said in the family that Avie had made a smart move in marrying first, avoiding the risk of becoming the "home daughter"—the one who is left at home to look after her parents. But the family influences were strong, for Avie and Harry returned to Mobberley, moving into a new house, named Rathlin, near Hobcroft House. George took a close interest in their plans, wondering if the garden at Rathlin would incorporate the sand pit where they had all once played: "How thrilling it was to leap down its little precipices."

In July George went to Pen y Pass with Hugh Wilson. The weather was abysmal and they managed just one day's climbing on Lliwedd, which included the Girdle Traverse, the horizontal crossing of the cliff first climbed by Archer Thomson and his partner E. S. Reynolds in 1907. Then George went to see Benson, who was taking a holiday at Loweswater in the Lake District. Benson complained about George's appearance: "Too much hair and not enough collar. He would be much more attractive if he only were not so determined to dress unconventionally." Once again Benson was revealing his own sensitivities, for his family doctor, Ross Todd, was at Loweswater too, and Benson suspected that he and George were attracted to each other. Even so George and Benson went on several energetic walks together, striding across the high tops to reach the summit of Pillar Mountain in a brisk four hours. "I never saw anyone show such ecstatic delight as George in the presence of the mountains," Benson wrote. During one descent George stripped off to swim in Crummock Water: Benson described him as "a fine figure, taking headers and racing in the sun." That evening George showed "a little more than usual of the inside of his charming and impulsive mind," Benson commenting that he still had the ability to bring a fresh perspective to familiar matters: "He is in the delicious position of finding all things new."

⚘

Two weeks later, George was back in the Alps. But the circumstances were in marked contrast to his glorious season with Young and Robertson the previous year. George had with him a fifteen-year-old boy named John Bankes-Price whose parents had engaged George to give him an introduction to alpine climbing—a relationship George called "bear-leading." Young had provided a reference which helped George secure the job, and George told him it sounded "rather pleasant." Once in the Alps, the reality was different, for Bankes-Price showed no aptitude or enthusiasm for climbing, and was further handicapped when he hurt his knee. But there was one enormous mitigating factor. After a few easy climbs above Bel Alp, George moved across to Zermatt, where he met Cottie Sanders.

Cottie, who was in Zermatt with her family, saw at once how frustrated George was. Bankes-Price could hardly have been a less suitable pupil: "He had no taste whatever for the pursuit; he was weak and clumsy, he disliked cold and heat and exertions, and it was impossible to kindle in him the smallest spark of enthusiasm." George also had to contend with the fact that Geoffrey Young was there, partnered by one of his former Eton pupils, Marcus Heywood. During a spell of glorious weather they climbed eleven peaks in twelve days, including the first ascent of the west face of the Zinal Rothorn.

What impressed Cottie, however, was the "superb conscientiousness" George showed in meeting his obligations towards Bankes-Price. She noticed him running his hands through his hair "in one of those nervous clouded moods that I got to know well" but George persevered and managed to get his pupil up two peaklets, the Trifthorn and the Riffelhorn. Cottie nobly took charge of Bankes-Price to enable George to dash off on a vain attempt to climb the Arbengrat, one of the ridges on the Weisshorn; when the group moved on to Arolla, George succeeded in a traverse of Mont Collon. As for Bankes-Price, he confounded all expectations by writing to George after the holiday to declare that he was looking forward to climbing again "whenever I can."

In intervals between watching over Bankes-Price, George spent as much time as he could with Cottie. She had confided to her diary, though not to George, her disappointment that he had not been at Pen y Pass the previous Easter. He told her about his visit to Paris and the writers he had met, whom he praised for the directness and honesty of their writing. They went to the Wega bookshop together, where George recommended the French romantic poet Alfred de Musset. Cottie was struck by George's enthusiasm for "the beauty and importance" of writing: "I had never heard anyone talk about writing like that before." It was an introduction, a "first instalment," she wrote, "of what I always got so much of from George. He was always opening my eyes to new things, putting me in the way of fresh pleasures and activities of the mind, touching things with a fresh light."

While Cottie conceded in her diary that George could appear dogmatic and intolerant, she felt he was innately modest underneath. Shortly before he left Zermatt she gave him a small linen bag to carry sugar while climbing, replacing a tin which invariably spilled its contents into his rucksack. George did not yet know how to respond to a gift from a woman, for when she told him she had made the bag herself, he was "speechless with embarrassment." On the evening before George left to return to England, he and Cottie strolled through Zermatt together. "I want very much to climb with you," he told her, "because I fancy we have rather the same attitude towards the mountains."

CHAPTER FIVE

Dear Cottie
1910–1911

Soon after George started at Charterhouse in September 1910, David Pye paid him a visit. George had been allocated rooms at a nearby building called Nercwys House, and Pye was amused to find his sitting room "a litter of books and papers." Scattered across the desk and floor were books in English and French, Fabian tracts and modern plays, photographs of Greek statues and reproductions of contemporary French paintings and, on top of all of these, "a sea of essays" from his pupils.

Pye interpreted the chaos at Nercwys House as a token of the enthusiasm with which George had plunged into his new career. He had been characteristically hesitant at first, telling his mother four days after he arrived: "I am enjoying life here, though there are moments of doubt." He found small boys "difficult to teach and control; but it amuses me, and that is the great thing." George had received no form of teacher training and instead followed the examples set by Irving, Benson, and Young, who had rejected the authoritarian methods of most British public schools and aimed instead to get to know their pupils as individuals and teach through mutual respect and trust. Benson wrote to reassure him that boys did respond if the teachers could work out how to be "both strict and kind"—some boys at least were "quite delightful."

George still faced considerable difficulties, some stemming from the nature and ambience of the public school system itself. Charterhouse, named after a

Carthusian monastery in the City of London, had moved to Godalming in 1872, occupying a site on the Surrey hills from which its grandiose neo-Gothic buildings and Italianate spires were visible for miles around. It did so at the time of the greatest expansion of the British public schools as they educated the sons of Britain's rising entrepreneurial classes and provided the young men who would administer the British Empire, then approaching its zenith. Their teaching methods, however, embodied an enormous contradiction. Ostensibly they aimed to supply an education based on such fair-sounding notions as muscular Christianity and *mens sana in corpore sano*—imbuing their pupils with physical fitness and a moral sense, a sane mind in a sound body.

The contradiction stemmed from the fact that most public schools were oppressive institutions ruled by cruelty and fear, with discipline enforced through floggings, bullying, and a bizarre caste system, known in Britain as fagging, where new arrivals were obliged to act as body servants to older boys. The headmaster of Charterhouse, Gerald Rendall, who had appointed George, was a mild-mannered man who did not believe in iron discipline. His views were not shared by many of his staff, who were conditioned to believe that teachers and pupils existed in a state of permanent war. Many were hostile to George, complaining that his informal approach threatened to undermine their own attempts to maintain control.

George had other problems. As Pye noted, his "absurdly youthful appearance" led visiting parents to mistake him for one of his pupils, although George claimed that this helped him in his teaching. His fast, nervous style of speaking could make him hard to understand. He had to contend with classes of up to thirty boys—far too many for advanced work, such as Milton's *Paradise Lost*, George felt. Most awkward of all, in view of George's strengthening agnosticism, was the requirement that he should teach scripture. "Imagine me teaching the smallest boys about the fall of man!" he wrote to Pye. "What the devil is one to say? It was such a wholly admirable business and God behaved so badly; mere petty jealousy!"

In Pye's view, George also had temperamental flaws. The counterpoint to his eagerness, enthusiasm, and optimism was "a tendency to depression, impatience, and disgust at any failure." George grappled doggedly—"heroically" was Pye's term—with the spectrum of difficulties. He took an expansive view of the curriculum, recommending his pupils to read widely, talking to them about literature and politics, and setting essays on discursive subjects such as candor, popularity, and hypocrisy. He also took them on out-of-school trips to scenic or architectural landmarks. Some of his pupils considered him a soft touch and did their best to wreck his classes. Others felt he was an inspirational teacher who had opened their eyes to far more than their formal subject matter. The poet Robert Graves, who was at Charterhouse from 1909 to 1914, said George was the best teacher and the first real friend he ever had.

As George struggled to find his feet at Charterhouse, he had to cope with the latest dramas in his emotional life, where the Stracheys were again occupying center stage. After his teaching at Dartmouth in May, George arranged to stop overnight at Belsize Park Gardens, where James was now living with his brother. As always, news of his impending visit spread fast, for James promptly told Lytton that George would be staying. Lytton must have appreciated the tip, as his ardor for George had not waned. Finally, in October, Lytton decided to press his case. With a sense that he was venturing into some unknown hinterland—"I wonder where Charterhouse is? I think probably in some semi-detached Surrey region"— he traveled down to Charterhouse for the weekend of October 15 and 16. And, just like George's encounter with James in Lowes Dickinson's bedroom, what ensued was soon semipublic knowledge.

"Lytton," his brother James wrote to Rupert Brooke three days later, "seems to have had a hot time of it with George." Lytton, James reported, had made a sexual proposition to George. But George had evidently found an entirely plausible excuse to turn him down, namely the lack of privacy at Nercwys House. "I gather that on Sunday he only didn't go through with it out of terror that someone would come in—as there [was] no key to the door," James related.

The following day George had invoked the debacle with James to make his feelings plain. "George said in fact that such things couldn't ever be repeated. They bored him so." Even so Lytton persisted, agreeing with George that there was "no point in anything short of actual copulation," but going on to argue that as he was "merely indifferent, he'd be obliging enough to allow that." George was adamant but Lytton persevered: "Just once?"

"No, never."

Lytton's own account, contained in a letter to Duncan Grant on the same day, reveals both confusion and hurt. "The copulation never came, though there were some singular moments. He has a fond of prudery—also of 'indifference'— but then why make a fuss? At least there was conversation which left me déchiré, and a little nearer love. Am I after all in love with him? I believe his feelings are as exquisite as his face. He was too charming, and his affection also killed me. I would have given worlds for an embrace, but it was too late—and I am not in love." As an act of retaliation, Lytton had told George "he never wanted to see him again on those conditions—as it would be simply boring." By James's account George had been "awfully upset in the end." James delivered a gratuitous barb of his own, implying that George had been deluded over Lytton's feelings. "It appears that the poor fellow had imagined all along that Lytton was deeply in love with him."

Lytton, for all his bravado, was clearly distraught. "I reached here yesterday in a state bordering on collapse," he told Grant. "I'm only now beginning to pull around. I wish you were here. I feel as if I'd enough to say to go on talking forever—and how can I write? The important things vanish, and there are some things which even I haven't the nerve to put on paper—not because of the last ineradicable relics of human shame which haunt me still."

From these overlapping accounts it is clear that George had no wish to repeat his experience with James Strachey, particularly as it was Lytton, not he, who was the suitor. The episode suggests again that "poor George" was out of his depth when dealing with such expert embroilers and manipulators as the Strachey crew. But he still found the strength not to succumb to Lytton's blandishments, and to assert what he wanted for himself. He also benefited from the episode as it furthered his friendship with Duncan Grant. Ironically, having been rejected himself, Lytton assumed the role of matchmaker and proposed that George should act as Grant's model. "Oh heavens! his body!" Lytton wrote. "The supreme beauty of the face has I'm afraid gone—that wonderful bloom—but it's still immensely attractive, with the eyes, and the colour, and the charming expression, and the strange divine ears, so large and lascivious—oh! . . . "

The proposal made sense, as Grant could not afford professional models at that stage in his career. Lytton had already made the suggestion to George, who had seemed "charmed" by the idea. Lytton suggested to Grant that he should visit Charterhouse so that George could pose for him nude: "The thought . . . overwhelms me in a flood," Lytton wrote feverishly. But if that proved impossible—"there are very many clergymen about"—why not paint "a small full length sitting, in romantic colours?" Fanciful as ever, Lytton even wondered if George was in love with Grant: but either way he was sure that George would welcome an approach. "So you see your course is clear."

It was George who moved first, inviting Grant to Charterhouse on November 1. "Lytton encouraged me to think that you might be willing to spend a weekend here. Why not come next Saturday?" Grant declined as he had to complete a portrait, but added: "Please ask me again if you will—I want to hear about how you enjoy being a schoolmaster." The next time Grant agreed, taking the train to Charterhouse for an afternoon at the end of the month. "I went to Godalming to see George," Grant told Maynard Keynes. "It was magnificent and the country looked extraordinarily beautiful. There was a very full moon by whose light I walked back to Guildford where I caught the last train to London."

From Grant's effervescent account, it is evident that he and George had enjoyed each other's company. Their friendship lasted until George got married in

1914, and continued on a more occasional basis after that. Precisely what occurred between them in that period is another issue that has preoccupied biographers. Non-mountaineering writers have asserted that George and Grant were "lovers" or had "an affair." But what an affair entails, as we have already seen, can be a contentious point. One Bloomsbury historian believes that it went as far as sex but Grant himself denied that this was so. In 1977, answering a question about George from the Everest historian Walter Unsworth, he declared: "I think I can tell you with assurance that he was not a homosexual." Although Grant was not always consistent in his recollections, we believe that where his relationship with George is concerned, his declaration rings true. Having suffered the embarrassment and scars of his affair with James Strachey, George was not going to become so intensely involved again.

Grant, in any case, had far more to offer George. Both he and Bloomsbury were, at that moment, becoming hot. It was the eve of the epochal exhibition, Manet and the Post-Impressionists, which opened at the Grafton Galleries on November 8, 1910. With its assembly of paintings by Cézanne, Gaugin, Van Gogh, Matisse, Derain, Roualt, and the young Picasso, it attracted massive crowds, enormous publicity, and praise and condemnation in equal measure—all the hallmarks, in short, of a triumphant exhibition. The organizer was Roger Fry, a friend of Grant and fellow painter Vanessa Bell, whose contacts drew them closer into the circle of British painters who congregated in and around Fitzroy Street. George's taste for the art of the time had been whetted through his stay with the Bussys, with their talk of Matisse and Roualt. He enjoyed its spirit of rebellion and modernity, the sense that it was questioning established aesthetic values and pushing into radical new territory. Through Grant, George could have access to all of this, stimulating his taste for excitement and adventure.

⸎

While George was developing his friendship with Grant, he was also fascinated by the possibilities offered by Cottie Sanders. He had never met a woman with her combination of attributes. Vivacious, expressive, outward-going, sharing many of his interests, above all climbing: here was yet more fresh territory to explore. There was an unpropitious beginning when he invited her to a reception of the Alpine Club, to which he had just been elected, on December 7. The reception was held in the Grafton Galleries, giving them a chance to inspect the post-impressionist exhibition, but George had not realized it was a formal occasion and arrived at Elm Park Gardens wearing a green tweed suit and a battered gray felt hat. When he realized his mistake he withdrew in embarrassment, and took

Cottie to the exhibition a few days later. She had been skeptical about the paintings but he attempted, "with great patience and eagerness," to explain the artists' intentions, advising her to look beyond their figurative distortions and consider the emotions their subject matter inspired. Cottie was converted. George, she said, made her look at the paintings, "and go on looking, seriously, and not treat them as a huge joke; and so in time I came to see something of what there was."

Two weeks later they met again at Pen y Pass. Cottie and her brother Jack arrived there on December 28; George spent Christmas with Avie and her husband at Mobberley and arrived on New Year's Day. On January 2, 1911, George and Young tried to take her on the Girdle Traverse on Lliwedd. Although Cottie protested that she was tired from her previous climbs, they persuaded her to start but she became frightened and asked to be taken to the top of Lliwedd by the easiest route. George seemed surprised: being frightened, Cottie wrote, appeared to be something "he had no experience of whatever." Once at the top Young stomped off along the ridge but George escorted her down the path to Pen y Pass until she said she could find the rest of the way herself. "I wanted to be alone to get over it. He was a little puzzled, but did as I wished."

George devoted several more days to climbing with Cottie. He led her and Jack up a route on Tryfan's Central Buttress, moving "like a great cat, scolding, exhorting and encouraging us." Next was Parson's Nose on Clogwyn y Person, from which George and Young had retreated in a snowstorm at Easter 1909. "We were rather feeble creatures and his patience with us was on the whole extraordinary," Cottie wrote. They lost the way in mist on the descent but George "was a comfortable companion in misadventure, unperturbed and full of optimism." He and Cottie talked avidly during their walks back to Pen y Pass, the topics ranging across literature, arts, and politics, especially education. George detested the "illiberality, smallness and cramping narrowness" of conventional schools and used climbing as a metaphor for what education could achieve: "His great desire was for the spirit of man to exercise itself as freely and fearlessly and joyously as a climber on a hill." On their last day they walked over the Glyders in freezing temperatures, reaching the top of Creigiau Gleision, a crag overlooking the Llanberis Pass, as dusk fell. To the west the sky was dotted with "tiny rose-flushed flakes of cloud." George said it was like a Corot sunset.

When Cottie left, George moved on to Ogwen Cottage, where Cottie sent him a pair of climbing breeches in gratitude for his help. "It is not for you to feel grateful," George assured her in reply. "It is a pleasure to climb with you—excuse my bluntness—because you are so obviously pleased with climbing." It was certainly a blunt statement by the standards of Cottie's circle. But she and George had made a strong impression on each other, strengthened through the shared intensity of climbing, bringing a sense of bonding George had previously known only with men. When George visited Cambridge, Benson was struck by how "contented and tolerant" he seemed.

Yet George held back. It is the view of Cottie's biographer, Benita Stoney, that she was an ingénue, ensnaring men's emotions without being able to manage the consequences. If so, it was an encounter between equals, for Stoney's judgment mirrors comments often made about George: Benson once called him an "Ion," a poet in Greek literature who was unaware of the seductive effect he had on others, while Duncan Grant described him as a charming innocent. George was evidently wary, for on January 30 he told Avie: "I didn't fall in love with Miss Sanders—which showed a considerable power of resistance, for her charms are not few and quite artless." His letter also marked a significant family event, for Avie was pregnant. "Very good news," George told her. "It is the finest thing in a woman's life." Trafford, by contrast, confessed to George: "I do not much relish being an uncle for the first few years, because I think that babies are simply horrible till they reach the age of 6 or 7."

Meanwhile George's friendship with Grant was proceeding on its intermittent course. It could hardly be otherwise, since Grant, in keeping with the Bloomsbury spirit, was doing his best to shuffle his relationships without entirely losing the plot. His principal current lover was Adrian Stephen, the youngest child of the illustrious Stephen family: his father Leslie Stephen was a man of letters and a prominent Victorian alpinist; his sisters included Vanessa Bell and the future Virginia Woolf. But Grant was still seeing his former lover, Maynard Keynes, as well as indulging in a series of flirtations. He and George exchanged notes and visits, although more often than not the complications of Grant's life led him to refuse George's invitations to Charterhouse. Shortly before the new term George called on Grant in his studio in Fitzroy Square. George was looking "very radiant," Grant wrote, and that evening they dined at Gourmet's, a fashionable West End restaurant. At George's suggestion, Geoffrey Young came too. Grant, who had not met Young before, was "fascinated" by him, although adding: "He seemed to be in love with George."

❧

The Easter gathering at Pen y Pass in 1911 was one of the most spectacular ever. Cottie called it "the apotheosis of the Welsh parties organised by Geoffrey Young—the biggest, the most catholic, the wildest." By now, in addition to top-level climbers such as Jones, Dickinson, Irving, Todhunter, Pope, Young, and George himself, illustrious families like the Huxleys and Trevelyans were being attracted by their renown. After days out on the crags and hills the evenings were filled with talk and music: sea shanties and boat songs, German Lieder and duets from Mendelssohn, folk songs from Ireland and Young's own compositions, often rounded off with negro spirituals, as they were called, such as "Shine, Shine Harvest Moon" and "Darkies Lead a Happy Life." Making her first visit to Pen y Pass was Eleanor Slingsby, the fifteen-year-old daughter of the distinguished climber Cecil Slingsby, who eventually married Geoffrey Young. She was there with her older brother Laurence but while her boyish good looks acted as a magnet for Young, she remembered George equally well from that first visit, later relating how she first saw him wearing a red shirt and leaning on the mantelpiece in the Gorphwysfa's smoking room. "He had a beautiful voice and was absolutely beautiful though not sexually attractive," she told Young's biographer, Alan Hankinson. She remembered Cottie—"also very beautiful, tall and elegant"—and how she and George "used to get very intense talking Shelley together." Sometimes, as Cottie observed, the gathering divided on gender lines. The men would stage an impromptu wrestling match in the smoking room, while "we girls [would] hold a gossiping meeting in my room." The evening came to an end only when Rawson Owen, the Gorphwysfa's tolerant and amiable proprietor, cut off the power supply.

George and Cottie climbed together only once, as he was in demand to escort the novices on the cliffs. She was in a party which he led up Great Gully on Craig yr Ysfa. The icy conditions required all her concentration and she, in common with her fellow climbers, felt unable "to give to the scenery the attention which George felt it demanded." The party was notable for another contretemps which has been frequently retold, often to George's detriment. Present at Pen y Pass was the alpinist Karl Blodig, a dentist from Austria who had made it his life's ambition to be the first mountaineer to climb all fifty-seven of the Alps' 4000-meter peaks (in 1911, he had just four to go). After Young and George had taken him for a day's climbing on Lliwedd, Blodig loudly declared of George: "That young man will not be alive for long." George was dismayed, not only because he had been criticized by a guest, but because he considered Blodig's insinuation unjust. While he accepted that rock climbing entailed risk, he felt confident in his judgment and his technical ability. Cottie was angry on George's behalf, believing that he was "prudent according to his own standards," although accepting that these were not the standards of "ordinary rock climbers." She recognized that George was more adventurous when climbing on his own, rather than when he was taking responsibility for beginners, but "never saw him do a reckless or ill-considered thing."

Blodig's accusation raised a serious issue, and George was chastened when, several years later, Young told him that he feared that his enthusiasm sometimes got the better of his discretion. The fact remained that George had only one serious leader fall in his career before Everest, when Young saved his life during their ascent of the Nesthorn in 1909. George reserved his own strongest criticism for incompetent climbers who, through "irresponsible folly or ignorance," put themselves into danger. The point was made when he and Young were called out that Easter to rescue a climber who became stuck, unable to progress up or down, on Clogwyn y Person. He turned out to be a German, living in Bradford, who had gone climbing in a long mackintosh and ordinary outdoor shoes. After George and Young escorted him to safety, he offered them a sovereign as reward but they refused to accept it. There was laughter among the watching climbers but George was too cross to see the funny side; mountaineering, he said, had been "brought into disrepute."

George had the last word. Dr. Blodig was in the party which George led up Great Gully on Craig yr Ysfa. When George reached an unpleasantly icy pitch Blodig announced that he wanted to go back, but he was outnumbered by the other climbers, including Cottie. George climbed the icy section by "combined tactics," which meant climbing on one of his partner's shoulders. "Unanimous cries of 'Hurrah' and 'Bravo' hailed this extraordinary performance," Cottie recorded, and the group—including a rueful Blodig—reached the top safely.

As the party broke up, Cottie told George he was welcome to stay with her family in Fulham whenever he liked. George came up to London on May 2 for the Alpine Club dinner, Cottie noting that he had brought his dinner jacket this time. When they visited a new collection of Chinese paintings at the British Museum, George was "fairly intoxicated with their beauty" and this time Cottie needed no coaxing: "I could go the whole way with George at once." They packed in visits to the National Gallery and then a concert, Debussy's *Pelléas et Mélisande*, even though George had to get up at six to catch a train back to Charterhouse.

A few days later George wrote to thank Cottie for her hospitality. He also broached an immensely delicate issue, doing so with such hesitation that it was clear they were approaching a watershed in their relationship. George told Cottie: "My experiences of friendship are with my own sex," adding that if she were a man he would know what to do. "To confess the truth I don't much understand women and they make me feel like a mouse. But I suppose one may be friends with a lady mayn't I?" Gradually, tortuously, George worked his way around to the subject. When addressing a woman he felt that surnames were a barrier, while the term "Miss" was hopeless because it suggested the woman in question was "either a goddess or a doll, which she generally is and consequently unapproachable." At last he came to the point: could he call her Cottie?

Cottie evidently gave her consent, for George's next letter, dated June 6, 1911, began: "Dear Cottie . . . " He told her he had been sleeping out during the hot summer nights, sharing a tent with a fellow teacher and his brother Trafford. "A farm supplies bread and eggs, a nightjar perches in the Scotch fir a few yards away, the mist is white in the valleys," George wrote, before adding: "I suppose there's no chance of seeing you in these parts . . . "

⚓

As the end of his first year at Charterhouse approached, George was more at ease. Benson felt he was more objective in his views, and George told David Pye that he felt more in control, both of his pupils and of himself. "This last term has been very agreeable: several things got better: I got less irritable and found it easier to be severe without being angry." He was managing his pupils better too, as he told Avie: "If I hate punishing rather more, I have far fewer punishments to give." He congratulated Avie on the birth of her baby son. "I imagine that you're lying in bed and just wondering and gloating—and are you already weaving strange dreams of glory for his manhood and all his future?"

Almost until the last day of term, George was uncertain where he would be climbing that summer. His old Winchester tutor Graham Irving wanted him to join a trip to the Alps with Harry Tyndale, the founder member of the Winchester Ice Club who was now Irving's brother-in-law. Cottie Sanders had invited him to stay with her in Mull, where her parents had rented a lodge near the village of Aros. Its peaks, she conceded, were not quite on the scale of the Alps, but they still offered enjoyable climbing and scrambling.

George told Cottie that although Mull sounded delightful—"white sails on a Highland Loch and blue hills unexplored in the distance"—he would prefer to go to the Alps. However there was a difficulty. A month earlier he had been overcome with exhaustion and compelled to take to his bed. His doctor diagnosed a bad heart and sent him for tests, whose verdict he now awaited. George told Cottie that if he could not go to the Alps on grounds of ill health, he would join her in Mull. Then his doctor told him that his heart problem, whatever it was, seemed to have cleared up and he was free to go to the Alps. When George broke the news to Cottie he did his best to cheer her up, as she was evidently disenchanted with the weather. "You didn't sound particularly pleased with Mull," George observed, "but I hope the sun has shone since then."

George spent two weeks in the Alps. The trip marked another stage in his mountaineering evolution. On his three main previous visits—excluding the disastrous bear-leading trip—he had been in a subordinate role, accepting the decisions of Irving and Young and following, at times literally, in their footsteps. Now he joined his two companions in mapping out the days, making judgments about the scale of the approach marches, navigational and safety problems, the technical nature of the ascents. They were ambitious in their objectives, avoiding the more obvious and frequented routes, venturing instead into remote and difficult territory, where the isolation and consequent psychological demands were all the greater. As Cottie had witnessed at Pen y Pass, George had acquired the ability to remember and visualize an alpine problem which he would work on, perhaps subliminally, and then suddenly announce a solution. "His memory, bad for a good many things, was almost perfect for this."

George and his partners, Irving and Tyndale, took the train from Paris to Modane in the Graian Alps. After an arduous crossing of the wild valley head named Pont, they climbed the Gran Paradiso, at 13,323 feet the highest peak solely in Italy, doing so via its steep, icy east face. On August 9 they made the first ascent of the western ridge of the Herbetet, a rock pyramid near the Gran Paradiso, with a particularly testing traverse on icy rocks below a gendarme, a rock pillar that sat astride the ridge, with almost no protection from belays. They reached the summit at 3:30 P.M. and descended to the resort of Cogne by nightfall.

Two days later came another massive day, covering fifteen miles and climbing a total of 15,000 feet as they made the first complete traverse of the main ridge of the Apostoli peaks. On August 14 they climbed the Grivola, a sharp, pointed peak vulnerable to storms, this time making a long exploratory new approach from the east and finishing up the north ridge. There were several troubling sections of steep ice but George led with aplomb, cutting a staircase of steps "with inimitable ease and grace," as Tyndale wrote. What struck him about George's climbing, which he had not seen since 1905, was his suppleness and economy of movement: "his movements appeared almost serpentine in their smoothness."

On August 18, having moved to Courmayeur, they set out to climb Mont Maudit, at 14,649 feet one of the highest peaks in the Mont Blanc massif. They aimed to do so by its long, sheaf-like east ridge, snaking its way across the glaciers, known today as the Frontier Ridge. What was already a bold enterprise became more difficult when, shortly after leaving the mountain hut on the Col du Géant at 3:30 A.M., George was affected by a stomach disorder that he blamed on drinking some sour chianti the night before. When they reached the crest of the ridge George passed out, kicking over the stove on which Irving was attempting to cook breakfast from oats and melted snow. To his intense embarrassment George passed out for a second time when he was supposed to be paying out Irving's rope. The most anxious moments came as Irving led up an icy stretch below the summit, where George and Tyndale knew that if Irving fell they stood no chance of holding him and would probably be dragged off themselves. It was with both elation and relief that they reached the summit in mid-afternoon.

They now faced a difficult choice. The normal descent route was to the Col de la Brenva, where they could continue down to the Grands Mulets hut. Alternatively, they could push on to the summit of Mont Blanc itself, another 1600 feet of ascent. When they reached the col, George's legs felt leaden and all three climbers were suffering from the altitude, but when Irving suggested going down, it was George who insisted that they should go on. At 6:30 P.M. they were standing on the highest summit in western Europe: "a solemn dome," George wrote, "resting on all those marvellous buttresses, fine and firm above all its chasms of ice." Ahead lay a long and demanding descent of a steep and highly crevassed glacier in the gathering dark, but they reached the Grands Mulets hut safely after a sixteen and a half hour day.

Apart from one further short climb, George's alpine season was over. But, much later, George revisited the trip. He had come to feel that much mountaineering writing was arid and impersonal, and that while most climbers were able to relate what they did, few could describe how they felt. In 1917, during a spell in an army camp in Winchester, he wrote an article for the *Alpine Journal* in which he explored his emotions during the Mont Maudit climb, attempting to relate the inner journey that accompanied the ascent. After drinking the sour chianti, George wrote, he felt ashamed at his lack of fitness and concentrated on not being sick. He was overwhelmed with guilt at falling asleep and this was made worse by Irving's anger when he kicked over the breakfast stove. He felt alarmed as Irving tackled the dangerous icy section below the summit of Mont Maudit, but accepted he had no choice but to give Irving his trust. When Irving proposed descending from the Col de la Brenva instead of going on to the summit of Mont Blanc, George would have felt too ashamed to accept. As they toiled up the final snowfield to the summit, George was afraid of an anticlimax, but then he was suffused with an uplifting awareness that even this most arduous stretch was part of the whole experience. "The dream stretched to the very end."

Once again George had invoked the idea of the dream to describe his aims and goals. He ended with a passage which has frequently been quoted, often without its source, and again uses the construct of the dream. "One must conquer, achieve, get to the top; one must know the end to be convinced that one can win the end—to know there's no dream that mustn't be dared . . . Is this the summit, crowning the day? How cool and how quiet! We're not exultant; but delighted, joyful; soberly astonished . . . Have we vanquished an enemy? None but ourselves . . . . "*

Once back in Britain, George was determined to squeeze in some more climbing. He spent a week with his Birkenhead friend Harold Porter at the Snowdon Ranger, a hotel at Cwellyn on the far side of Snowdon from Pen y Pass. Climbing with what Porter remembered as "that miraculous ease and grace which I had already learnt to admire," George put up a series of routes which placed him in the highest ranks of contemporary British climbing. The routes were on some lesser-known Snowdonia haunts, as Young and Archer Thomson were hoping to publish a guidebook to the outlying crags, and encouraged their friends to explore them.

The first was the jagged skyline ridge on Y Garn, the cliff at the eastern edge of the Nantlle Ridge to the south of Snowdon. Thomson had attempted it the previous year but had retreated from the hardest pitch, a sixty-foot section of vertical rock; Anton Stoop, another guidebook writer, had died in a fall from the same place. The footholds sloped disconcertingly and the handholds required awkward sideways pulls, marking a technical advance from the straightforward vertical pulls on most routes of the time. It was Porter who led the crucial pitch, which George sparingly described as "exciting."

The second new route was a 280-foot groove on the cliff of Llechog, an hour's walk from the Snowdon Ranger. The toughest section was the second pitch, a long V-shaped chimney, where the holds again sloped out awkwardly, and it was impossible to secure any protection. The third route combined two previous routes on Lliwedd, with a new direct finish.

When the issue of George's technical ability arose in 1999, two British climbers, Martin Crook and Ray Wood, decided to test it for themselves by climbing these three routes. They came away most impressed by the technical demands of the routes, and the commitment and courage George and Porter had shown, particularly in view of their primitive equipment and almost complete lack of protection techniques. The route on Y Garn, now known as George's Ridge, was both technical and bold, leading Crook to wonder how many modern leaders, accustomed to the comfort of their high-tech equipment, would have been able to cope with its psychological demands. Crook found that the crucial second pitch of Eastern Gutter on Llechog became harder and harder, with a poor belay stance at the top, and described it as "a brilliant route of great character." As for the Lliwedd route, Far East Cracks Direct Finish, Crook agreed with the guidebook description that it was "dirty, loose and difficult." He rated both it and

---

*The ellipses are George's, and do not indicate that any text has been omitted.

Eastern Gutter as "Very Severe," making them two of the earliest climbs at that standard, and reckoned they required a level of boldness and commitment that would be foreign to most rock climbers today.

⁂

Not long after leaving the Snowdon Ranger, George returned to Charterhouse. While in the Alps he had sent two postcards to Cottie on Mull, relating the latest feats of Geoffrey Young, who had been making a series of dramatic new ascents with Josef Knubel, Karl Blodig, and Ralph Todhunter. But Cottie was preoccupied with family concerns. She sensed that something was amiss although at first she could not work out what it was. First, the household budget had been reduced to a mere £4000 ($19,440.00) a year. While this sum was a fortune by almost anyone else's standards, Cottie viewed it as "astonishingly moderate compared with our previous expenditure." Then, instead of going to the Alps as usual, her parents had rented the lodge on Mull, while her father remained in London.

In early September, Cottie discovered the answer at last. Her mother wrote to her from London to disclose that four years before, her father had suffered a slight stroke. Although he seemed to recover, the stroke had caused permanent mental damage and from then on he had made all his investment decisions by pricking the pages of a bible with a pin. In that time, the family fortune of £250,000 ($1,215,000.00) had all but disappeared. "The plain fact," Cottie wrote in her diary, "was that we were ruined."

Cottie and her sisters returned to London just as her parents were packing to leave the mansion in Elm Park Road. The family's annual income finally dwindled to £1000 ($4,860.00), leaving her parents just enough to go to live in Cannes. Cottie and her sister Helen rented a flat in the Fulham Road and Cottie took her first ever job, working as a secretary in a charity organization for 23 shillings ($5.59) a week. For Cottie it was a profoundly disturbing episode, bringing with it the novel experiences of feeling hungry and having to work for a living. But help was at hand for, as she confided to her journal, George, her mentor in so much, would now be able to teach her "about being poor."

Chapter Six

A Strange Thrill
1911–1914

Once back at Charterhouse in September 1911, George had new conflicts to face. Gerald Rendall, the headmaster who appointed him, had been replaced by Frank Fletcher, a former head of Marlborough. Fletcher, who had a reputation as an enthusiastic flogger, had been instructed by the school governors to tighten what they saw as the lax and indulgent attitudes that had flourished under Rendall. His arrival did nothing to moderate George's increasing dislike of aspects of public school life. He became dismayed by the school's "mechanical atmosphere," particularly because the requirements of School Certificate examinations threatened to limit the scope of his teaching. He disliked the enforced division between school and home, suspecting that many parents were only too ready to discard responsibility for their children's upbringing. Quite remarkably, in view of his own sporting achievements, he turned against organized sport on the grounds that it was wrong to force boys to take part if their aptitudes lay elsewhere. He also took a personal dislike to Fletcher, whom he compared to a whale: "He often looks as though he were trying to vomit the prophet Jonah."

Despite all his reservations about the school, and the disruption his more recalcitrant pupils tried to cause, George was determined to remain true to his ideal of what a teacher should be. He held play readings at Nercwys House and lectured with lantern slides on Renaissance art. He participated in school debates, usually on the radical (and unpopular) side. He opposed capital punishment on the grounds that it was immoral and did nothing to reduce crime (the motion was lost, 13–34). He devised a strategy of focusing on pupils he thought would most benefit from individual attention, among them Robert Graves. In *Goodbye to All That*, Graves described how, as a scholar who came from a poor background and wrote poetry, he was bullied mercilessly. George treated him as an equal and suggested he read modern authors such as H. G. Wells, Samuel Butler, and Rupert Brooke. To Graves, he was one of the very few "really decent masters" at Charterhouse, sadly wasted because he was so much at odds with the system. "Yet he always managed to find four or five boys who were, like him, out of their element, befriending and making life tolerable for them." In a note of condolence to Ruth when George died, Graves wrote that he owed to George the recovery of his self-respect.

Throughout this time George was living a life that was as rich as he could make it. He maintained his diverse social existence, moving around England's literary and artistic worlds, making friends and forming useful relationships. He was keen to develop his writing and read through his Boswell essay again. Arthur Benson had suggested that he convert it into a book, and George dispatched it to the publisher John Murray. Murray sent a standard "thanks but no thanks" rejection letter: while the manuscript was "creditable and careful," he did not feel it revealed much that was new, etc. etc. In any case, a rival book could be in the offing: Boswell's descendants had unearthed some journals and letters and it was not worth publishing George's book until Murray was certain what they contained.

George was undeterred and sent the manuscript to a second publisher, Smith Elder. They responded with gratifying speed, telling George they would like to publish it as a book in spring 1912. They sent a list of suggested changes: George should amplify various points, reduce the length of his sentences, and cut phrases like "it will be remembered" which they considered "perilously near journalese." Most important, he should formulate his point of view more clearly, summarizing it in a single paragraph which he should use to "go through the book and embolden your sentences where they need it."

George showed Smith Elder's letter to Lytton Strachey, who had stayed in touch. He had come to Charterhouse in June to avoid "the terrors" of the coronation of George V, having first warned George that he had grown "a red-brown-gold beard of the most divine proportions." Strachey agreed with Smith Elder, telling George that many of his sentences were "overloaded" and that he should clarify his point of view. It was far preferable, Strachey felt, "to sacrifice comprehensiveness to lucidity, especially in prose. One can only hope at best to say a part of what one thinks, and so one may as well make up one's mind to choose the part that's simple." George accepted Strachey's diagnosis and agreed to submit a revised manuscript to Smith Elder by the end of the year.

Cottie Sanders, meanwhile, had been struggling with her newly straitened life. She was, in truth, a long way short of the breadline. She had moved in to a flat in Walsingham Mansions in Fulham but, although she considered it "minute," it had six rooms and enough space for one of her former nursery maids to live in as the housekeeper. Her parents had sufficient funds in reserve to pay her an allowance to supplement her wages. Even so, she discovered being "actually hungry, a rather surprising experience." George once again became her guide. He dined with her and her sister Helen at Walsingham Mansions and went with her to an exhibition of Persian pottery at the Victoria and Albert Museum. As for "being poor," Cottie found George "fertile in resource and expedient for the best economies and for the art of spending wisely." He recommended her to pawn her christening mug and then sell the pawn ticket as well. Revealingly, he advised her that when she did spend money it was important to do so "lavishly and without thought," and counseled her on her other new experience, the activity known as going to work. Cottie admitted to feeling frightened at the prospect of her former leisure time being "sold into bondage" but George helped stiffen her resolve. "Generally speaking, he was inclined to regard the whole business rather as an escape from futility and philistinism than anything else."

As for climbing, Cottie acknowledged that there could be no more three-month summer seasons in the Alps, and that even trips to Wales would require careful "actuarial calculations." Instead, fortified with the proceeds from her christening mug, she took to organizing walking excursions in the Home Counties. She and up to a dozen friends would take the train into the countryside, walk until tea-time, usually spent at an inn, and then catch the train back to London. Cottie took the opportunity to arrange several trips to Godalming. George met them at the station and would then "tramp rapturously along at the head of the straggling band, causing one to note the special loveliness of every choice place through which he led us."

⁂

There was another enormous Pen y Pass party at Christmas. The climbing was mostly undemanding and the weather kind. George had brought Trafford who seemed somewhat overawed by the other climbers. A large group spent Christmas Day on Tryfan under a cold blue sky. There was a misty start when they climbed Snowdon on New Year's Day 1912, but near the summit they came out above the clouds, to be rewarded with the sight of a Brocken Spectre, a phenomenon that occurs when low-slanting sunlight casts a haloed shadow of the peaks and climbers on to the clouds below. Having raised the necessary funds, Cottie was there, but climbed with George only once, as they prospected for routes on Clogwyn y Person. Although it was a dull day, George was in a buoyant mood: "Roaming about, generally unroped, seeking a way—pausing in that characteristic attitude, one hand almost stroking the rock, while his eye wandered up and down looking for clues and weighing possibilities, till he decided that something would 'go.'"

By now George's assurance as a climber and climbing leader was being reflected in a social milieu. When Cottie first met him she noticed how he could be detached and withdrawn in large groups, and susceptible to mood swings, sometimes exuberant, sometimes despondent and irritable. But she had been full of admiration during the Pen y Pass party the previous Easter when George took part in a heated debate on an ethical issue with Young's cousin Page Dickinson, one of the Irish climbers who sailed their own boat across the Irish Sea to attend the parties. George had the tougher case, as he was arguing that it was important to live by fixed moral tenets, while Dickinson contended that the best thing about moral principles was to be able to break them. George, who was sitting on the floor beside the fire, betrayed his nervousness by lapsing into a stammer and running his fingers through his hair. But he stuck to his position despite banter from the crowd and kept an even temper throughout. Now, Cottie observed, he was initiating conversations, telling jokes, and even—deploying one of humor's most risky weapons—"countering irony with irony rather neatly."

Our judgment is that George's growing self-confidence stemmed from his sense that he was restoring balance to his personal life. He and Cottie recognized each other's strengths and what each could bring to the relationship. George had opened up a new world of literature and the arts for Cottie, laying the foundations for her career as a writer which formally began when she wrote her first novel, *Peking Picnic*, published under the pen name Ann Bridge in 1932. At the same time he acquired a clearer understanding of women, how to communicate with and relate to them, a precursor to heterosexual relationships and love.

That did not mean that George had abandoned affectionate friendships with men, as he was still in touch with Duncan Grant. George traveled to Birkenhead from Pen y Pass and Grant, who was on his way to an exhibition of his paintings in Manchester, joined him there on January 3, 1912. Grant lost no time in revealing his bemusement at life in provincial Britain, telling

Maynard Keynes: "This is a most ghastly house, among others just like Harlesdon [sic] I should think, stretching for miles and miles. I only arrived last night at 10 and it is now only 10 A.M. The only other inhabitant is George's sister—extraordinarily like the 1,000,000 other energetic pretty young ladies that this island produces."

The sister in question was Mary, and the houses were not really like those to be found in the London suburb of Harlesden. Apart from the vicarage, they were standard inner-city terraces, clustered around the docks. George took Grant for a walk through the shipyards, but Grant found the proceedings risible, as his Bloomsbury companions learned when he returned. "Duncan came in fresh from Liverpool where he had been staying with the beautiful George Mallory," Vanessa Bell told Roger Fry. "He gave us an extraordinary account of Liverpool society."

By now George had accepted the danger, arising from friendships within the Bloomsbury set, of encountering shafts of sarcasm such as these. Grant was in any case one of the less affected Bloomsbury denizens, exhibiting George's own ingenuousness when personal entanglements arose. And it is clear that something untoward occurred between them at around this time, as a letter—or at least the draft of a letter—from Grant to George reveals. He wrote it in the waiting room of Guildford station, having left Charterhouse in some haste but missing the 7 P.M. London train by a few minutes. "I hope you did not mind very much what I did tonight," Grant began. " . . . I did not mean to suggest that I was in love with you. I am far too fond of somebody else I think to fall in love. But I cannot help wanting to express my feelings for people to them, and mine are so complicated towards you that I was somehow conscious that a kiss would somehow do it. When I say complicated I mean difficult to explain in words, I daresay it is really very simple. I think I want to show you that I think you are beautiful for one thing—but I suppose I should have reckoned with you . . . . "

From his explanation and semiapology, it is clear that Grant, who could behave impulsively, had delivered an impromptu kiss which left George uncertain and discomfited. The letter also makes clear that the kiss was not intended as a declaration of love, since Grant was already committed to "somebody else," namely Adrian Stephen. In comparison with the James Strachey entanglement, it appears a minor incident. In any case it would seem that the letter was not sent, since it was eventually found in Grant's own papers and not George's, and this was presumably because Grant concluded that it would only bring further complications: far better to let the matter rest. As his biographer, Frances Spalding, observed, Grant found it easier to put his feelings into paint, especially as George was a willing model, and these roles now provided a mainstay for the relationship.

It was almost certainly in this period that Grant, who had moved to a new studio at 38 Brunswick Square in November 1911, painted the portrait of George which, like Bussy's, was acquired by the National Portrait Gallery. It depicts George naked from the waist up with his arms encircling his knees. The eclectic Grant painted it in a pointillist style, and the angle of George's nose and eyes closely resemble those in the Bussy portrait. Grant made a second pointillist painting of George, naked once again and this time in a full-length pose, one leg resting over the other, an arm reaching down to grasp his ankles. The painting bears the date 1913 but the Bloomsbury expert Richard Shone believes that Grant, who could be uncertain over dates, added this later, as he had moved on from his pointillist style by the summer of 1912.

George also posed for a series of nude photographs which Grant took at Brunswick Square. The poses are similar to those of the paintings, one showing George sitting on a table, his legs drawn up and his hands grasping his feet. There are several full-frontal shots, the most striking showing George in a classic climbing move with one foot on the ground, the other poised on a hold at the height of his knee, while his right arm reaches above his head. It precisely matches the position described by Young when he wrote that George would "set his foot high against any angle of smooth surface, fold his shoulder to his knee, and flow upward and upright again in an impetuous curve."

Grant was delighted with the photographs and in January 1912 sent three prints to Maynard Keynes; he also used them as models for poses that appeared in designs for the Omega workshops, where the Bloomsbury group produced furniture, wall decorations, and other items of interior decor. Later Grant made it clear that George had enjoyed posing for him. In an interview near the end of his life, Grant said that George was "a beautiful creature [who] was perfectly willing to sit to me." He added that while George was not narcissistic, it was "obvious" he liked to be admired. This accords with a letter from George thanking Grant for sending him one of the photographs. George complained that it did not show enough detail and asked Grant to send him the negatives so that he could make some prints himself, adding: "I am profoundly interested in the nude me."

As 1912 progressed, George continued to use his spare time to capacity, taking pleasure from dovetailing as many visits as he could into trips away from Charterhouse. After leaving Birkenhead he spent a weekend with the poet Wilfrid Blunt at his home in Poundhill near Crawley. Then it was up to London to meet Cottie for lunch and further exhibitions and museums. Grant wrote with the latest news from Bloomsbury: Rupert Brooke had been to tea, Lytton had just dined with Lady Ottoline Morrell, and he had been asked to design the costumes for a new production of *Macbeth*.

In February, George made another significant new friendship. While visiting the artist Neville Lytton he met Eddie Marsh, another habitué of the Bloomsbury salons, and a prolific patron of literature and the arts. Marsh worked as Winston Churchill's secretary at the Admiralty and had a hectic and high-powered social life, dining inter alia with Henry James, Max Beerbohm, D. H. Lawrence, and the prime minister, Herbert Asquith. He become a literary editor of high repute, polishing the manuscripts of his boss, Winston Churchill, Rudyard Kipling, Henry James, and J. M. Barrie, and acting as literary executor for the estate of Rupert Brooke. Marsh was also an Apostle, with a taste for the bizarre, once letting himself be photographed as the martyred St. Sebastian, with arrows embedded in his gray three-piece suit.

Like so many before him, Marsh was immediately attracted to George. He told Brooke: "Besides his great beauty of face I think he has enormous charm of mind and character," and complained that Brooke had not introduced them before. (Brooke replied that although he was fond of George, he somehow felt "momentarily dull" whenever they met, and for that reason had never got around to visiting him at Charterhouse.) Marsh offered to edit the proofs of George's *Boswell:* he called this "diabolizing," because he played devil's advocate in suggesting textual changes to the author. When George accepted, Marsh went so far as to visit the British Library to check some of George's facts.

Easter brought the customary Pen y Pass party and one that marked the start of an intense spell of climbing for George. His old Cambridge friend David Pye came to Pen y Pass for the first time, as did another figure who would be significant in George's life, the Australian-born climber George Finch, who settled in England that year. Trafford was there too, making what proved to be his last climbing trip with his brother. The weather provided all the contrasts the British climate is capable of, from fresh snowfall over Easter, followed by a week of blue skies and sunshine, which Young called "basking weather." On one of the worst days, when it was wet and bitterly cold, George and Young led Charles Trevelyan, then president of the Board of Education, up Lliwedd's Far East Cracks. Trevelyan, who later became a keen walker, and as a Liberal MP sponsored the first mountain access bill, had been complaining of backache, but the day's exertions put it right.

❧

Four months later George made his sixth trip to the Alps. His partners were his Birkenhead friend Harold Porter and Hugh Pope, an engaging Old Etonian, then at Oxford, whom he had met at Pen y Pass the previous Christmas. They had intended to climb in the Bernese Alps but the weather was abysmal and after meeting Geoffrey Young, who was climbing with Josef Knubel, they all moved across to Zermatt. The mountains were still shrouded in mist and, after one day's climbing, Young departed for Chamonix, where he was due to meet Humphrey Jones, his partner during his spell of memorable first ascents in the Alps in 1911. Jones had married just a week before and was spending his honeymoon introducing his wife, Muriel, to the Alps.

On August 8 George and his companions got out at last, climbing the Pointe de Genevoise, a sharp 12,000-foot rock peak above the Val d'Hérens, and making the demanding 400-meter (1300-foot) traverse to the Dent Perroc. That night George wrote to Cottie from Arolla, telling her of the miserable weather and a night he had spent in a hut, "my head upon a straw pillow and some good soup brewing." Two days later came another setback, when George succumbed to snow-blindness after climbing the Pigne d'Arolla by its steep northern ice face, and he was ordered by a doctor to spend several days in a darkened room. On August 15 they traversed the Douves Blanches, a spiky spur off the main chain of the Grands Dents on the east side of the Arolla Valley. On August 17 they found a new line on the Dent Blanche, which George had climbed by the south ridge with Irving and Bullock in 1905. They followed a "delectable" series of chimneys on the 2000-foot rock wall above the upper Ferpècle Glacier. They arrived on the south ridge a short distance below the summit, which they reached at 10:30 A.M. Young later ranked the route as one of "the few great guideless ascents made in the Alps" and it confirmed George's ability to find demanding and original routes in remote territory, displaying confidence and boldness, as well as a high level of physical fitness.

The three men spent the rest of the day descending to Zermatt, arriving at seven o'clock. They were looking forward to an evening of food and gossip at the Monte Rosa but instead there was shattering news. Two days before, Humphrey and Muriel Jones had been climbing the relatively easy Mont Rouge de Peuteret. Their guide was above them when his handhold broke and he crashed down on to them, sweeping all three to their deaths. Their bodies were found by Young, distraught at losing one of his closest climbing companions and at the bright futures that had been destroyed. Jones had just been elected as the youngest member of the Royal Society; Muriel was the first woman fellow of the University of Wales. It was another catastrophe for the compact British climbing community, and a chilling reminder of the perils of mountaineering. Young organized their funeral in Courmayeur which George and Pope attended. Afterwards they and Young crossed back to Zermatt via the Col Tournanche, making what proved to be George's last alpine ascent for seven years. Although they were in a despondent mood, Young felt that George was at the peak of his powers as he found a new line up the steep rock leading to the col, moving in "a continuous undulating movement so rapid and so powerful that one felt the rock must either yield or disintegrate."

Just as in 1911, when he had been determined to capitalize on the fitness he had achieved in the Alps, George returned to Snowdonia in September, staying at the Snowdon Ranger hotel in Cwellyn with a remarkably varied group. His main partner was Ralph Todhunter, a man in his forties who was well known for wearing white gloves while climbing and had accompanied Young and Humphrey Jones during their historic alpine season in 1911. George brought two Charterhouse boys, Bernard Scott and William Stevens, to give them an introduction to climbing. His sister Mary came too, with a friend from Birkenhead named Henrietta Livingstone. As Mary later told it, Livingstone was one of the three women who interested George before he was married, the others being Olive Blood, the doctor's daughter from Birkenhead, and Cottie Sanders. Livingstone was intense and intellectual, the daughter of a shipping entrepreneur and—according to Mary—more attracted to George than vice versa. Mary's main memories were of a raw day spent walking over the Snowdon range and of trying to make tea on a primus stove while sitting in a boat in the middle of a lake. Even so, she told George: "I enjoyed it tremendously."

George spent three days climbing with Todhunter, once again seeking crags away from the established climbing grounds for Young and Thomson's proposed new guidebook. They spent their first day on Craig y Cwm Du, a shaded north-facing crag above Betws Garmon and easily reached from the Snowdon Ranger. They made three first ascents. Pis Aller Rib followed a 470-foot arête and was later rated as Severe; Yellow Buttress was similar. Adam Rib, a 400-foot Hard Severe, was especially notable, as they straightened out a route put up by Thomson the previous year, tackling difficulties he had avoided on the final pitch. They next inspected Clogwyn du'r Arddu, the black cliff high on Snowdon that then had just two routes, both put up in 1905, one by the Abraham brothers. George and Todhunter made the third, a 500-foot gully, now named East Gully, which although modest by today's standards gave an intimate perspective on the cliff's soaring architecture. The following day they made their most important discovery, visiting Cwm Silyn, a rock amphitheater hidden away on the north side of the Nantlle ridge on the southwest fringe of Snowdonia. They made its first recorded ascent, a 300-foot route named Four Pitch Gully and later rated as Difficult.

On Clogwyn du'r Arddu and Cwm Silyn, George and Todhunter had put down markers for the future: Cwm Silyn developed into a popular crag with a range of routes for all abilities, while Cloggy, as it was referred to, became the testing ground for a generation of British climbers in the 1950s and 1960s. Their routes were significant in another way. The earliest ascents of peaks such as Lliwedd and Tryfan had been made as an integral part of going to the summit, and many climbers considered it de rigueur to do just that. Now George and Todhunter were prospecting for routes that were self-sufficient and stood on their own merits, helping to launch the transition to what Young described as "a new type of calculated climbing for its own sake."

Soon after returning to Charterhouse, George learned of yet another death. After their parting in Zermatt, Hugh Pope had left for the Pyrenees, borrowing George's ice ax for the trip and writing to thank him for his introduction to the Alps. In early October, on the day of a memorial service in Cambridge to Humphrey and Muriel Jones, Pope was reported missing after setting off on a solo ascent of the Pic du Midi d'Ossau. Young dashed to the Pyrenees, recruiting Knubel en route, and found Pope's body where it had fallen, "looking like a young god, lying at rest on a rock after swimming." Young told George the full story when they met in London. "It has left the most gloomy picture in my mind," George told Cottie. "He was such a charming companion in the Alps this year."

⚘

George's Boswell biography was published in October, four months late. In his preface, in which he explained that it was intended not as "a complete Life of Boswell, but an explanation of his character," George thanked three people in particular: "Mr A. C. Benson, whose encouragement promoted this enterprise, Mr G. L. Strachey for many valuable suggestions, and Mr E. H. Marsh for correcting my proofs, which was no mean labour." It won a respectable sprinkling of reviews. The best was in the *Contemporary Review,* which called it "a thought-provoking and satisfying book"; the *Oxford Chronicle* considered it "a valuable footnote to the literary history of the Eighteenth Century" but spoiled the effect by referring to the author as "Mr George Sampson." George was delighted by a letter of praise from Cottie: "I never imagined that anyone would care about it except 'Boswell students,'" he told her, "so it's all the more pleasing to hear that you like it." Most heartening of all was a report from Birkenhead, where his father—"not a great reader"—had been perusing the book on Saturday afternoons instead of preparing his sermon. "I therefore consider it a great success!"

Meanwhile George moved effortlessly among his different worlds. In September he dined in Soho with Grant, Brooke, and Marsh, then stayed with Grant at Brunswick Square. In October he was invited to the Ladies Alpine Club Christmas dinner by Mabel Capper, a climber he had met in the Alps in the summer. Shortly after accepting, he had a similar invitation from Cottie, and had to write to tell her, with the greatest regret, that she was too late. As an alternative, he proposed a visit on the afternoon of the dinner to the second London post-impressionist exhibition which had just opened in London and should make "an agreeable afternoon." Cottie did not let George off easily, for she said it was unlikely she could meet him in time. George sent further proposals for dinners, teas, and walks around Godalming. "It struck me that one might spend a glorious day starting at Farnham for Milford or Witley." But although he appeared keen to heal the minor rift between them, their friendship never quite regained its former intimacy.

George's social round continued in the New Year, 1913. On January 15 he had lunch with Rupert Brooke and Eddie Marsh; the next day he and Marsh paid a visit on Duncan Grant, who offered to provide him with two paintings for his classroom (it is not clear whether they were ever done). On February 1 Marsh came to Charterhouse, where he and George took it in turns to read passages aloud from the new poetic work by John Masefield, *The Daffodil Fields*. George wrote to Cottie, telling her he had read a history of the Spanish conquest of Mexico, "by far the most thrilling story of adventure in the world." He had just come back from watching a football match at Winchester: "One of those stirring contests by which the character of the young idea is so stoutly moulded that we may never live to see the day when the British Empire is dragged in the mire, or when the bonds of this ponderous Empire are loosened."

There had been no Pen y Pass party at Christmas, 1912. The reason lay in the deepening personal trauma overwhelming Geoffrey Young, which was eventually to impinge on George. Although Young had become president of the Climbers' Club, that honor was far outweighed by his despair at the deaths of his friends: Pope and the Joneses earlier that year, and Robertson in 1910. On top of these had come the sudden suicide of Archer Thomson, who had killed himself during a fit of depression by drinking a bottle of carbolic acid. Young was further distressed by his increasingly fraught attempts to come to terms with his troubled sexuality. He was resorting more frequently to the homosexual dives of Europe, and after the Joneses' funeral in Courmayeur had gone directly to Berlin in the hope, as he wrote in his private journal, of meeting "sensation with sensation" and finding a "natural remedy for overdone nerves and deeper feelings." At the same time, he was increasingly attracted to Eleanor Slingsby, who was still a schoolgirl. Young feared that Pen y Pass would only accentuate the conflicts he faced, and he gratefully accepted an invitation to spend Christmas in the Alps with the writer and off-piste skiing enthusiast, Arnold Lunn.

In the climbing world Pen y Pass had been badly missed and, as Easter approached, Young's friends pressed him to revive it. Young was at first reluctant but the argument was probably clinched when Eleanor Slingsby—accompanied by her father and brother—agreed to come. Young still hoped it would be a limited affair but more than fifty people turned up, including Duncan Grant and Robert Graves. Grant had been invited by Young's brother Hilton, who had bought one of his paintings, *The Dancers*. He was frozen by the two-day journey in the sidecar of Hilton's motorbike and was further bewildered when he accepted an invitation to join a walk, rather than an actual climb, and found himself tramping across a barren and frozen landscape, although he did concede that it was all rather beautiful.

George, who arrived after Grant had left, came with Geoffrey Keynes and three more Charterhouse boys, Hugh Heber Percy, Robert Mühlberg, and Robert Graves. After a few days at Pen y Pass they walked across Snowdon to the Snowdon Ranger Hotel. The weather restricted the climbing and, although George revisited the new testing grounds of Cwm Silyn, Llechog, and Craig y Cwm Du, it was apparently without posting any significant climbs. Graves relished the new experiences to the limit, thrilled to be doing "real precipice climbing." He thought that George was a "magnificent" climber and afterwards wrote to say he had never enjoyed himself so much in his life. Young was still mulling over the implications of restarting the Pen y Pass parties, telling his diary: "Physically as strong as ever, and nerve as sound. Pleasure and romance left. Too many memories of those five faces of last year, now gone."

George, by contrast, seemed unaffected by memories of his fallen friends, writing to Cottie from Charterhouse: "My life even now is the most agreeable I know of. When we see the sun again in this green paradise, I shall effervesce into a spirit." He continued to watch over Graves, introducing him to Eddie Marsh, who told Graves he should abandon the dated diction he was using in his poetry and search for a more modern voice. In a collective act of rebellion, George and Graves, together with Graves's friends Raymond Rodakowski and Cyril Hartmann, staged a coup against the official school magazine, a rather staid journal known as *The Carthusian*. They produced a rival magazine, which they called *Green Chartreuse*, and published it on Old Carthusian Day, July 5. It contained a perceptive satire by Graves on the school's inbred customs and slang, but the greatest offense was caused by a poster inspired by the magazine's title and provided by Duncan Grant. Depicting a life-size monk draining a wine glass, all in vivid green, it was hung on the school cricket pavilion and caused, so David Pye recorded, "some flutter among the decorous upholders of public school proprieties."

Soon afterwards, Young asked George to go climbing with him in Cornwall and Ireland. His proposal placed George in a dilemma, for Cottie Sanders, who had evidently pawned more of her possessions, had invited George to join her and a group of friends in the Alps. George prevaricated for a time, asking Cottie: "Do you mind if I don't decide?" It all sounded delightful, he assured her; he would love to come but if he couldn't, Ralph Todhunter would be in the area and could probably join her for a time. Although George appeared torn, he felt that he owed his loyalties to Young, who had been compelled to resign from his post as a school inspector and was convinced that this was a further outcome of the vendetta conducted against him since leaving his job at Eton amid allegations of sexual impropriety. Although Young said he had been losing interest in the job anyway, it posed another threat to his mental stability, and he felt his best recourse was to indulge in a frenetic round of climbing. George turned down Cottie's invitation and agreed to spend a month with Young.

Young had climbed in Cornwall before, exploring the granite sea cliffs in search of routes with Ralph Todhunter, Humphrey Jones, and Arthur Andrews, a former North Wales regular who had switched his attentions to southwest England. George, who brought Raymond Rodakowski with him for part of the trip, met Young in early August and camped with him in a cove in Nanjizael Bay near Land's End. Much later, in 1951, having published nothing about the Cornish climbing trip for almost forty years, Young described their activities in his book *Mountains with a Difference*: swimming in the sea, plunging into bursting green rollers, and drying off by stretching out "under a hot sky" on the sand. They put up a new route on a cliff named Carn Lês Boel, which they had inspected by swimming out to sea. Then, wearing only sneakers, and assuming that they were unlikely to be seen, they ran across the beach and attempted—still naked—to climb the ridge. While they revelled in their "superlative lightness of unhampered joints," their lack of clothing posed some interesting technical problems on the abrasive crystalline granite at the top of the route, which compelled them "to keep well out from the rock, and to finesse our balance style."

It is hard to ignore the homoerotic undercurrents of Young's account, particularly as he photographed George on the route, his back to the camera as he reached for a hold. Young pasted the photograph in the Pen y Pass book, together with photographs of himself (rear view) and the climber Siegfried Herford (full frontal) in similar states of undress. He completed the page with a photograph of Wilbert Spencer, a Cornish schoolboy whom he described as his "real romance" at that time. George clearly enjoyed nudity and exhibiting his power-ful, muscular physique to those who appreciated it, such as Young and Grant. Yet we are certain that George's relationships with Rodakowski and other Charterhouse boys he was taking on climbing trips should be seen in an inno-cent light, as extensions of his belief that the role of the teacher should not be confined to the classroom or an expressly didactic role. He continued these friend-ships with his pupils after he was married, sharing the news of their careers with Ruth. When Rodakowski was killed in the war, George told her, "He was a won-derfully innocent creature and I haven't a doubt devotedly brave," adding: "I'm glad you were fond of him my dear—you are good at loving my friends."

George and Young went their separate ways to Ireland, meeting again in Kerry, where they were due to go sailing with Conor O'Brien, a member of the Irish contingent at Pen y Pass. A loquacious figure, celebrated for climbing in bare feet, O'Brien was a dedicated sailor of small boats, who later made a round-the-world voyage in a ketch named *Saoirse*. While sailing along the Kerry coast, Young proposed that they climb the sensuously beautiful Mount Brandon. George made his excuses and departed on an excursion of his own, thus passing up the opportunity to climb Brandon in his bare feet with Young and O'Brien. He met them during their descent: Young remembered him running up the hill towards them, his legs stained with mud, "young and light and radiant as the May weather."

While Young moved on to the next stretch of his odyssey, which took him to the Scottish Highlands, George completed his summer climbing in the Lake District, staying at Wasdale Head for a week with another Charterhouse boy, Alan Goodfellow. They were joined for a day on Scafell by Harold Porter and a friend, Nigel Madan, climbing O. G. Jones's classic Pinnacle Route and the fear-somely dank Collier's Chimney. After Porter and Madan left, George and Goodfellow put up two new routes. One, which became known as Mallory's Varia-tion, was on Abbey Buttress on Great Gable, where George completed the route by climbing a twenty-foot slab on delicate holds, rather than taking an easier exit to the right. The other was a 200-foot route on the west side of Low Man, a shoulder on Pillar Rock. George called it North-West by West, although it also became known as Mallory's Route.

By the time George returned from the Lake District trip, Cottie Sanders had delivered another surprise, for he began his next letter to her: "I hear you're going to be married." While his statement could be seen as an implied rebuke, since Cottie had evidently not told him herself, her silence concealed a new round of family dramas. In March Cottie had met Owen O'Malley, a diplomat from an aristocratic family of Irish landowners, who was then based at the For-eign Office in London. O'Malley, who was on the rebound from a broken love affair, had courted Cottie relentlessly and they had become engaged in June. Matters had not proceeded smoothly since. The respective fathers had been locked in wrangling over the marriage settlement; and in August, when Cottie and O'Malley joined friends at Courmayeur, Cottie was upset to discover that O'Malley disliked climbing and wanted her to give it up.

Despite her misgivings, the wedding, at St. Mark's church in North Audley Street on October 25, 1913, went ahead. Owen O'Malley proved to be a deeply disturbed figure, with flaws that inhibited his progress through the diplomatic service; and their long marriage, says Cottie's biographer, Benita Stoney, "was searingly unhappy." George knew none of this when he wrote to Cottie; his letter instead reveals that his own thoughts had been turning to the advantages of marriage. "Of course I can only profess to believe that maidens and bachelors have the best of life: but I don't mind admitting to you privately that I consider them only half women and men." In any case, he added, "you have the best wishes in the world from me."

⚬⚬

October brought George disappointment in the shape of a royalty statement from Smith Elder, showing that of the 1000 copies they had printed of the Boswell biography, only 207 had been sold (and a further 83 dispensed as presentation copies). In theory, George was due a royalty of twenty percent on the selling price of 7s. 6d. ($1.82), which should have netted him a princely £15. 10s. 6d. ($75.33). In practice, he received nothing at all. That was because the publishers had adroitly stipulated that he should not receive any royalties until they had recovered their entire costs, a point which would not be reached until 455 copies had been sold. "In sending you this statement," Smith Elder piously added, "we are anxious that you should not suppose that there is the smallest repining on our part over the publication of your Work which we still think has deserved a better recognition than it has received from the public."

The end of the year saw the last Pen y Pass Christmas before war in Europe broke out, and George's last for eight years. It provided the participants with one of those scintillating days that fuels the memories for years to come. Young had been staying in Italy, finding "real peace" in a remote house at Fiesole in the Apennines that he shared with the painter Will Arnold-Forster, but he returned to organize the party as if aware that time was running out. George and Harold Porter drove from Birkenhead to Snowdonia, stopping off in Bangor to pick up Siegfried Herford, who was attending his first Pen y Pass party. Young had invited him after meeting him one evening on the summit of Tryfan, where he had been struck by "the slanting light through his wild hair."

A reserved and sensitive figure, born in Wales of a German mother, Herford was the rock climbing star of the day, famous for his daring new routes in the Lake District and on the gritstone edges of the English Peak District. The day after he and George arrived, they set off with Young to climb the Girdle Traverse on Lliwedd. Llyn Llydaw was frozen solid and Lliwedd was blanketed with snow and ice; to the three men, Young wrote, it was as if they were flying across the holds, "ghostly figures in white sweaters, swinging, turning, belaying in a counterpoint of precision and force." When they reached the end they ate their lunch and then decided to return across the face at a higher level, striking up a rhythm, Young wrote, "which I never remember attaining again on stiff rock with a rope of three."

After the climb, Young took another photograph which has achieved iconic status. Leaning against the wall of the Gorphwysfa Hotel, with the outlying Snowdon peak of Crib Goch rising behind, Herford looks thoughtfully down at the ground as he rests his left foot on the rim of a bucket. George, dressed in knee-length shorts, long socks, and black leather shoes, his collar turned up, a scarf at his neck, has plunged his hands into the voluminous pockets of a tweed jacket as he looks away from the camera, a darkly handsome figure with intimations of a brooding inner life. Young wrote that they had climbed "on a frosty icy day, in gay heart, and at great pace" and called it "one of the great climbing days of my life."

Soon after leaving Pen y Pass, George wrote an article for the *Climbers' Club Journal* in which he addressed the unavoidable element of risk in climbing. Although he had appeared less affected than Young by the succession of climbing deaths, he had been trying to process them in his own way. He was in no doubt that climbing was dangerous, and accepted that when he was pushing his own personal standards, as opposed to escorting inexperienced climbers, he was liable to cross "the line," the notional yardstick climbers use to judge whether they are in control of the risk they are running. But what did climbers hope to achieve by taking risks, and was this justifiable? How much more pleasure and satisfaction did they find, for example, than someone who spent a fortnight's holiday at the seaside? His attempt to find answers took him back in familiar territory, the nature of the emotional experience that climbing inspires. This time he found a metaphor to represent climbing's aesthetic and emotional appeal: it was like a symphony, George proposed, which also provided a spiritual journey with a beginning, intermediary passages, and an ending. Both a symphony and a mountain climb could be described in terms of their themes and variations, pianissimos and climaxes, their "moments of supremely harmonious experience," and the ability of half-remembered phrases to inspire recollection of those emotions during subsequent tranquillity.

George was uncertain whether his article, which he called "The Mountaineer as Artist," had succeeded. He told Young he feared "the scale is all wrong—the first part too long and the second part too short to be interesting." It was in fact a powerful and prescient attempt to locate the emotional core of all sporting experiences, not only mountaineering, whose participants knew the elation of success, the depression of failure, the "long-spun vivacity of anecdote." It was published in March 1914 in what would be termed today a celebrity issue of the journal, edited by Trevenen Huxley, with articles by Aldous Huxley, Katherine Cox, one of the femmes fatales of Bloomsbury, and "Mrs. O'Malley"—the former Cottie Sanders—who wrote about "Mountains in Dreams."

⁂

Shortly before Christmas, Eddie Marsh visited George again, staying the night at Nercwys House and meeting Robert Graves over coffee the next day. In the New Year, 1914, George inspected the latest offerings from the Bloomsbury group, an exhibition at the Alpine Club Gallery of paintings by Duncan Grant, Roger Fry, and Vanessa Bell. Somewhat to his own surprise, George took against a painting by Grant entitled *Adam and Eve* and comprising an ungainly mélange of styles and influences, from Byzantine art to Picasso. George, normally so sympathetic to artists' intentions, complained that it was "aiming at some remote asceticism of the spirit beyond my horizon," and asked Grant: "Have you forgotten the value of simple enjoyment in life?" George was not the only critic. The painting was savaged in newspaper reviews and some of Grant's other friends were hostile, among them Lytton Strachey and Jacques Raverat. Afterwards George was stricken with guilt, but Grant wrote a magnanimous reply, beginning "My darling George" and assuring him that there was "no cause for a quarrel."

George may have been, in any case, rediscovering the appeal of classical painting. He had been lecturing on Botticelli at Charterhouse, reckoning that his shows, illustrated with lantern slides, were engaging the interest of around twenty boys. There seemed to be a new edge to his account of the central figure in Botticelli's *The Birth of Venus,* an appreciation of womanhood that bordered on the sublime. "A stray lock floats gently in the breeze, and no more than in so much is she perturbed by life. A strange thrill (you see it in the right hand) and a gleam of wonder: that is all of the deep disturbances of life—less than the faintest shadow on the calm surface of a sunlight pool. Surely she will forget even this light care when she steps ashore with the perfection of graceful balance."

The phrasing—a strange thrill, the perfection of graceful balance—suggests a new dimension in George's life. It was confirmed in a letter he wrote on March 30. Young, who had gone back to stay with Will Arnold-Forster at Fiesole, invited George to join them at Easter: Arnold-Forster was "the best company," Fiesole "one of the loveliest places in the world." Not for the first time, George had received an alternative proposal. He told Young that, although he would be in Italy at Easter, he would be unable to join him. "I am to stay in Venice with a family consisting of one man and his three daughters. Did you ever hear the like of that?"

CHAPTER SEVEN

Immortal Love
1914–1916

The first thing George noticed about Ruth Turner was that when she ate grapes she crunched the seeds and swallowed them instead of spitting them out. Ruth could not help noticing how handsome George was, in particular his eyes, which she later described as "pellucid grey." But she also supposed she wouldn't like him, as he was so good-looking that she felt he was bound to have been spoiled.

George Mallory and Ruth Turner met for the first time at a dinner held in the autumn of 1913 by Arthur Clutton-Brock, a lawyer and writer who lived in Hindhead Road, which wound up from the Wey Valley towards Charterhouse school. Ruth, who was then twenty-one, lived with her father and two sisters at Westbrook, an elegant mansion on the far side of the Wey Valley, staffed by a retinue of servants and surrounded by gardens, orchards, and farmland. Her mother, Mary, had died six years before, leaving her father, Thackeray Turner, a prosperous architect, to bring up their three daughters. Like Ruth, Turner was drawn to the handsome young schoolteacher, then twenty-seven, and invited him to Westbrook to play billiards. George sent the family invitations to a play-reading at Charterhouse; and he, Ruth, and her sisters, Marjorie and Mildred, acted in a country-house performance of *The Princess*, a dramatic poem by Tennyson whose romantic storyline overlay a plea for women's freedom. George took the part of Cyril, the companion of a prince who is betrothed to a beautiful princess, while the Turner sisters played the princess's maidens. George had a checkered acting career at Cambridge, and his daughter Clare believed that her mother would have made a poor actress too. "She couldn't act in anything she did," Clare remembered. "She was too honest."

George and Ruth fell in love in Italy at Easter 1914. In March Thackeray Turner invited George to join him and his daughters on a family holiday there. All three of his daughters sent him instructions from Venice. Mildred told him they had reserved him a small but airy room in the Casa Biondetti, with a view down the Grand Canal. Marjorie told him the room was not on the same floor as theirs, but it was the same price. Ruth, who sent him two letters, told him they would meet him at Verona station at 10 A.M. on Friday, April 3, and would return to Venice with him that evening. George spent a week with the Turners in Venice. One morning he and Ruth took the train to Asolo, a romantic town with a medieval castle in the hills northeast of Venice, where Robert Browning once lived. They spent a day there, walking in the hills and dallying in a meadow rich with alpine flowers. By the time they left Venice they were passionately in love.

While Ruth returned to Godalming, George moved on to Fiesole. Young had returned to Britain for the Pen y Pass party, but Will Arnold-Forster was still there, together with two friends, George Trevelyan and Stephen Tallents. George told them about Ruth, and thought the best word to describe her wistful, innocent beauty, with her fair skin, her china-blue eyes, and her luxuriant light-brown hair, was Botticellian. It was an adjective rich with associations, as it had been applied to him, by both Graham Irving and Lytton Strachey, and was also used by E. M. Forster of Lucy Honeychurch, his heroine in *A Room with a View*, who fell in love in a meadow of flowers at Fiesole. George wrote to tell his sister Avie that Venice "was a wonderful place—and then my companions were perfect." He received a letter from Ruth: "How wonderful it was that day among the flowers at Asolo! I hope you are having a lovely time among the mountains, little towns, and flowers."

Nothing in George's life had prepared him for this. By comparison, his early romances had been little more than adolescent infatuations. His Cambridge friendships had enabled him to explore and find a language for his emotions, although they had led to the blind alley of his distressing affair with James Strachey. His relationship with Cottie Sanders had helped him overcome his diffidence towards women but had remained within safe limits defined by the climbing and aesthetic worlds. Now he had been utterly overwhelmed by an explosion of feeling whose intensity he could not have guessed at. On Easter Sunday he completed a sonnet in which he attempted to understand and express what had happened to him. It ranks as perhaps his finest piece of writing, working with the discipline of the sonnet form to encompass the profundity of his love.

To Ruth:

> I remember a passionate lark, from fields at home
> Launched in the fern-spread cradle of summer air,
> That filled, as no bird but the proud lark dare
> With life of liquid sound the whole heaven's dome.
> But this lone mystic of Italian hills,
> With wings beating at the doors of Paradise,
> Not only charms my wakeful ear, but fills
> With fire of the one true vision, my smouldering eyes.
>
> Now I am lost in listening, and the streams
> Of pure music suspended at a great height
> Drop even to me, then borne through quivering light
> Float o'er unmeasured space, until it seems
> That the same lark winging the universal blue
> Wakes the same trembling ecstasy in you.

It was a beautiful evocation of love and longing, using images of the wild drawn from the past and present to help bridge the temporary gap between them. Even so George felt diffident about it and did not send it to Ruth, although he told her he had written it. But barely ten days after he returned to Godalming, and following what can only be called a whirlwind courtship, they decided to get married. "What bliss!" George told his mother on May 1. "And what a revolution! Ruth Turner—she lives just over the river from here in a lovely house and with lovely people, and she's as good as gold, and brave and true and sweet. What more can I say!"

It looked like a perfect match. Ruth was generous and sympathetic, always trying to put herself in other people's place, and feeling their hurts as if they were her own. She believed in the importance of honesty and of telling the truth. Ruth saw these qualities reflected in George, especially his emotional honesty and his readiness to bare his soul. The Mallorys' daughter Clare sometimes felt her mother carried her goodness to excess, and wished she would be less self-effacing and think of her own needs more often. Clare also felt she could be too honest for her own good. "She was the terror of her friends," Clare related, "because she didn't have any of those little social lies that most people have to gloss things over and make them run smoothly."

Where their interests and practical matters were concerned, Ruth and George complemented each other neatly. They both had a love of the outdoors, of beautiful landscapes, and especially of flowers. Unlike George, Ruth had not read widely and had only an instinctive approach to politics. But she could speak French and Italian, had a strong artistic sense, and was skilled at handicrafts, especially knitting. They shared similar attitudes towards their bodies: Ruth's father was a nudist, which he held to be one aspect of being honest, and Ruth was brought up to talk about her body and its functions without embarrassment. The biggest potential difference between them lay in financial matters. Unlike George, who had the profligate example of his parents before him, Ruth had been taught to be careful with money, even though she came from a family that maintained what Cottie Sanders was to describe as medieval standards of hospitality. This apart, George's friend David Pye felt that his partnership with Ruth, matching his attributes and compensating for his deficiencies, had made him a whole person. "Seldom were two people more perfectly adapted to the purpose of modifying, rounding off, and completing each other."

Ruth owed to her mother, Mary Powell, many of the characteristics that appealed to George. Mary Powell came from a prosperous family that made its money through investing in American mines and railways just as the great American hinterland was being opened up to industrial developers and speculators. Her father Thomas Wilde Powell—Ruth's grandfather—took great pains to protect his investments, crossing the Atlantic on paddle-steamers in the 1850s to check on their progress. Mary was one of nine children who grew up in Charlton in southeast London before the family moved to Guildford. She was the most sensible and down-to-earth of the nine, setting her daughters further examples through her selflessness and generosity. Ethel Burton-Brown, the headmistress of Prior's Field school which both Ruth and Marjorie attended, said that Mary was "one of the finest and noblest women I have ever known, as well as the most unselfish." She was radical in her views of the rights of women and had a strong artistic and practical side. She set up the Women's Guild of Arts with May Morris, daughter of the great William Morris. She and her father belonged to the Society for the Protection of Ancient Buildings, founded by Morris to save historic buildings from the ravages of developers who even then had little regard for Britain's architectural heritage.

It was at the society that Mary Powell met Hugh Thackeray Turner, who had helped Morris found the society and acted as its secretary for a time. Born in 1853, the same year as Mary, he was one of seven sons of a Wiltshire clergyman, and a distant relative of William Makepeace Thackeray. He was a multitalented figure who made most of his money as an architect through designing buildings in central London for the prosperous Grosvenor Estate. In his spare time he painted china and played the flute. He was something of a dandy, with a trim beard and mustache, and wore breeches and a bright blue tie to match his blue eyes. His family was equally talented. His brother Hawes was director of the National Gallery; another brother, Lawrence, was an accomplished wood carver who became prominent in the Arts and Crafts Movement; and several of his sisters were talented artists and copyists. He and Mary married in 1888 and went to live in a spacious house in Gower Street, close to Bloomsbury, where their three daughters—Marjorie, Ruth, and Mildred—were born.

In the mid-1890s Turner began planning his masterpiece, a family home to be built in Godalming on the site of a mansion named Westbrook House, which had stood on the crest of a ridge overlooking the river Wey. Its architectural style showed the influence of the Arts and Crafts Movement, with its belief in the vernacular, using local materials such as the creamy Bargate stone to be found in the southern Weald. It had prominent external chimney pieces, steep red-tiled roofs, a grandiose entrance porch, and extensive gardens consisting of a series of flower beds and lawns, with an avenue of limes and a sunken water garden, occupying thirty-seven acres in all. It had around twenty rooms, decorated with carved oak paneling, tiled fire surrounds, and elaborate plasterwork ceilings. Turner's painted bowls and plates, embellished with patterns of flowers and magical animals, lined the mantelpieces and windowsills. Later this became a family activity, Turner teaching his daughters how to paint china too, an activity in which Ruth excelled. After the bowls had been painted they would be sent away to be glazed and fired, and the family would gather around to remove them lovingly from their packing cases when they were returned. Gardening was another communal passion, and there were regular family conferences to decide what to plant and where. But the design of the house was marked by one of Turner's eccentricities. For some unknown reason he disliked bathrooms and installed just one, at the very top of the house. At the same time he reserved for himself the privilege of having a hip-bath in his bedroom which was filled by a succession of maids bearing hot water in jugs.

Westbrook was completed in 1900 and the Turners moved in soon afterwards. They staffed the house with eight or nine servants and gardeners. They were fond of entertaining and did so on a lavish scale, inviting twenty guests or more to dinner. The three girls would fill the vases with armfuls of flowers from the garden, while Mary presided over the cooking. The two oldest girls, Marjorie and Ruth, went to Prior's Field, a free-thinking school close by that was founded in 1902 by Julia Huxley, the mother of Aldous Huxley. Although Ruth did well in French and Italian, she suffered from a learning handicap that may have been a mild form of dyslexia, although the term was not used in those days. She had great difficulty throughout her life with spelling, and Clare recalled how, when she was ten, Ruth would ask whether the word for sand on the seashore was spelled "beech" or "beach."

In 1907 tragedy struck the family. Ruth's mother, who was fifty-four, developed pneumonia. Instead of taking to her bed at once she struggled on until it was too late and died a few days later. Marjorie was brought back from school to help run the household, but Ruth, then age fifteen, was allowed to stay on. She found solace in the church, praying every day, teaching at Sunday school when she was eighteen, and looking to her religion to find moral signposts for her life. In Clare's view, that was something else that attracted George to her, even though he was an agnostic. "He was brought up as a Christian by a mother and father who didn't really live up to their beliefs," Clare said. "He thought that Ruth was pure and true and wonderful."

℞

In May 1914, a few days after they became engaged, Ruth was required to accompany the rest of her family and some of her father's friends on a long-arranged holiday in Ireland based at Letterkenny in County Donegal. Uncles Lawrence and Hawes were there, as were Marjorie and Mildred. The women spent most of their time rowing the men out into lochs on fishing trips, although they did all climb a nearby 2000-foot hill, only to be hit by driving sleet as they neared the summit. George and Ruth had pledged to write to each other every day, and his letters were suffused with both excitement and wonder as he struggled to come to terms with what had happened between them.

George retailed the daily gossip from school as if he were already talking to an old friend. One afternoon, he had spent two hours trying to teach some "exceptionally irritating boys"; on another, he had escorted the Charterhouse school eight on the river almost as far as Somerset Bridge. In an English class he had conducted a reading of "the great third act of *King Lear*." He had taking the part of Lear himself—"I really felt a bit mad"—but despaired of his pupils' inability to appreciate Cordelia: "blighted little arses," he called them, with "shallow little minds." He had more success when he read poetry to a younger class, including "The Lady of Shalott" and "Full Fathom Five": "they seemed enchanted."

Time and again George returned to his own tumultuous emotions. "How can I tell you what it feels like to read the loving things you say," he wrote on May 18; "it's too too wonderful that you should love me and give me such happiness as I never dreamt of . . . My sweet Ruth, how I love you! And want you now at this moment and always." "Dearest Ruth," he began on May 21, "Your letter this morning was a great joy—almost more so than usual. It is a wonderful thing to know that you love me and want to know me and that my letters have a meaning for you." Most passionate of all, on May 25, as Ruth's return neared, he wrote: "My darling, I am longing for you. Oh! why aren't you here—I would kiss your lips and look into your eyes and you You You all near me and with me, strong and glorious and loving and laughing. Oh! my arms are aching dear for you—to draw you swiftly and firmly close to me . . . And yours! You would like to feel me there wouldn't you? I would be splendid, all on fire, a man in heaven already. And you would look down from your heaven to me in mine and two heavens would meet in our eyes and on our lips dearest Ruth."

Ruth's letters were not quite so lyrical. She wrote in a painstaking script, a consequence of her spelling weakness, and usually committing several endearing mistakes per letter: Saterday, possable, glassiers. She was reading Edward Whymper's *Scrambles Among the Alps*, which George had given her: not knowing the outcome, she was horrified when she reached Whymper's account of his descent from the summit of the Matterhorn in 1865, when four of his companions were killed. After that she started on a biography of William Morris written by Arthur Clutton-Brock. She asked George to send her the sonnet he had written on Easter Day and he dispatched it with a letter instructing her to read the last six lines more slowly than the first eight, taking particular care to pause before the final two words, "in you." He added that he did not need to explain the identity of the "one true vision," adding: "My darling Ruth, I do hope you'll like it—it cost so much!"

Ruth did like the sonnet: "I like it very much, quite how much I cannot [tell] till I know it better." Although she lacked George's vocabulary and grammar, a voice of sweetness and lack of guile invariably came through in her letters. "What I really want is to know you and to love you more and more," she continued. "All the other things that people often speak of as though they matter, matter so little compared to this." On May 16 she lamented that she did not have a photograph of him. "But I think I can remember you pretty well, not proberbly with the exactness of detail that Mildred would, but your expression and love and goodness the parts of you that matter most." On May 21 she told him she had been reading his sonnet again. "The more I read the poem you sent me the more beautiful I think it is, there is more I would like to say here only I cannot find words that would be sure to convey what I feel about you."

On May 28 Ruth had a premonition about "people who have to be away from each other for a year sometimes even more." She felt "it must be awfully dreary and worrying, the exchange of ideas, the answers to questions, everything in writing is so slow." On May 30, two days before leaving for home, she revealed her most profound desires. She had been putting George's letters into order—"a lovely occupation"—and found herself thinking of him "till I go to sleep and the minute I wake up." Then she told him: "To make a beautiful thing is one of the greatest happinesses one can gave, George dear think what a beautiful child would be, it is almost too sacred a thing to say, please kiss the place where I have written it."

⚘

Among George's family and friends, the news of his impending marriage was greeted with surprise and delight. "This is good news indeed," wrote Trafford from Magdalene College, where he was in his final year. "I am very pleased to hear it; heartiest congratulations! I must say that I was extraordinarily surprised. However I suppose the influence of spring and Italy, combined with meeting the right person, fairly laid you by the heels." "This is news indeed," his mother wrote. "I do congratulate you most truly and heartily—I am sure you made a good choice. God bless you both. I feel He has guided you—I wish I could come to see you with all my heart but I can't till I'm better—I am pretty helpless at present." His father—"very pleased you have decided to break out into matrimony"—called him "a sly old thing—I always thought you were cut out for a bachelor." Of his climbing friends, Ralph Todhunter was "quite overcome"; Nigel Madan called it "the best possible news—altogether sudden and splendid." One of the first to meet Ruth was Geoffrey Young, who told George: "I have never met anyone who brought such an atmosphere of reality, such a certainty of true nature." From Prior's Field, Ethel Burton-Brown wrote to tell him that Ruth was "all that is good and sweet and womanly."

A little cautiously, George began the task of introducing Ruth to his other worlds. She now knew about mountaineering, but there were the Bloomsbury friends too. On May 2 George broke the news to Grant. "My dear Duncan," he wrote, "I have fallen in love and we're going to be married. What am I to tell you about it? You must come and hear—and see. Of course I can't guarantee that she'll interest you; but she'll like you and you'll not dislike her. Anyway it can't make any difference to us and I told you before what I think about you." The letter arrived at a bad moment for Grant, as his affair with Adrian Stephen had just come to an end, and his reply to George sounded like a valediction, as if an episode in his life was coming to a close: "Dying to meet her. Is she sweet or is she fair? Goodbye dear old creature—yr ever affct, D.G."

There were also the Stracheys: George was no longer in touch with James, and had not seen Lytton for more than a year. Then he learned that Lytton was contemplating a visit to Charterhouse and did his best to warn Ruth about him first. While Lytton looked "very striking," he spoke in a falsetto voice, which made people think he was shy. "He is very, very queer—not to me of course because I know him as a friend—but to the world." George told Ruth that because he had profound respect for Lytton's intellect, and "much love for him as a man of intense feeling," he was prepared to tolerate his foibles. He also told Ruth about the Charterhouse boys he felt closest to, among them Raymond Rodakowski, who had told him that engaged couples should write to each other every day; and Alan Goodfellow, a delightful boy, "who climbed with me in the Lakes last year."

As for a wedding date, George and Ruth saw no reason to linger and favored the end of July. But complications were mounting, not least because Europe was sliding inexorably into war. The arms race between Britain and Germany was intensifying, other European powers were building up their armaments, and the squabbling among the Balkan nations was increasing. The most immediate effect was to catapult George's sister Mary into marriage. In February she had become engaged to Ralph Brooke, an artillery officer in the British army, and had talked then of getting married in 1915. They now urgently brought the date forward to July 22, the wedding to be held in Birkenhead.

The prospect of two weddings taking place in such short order brought near panic to the Birkenhead rectory. George's mother was already bombarding him with letters. Why hadn't he written? Did he want any night-shirts, or vests, or drawers? Why hadn't Ruth replied to a note she had sent? Did they need any furniture? What about a bureau, or a bookcase? Should she order it for them? Would they like some house-linen? Shouldn't she and Ruth choose it together? Would they like her to come down to Godalming? Next Wednesday, perhaps, or Saturday? And what about the wedding date itself? How about July 30? Wouldn't August 4 give them all more time? On June 22 she wrote despairingly: "We are so *very* agitated at *not hearing from you!*" and signed herself: "Yr loving mother (but sadly aged) Annie B. Mallory—in haste for post and rather tired!"

The date was finally fixed for July 29. But there were several outstanding items of business to be addressed. The first concerned the delicate matter of money. It was clear to Thackeray Turner that a schoolmaster's salary was not going to be adequate to keep his daughter in the manner to which she was accustomed. When he asked George how he intended to support Ruth, George valiantly told him: "I couldn't possibly marry a girl if she had her own income." Turner quickly put him right: "You couldn't possibly marry her if she hadn't." In the end George consented to Turner providing Ruth an income of £750 ($3645.00) a year.

Turner also made a decisive intervention over where they should live. On the far side of the valley from Westbrook, a few doors from the Clutton-Brocks, they had found a house that they loved. It was built in 1872 and was thought to be the oldest house in the top part of Hindhead Road (later renamed Frith Hill Road). Like Westbrook, it was built of the local Bargate stone, and had a large gabled roof, six bedrooms, an elegant dining room and a light, airy sitting room that opened onto a loggia, a covered terrace room where you could sit out and be shaded from the sun and shielded from the wind. It had a conservatory, a lawn that stretched along the top of the hill, and gardens that dropped steeply down the hillside, with shrubs, wild flowers and a thicket of trees. The house was called the Holt which can mean either a copse or an otters' den.

Turner himself conducted the negotiations with the owner, a Mr. John Marshall, who had paid £375 ($1807.00) for the house in 1878. They settled on £1600 ($7776.00) and Turner put up the money, on one important condition: the house would formally belong to Ruth, and her name would appear on the deeds. There was a snag, which was the house would not be available until January 1915, and the Mallorys would have to rent somewhere to live before then. But they were already full of plans for improving the house and adapting it to their needs, and Turner's brother Lawrence offered to add some decorative touches of his own as his wedding present.

The remaining issue concerned their honeymoon. George wanted to take Ruth to the Alps. She had warmed to the idea, despite reading *Scrambles Among the Alps*, and George had been taking soundings among his family and friends. There was one sensitive topic preoccupying George, which he cautiously referred to as "the physical state of girls immediately after marriage." George evidently believed that women were somehow delicate or vulnerable after their first sexual experience. Yet his mother—who was "most particular in such matters"—had advised that "it was a period when women ought to take more exercise than usual." A doctor married to one of Ruth's aunts had confirmed the diagnosis: "He had no qualms for Ruth (whom he knows well) if she takes a full day's rest after an expedition."

Geoffrey Young expressed qualms of another kind. Recalling how he had found the bodies of Humphrey and Muriel Jones in the Alps, he claimed in a letter to George that the accident had occurred because Jones had been distracted by having to watch out for his new wife. It was an indication of how strongly Young felt that he voiced some remarkably forthright criticism, telling George that he was sometimes carried away by his "extraordinary physical brilliance in climbing." This could cause him to lead weaker climbers "to take risks or exertions that they were not fit for, and which, had the crisis come, neither you nor any man in climbing could have the margin to cover for both."

The strength of Young's comments had clearly been influenced by his own reconsideration of the risks and rewards of climbing, for he concluded: "This is all to my loss, and a horrid thing to say; but, if I've got anywhere, it is to seeing that human relations are more precious than mountains." George had always felt that he stayed within his safety margins when leading less experienced climbers. But the criticism from Young, usually so ready to offer his support and reassurance, came as a shock. George hastily assured him that he hadn't been thinking of taking Ruth on any major climbs, only to some of the beginners' peaks in the Oberland, with perhaps a stay at the Montenvert, a hotel on a mountain shoulder above Chamonix that was a popular starting point for climbs in the Mont Blanc range. He conceded Young's point about being distracted: "I see it very clearly now you have put it to me." But he did not renounce the idea of going to the Alps, for he asked Young to suggest some easier climbs, and whether they should employ a guide. In the end, these were to prove academic questions. On June 28, a gunman named Gavrilo Princip assassinated the Archduke Franz Ferdinand, heir to the Austro-Hungarian crown, in the Bosnian capital of Sarajevo. Within five weeks Europe was at war, overshadowing such minor matters as trips to the Alps.

George took Ruth to meet his parents in Birkenhead at the end of June. His father told him that their visit had "left a very pleasant impression. We all like Ruth so much and it is delightful to see you both so happy." On the eve of the wedding a number of their friends gathered at Westbrook, including Duncan Grant and Geoffrey Young, who was to be best man. There may have been some communal nude swimming since Grant said later that it was the last time he had seen George naked. The wedding took place in Godalming, on a day of sunshine and clouds, and was officiated by George's father. Just three months had passed since the crisis over the Mallory family's name that had so troubled Herbert, and he told his son to be sure to sign the marriage certificate as "George Herbert Leigh Leigh-Mallory."

For their honeymoon, the Mallorys went to Porlock in Somerset, a place where, George wrote, Exmoor meets the sea, and where Ruth wanted "to sleep under the stars." On August 3 Germany invaded Belgium and the next day Britain declared war. There is a story that the newlywed couple were questioned by a zealous policeman who suspected that they were German spies but the location varies: some suggest that this occurred in Somerset, others that it was during a subsequent camping trip to Sussex.

⚘

Either way, George was anxious to get back to Godalming to learn news of the war. The German army was storming through Belgium, great battles were taking place in the east, and prime minister Asquith was calling for a new army of over a million men. Volunteers were flooding to the recruiting offices and reports came from George's family of recruits packing the streets of Liverpool and Birkenhead. Among those who responded to the call in the first week were Trafford, Robert Graves, and Geoffrey Young, who at the age of forty became a war correspondent, sending dispatches from the battlefield to the liberal newspaper the *Daily News*.

George was simultaneously excited and appalled by the outbreak of war. In his history classes at Charterhouse he had tried to teach a constructive view of international relations, arguing that as humankind progressed, problems could be solved by a combination of diplomacy, intellectual rigor, and concepts of shared morality. David Pye felt that for George the outbreak of war was a "supreme disaster," since it represented the breakdown of the system—however faulty and ridden with compromise—on which he had pinned his hopes. Then George became more optimistic, believing that if Prussian militarism could be defeated, the positive aspects of German civilization could flourish. "I feel almost as if a tide of centuries has swept over us in the last fortnight," George grandiosely wrote. "We are basking in the sun and watching the dawn of tremendous hopes." Like many of his friends, George's first instinctive reaction had been to take part, and he sent a cable to Young asking if he could help find him a similar role. But it was soon clear that teachers would be required to stay at their posts: education had to go on, and in any case most people expected the war to be over by Christmas.

In September, shortly before the new term at Charterhouse, George took Ruth on her first climbing trip. They spent a week at the Wastwater Hotel at Wasdale Head. Harold Porter came too, usually occupying third place on the rope, to give Ruth a feeling of added security, particularly on traverses where she was protected from both ends. Ruth, Porter recorded, showed "remarkable enthusiasm and complete freedom from any trace of beginners' nerves"—a token both of how game she was and of her trust in George. Her very first climb was the great monument to English rock climbing, Napes Needle on Great Gable, which had been George's own second Lake District ascent. The next day they climbed New West, the imposing direct line on the west face of High Man, a 290-foot route graded today as Very Difficult. Then came an exploratory day on Scafell, similar to the one George and Porter had spent in 1913, working their way up and down the classic routes.

September 11 brought a howling gale but, while Porter hesitated, both Ruth and George insisted they should go out, walking to the top of Esk Hause, then dropping down for tea at Seatoller and returning via Sty Head. They went blackberry-picking on September 12 and the next day, their last, they climbed Eagle's Nest Ridge on

Great Gable in wind and cloud, then descended Needle Ridge. In a week Ruth had covered a gamut of techniques and experiences that would stand her in good stead if she were ever to climb with George in the Alps, particularly having learned how to climb down routes. She said she had enjoyed it all.

Once back at Charterhouse, George felt renewed ambivalence about the war. He was dismayed by the jingoism of the national press, especially the *Morning Post* and Lord Northcliffe's *Daily Mirror* and *Daily Mail*. He delivered a lecture about the causes of war in which he tried to present a considered view but it was his passages about defeating German militarism that were most enthusiastically received. "It bucked me up," he told Young, after the unusual experience of being cheered by his pupils. Ruth went to perform menial work at Godalming Hospital, which was treating casualties shipped back from France. George visited the hospital and listened to the soldiers' tales from the front. Their accents and dialect struck him as "queer talk," coming as it did from the far side of the class divide, but he found them "very good folk, most of them." Otherwise he and Ruth did their best to carry on a normal life. George wrote to congratulate Young on his latest book of poems. Grant offered to send them a picture of some paper flowers as a belated wedding present. Mary Anne O'Malley, as Cottie Sanders now called herself, asked George to be godfather to her baby daughter Jane, who was born on August 9; George missed the christening on October 1, but sent the baby a lapis lazuli necklace.

Meanwhile there was dramatic news from France. The German advance into France had been halted at the Marne, but there had been heavy casualties on both sides. More of George's friends were joining up: Hugh Wilson, Ralph Todhunter, Siegfried Herford, Rupert Brooke, even Rawson Owen, proprietor of the Gorphwysfa Hotel, despite the fact that he had been badly wounded in the Boer War. Mabel Capper, his host at the Ladies Alpine Club dinner in December 1912, had gone to France as a nurse (she was later awarded the Croix de Guerre). Even Duncan Grant, although he was a pacifist, wanted to help in some way. He told George he had wanted to become an interpreter, but was turned down because he could not speak German; he had thought of joining the navy, but the problem was that he was invariably seasick; his latest idea was to become "a sort of railway guard" on trains carrying troops to the front.

In November George was astonished to find that Geoffrey Young was running an ambulance unit in Dunkirk. Young had abandoned his role as war correspondent and was helping to transport both casualties and refugees away from the front. George's conscience was more troubled than ever, as he told Young on November 22. It was "increasingly impossible to remain a comfortable schoolmaster," he wrote. "Naturally I want to avoid the army for Ruth's sake—but can't

I do some job of your sort?" Ruth was talking of going to France herself: "She is very strong and competent, but I don't suppose it is so likely that [you] could find a job for her." But George still faced the problem that the government wanted teachers to stay at home. On December 9 the war minister, Lord Kitchener, instructed headmasters not to let teachers join up if this would impair the work of their schools, in particular their contribution to the war effort through the schools' Officer Training Corps. When George inquired, Fletcher firmly told him he was needed at Charterhouse.

At Christmas George and Ruth made another climbing trip, this time to North Wales, where they stayed at the Pen y Gwryd Hotel, a more luxurious climbers' venue a mile or so from the Gorphwysfa on the east side of the Llanberis Pass. This time they were accompanied by David Pye, who had been prevented from enlisting through ill health. The weather was hideously bad, with westerly gales and blizzards sweeping through the Snowdon range, accelerating over the ridges, scouring the tops, threatening to blow climbers from their holds. Pye called it "a most severe initiation, enough to daunt any but the stoutest-hearted novice."

In breaks between storms they managed two routes on Lliwedd and others on Glyder Fawr and Tryfan. The most testing day came when they climbed Parson's Nose and tried to press on up the ridge to the summit of Snowdon. The wind was like a tornado, driving into their faces with such force that it was impossible to speak. When they reached Bwlch Glas, the dip in the ridge above Llyn Llydaw, the whirlwind of snow intensified and George decided they should give the mountain best. He pointed down the slope, indicating that Ruth should set off, but this time her implicit faith in his judgment faltered and she hesitated. George simply grasped her shoulders and pushed her bodily over the edge, while Pye held her rope. There were other dramas, most notably when her boot was scorched through being placed too close to the fire to dry, and it had to be patched up with leather cut from a handbag. But Ruth, Pye concluded, was as unperturbed and trusting as ever.

Back in Godalming, work on the Holt was still under way. Unsurprisingly the builders were taking longer than expected, and Uncle Lawrence was struggling with the design of some ceiling work that was proving more complicated and expensive than he had intended. George offered to help meet the cost but Lawrence turned him down. The work had not been finished by the time they had to leave their rented accommodation, and so they moved into Westbrook. George did not feel comfortable staying with Ruth's family. He was back in touch with Benson, and wrote to tell him: "They are very good people, but one doesn't want to live that way when one is married."

George and Ruth moved into the Holt on March 10. Just two days later Ruth was admitted to a nursing home. She was three months pregnant, and suffered from acute morning sickness that persisted for two months. Otherwise she was thrilled that her wish, so devoutly expressed in her last letter to George from Ireland, had been fulfilled. George was excited too: as he told Benson on April 25, domesticity and fatherhood were his latest challenge. "To 'settle down,' that is what one wants; it sounds dull; in reality it's a sort of deliberate adventure." Marriage, he added, drawing on an image from weaving, was like batting a shuttle "that seems to carry a variety of gay threads between the two until both are partners in a flexible parti-coloured web."

David Pye witnessed the transition to domesticity too. Previously literary and intellectual matters had been paramount in George's life, with practical concerns relegated to a secondary place. "Now, in the house which they had made beautiful with such ardent and delighted care, he found himself surrounded to an unprecedented extent with what he called the apparatus of life . . . His companion in his new life was a person of the wisest simplicity and a transcendent practicalness who dealt with all the everyday concerns of life with a prompt efficiency, and was wont to dispose of more weighty problems with summary and almost irreverent common sense."

George's letters reflected this air of partnership and tranquillity, which provided an antidote to news of the war. The Holt, he told Young, was "a charming little place." Its drawing room and dining room opened on to the loggia, with its tiled floor and low brick wall "to lean your elbow on." The bank below the house, dropping down to the copse, was covered with primroses, daffodils, celandines, bluebells, and anemones; "When the sun blazed out," he wrote, "I felt like lying naked on our grass bank." Ruth had recovered from her morning sickness, and was "expanding her absolute plumbwellness." The house was furnished and decorated in the most fashionable of styles, with bright colors, William Morris patterns for the fabrics and wallpaper, a mixture of dark old oak and new unstained oak, and a scattering of rugs. It was all, George said, "what life ought to be like."

But it couldn't be, as George sensed. The war that would supposedly be over by Christmas was becoming a siege, with the Germans and the Allies digging in to a line of trenches, extending from the North Sea to Switzerland, that would remain essentially unchanged, despite the deaths of millions of men, for the next four years. George had just heard that Rupert Brooke had died of blood poisoning on the way the Dardanelles: "It seems so wanton," he wrote. Jack Sanders was killed on the very same day, April 22, in the first German gas attack of the war, at Ypres. Wilbert Spencer, Young's Cornish friend, who had became an infantry officer, was killed on the western front. Then came news from Trafford, contained in letters that revealed a soldier's disillusionment as the horrors of war struck home.

Having joined up as a private in the first week of the war, Trafford became a second lieutenant with an infantry regiment that went into the front line near Ypres in May 1915. His first accounts of action in the trenches barely a hundred yards from the Germans were suffused with excitement: the crack of rifles, bullets whistling past, star shells that make it almost "as light as day," the "wonderful" explosions of German shells that sent up "great clouds of red and white dust" and left neat holes in the ground. Despite the foul latrines, and the smell of rotting bodies that had been mixed into the clay of the trenches, Trafford told George: "I must say I am extraordinarily happy here. I never thought I should enjoy it so much."

Within a few days, Trafford's tone changed, as he and his men battled with exhaustion, contradictory orders, and the horror of gas attacks. "You have an alternative of putting your head down in the trench and being asphyxiated or putting it up over the trench into rapid fire. We have got gag things to put over our mouths, but still many seem to get killed." English press reports that the Germans were running out of ammunition and facing defeat were "unmitigated bosh." On May 12, after a particularly ferocious battle, there were "dead bodies all about the place," and the stench was almost overwhelming. One of his fellow officers "got the back of his head shot off," another was fortunate enough to get a "cushy wound" in his arm and was shipped back to England. On June 11, after a day spent trying to dig an emplacement in the ruins of a shattered building, Trafford recalled his stay with George in Snowdonia in August 1908. "I often think of the cowshed days and the nights when we used to sleep out," he told George. "How jolly they were." On June 16 Trafford was wounded in the leg during an attack on the German trenches and within a few days was in the hospital in Oxford.

While his brother was now safe for the time being, George was more and more troubled by the fate of his friends and relatives, more and more certain where his duty lay. In March, due to Fletcher's objections, he had missed an opportunity to work with Will Arnold-Forster, who was running an anticontraband department at the Admiralty. George wrote a pamphlet, "War Work for Boys and Girls," aimed at telling schoolchildren that they could help the war effort by using their education to develop self-discipline, spiritual growth, and clear thought. George warned them to beware of excessive propaganda but ended on a suitably patriotic note, telling them to "think and, when we think, devote ourselves to learning what is right for England." Arnold-Forster and Eddie Marsh visited him and suggested he join the Royal Naval Air Service. Fletcher got wind of this and told George that he was permitted to make preliminary inquiries about a possible role with the forces, "so that in case the War Office asked us for more officers you might be ready among others." But until then, Fletcher warned, "I cannot consent to your going."

In July, Ruth, who was seven months pregnant, insisted that George should go up to Pen y Pass. He arranged to take his former Charterhouse pupil Hugh Heber Percy, who was about to start an officers' training course at Sandhurst. Mary Anne O'Malley had invited George to spend a week with her and her husband in Scotland but he made the counterproposal that they come to Wales and, after some cajoling, Owen O'Malley agreed. They stayed at Pen y Pass and were joined for a time by a friend of the Turners, a music teacher, Ursula Nettleship. They mostly climbed standard routes on Tryfan and Lliwedd, with a long day spent walking over the tops, including Lliwedd and Mynedd Mawr.

George wrote to Ruth almost every day, providing her with a running commentary on the trip. The war had thrown up some tiresome obstacles. Soldiers were guarding the water pipes running from Llyn Llyddaw to the nearby power station and an officer told them they were forbidden to pass. They ignored him and dodged the sentries, reaching Lliwedd unharmed. He enjoyed climbing with Mary Anne, although she was not very fit, but found her husband Owen "a queer cuss, something of a professional pessimist." When Ruth revealed she was anxious about his climbing, asking him to take "very extra care," he reassured her: "It's a very mild affair altogether and I'm very strong." He had left his spectacles behind and asked her to send them to him: she included some socks, his belt, and a shoehorn, which she suspected he had forgotten as well. He called her "my dearest, my far away enchantress" and told her: "I do miss having you here to enjoy it all."

Ruth addressed her first letter to "My own much the dearest in the world." She had left the Holt and gone to stay at Westbrook, where she picked fruit, went for walks, or rode in the family pony and trap with her aunts. She painted china, like her father, and pointed out that she had remembered to spell the word china without an "R" on the end. She had looked in at the Holt to inspect the garden: "there are some nice double opium poppies out in the bed below the loggia." She was knitting him some socks, as she liked to have something else to do while she was reading. As for the baby, she could feel it moving more vigorously than before. She was having a sleep in the afternoons, "for its sake rather than mine."

From Pen y Pass George went on to spend a brief holiday with his father in Yorkshire. They had planned to stay in Ripon, but found that 50,000 troops were quartered at the nearby base at Catterick, creating scenes of "barbaric turmoil" in the streets. They moved to the Yorkshire dales, staying at Pateley Bridge, where they were put up in a converted railway carriage in the grounds of a hydro-hotel. They hired bikes and rode out to Fountains and Jervaulx Abbeys. George found it a shock to spend time with his father again: he was "a terrible snob and timid and rather greedy too."

There was family gossip to exchange. Trafford, who had recovered from his injury, was getting married on August 18 to Doris Sawyer, a woman from south London whom he had met at a dance; and Mildred had become engaged to a Captain Robert Morgan, who had been on the holiday with the Turner family in Ireland the previous spring. As for the war, Ruth was "thrilled" by new landings at Gallipoli but worried that Warsaw had fallen to the Germans. "I wonder when this war will end."

As George's return approached, Ruth was more and more preoccupied by the impending birth. "I do wish I knew more about our baby," she wrote. "I want to think about it and I like to. But there is so little to think about its all speculation and imagining. I don't even know what its like to have a baby of my own not counting what sort of a baby, and what sort of character it has." On August 10 she was looking ahead to the days when they had several children. "I wonder dear how much we shall keep up with the times and be able to be proper companions for our children. Lets try and remember that they must educate us as well as we educating them then I think we may not go so far wrong, we mustn't hate every new thing that comes along until its got old."

The Mallorys' baby was born on September 19 and they called her Frances Clare. Ruth's contractions were weak and the labor lasted almost forty-eight hours. After the birth there were complications with the placenta; Ruth's temperature soared, and she had to spend several weeks in bed. George was shocked by how much Ruth had suffered. "Poor Ruth had a terrible time," he told Young. "I had no idea it could be so horrible." He admitted that he felt curiously unaffected by his daughter—"I can't claim any great interest at present"—but Ruth was delighted, "which is the great thing." George's confession was certainly in keeping with the cultural climate of the time: men were not expected to be involved in their children's upbringing, even if George's own childhood had done anything to prepare him for fatherhood. Ruth had expected to follow the practice of handing over responsibility for her children to nurses and nursemaids, but she was taken unawares by the strength of her affection for Clare and the bond they formed.

The conventions of child-rearing at that time are illustrated by a unique record of Clare's early life, a picture book consisting of a dozen watercolor paintings made by Ruth's younger sister Mildred, Clare's Auntie Mill, who gave the book to Clare. The first painting depicts Ruth sitting with Clare on her lap in the nursery at the Holt, its red and blue wallpaper decorated with birds and flowers. Facing Ruth, with a baby's bath between them, is a uniformed Nurse Munro

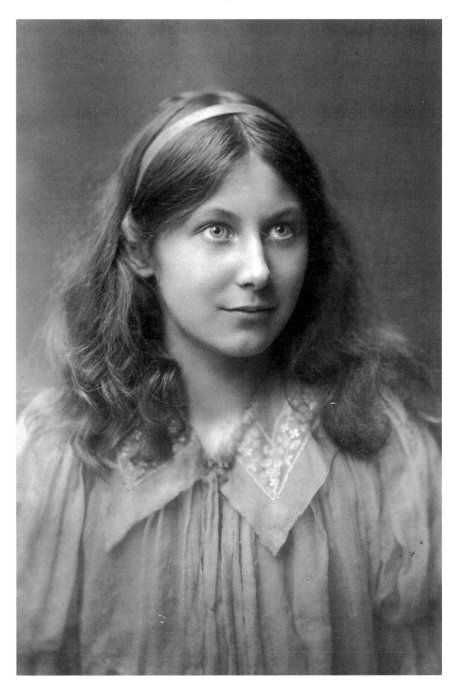

Ruth Turner, George's "one true vision . . . brave and true and sweet," as a teenager. He was twenty-seven, she twenty-one, when they fell in love in Italy at Easter, 1914.

Ruth and George were married at Godalming on July 29, 1914, six days before Britain and Germany went to war. Photographed here in his army uniform, George survived sixteen months on the western front.

The Mallorys' first child, Clare, photographed with Ruth at around three months old, was born at the Holt, their home in Godalming, in September 1915.

(Below) In May 1917, George was sent home from France to have an operation on the ankle he broke in a climbing fall in 1909. As depicted in the watercolor painted by her sister Mildred (Clare's "Auntie Mill"), Ruth and Clare visited George in the Officers' Hospital at Portland Place, London, after the operation.

George, photographed at Westbrook with Clare in 1917, spent seventeen months in Britain before returning to the western front in September 1918 for the final push of the war.

In 1919, after demobilisation, George returned to his teaching post at Charterhouse school, whose towers are visible in the background as he sits on the wall of the loggia at the Holt.

At Easter 1919, the Pen y Pass climbing parties were revived. George bought a second-hand car, an American Studebaker-Flanders (1912 model), for the occasion: helping with a push start, while George takes the wheel, are Ruth (left, at rear), Len Young (seated, left of George) and Geoffrey Young (to George's right).

The Pen y Pass party, Easter 1919. Back row standing, left to right: W. R. Reade, unknown, unknown, Ursula Nettleship, Marjorie Turner ("Aunt Marby"), Kitty O'Brien, Ruth Mallory, Raymond Bicknell, Conor O'Brien, Harold Porter, Geoffrey Winthrop Young, Claude Elliott, Colonel Rathbone. Center row seated: Len Young (wearing scarf), Glen Bicknell, Mrs. H. V. Reade, H. V. Reade, George Mallory. Front row seated: unknown, Mrs. Bartram (wearing white jacket), unknown, Rivers Arundel, Rupert Thomson, Ferdy Speyer, F. H. Slingsby, Geoffrey Bartram.

After George's death in 1924, Ruth and the children returned to live with her father at Westbrook. (Above) Ruth took the children—left to right, Berry, John and Clare—on seaside vacations, and (below left) on picnics: Ruth is wearing a floral hat, front left, and Berry, Clare, and John form the trio at the back. (Below right) Ruth, about age forty here, remarried at forty-eight in 1939, but died of cancer three years later.

Ruth brought up the children as free spirits. "She made a conscious decision not to over-protect us," recalled John, who is to the left in the picture, with Clare and Berry above him, photographed on a family vacation, possibly in Brittany.

Clare, photographed in California in 1999, kept and treasured the pottery her mother had painted.

In 1999 John Mallory, on a visit from South Africa, returned to the Holt in Godalming and, for the first time since 1924, saw the room where he was born.

who, the caption says, "usually gave Clare her bath"—although it adds that on this occasion Nurse Munro was showing Ruth how to bath Clare herself.

Nurse Munro stayed with the Mallorys for a month. After that her place was taken by the redoubtable Violet Meakin, who was nursemaid to all three of the Mallorys' children and remained close to the family throughout her life. More than eighty years on, Clare remembered Vi well, and recalled Vi's story of how she first saw Ruth with a spring-green ribbon in her hair. Ruth was equally taken with Vi's "dark Spanish beauty" and hired her even though she had no formal training as a nursemaid. "She was a decent, upright, working-class woman," Clare recalled. "She was very pernickety, made us show her our fingers, and warmed up our clothes on the fireguard before we got into them. She looked after us well." The Mallorys had three other servants, a cook, maid, and gardener. By Westbrook standards this was far from excessive and it certainly facilitated the Mallorys' lives, as it enabled them to have holidays without their children, and eased George's conscience over leaving Ruth to go climbing. Yet Ruth always felt torn when she handed over the children to Vi, and she told George how much she enjoyed having the children to herself when Vi was away.

⚭

When the new Charterhouse term began, George, so he admitted to Mary Anne O'Malley, felt "rather distressed." He was more critical than ever of the school curriculum, and had told Fletcher that the distortions caused by the School Certificate examinations were bringing "deplorable" results. Weighing down on him far more was the news from the front. Hugh Wilson had been shot in a clash with a German patrol and now his Charterhouse boys, including Raymond Radokowski and Alan Goodfellow, were going off to fight: to lose them, he told Mary Anne, would be "like cutting off buds."

At last George had his way. His brother-in-law, the artillery officer Ralph Brooke, offered to help him get a commission in the Royal Artillery "if and when you manage to arrange things satisfactorily with your headmaster." George accepted his offer without knowing if Fletcher would agree, and Brooke wrote to a friend who ran an artillery training course in Weymouth, recommending George on the grounds that he was an expert in trigonometry and maths. At last George's persistence wore Fletcher down, and he found a teacher who could take George's place. When George discussed it with Ruth, she told him he should follow his conscience and join up. On December 13 George wrote to tell Avie that Ruth was "perfectly happy" that he had done so; she wanted "to make her part of the sacrifice, which indeed is far the largest." George himself had been "as keen as possible to become a soldier, and now I am one I feel really happy."

George was due to start his training at Weymouth in January 1916. He traveled to Birkenhead to spend Christmas with his parents, followed by a few days at Pen y Pass and a visit to Avie in Mobberley. If it seems odd that George should be away from Ruth over Christmas, there is barely a hint of dissatisfaction in their letters. Ruth told George she had "quite a happy Christmas": her father gave her a pair of bellows decorated with an "Uncle Lawrence pattern" for the fireside at the Holt, and they went to church together. George sent Ruth a carved boy-angel's head as a present, which Ruth considered "very sweet." The one possible note of recrimination came when Ruth told him: "We will make some lovely Christmases for baby Clare and perhaps other little babies in future years."

After "quite a happy and successful" visit to Birkenhead, George stayed at Pen y Pass with Conor O'Brien, the Irish sailor, and Herbert Reade, another former Pen y Pass regular, who had often climbed there with his wife. The weather was poor: cold, a stiff east wind, and on one day continuous rain. They combined two existing lines on Clogwyn y Ddysgl to put up a new route which they called Black Gates: "a gorgeous climb," George wrote, "one of the very best." On the west peak of Lliwedd they added a fresh start to an old line to produce Three Pinnacle Face: "My lead," he told Ruth; "you may imagine if I enjoyed it."

Once off the rock, however, George's thoughts turned to his impending departure to Weymouth. He and Ruth had decided to let the Holt while he was away, with the idea that Ruth and Clare would stay at Westbrook. George came up with another plan: why didn't they join him in Weymouth instead? "Please think this over very hard," George urged. Ruth was enthusiastic. She was already distressed at the thought of leaving the Holt after only nine months, and although she suggested that George should find out how much time he would be able to spend with her in Weymouth, she told him: "Oh dearest I am not going to be away from you two months on end if I can possibly help it." The Mallorys left the Holt in early January. Another of Mildred's watercolors shows Ruth in her green dress stuffing a red item of clothing into a suitcase, while George, wearing a light-brown suit, kneels on top of the suitcase to force it shut. Vi, in her blue and white uniform, is carrying Clare out of the room. Their last days together at the Holt, George told Ruth, "were good. You were more wonderful and more lovable than ever."

At first, Ruth and Clare lived at Westbook while George looked for a place where they could stay in Weymouth. He was billeted in a cramped guest house overlooking the harbor, sharing a room with a fellow recruit named Hooper whom he found "not interesting but quite unobjectionable." Training as an artillery officer consisted of an endless round of lectures in a drill hall that reeked each morning of stale beer and cider. Then came drill with a rusting six-inch gun, the most difficult part manhandling 100-pound shells into its breech. There was a great volume of mathematical calculations to absorb, a new vocabulary to learn: "spars and guns and capstans and handspikes and skiddering and sleighs and parbuckling," as he told Ruth. The most exciting moments came when the gun was actually fired, creating a deafening noise; the worst aspect was the end-less standing around, which George found almost intolerable: "How we waste the hours!"

The best news was that his weekends would be free, and—after a long search—he thought he had found a suitable cottage in a village near Dorchester. The sitting room was dark but comfortable; none of the rooms were very big, "but big enough I think." The rent would be 30 shillings ($7.14) a week and George suggested that Ruth should try it for two weeks. Later they found better accom-modation at Abbotsbury, a village five miles along the coast from Weymouth. Auntie Mill's next watercolor depicts Ruth and Vi, Clare in her arms, arriving at Weymouth station, where a porter is loading their baggage onto a trolley. George spent his weekdays training at Weymouth, his weekends at Abbotsbury, while Ruth came into Weymouth twice a week to have lunch with him. "It's not too bad," George wrote, particularly as Ruth had "a very good landlady." Yet there was a solitary mood to Auntie Mill's next painting, which shows Vi and Ruth holding Clare standing among the windswept pebbles of Chesil Beach, suggest-ing that Ruth was steeling herself for the absences to come.

George expressed similar sentiments in a letter to Mary Anne on February 27. Military education, he found, consisted of "training in patience under en-forced inertia" but he expected to be sent to France by the end of April, after a further spell of training at the army's artillery school in Kent. "I feel so mixed up when I think of it—not wanting perfect safety for my own sake because I prefer adventure and want anyway to share those risks with my friends; but thinking so very differently where Ruth comes in. I'm afraid she'll feel very sore when I'm out there." Mary Anne had been arranging to have his pamphlet about war work for young people published by Allen and Unwin—it was to be sold at 6d. (12 cents) a copy—and she sent him a contract to sign: "You've really been wonderfully efficient as well as kind about it and I feel very grateful," George told her. He passed on news of the death of Siegfried Herford, his partner with Young on the magical Girdle Traverse on Lliwedd at Christmas 1913, another to have been killed at Ypres.

On April 1, George traveled from Weymouth to Lydd, spending the night at the Grand Hotel at Littlestone-on-Sea. Ruth returned to Westbrook in the hope that George would be able to visit her there at weekends. George quickly discovered that was impossible, as he only had Sundays off. Ruth was not to be denied, and George found a tiny flat in Littlestone where they could stay together, with a garden full of celandines, narcissi, and hyacinths. It was a brief stay of execution. On May 4 George crossed the Channel to France, arriving in the early morning at le Havre. That evening Ruth wrote to him from Westbrook.

> My own beloved darling,
>
> I think I must write to you tonight it makes me feel less far from you. I am allright dear. I am cheerful and I havent cryed any more. I had baby as soon as I got home till she went to bed and it was very comforting. She is more of a comfort than anything else I could have . . . .
>
> > Dearest and most beloved,
> > be happy—your loving Ruth

Two days later, when she had still not heard from him, she wrote to him again. Her letter expressed the conflict she felt between love and duty, and how she had attempted to resolve it.

> My dear one, what is happening to you I wonder so much. Are you happy and are you well? You should have peace of mind because you are doing what is right. Hard as this is I would not for anything go back to the peaceful days before I knew and loved you. I thought then that I would rather live a peaceful painless life than a full one with all the pain that comes with it but I did not know the wonderful happiness. I love you, I love you and you love me and that ought to be happiness enough for a life time, but I do want you. We want to live together all the time and share thoughts and joys and sorrows, and we can't apart as we can together, but we shall have to try very hard. I don't need to be parted from you to know your loveliness. I know it when I am with you, constantly. Dear, dear one good night. All the immortal love my soul has is with you.
>
> > Ruth

CHAPTER EIGHT

The Pity of War
1916–1918

Less than twenty-four hours after parting from Ruth, George was having break-fast at an open-air cafe near le Havre. There was a familiar bustle around him, of clattering plates, clinking glasses, waiters taking orders, all so much like the France he had known on his trips to the Alps. As he told Ruth, he knew it could not last, for he would be moving on that afternoon. "I thought much of you, dearest, during the long night," he added. "You were so beautiful and splendidly brave yesterday afternoon. Those last moments will stay with me, dear Ruth . . . . " He had a confession to make: he had gone off with her return train ticket to Godalming in his pocket. In her next letter Ruth—scrupulously honest as al-ways—told him that although she had managed to get home without it she felt obliged to send the railway company a postal order, unless George could send it to her now. It was too late. George's next letter said he had been surrounded by some importunate French children who wanted his buttons and badges as souve-nirs, and he had given them her train ticket instead.

One of the most surreal aspects of the First World War, which saw the nation-states of Europe locked in a titanic struggle that lasted more than four years, was that life away from the battlegrounds, as at le Havre, could continue in a plau-sible facsimile of normality. During George's first week in France, when he re-mained at a camp near le Havre, some of the realities of war intruded. He learned how to use a revolver—"If I saw a German 20 yards off and he gave me plenty of time to aim, I might hit him"—and attended a church service in the village of Montivilliers, where seventy-five of the men had been killed and most of the women were dressed in black. But it was not until he took a troop train to Armentieres, some hundred miles to the east, that he learned the full truth. He had been assigned to the 40th Siege Battery, then positioned in the northern sector of the western front. A short distance away was the front line itself, the snaking lines of trenches, with sometimes as little as fifty yards between the opposing sides, which were the true killing grounds.

George knew, as he admitted in a letter to Avie, that he was fortunate to have been assigned to the artillery rather than the infantry: "The chance of survival in my branch of the services is very large." But over the next twelve months he was exposed to the full compass of wartime life: the physical drudgery, continually digging into new positions, the cold and the wet, the fight to preserve dignity and self-respect, punctuated with passages of intense action as the great set-piece battles unfolded. As ever, George endeavored to absorb and process all of this as another of the shaping experiences of his life. He was better suited to do so than many of his colleagues who had been pitched into war after working in offices and factories; George had spent days and nights in wild mountain environments, often sleeping rough, and this was another test he was determined to come through. His greatest hardship was his separation from Ruth. He understood her anxieties and often minimized his own danger and discomfort for her sake.

George and Ruth expressed all of this in a remarkable cycle of letters that was the most constant and frequent of their relationship. The letters became the means by which they sustained their marriage, covering everything from day-to-day minutiae to their most profound fears. Ruth, who wrote daily, conveyed her news as if George had just come home from Charterhouse, relating her tasks and errands, her conversations, news of her father and sisters, her social encounters. She told him about Clare, how she was crawling, then walking, the pleasure she had from feeling "her little body close to mine—it's a little different sort of love to any other, in a kind of way it's more felt and less thought."

The demands on Ruth were intense, for at Westbrook she became the de facto head of household affairs as well as helping to minister to her father's needs. She and George had eventually found tenants for the Holt, a couple named Mr. and Mrs. Green, and she had to deal with such issues as how much coal they were using, as well as visiting the house and inspecting the gardens to see that all was well. She became exasperated with the Greens when they kept summoning her because the cellar was flooded after a spell of heavy rain. When she learned that the O'Malleys were looking for somewhere to live, she asked the Greens to leave and the O'Malleys moved in, presenting Ruth with fewer problems than before.

Most important of all were her obligations to George. The British forces were supported by an army of women back home, sending parcels of food and provisions that helped sustain their strength and morale. Ruth had told George she would send him anything he asked. She dispatched packages of tea, sausages, potatoes and butter; homemade cakes, marmalade, anchovy sauce; whisky, gin, Grand Marnier, Idris water, Turkish cigarettes; books, newspapers, warm clothes, matches, a loofah; and notebooks, pencils, and an eraser, so that he could continue to write to her. She often carried his letters with her, wrapped in a red ribbon; and she read them again when she went to bed. "It is nice having them then," she told him, "and I go to sleep thinking about you."

George's first letter to Ruth after he had joined the 40th Siege Battery was addressed from "a dilapidated old town in France." (He was not allowed to mention any place names in his letters, although later the censorship rules were relaxed.) He had been billeted in a cottage in the town's main street, with the battery's four guns close by. He shared the cottage with a Lieutenant Bell, who impressed him greatly: he and several fellow officers had been promoted from the ranks, and George felt they had "a marked refinement of feeling, living in harmony with life in some queer rare way quite their own." Bell in particular was a "quiet, observing man" who eschewed "the hard-driving manner associated with school-masters and Prussians" and instead commanded calmly, without "shouting or swearing or drilling the men."

As a second lieutenant, George was third in the line of command, behind the commanding officer, Captain Lithgow, and Lieutenant Bell. His responsibilities included taking charge of the firing of the guns and manning the observation posts from where the fire could be directed. The OPs, as they were known, could be in a tree, or church tower, if there were any left standing, or in a shell-hole in no-man's-land between the two front lines. This was by far the more dangerous activity, especially as the OPs themselves became the targets of the enemy guns.

For the time being, the most immediate problem was a lack of food. Another of George's tasks was to visit the local markets to buy supplies, taking advantage of his fluent French. Ruth began sending him tea, cakes, and vegetables from Westbrook's kitchen garden. She also sent news of his pamphlet, which had just been advertised in the *Times Literary Supplement*, and there was praise for it from his friends, among them Herbert Reade, Arthur Benson, and the Clutton-Brocks.

As yet, George told Ruth, there was "no sign of Fritz." His first intimation of warfare came when he was roused at 12:30 A.M. for a gas drill. Then the first German shells landed nearby, showering the street with shrapnel, and George dived into a building. "There is plenty of time to take cover," he assured Ruth, adding that he was already accustomed to the noise of passing shells and could recognize the change in tone that spelled danger. "One just goes about one's business without worrying about such things." Of greater concern was the effect of war on the landscape. "When I have looked upon the good gardens and blossom of spring in this beautiful country war has seemed more than ever inconceivable and monstrous." Even so, he was looking forward to the prospect of action: "This is a great adventure and a rich experience for me dearest and you'll love me more for it I hope when we meet again. I'm prepared for whatever may happen and there's no going back on that." When Ruth sent him a photograph of herself, as he had asked, he told her: "Dearest one, I salute your image with kisses."

One of Ruth's earliest letters contained disappointing news: she had hoped she was pregnant again, but her period had just started. A few days later she, Clare, and Vi made a trip north, staying with Avie and Harry Longridge in Mobberley and then with George's parents at the vicarage in Birkenhead. She felt at home with the Longridges but uncomfortable at the vicarage: "the atmosphere is not happy," she told George. She was dismayed that his parents' behavior was so much at odds with their supposedly Christian beliefs. She was astonished when George's father claimed to have cured himself of an outbreak of warts by placing an equivalent number of stones in a bag that he hid beside a crossroads: "If a person can believe that, they can believe anything." Ruth was angered by his mother's failure to keep a secret, her criticisms of the way she was bringing up Clare—"I wonder how she first got hold of the idea that she knows every one elses job better than they do"—and her inability to tell "the accurate careful truth . . . she is an odd one, you know." Ruth added, even so, that his mother had probably brought up George as best she could. "I think leaving you alone was in the circumstances probably the best thing. People do grow up with character when they are left to do it more or less their own way. Not that I think it would have been very easy to crush your character out of you . . . ."

One evening Ruth watched the ships on the Mersey: "Dirty funny little steamers, black torpedo boats, and a still, naked, sailing ship waiting to be painted." She had Clare with her: "She was so sweet," she told George. "She seems so part of me, and I am so very proud to have her. Darling I am so glad you gave her to me before you had to go away. And yet I don't love her like I love you and she does not make up for not having you at all. I do want you so much. And yet I am glad you are doing what you are. I think very often of the time when you come back. I do hope it will be soon . . . ."

On May 29 the unit moved south to "a hot part of the line." A British infantry attack was imminent and the battery had to haul its guns into position with horses. On May 30, when the attack was launched, the battery fired off more than 600 shells. But the most dramatic news was elsewhere. George was gripped by reports of the battle of Jutland, when the British lost three battle cruisers, although the long-term effect was to pin down the German fleet for the rest of the war. "Though one might have hoped for better news I don't feel at all depressed," he told Ruth. "Will they come out again I wonder?"

George was now living in a dugout, carved into the Picardy clay, and he sent Ruth a diagram to show its cramped dimensions. It was also infested with rats. She sent him cakes and soup tablets; he told her he had gone foraging for bread and potatoes, and had found a field of "delicious" wild strawberries. He was unable to send her a present for her birthday on June 10 (she was twenty-four) and asked her to buy a copy of Shakespeare's *Sonnets* as "a reminder of my love dearest as they talk of little else." Her letters, he told her, were like "great shafts of light which come pouring in on me. I want you in my arms so that I can kiss you; no other way expresses my feelings." On June 14 the battery was on the move south again, taking up a new position near Albert, just north of the river Somme. Having come thus far, George admitted that he had a longing for real action: "It is extraordinary how the desire is growing with me to take part in an offensive."

Ruth was troubled by feelings that she should be doing more to help the war effort. She had worked for a time at a goods depot near Godalming but had stopped doing so because she was afraid she might catch an illness or infection that would be transmitted to Clare. Vi was talking of working in a munitions factory, although her father was trying to stop her because the work was so dangerous. The possibility plunged Ruth into confusion. She told George that she liked it when Vi was away, as she had Clare to herself: "I do love having her, and holding her, and doing everything for her . . . I should like to have [her] all the time." But, she conceded, that could be "very inconvenient" at times—"especially when you come home on leave." In the end, Vi stayed.

❧

On July 1, the greatest British offensive of the war began, when nearly 300,000 soldiers attacked the Germans along the Somme. George's battery had been delivering a preliminary bombardment for a week and at 6:30 that morning its firing intensified with the aim—in which it failed—of cowing the German forces and smashing their defenses. For several hours, George wrote, he had no idea how the attack was faring, but then the walking wounded began to pass their position, followed by German prisoners under escort. In a brief lull George wrote: "It is a battle of which we see as it were only the rim of a seething cauldron. Things have probably gone fairly well to the south of us, but badly here, and altogether very disappointing." It was, he added, "an exciting and very awful time." Later he heard that the attack had been held up by intense machine-gun fire; by that night, although no one yet knew the full scale of the catastrophe, nearly 60,000 British soldiers had been killed or injured. "To me this result together with the sight of the wounded was poignantly grievous," he told Ruth. "We were profoundly depressed that night—our hope of moving forward immediately seemed to have vanished."

The British slaughter on the first day of the Somme was, paradoxically, a watershed in the war, a moment of truth that not everyone grasped. George was among the more prescient observers who realized that there could be no quick victory, and that the winners would be the side which could sustain the fight the longest, no matter how much time it took. "We shall make [Germany] fight to exhaustion," he told Ruth. Meanwhile the battle raged on. On July 6 the battery fired all day to support another British attack, and George watched German prisoners being brought back. Some were fine soldiers, he observed; others "look as if they could hardly hold a rifle." A few days later he moved to a new dugout whose ceiling was shiny with moisture; he made himself a table from an ammunition box and placed on it his favorite book, a collection of four Shakespeare plays: *Romeo and Juliet*, *King Lear*, *Hamlet*, and *Othello*. "It is the greatest comfort of life that I have such a sanctum," he wrote.

On July 15 George saw flamethrowers in action, used by the French for the first time: "a sort of liquid fire, a long line of trenches apparently on fire and exploding with great flashes and clouds of sparks." By now the battlefield had been reduced to a "state of complete desert, with only ragged remnants of trees." At intervals he had to go into the British trenches to lay out telephone wires and to judge the effect of the battery's fire, and he was disturbed by the sight of British casualties. "'Oh the pity of it!' I very often exclaim when I see the dead lying out, and anger when I see corpses quite inexcusably not buried." His words curiously foreshadowed the line "The pity of war, the pity war distilled" in Wilfred Owen's semimystical masterpiece, "Strange Meeting."

Despite the force of George's description, he was making efforts to spare Ruth the worst of the horrors and to minimize their effect on him, usually ending his letters on an upbeat note, together with an expression of his love. He wrote more starkly to his friends and even to his parents, telling his father it could be "as harrowing as you can imagine when one sees the dead and the dying and hears of regiments being cut up by machine guns." On July 17 a letter to Ruth suggested that the conflict and the slaughter was troubling him more than he was willing to admit, for he had lost his customary show of equanimity and was clearly on edge. After relating the latest news, he asked her to read through her letters before posting them, as it was sometimes hard for him to tell what she meant, especially because of her tendency to omit important words. "I hope you treat other people better than you treat me in that respect because I really don't think it nice to let your thoughts go forth in a careless fashion," he admonished her. He also told her that he still felt a "mild shock" on reading her miscreant spellings: boddy, pail (for pale), loosing (for losing).

Although George told Ruth that she really wrote "very good letters," his criticisms brought a spirited response. "The carelessness I do humbly apologize for. I know I ought always to read my letters through and sometimes I do. When I don't its usually because I am hurried, but I wont be any more if I can help it . . . As for the spelling I'm afraid you must take that as one of the worses, in the 'for better or for worse' of the marriage ceremony. I never tryed to conceal the fact from you."

It remained a rare lapse into discord, for what was impressive was the extent to which they were able to replicate the customary interchanges of married life. They discussed the progress of the war, the outcome of battles on other fronts, the politics of Europe, and how they might affect a settlement. They were both reading whenever they could, and swapped views about their latest books. George enjoyed George Eliot's *Felix Holt* and the socialist-realist novel *The Ragged Trousered Philanthropists* by Robert Tressell. Ruth read *War and Peace*, which she thought was wonderful, and *Sense and Sensibility*, which she had first read at school. She sent him the left-wing weekly the *Nation* and a journal about international affairs. They also conducted a long-running debate about their religious beliefs and how they should introduce the subject to Clare. It was a potentially contentious subject, since Ruth was still a committed and instinctive Christian, and George was best described as an agnostic in so far as he rejected the appurtenances of organized religion and church hierarchies, although he did believe in the essential morality of Christianity. Ruth too was angered by shows of hypocrisy and dishonesty—particularly as embodied by George's parents—and she and George moved towards each other until they found common ground. Ruth remained concerned about what kind of religious upbringing Clare should receive and she sent George a list of core principles she felt Clare should be taught, from which he did not dissent.

On July 29 George and five of his men went up to the front line once again. After renewing the telephone wire they were crossing open ground when they heard an incoming shell and dived into a trench. But two men who were carrying the coil of wire and had fallen behind were hit by the blast. George hurried back and found them lying face-down in the mud. Both were dead. "They were very nice fellows," he told Ruth; one in particular, with whom he had spent most of the day, "was the most agreeable of companions and the best of our signallers." It was now that George revealed that on his very first day with the battery a bullet had passed between him and a man walking barely a yard in front. He had been reflecting on his own mortality, the notion that he too would join the clay. He realized that he was becoming hardened to death—"It is an accepted fact that men are killed and I have no more to learn about that"—but not to the wounded. "It always distresses me to see them."

Ruth received his letter about the death of his two men on August 1. "My dear, it must have been awful, I am so sorry. Yes, it does make me more anxious, I can't help it." She wondered why they had been walking alongside the trenches instead of in them. "Do be as careful as you can dear. And keep well."

In the middle of August, after six weeks of battle, George was sent to a rest camp near Amiens for ten days of rest and recuperation. He went for a walk that day, wondering at the rolling farmland, the corn in sheaves, a valley full of un-damaged trees. "The colours were deliciously fresh in the pleasant breeze," he told Ruth. "I wondered when I felt so divinely happy what the further bliss of your presence could have done or what sort of joy I should feel if I were at home with you—my belief is that when that does happen I shall simply burst with overfulness." He told her about visiting Amiens Cathedral, and finding a lake where he could swim. "Why don't you walk in here and sit down beside me and talk to me beautifully in a low voice?" They adopted a new term, "P.B.," which stood for post-bellum, after the war, and they discussed what they would do: George wanted to take Ruth to Brittany. Ruth told him she had dreamed of being in France with him. "We were digging something," and she suddenly be-came afraid of being shot. "Oh I wish I were with you, to love you, and talk sleepy nonsense about all the happy things that are all to happen—*when*!!"

And so it went on. George returned to the front at the end of August and the digging in, the foraging for supplies, the bursts of action, the lulls, the momentary consolations followed the same pattern as before. He expanded his dugout, telling Ruth he had hit upon "a cunning arrangement," which he illustrated with a dia-gram, so that it could seat three people at once. For a time the water supply was foul, and he found lice in his clothes. Ruth's parcels continued to arrive, with cakes, fruit, books. George was reading H. G. Wells and Henry James and dipping into Shakespeare, as always. He still had eyes for beauty in unexpected places. While musing about life "P.B." at the Holt, imagining a return to drawing-room manners after the elemental nature of life in the trenches, he described a soldier who was "sitting quietly beside his signaller waiting on events; he had a rare dig-nity; for him clearly there were things beyond his surroundings, he had beautiful visionary eyes which looked at me thoughtfully before he answered my remarks."

At about this time he began another new project. He started to write a novel, although he did not call it that yet. It already had a title, *The Book of Geoffrey*, and he intended to explore some of the subjects that concerned him most: morality, the emotions, the purpose of education. He was beginning to devise the narrative form, using a father's concern for his son to construct dialogues with a teacher. It was an intriguing device, for it enabled him to voice his criticisms of the school system as well as to represent his desire, which he had expressed to Ruth, that they should have a son of their own.

There were more battles in mid-September, "far the most exciting day since the bitter disappointment of July 1," he wrote. After attack and counterattack the British seemed to be gaining ground, their losses showing some decline, the Germans' increasing. The names of the battlegrounds were passing into history—Menin Road, Polygon Wood, Passchendaele—as the British occupied wastelands of mud and craters, George wrote, with not a blade of grass to be seen. At last he saw clear fresh ground ahead, land sloping downwards as the battery moved on to a ridge between Martinpuich and High Wood, where it would be easier to range the guns. The dates of the new term at Charterhouse passed as autumn arrived, and he dreamed of swimming with Ruth in Ffynnon Llugwy, the "little black lake" below the ridge of Craig yr Ysfa.

On September 19 Ruth wrote to tell George about Clare's first birthday. She had enjoyed her presents, particularly a rattle George's mother had sent her: "She smiled and laughed over each one." Clare's sixth tooth had just come through and she was "enchanting and most awfully pretty," Ruth related, "with soft yellow hair and bright cheeks, blue eyes and dark lashes." George had sent her two presents. The first was a book of rhymes that she looked at eagerly; the second was a letter he had written five days before, in the knowledge that she might never see her father again. He was particularly keen that she should not think of him as a soldier, for that was only a temporary aspect of his life, a sentiment that also allowed him to view the war as a finite event that should soon end.

> *My dear Frances Clare,*
>
> *This is to wish you many happy returns of the day, Daddy's good wishes! I'm afraid they mean very little to you; you know even less of Daddy. You are not even aware of the grave fact that you are blessed with a parent who has theories about education and might mean God knows what high sounding doctrines by his simple greeting. But he doesn't in fact mean more than he says and it is surely enough; for to be happy means much.*
>
> *I hope you will be enjoying your birthday; I imagine you will be subjected to*

even more than the usual number of kisses, and probably also to more elaborate and more frequent dressings with many types of pink ribbon. To submit grace-fully to all this is more than I would venture to ask of you—though your stern mother might. As mere worldly wisdom however I would advise that if you curse somewhat (as your great uncle Hawes assures me you do curse sometimes) you make up for that by distributing your smiles in a generous fashion, and, for the sake of harmony, quite indiscriminately.

One thing you must understand about Daddy. When last you saw him in a uniform you may have begun to think of him as a soldier and you may see him in the same disguise before so very long. But for better or for worse Daddy is not a soldier and nothing that concerns a soldier as such has any interest for him: there-fore if ever you give your heart away to Daddy it must not be, after the custom of the sex to which you belong, for that he wears khaki—but rather because he has such a nice way of holding silk for mummy to wind and of making the kitten purr.

From your ever loving father,
George Mallory

On September 26 the British at last captured Thiepval, their goal on July 1, the first day of the battle of the Somme. George watched the infantry launch an at-tack. "It was thrilling and indescribable to see the hamlet they were attacking smothered with shellfire, running down a slope waiting until the barrage lifted and then pressing on again to reach the abandoned trench which had been their objec-tive." In October two new concerns took over. One was the weather, as the worst European winter in almost forty years arrived. It brought drenching rain, daytime temperatures hovering a little above zero, bitter cold at night. Ruth sent George extra socks and shirts and his climbing boots; from his mother came a waistcoat. The other concern, an increasingly dominant theme, was the prospect of leave.

The battery sent its men home according to a rota but George could not detect what principles it followed, whether seniority or length of time away: he assumed his turn would come but did not know if it would take weeks or months. He began to hope he would be back for Christmas but then warned Ruth they might have to wait until spring. He started to plan the unit's Christmas meals: breakfast at 9 A.M., an hour later than usual, with porridge, sausage, and mash; lunch of roast pork and plum pudding; tea, fresh butter and new bread, jam, biscuits, and celery; supper of soup, bread, and cheese. He was also organizing a football match with another battery, and needed to clear the farmer's field that would comprise the pitch. Sud-denly, on December 9, his leave came through. "Oh! My darling," he exclaimed to Ruth. "I do hope there'll be no delay this time." A few days later he was home.

George spent just ten days with Ruth and Clare at Westbrook. He returned to France on Boxing Day, leaving Ruth to try to contain her grief. "I went up the steep way, through the little gate I showed you, after I left you," she wrote. "I could cry that way; I simply had to a little, you know. Then I leaned against the ivy wall and looked through tree twigs into the mist; and I tried to pray in silence, just getting near to God and to you and to everything. I don't think I did it very well, but I feel wonderfully soothed and better."

George reached the battery on December 29 to find that it had been in action on Christmas Day. The Christmas lunch had been postponed to 3 P.M. and the mud was worse than ever. In his first letter to Ruth he dwelled on their ten precious days together, the scenes they had enjoyed, the "visions of you" he cherished, his pleasure that they had bridged "all sorts of gaps" caused by his absence. It only remained, he added, "to hear that you are going to have a baby." A week later came the answer. Ruth told him that all the signs were positive: her period had not come, she had "little feelings in my breasts and you know last time they were one of the first signs I had . . . Oh darling I did not think it really would happen." They had evidently made other feelings clear, for Ruth was anticipating his reaction: "I hope after caring for it tenderly for nine months I shall be able to give you back a lovely boy. But a girl is not to be unwelcome to either of us . . . " George was delighted. "I was hoping and hoping for this news," he told her. "I am glad dear one—for all reasons. I some how thought it would be all right . . . We won't worry about whether it's to be a boy or a girl."

George had good news for Ruth in turn, although he did not entirely see it that way. He had been transferred to the brigade headquarters that had been installed some three miles behind the front line. His assignment was to act as assistant to a colonel but, since the colonel hated delegating, George only had menial chores to perform. He did have to learn how to ride a horse to accompany the colonel on inspections but regarded that as a "footling old woman's job." He had a batman (a British officer's personal military servant) who had been a barber in civilian life and who shaved him in bed every morning, cleaned out his chimney, and kept his underclothes washed and dried. One night, in a rare burst of activity, George helped to clear mud and water from a half-dug observation post; another evening he walked four miles to visit one of his Cambridge friends, Cosmo Gordon. "I like Cosmo," he told Ruth. "He was always very attractive—but much nicer now than he used to be." The weather got ever colder, there was snow on the ground for a fortnight, and the motor vehicles were harder to start each morning. He found reward in a walk across frozen marshes in a gleaming blue light: everything was "hard and clean and beautiful," reminding him of the Alps. Then came the distressing death of a fellow officer named

Boal who was hit by shrapnel from a shell as he left an observation post. "He died of his wounds in less than 24 hours after suffering a lot of pain I fear; I understand his case was practically hopeless from the first."

In February George was cheered by a brief new assignment as liaison officer to a nearby French unit. He was amused to discover that the French considered the English "happy-go-lucky, ill-organized and slow to change our ways"—luckily, George told Ruth, "They don't know the worst." He played poker with the British officers and chess with the French: "So far my duties have been far from arduous." Ruth's food parcels continued to arrive, bringing cakes and sausages, although his mother wrote to say that a Cheshire cheese she had dispatched weeks before had just been returned to her, "half eaten by rats." The Germans were retreating to the banks of the Somme, bringing brief hopes that perhaps the war would end that year after all, although George suspected they were merely consolidating new positions. He walked over the land they had abandoned, and was filled with "unspeakable rage" at the desolation: shattered churches, villages in ruins, even the cherry trees lying on the ground, their blossom despoiled. For George, it drove away "every feeling about the enemy except the desire to destroy them."

Ruth's letters at this stage were more composed: she was relieved that George was away from the front line, and she had settled into more of a routine at home. She was apprehensive about an impending visit from George's mother, particularly because his sister Mary had just had her first baby, a daughter named Barbara. In comparison with Clare, Ruth predicted, "She will probably tell me how lovely and very intelligent and how much more forward Barbara is." But the visit proved uneventful. Ruth was already looking ahead to September, when their second child was due, and George anticipated that she would be "wonderfully happy" when the baby was born. "I suppose you'll go clucking about like any young hen and puffing out your feathers," he predicted, adding: "It's astonishing what may happen to what one marries." Not for the first time, he drew a vigorous response. "You say you never know what will happen to the person you marry. Are you really surprised that I have turned so henny? It only shows there was a lump of me you didn't know."

At the end of March George applied to return to his battery, which had moved to a new position. With the Germans seemingly in retreat, all the talk was of the Americans entering the war, bringing "assurance of victory." George explored a wood in search of a new observation post, and found it carpeted with wood anemones and cowslips. He sat down for breakfast behind a shattered tree trunk, boiling water for coffee on a "small, bright fire" and frying sardines in the embers. Then came a new panic, when he lost a secret code book. George told Ruth he could have claimed that the book had gone missing in the chaos of moving to a new position, adding, with spectacular lack of self-knowledge, that the excuse would have worked "as I very seldom lose things." However a very senior officer was asking for the book and George wondered if he would be shot at dawn. The book was found, and George escaped retribution.

In their letters George and Ruth still looked ahead to the time he might return, counting the days to some notional date when he might get more leave, hoping against hope that the war might end that year. "I would like to find you waiting for me at the Holt!" George wrote. "How happily we would step out into the loggia and watch the play of sunlight in that lovely valley." In fact, it was neither leave, nor the end of the war, that would take George home. Since his return to France in December, George had been increasingly troubled by pain in his right ankle. It felt as if one of his bones had acquired a sharp edge and was cutting into his flesh, and he was finding it more and more difficult to walk. A doctor told him the damage had been caused by his fall from the sandstone out-crop in Birkenhead in 1909. The fracture, which had never been diagnosed and had healed badly, was coming apart. "For the present he advises bandages to hold it together and restrict movement," George said. "But he says after the war I ought to have an operation."

Mid-April brought snow, and George told Ruth that, although spring might have arrived at Westbrook, there was still a cold wind in France. In front of him as he wrote was one of her hand-painted bowls, decorated with yellow polyanthus and grape hyacinths, which had somehow survived being mailed to him in France: "It perpetually reminds me of you." Three days later he told Ruth he had been reading an article by H. G. Wells, who was arguing that air power held the key to victory; he thought Wells could be right, "But it's a very slow way of winning." He was afraid that rationing might be introduced in Britain and suggested that Ruth should stop sending cakes. On May 4 he opened fire at some German troops moving behind their lines, but missed; a pair of swallows, unable to find any eaves among the shattered houses, made a nest in the battery's mess. George told Ruth that his ankle was getting worse. "It is behaving very badly and I'm again more or less crocked. I'm going to try wearing shoes consistently for a time—that may help." One of the doctors reexamined the ankle and concluded that if George was going to be of any further use to the British army, he needed an operation.

⤐

The next of Auntie Mill's watercolors shows George in a bed at the Officers' Hospital at Portland Place in London. His ankle has been operated on—the fractured bone was separated, the edges smoothed and then reset—for there is a protective frame, covered by the blue bedclothes, resting over his feet. George, wearing red-striped pajamas, is sitting up in the bed, while Clare sits across his lap, her face turned towards him in a smile, a blue ribbon tying her golden hair. George is smiling at Clare and has a posy of Westbrook flowers in his hand. Ruth is sitting on the far side of the bed, wearing an extravagantly broad-brimmed blue hat and a long blue V-necked dress, but Mill has placed her in a position that conceals the fact that she is five months pregnant.

There is something of a wistful look, a cautious smile, on Ruth's face, as if she cannot quite believe the good fortune that has brought George home. Although he was still in the army, she would no longer have to wonder from one moment to the next whether a delivery boy was about to bring a telegram with the direst news. More than a year would pass before George returned to France, a hiatus caused by a chapter of accidents and fortuitous postings that made it appear that he had a guardian angel to watch over him. As always George did everything he could in that time to find stimulating activities which would offset the tedium of army life away from the front.

When George was discharged from hospital he went to Westbrook to convalesce. By July his ankle was sufficiently recovered for him to decide to test it by a visit to the mountains. He and David Pye, an experimental engineer with the Royal Flying Corps, schemed a trip to the island of Arran, off the southwest coast of Scotland; there was no question of Ruth coming, as she was seven months pregnant and so troubled by the heat that she declared she did not want to have any more babies in the summer. Before taking the ferry to Arran George spent three days with Cosmo Gordon's in-laws at their country house at Skipness on the Mull of Kintyre: "I slept under the trees and bathed about four times a day and went up the burns and on to the moors," he told Ruth. He met Cosmo's wife Frances and their baby boy—"it was very nice to make friends with them"— and Frances drove him in a pony and trap to catch the steamer ferry from Carradale. Pye had invited Will Arnold-Forster and the three stayed at a hotel at Corrie on the east coast, looking towards the Scottish mainland.

It was the first time George had been into the Scottish hills and, although there were no peaks on Arran even 3000 feet high, he was enthralled by the soaring, rocky landscape. "The mountains themselves are so lovely, and when one gets up high . . . the view of all the islands & peninsulas in those parts is like being in some enchanting country—nothing I have seen beats it for colour." Apart from one tentative rock climb, George spent most of the time roaming the peaks and moorland, exploring tunnels and caves, swimming in streams and the sea. His ankle still gave him cause for concern. "It just managed to do all that was required of it," he wrote to Avie on August 29, "but with many signs of weakness: it used to be very stiff in the evenings and had to be rubbed vigorously before use." After the trip it had seemed "weak and crackly" but had improved since.

In September the army doctors passed George fit for duties again. For the moment, it seemed, he was spared a return to France and sent to an army camp at Avington Park, near Winchester, to train on the new sixty-pound guns the Royal Artillery was acquiring. Compared to the western front, George found the camp preternaturally calm, a world away from the fighting. He was bewildered by the unconvivial silences at mealtimes and frustrated at the jobs he was given, which included watching over the army's horses and checking through discarded socks to see if he could make up wearable pairs.

There were consolations. He visited his old school, meeting former teachers such as Graham Irving, and undertaking walks he remembered from his school days. Above all, Westbrook was just thirty miles away. Ruth wanted to visit him at Avington Park but he advised her not to come as the visiting procedures were hopelessly bureaucratic. Instead, he would come to her. He borrowed a motorcycle from one of the Winchester teachers and, after a cursory spell of self-instruction, rode it to Westbrook on weekends. Ruth was delighted to see him, particularly as their second child was imminent. They discussed names and settled on Arabella for a girl, Edwin for a boy.

Their daughter was born on September 16, emerging far more readily than Clare. They promptly overturned their decision on her name and called her Beridge Ruth. Berridge—with two "r"s—was the name of the evangelist preacher who was one of Annie Jebb's forebears and Ruth, perhaps to avoid the confusion over the spelling, soon took to calling her Berry. George did his best to conceal his disappointment at not having a son. Ruth was more concerned over the dangers of sibling rivalry and arranged for Berry to be in a crib the first time Clare saw her. Auntie Mill's next picture shows Clare standing on a chair to peer in at Berry as she lies in her crib in the dressing room off her parents' bedroom.

Geoffrey Young had agreed to be Berry's godfather but on the very day she was born George heard shattering news. After helping to set up the Quakers' ambulance service in France, and running an entire medical unit at Ypres, Young had gone to Italy—one of the western Allies—to establish an ambulance service in the mountains of the Italian-Austrian front. On August 31 he was hit by an Austrian shell, wounding his left leg so badly that it had to be amputated at the knee. On the evening of September 16, George sent his condolences to his mother, Lady Alice Young. A few days later, having obtained Young's address, George wrote to him, doing his best to express his sorrow without casting the future in too bleak a light. Young replied on September 26, telling George he was already planning to climb with an artificial leg. "Now I shall have the immense stimulus of a new start, with every little inch of progress a joy instead of a commonplace. I count on my great-hearts, like you, to share in the fun of that game with me."

In early October George, having been elevated to the rank of full lieutenant, started a course at Avington for newly promoted officers. Hovering over him, as he and Ruth well knew, was the prospect of an imminent return to France. "My dear one," he told Ruth, "I am bound to say I feel it's high time I should go out again: the present events in France just put that into my blood." He added that Ralph Brooke, their brother-in-law, who was commanding a siege battery in France, was "keen to get me into his battery and is moving all he can." But just five weeks after Young lost his left leg, it was George's turn to injure himself. George was riding into the camp on his borrowed motorcycle, after the usual breakneck dash from Westbrook, when he crashed into the gatepost, crushing his right foot. His explanation to Ruth sounded embarrassingly thin: "As I turned into the camp my brake which I endeavoured to apply as I hadn't quite suffi-ciently slowed down failed to act." He did his best to play down the injury, tell-ing Ruth that although he had a nasty wound and would be unable to walk for several days, the camp doctor was "*absolutely* happy" that there would be no lasting damage. George in fact spent a month in the hospital, followed by a second month before he could walk in comfort again. Since he had barely recov-ered from the operation to his ankle, he felt "like a school-boy in disgrace."

Still using the motorcycle, George resumed his visits to Westbrook as soon as he could. From time to time events in France impinged: in early November, when the British lost thousands more men in the latest battle at Passchendaele, all leave was cancelled in case urgent replacements were needed. "Just one of the periodical scares, I expect," George told Ruth, explaining that he could not take the risk of leaving the camp without permission. George used some of the time to complete his experimental account of his emotions during his 1911 ascent of Mont Blanc: in a letter to Young, he described it as an attempt "to treat an expedition as a spiritual experience." He had sent the article to the editor of the *Alpine Journal*, George Yeld, who—as George related with wry amusement—did not know what to make of the article as it differed so radically from the journal's regular fare. Yeld sent it for a second opinion to the president of the Alpine Club, Percy Farrar, who did not understand it either and forwarded it for yet another judgment to George's friend and climbing partner, Herbert Reade. It was finally published in September 1918.

By the end of 1917 George had been passed fit for military service again. He was firmly expecting to be sent back to France but, after further delays, he was deemed to need a further spell of training and was dispatched to take a battery commander's course at the artillery school at Lydd. There, it so happened, he came under the aegis of Ralph Brooke, who had just been posted back from France to take command of the school. When George transferred there Ruth and the children went with him. They stayed with Mary and Ralph and their three children at Littlestone, a seaside village five miles from Lydd. The children built sand castles on the beach while George and Brooke enjoyed occasional rounds of golf during breaks from training.

George and Ruth were also able to pick up some of the strands of their old social life. They spent Christmas at Westbrook and in January attended the wedding of Robert Graves and Nancy Nicholson in London, where George was best man. There was another wedding at Easter: Geoffrey Young had finally prevailed in his wooing of Eleanor Slingsby, known to all as Len. The culminating indulgence for George and Ruth came at the end of July 1918, when they spent a week in Skye, leaving Clare and Berry at Westbrook with Vi. They made a rendezvous at Inverness with David Pye, on leave from his work with the Royal Flying Corps, which had become the Royal Air Force that year. Pye brought with him a most useful climbing partner in the figure of Leslie Shadbolt, a Pen y Pass man who had made some of the first rock climbs before the war on the beautifully adhesive black gabbro rock of Skye's Cuillin hills. His greatest distinction was to have taken part in the first end-to-end traverse of the Cuillin Ridge, which snakes its way for seven miles across the south of the island and is still the longest test piece for climbers and scramblers in the British Isles. From Inverness they crossed Scotland by train to the Kyle of Lochalsh, passing through a landscape of glens and peaks and running along the sandy shoreline of Loch Carron, "shining and studded with small islands under a faint blue haze," Pye wrote. They took the Skye ferry to Kyleakin and from there drove to the Sligachan Inn at the northern end of the Cuillin Ridge.

The weather, so often the bane of Scottish climbing, was almost perfect throughout, the one drawback being the clouds of midges that enveloped them, particularly when they stopped to swim. Their first climb was the classic Pinnacle ridge on Sgurr nan Gillean. They crossed the dauntingly exposed gap near the third pinnacle just as the last of the morning mist blew away, revealing the entire ridge in its "peculiar magic and grandeur," Pye wrote, with its "quality of superb simplicity, unique among mountains." The next day they climbed on the north face of Sgurr a'Mhadaidh, one of the peaks at the center of the range. They had intended to follow a route which Shadbolt had climbed with Archer Thomson in 1911 but were attracted by a new line which zigzagged across the foot of the face and then took a direct line to the top. It was typical of the age in following long pitches with no belays and although the climbing was not demanding it was often on steep rock where care, Pye dryly observed, "was essential."

On July 29 they left Sligachan to walk to Glen Brittle at the western end of the range. It was one of George's ambitious outings, typical of those he undertook in the Alps, filling every hour of the day. They walked down Glen Sligachan, crossed the subsidiary ridge of Druim nan Ramh, and stopped for lunch at Loch Coruisk, one of the most isolated lochs in Britain, with peaks curving steeply around it on three sides, the innermost sanctum of the range. From there they could have followed the seashore to skirt the southern end of the ridge but instead headed straight up the east face of Sgurr Coire an Lochan to the crest of the ridge 3000 feet above. The view, down to Glen Brittle and out to the islands of the Outer Hebrides shimmering in the Atlantic, took their breath away. They scrambled along the ridge to reach the notch between Sgurr Mhic Coinnich and the highest peak, Sgurr Alasdair, and from there made the descent to Glen Brittle, where they had arranged to stay with Mrs. Campbell, the formidable keeper of the Glen Brittle post office. Before supper they went swimming, "the crowning moment of the day," Pye wrote. For Ruth especially it was a long and demanding day, but she told Pye that it was far less testing than the occasion when a blizzard drove them off the Snowdon ridge.

However, Ruth asked to be excused climbing the next day. The three men walked up to Sron na Ciche, the huge crag that overlooks Coire Lagan above Glen Brittle, and well known for the strange rounded buttress jutting from its face known as the Cioch, first noticed by Norman Collie when he saw the evening shadow it cast. While Pye lazed in the sun, George led Shadbolt up a line close to the Cioch which was probably the route known as Cioch West and may have been the first ascent. The next day George led an indisputable first ascent following some prominent crack lines up 1000 feet on the western buttress of Sron na Ciche. It took six hours, and the most difficult moves, described by Pye as "a crab-like movement over slabs," came when George had led out almost seventy feet without a belay, and was out of sight of his partner. Known as Mallory's Slab and Groove, it was later graded as Severe. George and his partners celebrated with a swim—"a glorious bathe, a bathe beyond words," Pye wrote—in a burn during the descent. They tried to evade the midges by staying underwater but this method, Pye wrote, was "of limited usefulness."

For George and Ruth it was the end of the holiday. While Pye and Shadbolt stayed to put up Crack of Doom, the finest line on the Cioch, they traveled back south. In France, the final push was on. In the spring the Germans had launched their last, most desperate offensive. They succeeded in driving through the Allied lines and advancing on Paris, just as they had in 1914. But they did so at the cost of more than a million men, fatally draining their final reserves. In the summer, with the Allies assisted by the newly arrived U.S. forces, the Germans were driven inexorably back to the Hindenburg line, their line of last defense. But the Allies were losing men in tens of thousands too. At the end of September, after a further spell of training in Newcastle, where he was once again accompanied by Ruth, George was among the troops sent back to France to ensure that the final victory was secured.

℞

Having had George with her or near her for sixteen months, Ruth found another parting almost unbearable. But she had become practiced in her stoicism, relating on September 23: "I did part from you cheerfully in true British fashion, didn't I. I am getting stronger at those times than I used to be. I suppose the adversity of war hardens ones fibre." She had gone to stay at Birkenhead: George's parents "welcomed me very much, it was nice after the gloom of parting with you." She ended on an optimistic note, acknowledging that the war was drawing to a close at last. "I hope more than I can say that you will come home soon to a world at peace."

George had been assigned to another siege battery, the 515th, which was positioned between Arras and the Channel coast at a comfortable distance from the front line. The commanding officer was a Major Gwilym Lloyd George, who happened to be the son of the British prime minister. George's immediate task was to furnish his new quarters, a cabin in a railway truck. Its greatest shortcoming was a lack of curtains, which he asked Ruth to provide. His next assignment was to organize a sports day for the men beside the sea. He arranged a football match, followed by a program of sprints and obstacle races, including one which required the men to strip off their clothes, run into the sea, roll in the waves, then run back. All the fighting was to the south and by mid-October Germany began to sue for peace. George and Ruth were in a high tension for the next three weeks, as the two sides exchanged diplomatic notes while the death toll continued. On November 10 George was with Geoffrey Keynes, whom he had tracked down to a unit near Cambrai, and they were just turning in for bed when they heard shouts—"confused and dispersed"—that the armistice was imminent. Neither of them could quite believe it.

The following morning, November 11, Ruth started a letter to George. "I don't know what to do I can't settle down to anything. We are simply waiting and listening to hear the first thing that shall tell us that the news of Peace has come. We may hear any time now. I don't think I can possibly write you an intelligent letter I am too full of waiting emotion." She told him she wanted to get back to the Holt as soon as she could, and said she was sorry she had not yet been able to send him some woodworking tools, a plane and a chisel. Then, shortly after eleven o'clock, she wrote a single line that recorded an epochal moment in the world's history: "It's come dear the bells have begun."

Ruth put down her pen and hurried to a thanksgiving service at Godalming parish church. It began with the national anthem, and included the hymn "Now thank we all our God." "It was really very nice," she told George. That afternoon she and Vi took Clare and Berry into Godalming to see the flags decorating the High Street, Clare and Berry each waving a miniature Union Jack. "I hope Clare may manage to remember it. Anyway she knows its because you are coming home soon."

George celebrated the end of the war with his brother Trafford, whose career had followed a spectacular path since he had been invalided home in 1915. He had resolved not to return to the trenches and had trained as a pilot instead. In 1916, the year he got married, he joined the fledgling Royal Flying Corps and by the end of the war was a Royal Air Force squadron commander. On Armistice Day he sent a car to fetch George and they spent the evening at the officers' club in Cambrai. "It was a good evening," George told Ruth, "with much hilarity and no drunkenness." The predominant feeling, he wrote, was one of release. "What a freedom it is now! I seem to be inundated by waves of elation and to be capable now of untroubled joy such as no one [has] known during these 4 years since the war began."

George also talked of the cost to themselves, the penalties and strains their marriage had suffered, and the anxieties they had struggled to bear: this victory, he told her, was for themselves. "What a wonderful life we will have together— what a lovely thing we *must* make of such a gift. I want to lose all harshness of jagged nerves, to be above all gentle. I feel we have achieved victory for that almost more than anything." He ended: "Farewell then my love for the present. 'I shall clasp thee again o thou soul of my soul.' Your loving George."

On the day after the armistice, Ruth was taken ill with pneumonia. She spent a week in bed and it was several weeks before she fully recovered. Five days passed before she was able to write to George again, by far the longest interruption in her letters during the war. George told her that he hoped to be home very soon, but two months were to pass before that hope was fulfilled. The British had more than a million men to demobilize: apart from the gargantuan problems of administration, there was only a limited number of ships to transport them back across the English Channel. As a schoolteacher George was supposedly in a priority group but it appeared to make no difference. While he and Ruth lamented the delay he filled his time as best he could. He paid several visits to Trafford and was treated to a spin in one of his squadron's planes. The pilot, who was Canadian, indulged in some aerobatics, George enthralled as always with the physical sensations: "At the critical moment something seemed to grip one's whole body." But when the pilot proposed looping the loop George hastily refused, as he had failed to fasten his safety belt.

On November 15 George wrote to his father, a letter suffused with a sympathetic rendering of the spiritual terms his father would have used. "Life presents itself very much to me as a gift. If I haven't escaped so many chances of death as plenty of others, still it is surprising to find myself a survivor, and it's not a lot I have always wanted. There has not been so much to be said for being alive in the company of the dead. Anyway, it's good to be alive now." He spent a week in Paris, going to the theater, buying books, meeting a painter, and delighting in a city readjusting to peace. He spent Christmas with his men, performing a song he had written for the battery concert, a parody of "Widdicombe Fair" based on the life of a gun crew. Although the day went well, George was beginning to feel that if he could not be with Ruth, he would rather be alone. He rented a room in Calais and spent time there writing. But there was something wrong, as he told Ruth, for the room had a double bed; if only he could share it with her.

On January 7, 1919, Ruth picked up the theme. There had been problems negotiating the date of the O'Malleys' departure from the Holt but they had now left. "It was so nice to feel that it belonged to us again properly," she told George. "I did wish most awfully that you were there with me . . . It was worse than sleeping in a double bed without you. I too am doing that and have been longing and longing for the night to come when you would be with me." She had been hoping that they would be able to share the first night back at the Holt, and the chance seemed to have gone. But this was not an occasion for grief: "I think so often that at any rate you are alive and coming back soon and think what this would have been if you had been killed and I had been going back to live there alone with the children." It was the last letter she wrote to him in France.

The penultimate page of Auntie Mill's picture book depicts Armistice Day afternoon in Godalming. "One day," runs Auntie Mill's caption, "Mummie and Vi took Clare and Berry into the town to see all the flags because it was Peace and they each had a Union Jack to wave." Lines of flags and bunting are strung across the street. Clare, a black bonnet over her curly fair hair, is carrying a Union Jack as she walks beside Vi, who is pushing Berry's baby carriage. Ruth, who wears a gray coat, blue stockings, and a brown cloche hat, is walking alongside. Auntie Mill has not forgotten the cost of victory, for at the center of the picture is a woman dressed in black leading a small child by the hand. And Ruth is looking towards a solitary soldier leaning against a building, perhaps thinking that he reminds her of George.

George came home in the second week of January, and Auntie Mill's final picture shows the moment the family returned to the Holt. A pony and trap is pulling out of the gates of Westbrook carrying Ruth, Vi, Clare, and Berry. George, wearing a gray suit, red tie, and panama hat, is astride a bicycle, its spokes a blur as he strives to keep up with the pony and trap. "As the war was over," Mill wrote, "Daddy came home and stopped being a soldier. So they all went back to live at the Holt again."

Ahead, it seemed, lay the time that they had been waiting for ever since they had got married, when the world was not at war and their lives were not blighted by fear and uncertainty. They had reclaimed their home at the Holt, were reunited with their two children and nurturing plans for a third—preferably a son. George was within Ruth's reach, working at Charterhouse, its spires in sight from the loggia at the Holt. When they stretched out an arm at night, they would no longer find their double bed empty. There was just one doubt to cloud this prospect of the future. "The only possible jar to our happiness will be my personal ambitions," George had written to Ruth shortly before returning from France. "You must be patient with me, my dearest one."

CHAPTER NINE

Any Aspirations?
1919–1921

The first aim for George and Ruth, once they had returned to the Holt, was to make it their home again. No matter how careful their tenants might have been, the two years of occupation by the Greens and the O'Malleys had left the unmistakable patina of someone else's presence: the busiest rooms had to be repainted and the stair-carpet replaced. Now that the family was reunited, the rooms had to be allocated too. Clare and Berry were given a bedroom under the eaves on the top floor, with views of the garden and the valley. It was furnished with a chest of drawers, a table and chair that Ruth's father had given Clare, and new blue linoleum for the floor. George reclaimed his study, which the O'Malleys had used as a lumber room. He had several boxes of new books to unpack, including those Ruth had been sending him in France and a batch he had bought during his Paris trip, and these he now arranged on the shelves.

As they settled back into the Holt, there were problems stemming from the effects of war. There was still rationing, with sugar and coal in short supply. There was also what Ruth, in common with many other middle-class households, referred to—with no trace of irony—as the servant problem. The women of Britain had found new work in offices and factories, and many of them were still needed in those roles, as around 750,000 men had not returned from the war. In a broader sense, the war had begun the erosion of Britain's great social divide, and many women were no longer prepared to go into service, as it was called. Those who were willing to do so were in a seller's market and when Ruth found a cook named Maud Mercer she asked for £35 ($152.00) a year. Ruth felt she had no choice but to meet her demands which meant, in equity, raising Vi's annual pay from £28 ($121.80) to £35 ($152.00) too. Ruth also found a live-in parlor maid, a gardener who would work two days a week, and a cleaning woman who would come every Friday. The cook and parlor maid would sleep in two attic rooms alongside the children's bedroom, while Vi would sleep with the children.

Ruth took the lead in raising the children. She mostly followed her instincts, as there were no child-rearing manuals, no Spocks or Leaches, to guide her, and she did not have her mother to offer advice. Fortunately, as she had told George, "I really like having the children to look after—so many mothers who have nurses seem to dread their time with them." As she had remarked during the war, she especially enjoyed it when Vi was away and she could feed and bathe the children herself: on Christmas morning at Westbrook, when Vi was attending an early-morning service, she had snuggled into Vi's bed for a cuddle with Clare. She made the children's clothes, including a cloak and bonnet for Clare, and a winter frock for Clare's doll. She was developing her ideas on education, espousing the theories of Maria Montessori, the Italian educationist who believed in encouraging children's spirit of discovery to motivate them to learn. Ruth had been buying the Montessori beads, blocks, and frames that helped young children learn how to classify, count, and manipulate. She delighted in watching Clare's rapid progress, although Clare herself later said that she had found the equipment far too easy and wished for something more challenging.

Ruth also believed that she and George should relate to their children as equals, listening to them and respecting them as friends. While George approved of Ruth's approach, which matched his own educational philosophy, there were difficulties caused by his periodic departures that were to worsen throughout the marriage. Each time he went away, Ruth had to manage the children and household herself; each time he came back, it became harder to readjust. What made it worse was that Ruth, as her daughter Clare remarked, was a lenient mother—perhaps too lenient for her own good. There was already a contrast between Ruth's approach and that of Vi who was less indulgent; George's return upset the balance still further. Clare had memories that gave the impression that George could be a strict father who also wondered how he fitted in. Once he became exasperated when Clare was protesting at having her hair brushed and abruptly turned on his heel and walked out of the nursery. There had in fact been little to prepare George for fatherhood. Although he was a modern man, concerned about women's position and rights, it was still a time when fathers were not expected to play any significant part in their children's upbringing. Yet there can be no doubting George's affection for his children, and a photograph taken at Westbrook during the war shows him extending a hand to Clare, admiration manifest in his eyes. It also reveals the privations he had suffered, for his cheeks are hollow and his face is gaunt.

Less than two weeks after his return, George took up his old job at Charterhouse. Although he and Ruth felt angry that Fletcher had not done more to secure his early demobilization, the headmaster had written a letter welcoming him back. Ruth had looked ahead to the time when George's pupils would be visiting the Holt again, and so it soon proved. At the same time their social life, which Ruth had kept going by proxy when George was in France, was rapidly revived. Their former tenants, the O'Malleys, returned as guests: Ruth enjoyed Mary Anne's sparkle and sense of fun, and she and George were prepared to tolerate Owen.

As the dedicated chronicler of her friendship with George, Mary Anne recorded her memories of the Mallorys' return to the Holt, which became the picture of bustling domesticity as they set about recreating the shared haven they had always wanted. She especially remembered the drawing room, with its air of repose, even when the children burst in; and George's study, with its deep armchairs that soon acquired a "mellow and agreeable shabbiness," and the Scots pines visible from the window, swaying in the wind. Ruth welcomed all who came, whether they were invited guests, colleagues he brought back from school, or his favored pupils, as Mary Anne described. "There was always a welcome and a meal, and a sense of freedom and well-being for mind and body in that house—with any amount of good talk—over the fire, or in the loggia, or strolling idly about the garden, perching on the low wall or on the great oak seat." George once told her: "It is a good house to live in."

❧

At Easter 1919, at the instigation of Geoffrey Young, the Pen y Pass parties were revived. Young was determined to try to climb again, using the artificial leg he had designed with a detachable foot and a variety of soles, including a rubber pad and a steel spike studded with nails. He asked George to help: while he and Len would handle "the social side," he needed George, "as almost the only survivor" from his generation, to recruit the climbers. Young calculated that out of sixty climbers mentioned in the Pen y Pass book up to 1914, twenty-three had died in the war and eleven had been injured, including himself. One of the most remarkable stories was that of Rawson Owen, the Gorphwysfa's proprietor, who had joined up in 1914, landed at Gallipoli, fought the Turks in Palestine, was in France on Armistice Day, and returned to Pen y Pass "sound and unwounded, one of the few original survivors of his regiment."

George and Ruth bought a secondhand car for the occasion, a rather flamboyant 1912 American Studebaker-Flanders, a four-cylinder, five-seater tourer with acetylene headlamps and oil side lamps. (From a photograph showing a Pen y Pass group trying to push-start the car with George at the wheel, they appear to have had trouble with it, and they sold it soon after the trip.) They left the children with Vi and took with them Ruth's sister Marjorie—usually known as Marby—and Ursula Nettleship. The party, in Young's words, "exceeded all expectations." Twenty-eight people stayed at the Gorphwysfa, including Herbert Reade, Claude Elliott, Harold Porter and David Pye, and several wives. The most notable absentee was Mary Anne, whose climbing career—at her husband's insistence—was at an end. Young could not help ruminating over the faces missing from the prewar years, but on Easter Sunday he faced his own biggest test. Watched and encouraged by many of his colleagues, George among them, he attempted to climb Gashed Crag on Tryfan. Relying mainly on the strength of his shoulders and arms, and using a top-rope for protection, he reached the top in safety.

The next day George made a new traverse on Lliwedd's East Buttress. His partners were Pye, Elliott, and Ruth, gamely trusting George's assessment of her abilities once again. They started by following George's Slab Climb to the Bowling Green and striking rightwards across the buttress at a height of around 200 feet. The toughest move was a short pendulum on handholds into an awkward right-angled corner, and they completed the route in four hours. Harold Porter, who repeated the climb and photographed some of the key moves at Easter 1926, wrote that it demonstrated George's "fertility in invention and his resourcefulness in action." He considered it a better climb than Thomson's Girdle Traverse, although subsequent guidebooks graded it as Very Difficult, against Severe for the Thomson route.

Three months later, George, together with Porter and Claude Elliott, went to the Alps, crossing the English Channel on July 27. George had been dwelling on his mountaineering memories through the war but as their train approached Chamonix he found that nothing had prepared him for his first sight of the Alps after seven years away. "The thread of experience had been broken," he wrote in an article for the *Alpine Journal*. "To me they were a vision startlingly fresh and new—new as when I first saw them, and so overwhelmingly greater than the images I had conjured up that I seemed never to have seen them before."

At first, it appeared that the trip had been blighted. The weather was poor, and both George and Elliott were affected by altitude sickness. Elliott was carrying a knee injury and on August 1 he gave up and went home. George was distressed on his behalf: "He had so set his heart on the mountains." The next day he and Porter attempted a new route on the east or Mer de Glace face of the Grand Charmoz, one of the Chamonix Aiguilles, following a rocky rib that joined the main crest of the mountain near a prominent spire known as the Aiguille de la République. As he struggled to readjust to the mountain environment, George felt he was climbing badly, with "no fizz." He stumbled and shattered their lantern, cutting his hand on the glass, found step-cutting awkward, and made several routefinding mistakes. Then, as he and Porter looked up at the final 1000 feet, they felt suddenly elated by the challenge. They followed a line of flakes, slabs, and cracks, George fashioning holds by twisting his ice ax into cracks, at one point standing on Porter's shoulders to overcome a steep, holdless slab. The last pitch, a granite wall plastered in ice, was the hardest, but in a few minutes they were at the top. Although the route had been mostly on rock, lacking the radiance of a snow-and-ice ascent, George felt it was a worthwhile achievement. He called it "a proper expedition for two guideless climbers," who had "rubbed their noses against the rocks."

On August 5 they attempted a new mixed route on the north face of the Aiguille du Midi. Two previous parties had climbed the prominent couloir at the center of the face but neither had reached the final summit rocks. George and Porter followed a line to the left of the couloir and reached the top, after climbing almost 3000 feet, just after midday. Their final ascent was a route on Mont Blanc, made with two other British climbers, Professor Arthur Pigou and William McLean, whom they had met at the Rifugio Torino, a hut on the Col du Géant. They began at the Italian Val Veni and ascended the Miage Glacier to the Sella hut, and there followed the Rochers du Mont Blanc route, which finds an elegant mountaineering line up a complicated face. George wrote of their "smooth, unchecked, harmonious advance" and of the undiminished reward of climbing Mont Blanc. "A great mountain is always greater than we know; it has mysteries, surprises, hidden purposes; it holds always something in store for us"—words which could be applied to a future mountain.

With some reluctance, George turned for home. He had wanted to stay longer but Porter was suffering from hemorrhoids, an affliction all too common among climbers, and George was unable to find another partner. Even so, it had been an accomplished return to the Alps for George, putting up two new routes despite indifferent weather, and finishing with a strong route on Mont Blanc. He wrote to Young, telling him that, although it grieved him to leave at a time of "perfect weather and perfect snow," he was pleased that he had been fitter than he had expected. "It seems a very small record for the first great chance after the war," he wrote. "But I have a host of lovely visions and one climb to dream about."

George took advantage of his premature return to join Ruth and the children at the end of their seaside holiday. In September he and Ruth left the children with Vi and went walking near Gloucester, exploring river valleys, including the Wye, Severn, and Teme, and covering up to thirty miles in a day. It was an idyllic time, George wrote, lingering for a meal in a country inn or on a grassy bank, picking apples in an orchard: "enjoying all the detail and the distance till some golden beauty seemed to have been distilled all about us."

⁂

On the face of things, George and Ruth seemed to have all they could have asked for. But there was still the question of Charterhouse. The euphoria of his first six months back home had helped George overcome his frustrations and his dislike of Fletcher, but his views of the inadequacies and flaws of the public school still held. He had made the point with some force while drafting his novel, *The Book of Geoffrey*, when he was in France. In one passage a father confronts a teacher and accuses him of destroying his son's innocence and inquisitiveness. Previously the boy had been "a pleasant companion full of young curiosity, a healthy animal, a proper English boy"; now he was selfish, prejudiced, and dull, a mental coward full of contempt for other people's views. "Superficial and self-satisfied, he is disastrously ill equipped for making the best of life."

Even more forthright, and strengthening the suggestion that George was evoking his own estrangement from his parents, is the father's accusation to the teacher: "When I gave him to you, he was lost to me. I knew him no longer and couldn't know him . . . His lips indeed spoke but his heart was closed from me and his mother." David Pye suspected that George was also affected by guilt, as he had been reconsidering his own approach to teaching, and wondering whether he could have done more for the majority of his pupils rather than the favored few. "Armed with his own experience, he would not attempt the same methods," Pye recorded.

As always, George tried to build on the lessons of frustration and disappointment. He, Pye, and Geoffrey Young began to consider opening a school of their own. Together with Ruth and Len Young, they met several times at the Holt to discuss the idea. George went so far as to prepare a draft prospectus for the school that made four key points. First, parents and teachers should work closely together. Second, rather than inhabit oases of privilege, pupils should learn about other worlds across the social divides. They should be taught about craft and design, about farm work, and "the obligations of responsibility and disinterested effort." Third, there should be less of a distinction between lessons and leisure. Pupils should be under less pressure from the demands of the formal curriculum, and should be encouraged to develop initiative and self-reliance. Fourth, there should be fewer compulsory games. Pupils should be allowed to follow other pursuits and crafts, including walking and navigating through the countryside.

What was impressive about George's prospectus was the extent to which it addressed faults in a divisive and examination-obsessed education system that has persisted in Britain since. The issues he raised are still relevant in the continuing debate between theories of child-centered and didactic education. Nor was the project unduly fanciful, since Prior's Field, which Ruth had attended, had been opened by Julia Huxley with just six pupils and similarly progressive principles in 1902, and was still thriving almost a hundred years later. What was more, Julia Huxley's husband had been a teacher at Charterhouse. George, Young, and Pye drew up more detailed plans but in the end they lacked the collective will to see the scheme through. Pye eventually became provost of University College, London, while Young helped the German refugee Kurt Hahn when he founded Gordonstoun, the school in Scotland that emphasized the importance of honesty, integrity, self-reliance, and naked swimming.

⸎

The Mallorys spent Christmas at Westbrook. Soon afterwards, Ruth announced that she was pregnant again. George was unabashed in declaring that this time, as he told Young on January 11, 1920, they hoped for a boy. He also revealed his continuing incomprehension of the practicalities of motherhood. "It's been rather annoying to me both times that so much remained to tie Ruth after the baby was born," he told Young, "so that the whole business took not nine months but something like fifteen."

George's letter, like others he wrote in this period, also demonstrated his closeness with Young. Although he and Ruth were ready to bare almost all to each other, there were still significant areas—climbing in particular—where George sought advice and reassurance elsewhere. Young, for his part, needed a younger ally in the climbing world, and he enlisted George for a project that combined climbing and writing. When Young became president of the Climbers' Club, he found it in a near-moribund state, and he asked George, who was already a member of the club committee, to edit the next issue of the *Climbers' Club Journal.*

George readily accepted the new challenge and was full of plans, but soon discovered the realities of life on the other side of the editor's desk. Arthur Andrews, the Cornwall expert, submitted an unusable report on recent climbs. A whimsical piece by William McLean, George's partner on Mont Blanc the previous summer—and later assistant doctor on the 1933 Everest expedition— was "schoolboy stuff." Even an article by Pye about camping in the New Forest was dull. While George Finch had written an entertaining account of traversing the Petit Dru, with some excellent photographs, too many members had declined to contribute. In the end, George appealed to his friends, garnering articles by Conor O'Brien, Raymond Bicknell, and Young himself, who described their first ascent on the Nesthorn in 1909. George reviewed the book *Mountain Craft*, a summation of mountain knowledge of the time, which Young had edited as well as writing several chapters. Its publication had been delayed by the war, and George hailed it as "the most important work on mountaineering which has appeared in this generation." His review comprised an implicit tribute to Young, praising him for enriching George's climbing through his wisdom and companionship. It ended with a metaphor that accommodated Young's disability: where previously Young had occupied the summit of Mount Olympus, climbers would now meet him on the plains, "ready . . . to be kindled once more to a fresh desire for mountains." (Young in fact continued climbing for another fifteen years.) The issue of the journal finally appeared in November.

At Easter 1920 George went to Pen y Pass, this time without Ruth, who was four months pregnant. He took a group of Charterhouse boys and another teacher, and his climbing partners at Pen y Pass included Harold Porter, Herbert Reade, and Claude Elliott, who was there with his wife. For once the records of the Pen y Pass parties are sparse, for only one climb by George was recorded, Roof Route on Lliwedd, a Difficult first climbed by Young, Reade, and Andrews in 1907.

As yet another Charterhouse term approached, George saw that the scheme for starting a new school was losing its momentum. He now turned in another direction to find an outlet for his aspirations. The peace conferences that concluded the war had spawned a new international body, the League of Nations, which would supposedly prevent future conflicts. Although the League was fatally undermined by the refusal of the United States to take part, its opening sessions were conducted in a spirit that appealed to George, with talk of collective security, procedures to thwart aggression, and notions of world citizenship. He had maintained his interest in politics since leaving Cambridge, and his wartime letters to Ruth showed a shrewd grasp of the war aims of the respective national leaders and their maneuvers as the peace settlement approached. Both he and Ruth supported the Labour Party, and in December 1918 Ruth told him how impressed she had been by an election meeting in Godalming which had been chaired by Arthur Clutton-Brock. A Labour MP had made "just and reasonable" arguments for a Labour victory at the imminent general election and Clutton-Brock had talked of the "paramount importance" of the League of Nations. "His speech was good but I do not think he said much that you and I do not already feel strongly," Ruth told George.

On June 14, 1920, George sent a speculative letter to Gilbert Murray, the Regius Professor of Greek at Oxford University. Murray, a radical figure who was active in the women's suffrage movement as well as a climber, was secretary of the Union of the League of Nations, a voluntary pressure group formed to support the League of Nations. George asked Murray if the union "could find any use for my services—it is a cause which I want to serve, and I am prepared to give up my present job." He cited his experience as a lecturer and historian and his interest in literature and writing. "Perhaps the most important thing about me which I ought to tell you is that I think and feel passionately about international politics." The letter was couched in familiar terms, and referred to several mutual acquaintances by their first names, as well as to Murray's son Basil, who was then in his final year at Charterhouse. The letter revealed George's sense of urgency, for he offered to visit Murray in Oxford that weekend; and he had told Fletcher that if his application succeeded he could be leaving Charterhouse at the end of the summer term. However, the approach to Murray did not produce a job, although it may have had a bearing on a decision by George to visit Ireland at the end of the year.

At the end of term the Mallorys went on holiday with Avie and her growing family—she now had four children—at Trearddur Bay in Anglesey. On July 24 George departed for the Alps. Ruth was nearly eight months pregnant but George assured her that he would be back well before the baby was due. He went with Herbert Reade, Claude Elliott, and David Pye and, as in 1919, the trip was plagued by bad weather and his partners' infirmities. At fifty, Reade was feeling his age, Elliott was still troubled by his knee, and Pye dropped out of several climbs. Even so, George was in an ambitious frame of mind, leading his partners up to the Gamba hut beneath the south face of Mont Blanc, the wildest and most savage aspect of the mountain.

Pye later wrote that they had aimed to make the first ascent of the Innominata arête, although—unknown to him—it had in fact been climbed the previous year. George told Young, on the other hand, that they had hoped to follow the

Eccles couloir to the upper basin of the hanging Frêney glacier and from there ascend "by ribs west of Peuterey." If so, it was an audacious plan and one that was almost certainly out of reach at that time, for these were the Pillars of Frêney, the first of which was not climbed until 1940. They spent several days at the hut waiting in vain for the weather to clear before abandoning their attempt. By the time Pye and Elliott departed, they had climbed only the Aiguille de Talèfre and the Pré de Bar face of the Aiguille de Triolet, although both were satisfying routes.

One of George's most marked characteristics was his perseverance. In 1919 he had been intensely frustrated at failing to find new partners when Porter was afflicted with hemorrhoids. This time he persisted until he came upon George Finch, whom he had met at Pen y Pass in 1912. At thirty-two, Finch was regarded as one of the maverick figures of alpinism, both for his unconventional methods and for his long hair. Born in Australia, he had studied chemistry in Zurich and was awarded the MBE for his bomb-disposal work in Egypt during the war; later, he would be at the center of controversies over Everest in which George was involved. George teamed up with Finch and his companion Guy Forster to climb the Matterhorn and the Zinal Rothorn before they were compelled to spend another four days sitting out bad weather. Finch later recalled how restless George was at being thwarted. In the end he persuaded Finch and Forster to return to the Gamba hut for another attempt on his proposed new route, but they were again defeated by the weather.

George set off for home with mixed emotions. While he was disappointed at not having achieved more, he had been exhilarated at the wild mountain prospect from the Gamba, and filled with a sense that he had been "seeing" the mountains from a new perspective. They were no longer composed of fragmentary, disparate routes but were crystallizing into a wholeness, an essence, that he could read and grasp. Young came to a similar view of George's increasing maturity, describing it in a way that showed how the terminology of war was informing the language. Previously, Young wrote, George's approach to leadership had been to go "over the top" at the first impulse. Now he had acquired the wisdom of a battle-hardened officer in evaluating possibilities and risks.

George reached the Holt early in the morning of Saturday, August 21. He was half an hour late to greet his third child and first son, who was nearly two weeks premature. Ruth had been at Westbrook when her labor began and she was driven to the Holt in a neighbor's motor car. The midwife arrived with barely an hour to spare. The baby was named John. George, as he told Young, was far more moved than when his daughters were born. John was "a thumping great bruiser of a boy with fists and feet, a chin and very fat cheeks as salient features. We're highly delighted and Ruth is as bright and well as possible."

⚮

In December, George paid a visit to Ireland. Although his reason for doing so seemed clear, the precise impetus has never been established. His aim was to report on the reality of life at a time when Ireland was gripped by the "Terror," the battle between Irish republicanism, in the shape of Sinn Fein and the IRA, and the British government and its ruthless counterinsurgency force, the Black and Tans. The British, having developed their skills in black propaganda during the war, were highly adept in disseminating atrocity stories against the republican movement, and George declared that he wanted to find the truth. It may be that he was exploring the possibility of making a living as a writer: he and Ruth had now firmly decided that he should leave Charterhouse that summer, and the Irish trip gave him a chance to try his hand as a reporter. But the most recent evidence, unearthed by the historian Roger Croston, suggests that his trip may equally have stemmed from his approach to Gilbert Murray at the Union of the League of Nations in June. Both Murray and the union's management committee were closely following the issue of Irish home rule. The union's supporters were asking it to clarify its policy on home rule and it seems quite likely that Murray asked George to supply them with information to help the committee decide its line.

Whether as journalist, or political consultant, George possessed one priceless asset for his visit in the shape of good contacts. The Pen y Pass climber Conor O'Brien had been a republican gun-runner, using the boat George had sailed in during his visit to Ireland in the summer of 1913. O'Brien passed George on to leading figures such as Erskine Childers and Desmond Fitzgerald, who had been in prison with Eamon de Valera, the president of Sinn Fein. Fitzgerald was "director of propaganda" at the Dail, the provisional Irish government assembly, and he provided George a laissez-passer, writing an inscription on the back of a photograph of George which read: "Mr G. Mallory is anxious to have firsthand information as to acts of oppression and terror. I shall be glad if he can be assisted."

George arrived in Dublin on a Sunday morning, finding a deceptive air of calm. Although some buildings had been damaged, it did not compare with the destruction he had witnessed in France. But over the ensuing week he became acquainted with the insidious fear affecting the city. He was roused from his bed at 1:30 A.M. in a raid by British security forces, and saw the body of a child who had just been shot by excitable British troops. He was escorted on a trip into

165

rural areas where he met the families of republicans who had died fighting the British and heard about the summary executions performed by the Black and Tans. George's report was tighter and more economical than his recent climbing articles, and he ended it with a plea to understand both the justice and the passion of the republicans' cause. "We [should] think of Irishmen as human beings of like nature with ourselves and not a pack of savages and liars into the bargain," he wrote. It was true that violence had been used by both sides: "But how should men behave whose national spirit is being suppressed?"

There was no visible outcome of George's trip: his article was not published, and there is nothing in Murray's archives to show whether it ever reached his committee. This remains an academic question, for on January 23, 1921, George received a letter that changed his life. It came from Percy Farrar, the secretary—and former president—of the Alpine Club, who was also a member of the newly formed Mount Everest Committee. "It looks as though Everest would really be tried this summer," Farrar wrote. "Party would leave early April and get back in October. Any aspirations?"

CHAPTER TEN

The Opportunity of a Lifetime

1921

From the very start, Everest was a British affair. It was the British who established its height and the British who gave it its name. And it was the British who insisted they had the preeminent right to climb it, blocking other countries' attempts to do so for decades. For many of the surveyors, geographers, and climbers involved, it was a symbol of Britain's limitless colonial reach and a marker of British supremacy as a nation of explorers and mountaineers.

For George Mallory, it was more personal. He was cynical about many of the aspirations of the organizers of the first Everest expedition, who came from a different era and caste. For him Everest was, minimally, an opportunity to supplant the growing drudgery of his work as a schoolteacher and find the new direction to his life he was searching for. As a mountaineer, no summit he had ever seen remotely compared for grandeur and the challenge it represented. For the explorer of new worlds and new experiences, it represented the final frontier. But when George received his invitation to join the 1921 Everest expedition, he was not even sure that he should accept. And nor was Ruth.

The British who established the identity of the world's highest mountain were the officials of the Survey of India, methodically working their way across Britain's imperial possession with their calibrated chains, measuring rods, and theodolites in their task of completing what was known as the Great Trigonometrical Survey. They had long been curious about the height and location of the great snow peaks of Nepal, to India's north, which had been rumored to contain the world's highest mountain ever since infantry officers sent back crudely drawn charts and sketch maps in the first years of the nineteenth century. But the surveyors were banned from entering Nepal, as its rulers feared that they were the vanguard of an attempt to annex the country as Britain's latest colonial outpost.

The surveyors had to make their observations from a mosquito-infested tract of northern India known as the Terai. The problems were immense: the mountains were up to 150 miles away and often blanketed with clouds, and many of the surveyors died of malaria or had to be invalided home. In 1849 a surveyor named John Nicholson, using a theodolite so large that it required twelve men to carry it, made a series of sightings of what was suspected to be the highest peak. Nicholson's boss, Surveyor General Andrew Waugh, took a further seven years to check his measurements, making due allowances for the problems of light diffraction and variations of heat and barometric pressure. In 1856 he finally calculated that the peak's altitude was 29,002 feet: "higher than any hitherto measured in India," Waugh declared, and "most probably the highest in the world." (The measurements have withstood the test of time. Surveys by the Indian government in the 1950s, working from far closer than their predecessors of a hundred years before, produced a figure of 29,028 feet. The most recent figure published by the American National Geographical Society and based on global positioning satellites yielded a marginally revised height of 29,035 feet.)

Now that the British had identified the world's highest mountain, the next question was how it should be named. The Survey officials were keen to preserve local names, not least because it helped avert suspicion that the Survey was a mere appendage of British rule. There were several strong local candidates: the name Chomolungma, Tibetan for Goddess Mother of the World, had been current for centuries, and had appeared—as Tschoumou-Lanckma—on a map published in Paris in the 1730s. Other names, including Devadhunka and Chingopamari, had appeared in ancient Nepalese texts. But the Survey's naming committee professed itself unable to decide between these alternatives and so Waugh made the call, announcing that he would "name it after my illustrious predecessor"—the previous surveyor general, George Everest. Everest, a resolute if sometimes intolerant figure, was appalled by the proposal, as he too believed that the British had no right to impose their names on the geography of the region. He told the Royal Geographical Society (RGS), which decided these issues on behalf of the British government, that the word Everest could not be written in Hindi or even pronounced by Indians. But the RGS would not be deterred, and Everest it was. It remained the predominant name until the 1960s, when the Chinese revived Chomolungma, which is increasingly used today.

The British effectively staked the first claim to climb Everest when Clinton Dent, an Alpine Club president, declared in his book *Above the Snow Line* that, although the mountain was remote and any attempt could prove both expensive and dangerous, these obstacles should not deter "the ambitious mountaineer." Dent went on to predict that Everest would be climbed in his own lifetime. (Since he died, at age sixty-two, in 1912, he was forty-one years out.)

The first British climber to consider an attempt was the explorer, adventurer, and diplomat Francis Younghusband, who laid plans in 1893 to reconnoiter the mountain's approaches with a young Gurkha lieutenant named Charles Bruce. The plans came to nothing, but in 1903–04 Younghusband led a military mission to Tibet that secured the Dalai Lama's allegiance to Britain in its territorial rivalries with Russia and China. Younghusband used the opportunity to dispatch two of his officers to western Tibet, enabling them to examine Everest from the north. They saw the north face from a distance of sixty miles and thought it would be possible to climb the north ridge. Another of Younghusband's team, the political officer Claude White, took a photograph of Everest from the fortress town of Kampa Dzong, ninety-three miles away, the first in which Everest was clearly identified. When Younghusband camped at Kampa Dzong, he described how from his tent he could see dawn breaking over Everest, "poised high in heaven as the spotless pinnacle of the world."

The mission's success in establishing British precedence in Tibet, for which Younghusband was knighted, ensured that no other country's mountaineers would be allowed to approach Everest from the north until well after the Second World War. Ironically, it thwarted any British attempts in the next ten years too on the grounds of what Secretary of State for India John Morley called "considerations of high Imperial policy"—namely that any incursion by British mountaineers could threaten the delicate political balance of the region. British mountaineers were climbing elsewhere in the Himalaya during this time, reaching heights of around 23,000 feet, although it was an Italian expedition that had the most impressive achievement of the prewar era when the Duke of the Abruzzi reached 24,600 feet on K2—the second-highest mountain—in 1909. In general the new scale of mountaineering, with the distances, the climate, the sheer size of the mountains, only slowly dawned on these Himalayan pioneers. Their clothing was little better than they had worn in the Alps, and although they became familiar with the declining ratio of oxygen in the air no one had yet gone high enough for this to be a decisive factor.

In 1913 British interest in Everest was revived when a young army officer, John Noel, made an illicit foray into Tibet disguised as an Indian pilgrim. He obtained one tantalizing glimpse of its summit from sixty miles away, "a glittering spire of rock fluted with snow." Although Noel was an expert photographer, he was unable to take a picture because of the high winds. In 1914 he was one of a group of climbers and surveyors who started to plan a two-stage attempt on Everest, a reconnaissance followed by a full-scale attempt, to take place in 1915 and 1916. They were backed by the Royal Geographical Society and the Alpine Club, who prepared a diplomatic offensive to overcome the objections of the British government. All further preparations came to a halt in August 1914.

It has been argued that the attempts on Everest in the 1920s had a redemptive quality, an attempt to salvage something from the slaughter of the First World War and atone for the loss of such a staggering proportion of Britain's manhood. It can equally be argued that for the Everest enthusiasts the war represented merely an inconvenient hiatus, for it was only a few weeks after the armistice in 1918 that the Royal Geographical Society and the Alpine Club resumed their diplomatic efforts, asking the new secretary of state for India for permission to make a fresh attempt. Once again they were turned down, but the RGS and the Alpine Club were not to be thwarted, and embarked on a twin-track policy of preparing an expedition and tackling the political problems simultaneously. The diplomatic track was entrusted to Charles Howard-Bury, an old Etonian and former army officer of aristocratic lineage with a large estate at Mullingar in Ireland, who had offered to go to India and Tibet at his own expense. He spent almost six months hustling, cajoling, sweet-talking his way around officials and dignitaries. He tried to mediate an arms deal with the Tibetan government to secure its approval but the deal was blocked by the Indian government. He attempted to persuade the Handley Page air service to lay on a reconnaissance flight in return for publicity, but that too foundered. In the end Howard-Bury simply made so much of a nuisance of himself that the British political officer in Tibet went to meet the Dalai Lama to obtain his consent. The expedition was on.

A celebratory meeting staged by the Royal Geographical Society in December 1920 provides a tenor of the spirit with which the news was greeted. Younghusband, whose observations on the natural world tended towards mysticism, pitched it in grandiose terms, declaring that the expedition would help "rid ourselves of the ridiculous idea of the littleness of man in comparison with mountains." The president of the Alpine Club, Norman Collie, pointed out that no white man had been within forty or fifty miles of Everest, and that the surrounding country was unknown. Now the Alpine Club should take its due. Its members had "taught the way to climb mountains," and so it should be "not only English people, but members of the Alpine Club, who must have the first say in the matter of climbing Everest, the highest mountain in the world." When the RGS formally announced the prospective expedition on January 10, 1921, the press reflected the speakers' euphoria. "On Top of the World—Britishers' Great Adventure," trumpeted the *Daily News*. Collie's speech had provided the best sound bite and several newspapers headlined the phrase: "Where White Man Has Never Trod."

⁂

It was just thirteen days later that George received his letter from Percy Farrar, one of eight members of the newly formed Mount Everest Committee, sounding him out over joining the expedition. It was not entirely unexpected, for Geoffrey Young had been following events in the higher reaches of the Alpine Club and had tried to arouse George's interest in Everest during the Pen y Pass party of Easter 1919. It was almost certainly Young who recommended George to the Alpine Club, but when the letter arrived George hesitated, and it was all too clear why. He had already been separated from Ruth for sixteen months during the war and knew only too well how much anxiety she had suffered, despite his attempts to minimize the risk. Now they had three growing children and a home that he loved. He also had doubts about the viability of the expedition and the flag-waving with which it had been launched. He told his sister Avie that he wondered whether it was all "a merely fantastic performance" and made clear to David Pye the scale of the decision confronting him: "I am faced with a problem which throws all others into the background—Everest."

At this watershed in George's life, Geoffrey Young intervened. His own perspective on the expedition was tinged with regret, for he would have been a leading contender for one of the climbing places and even briefly wondered if he could take part on his artificial leg. Since that was out of the question, George offered the best alternative as his protégé and a youthful surrogate through whom he could live the experience. When Young learned of George's hesitation he paid a visit to the Holt, where George told him that he intended to defer to Ruth's wishes and turn down Farrar's invitation. Tactfully but inexorably, Young laid out the advantages of taking part. During a twenty-minute conversation he talked of "the label of Everest," a reference to the cachet Everest would bring, especially if George should reach the summit. This renown would help George in whatever career he chose, including education if he decided to remain in that field. "Ruth saw what I meant," Young wrote. "She told him to go."

George's moment of truth came on February 9, when he met three of the most significant figures in the venture. One was Sir Francis Younghusband, who now chaired the Mount Everest Committee. The second was the expedition's climbing leader, Harold Raeburn, who had put up some of the classic routes on Ben Nevis, including Observatory Ridge and Observatory Buttress, and had been to the

Himalaya the previous year. The third was Farrar himself. Over lunch Younghusband formally invited George to join the expedition. Somewhat gravely, George accepted, puzzling Younghusband that he did so "without visible emotion" and was not "bursting with enthusiasm." Younghusband was in fact seeing George in the mode that characterized his first encounter with new people and a new world: observe, evaluate before you commit. George revealed more of his feelings, among them a hint of his persistent reservations, when he wrote to Young the next day. "It seems rather a momentous step altogether, with a new job to find when I come back, but it will not be a bad thing to give up the settled ease of this present life . . . I expect I shall have no cause to regret your persuasion in the cause of Mount Everest. At present, I'm highly elated at the prospect, and so is Ruth—thank you for that." He told Avie that it was "the opportunity of a lifetime."

With barely two months to go before his departure, George had much to do. His first move was to tell Fletcher that he was leaving Charterhouse at the end of term. While working out his notice, he had to assemble his equipment—and deal with the problems that stemmed from the composition of the Mount Everest Committee and the foibles of its secretary, Arthur Hinks, who had been seconded to the post from his job as full-time secretary of the RGS.

While the Alpine Club and the Royal Geographical Society had agreed to pool their energies into what was effectively a combined operation, the expedition was vulnerable to the problems such operations usually produce, including conflicting aims and personal rivalries. To the RGS, the most important task was to survey the area around Everest and produce the best possible map of the mountain and its approaches. (The only map to date, drawn up by the Younghusband mission and covering the region to the north, stopped some forty miles short.) Of the nine men who would comprise the expedition (and there was absolutely no question of selecting any women), three would be surveyors, to be nominated by the RGS, and a fourth, doubling as a doctor, would be a naturalist. They were clear in their minds that the 1921 expedition was a surveying trip, with a full-scale mountaineering attempt to follow, probably in 1922. To the Alpine Club, by contrast, the task of surveying was a precursor to the paramount goal of going to the top of Everest. The club had the right to appoint four climbers—one of these too was a doctor—and while they were ready to acknowledge the surveyors' aims, they were there to climb Everest. They viewed the plan for a second expedition as a fall-back device, to be brought into play if they did not reach the summit in 1921.

In the overall scheme of things it was probably the surveyors who had the edge, a judgment reflected in the committee's choice of Howard-Bury as expedition leader. He had impressive credentials, for as well as having secured the Dalai Lama's permission for the expedition, he had traveled in Asia, had been a professional soldier, and had escaped from the Germans after being taken prisoner at Ypres, although recaptured and held for the rest of the war. His main personal interest was in exploration, and he was certainly not a mountaineer. And, as he knew himself, he was a stopgap leader, for the committee had really wanted Charles Bruce, the former Gurkha lieutenant, by then a general, who had discussed an attempt on Everest with Younghusband almost thirty years before. Bruce had just accepted a new military appointment and had to turn down the opportunity, although he did so on the understanding that he would lead a second expedition if one proved necessary.

It was not long before these difficulties impinged on George. On February 18 he received a pro forma letter from Hinks that raised issues of vital concern to him and Ruth. It also led him into a wounding personal battle with Hinks, an irascible, dogmatic, and intolerant man who disliked climbers and did his best to favor the RGS faction on the Mount Everest Committee, where he frequently clashed with Farrar, who staunchly defended the interests of the Alpine Club.

The letter first required George to agree to be bound by the wishes of the expedition leader, Howard-Bury: put bluntly, he was to obey orders. This troubled George, as he felt that on the mountain Raeburn should be calling the shots, and he made his priorities clear in his reply to Hinks. "I understand that while reconnaissance is the first mountaineering object, an attempt is to be made to scale Mount Everest this year provided that, in the opinion of Mr Raeburn, such an attempt can be made without jeopardising the chances of success next year; and that my services will be used in this attempt unless I am pronounced physically unfit by the medical officer."

The second issue was, in its potential effect on the lives of both George and Ruth, far more serious. Hinks had stipulated that expedition members were "to hold no communication whatever with the press, with no photographic news agencies or with any cinematograph company, and that no undertaking shall be entered into to publish any book or other writing upon the expedition until a specified time after publication of the official account." Hinks's concern was to some extent understandable, as the committee was negotiating a deal for exclusive coverage with *The Times* and a book contract with the London publishers Edward Arnold. But he also nurtured considerable personal animus against journalists, whom he dubbed "sharks and pirates," a barely necessary evil who ranked even lower than climbers.

Hinks's attempt to stifle all publicity was misplaced, since the expedition required public support, not least in its need to raise funds. For George and Ruth, the issue was all-important, since George hoped to base a future career on writing about his exploits; and here was Hinks attempting to suppress any such enterprise until an unknown date which remained in the committee's gift. Hinks's attitude reflected an astonishing insouciance towards the practicalities of everyday life, further exposed when he asked George whether he wanted the expedition to pay for his boat ticket to India. Hinks came from the world of the gentleman traveler, exemplified by the expedition leader Howard-Bury, who had agreed to pay all his own costs. The surveyors themselves were salaried employees of the Survey of India and its counterpart, the Geological Survey of India. George, by comparison, would be receiving no pay or other income while he was away, and it was only by grace of Ruth's allowance from her father that he could afford to join the expedition at all.

In a longer letter to Younghusband on March 11, he spelled out his anxieties over not being able to write about the expedition. He pointed out that the proposed agreement was unclear and had no time limit: and was he really being asked to submit anything he did write to the committee for approval? It was Hinks who replied to George, and his letter showed no sympathy for George's concerns. "It is impossible to make a definite detailed agreement, and I am sure you will realise this and be content to rely on being treated with every consideration." In other words, Hinks was saying, trust us. George swallowed his anxieties and duly signed the agreement, but his trust in "being treated with every consideration" was to be sorely abused.

George was booked to sail from Tilbury on the SS *Sardinia* on April 8. But as March went on, further problems arose. Hinks was niggling away at the cost of the climbers' equipment, including not only their boots and protective clothing but also their sleeping bags. He paid them only £50 ($192.00) as an advance, roughly half what was needed, leaving them to put up the rest of the cash themselves. It took the combined intervention of Farrar and Younghusband to persuade him to be less miserly: after all, as Farrar pointed out, "the risks of this expedition are at least as great as those of a Polar expedition" and they would be open to criticism if they tried to economize on the equipment for the men who would be making "the final push."

On March 17, George had a medical examination in Harley Street. He passed it on all counts: his physique was considered "well developed," there was no trace of a heart murmur or other irregularity, following the problem he had experienced in 1911, and the doctor concluded, "This man is in every respect fit." It was George Finch, one of George's three fellow climbers, who was the focus of the problems. Finch had financial anxieties that were more acute than George's, the result of hideously complicated personal difficulties. In 1918 he had divorced his wife after she had an affair. He was awarded custody of their son Peter—the future cinema actor—although it was not clear whether it was Finch or the lover who was his father. When Finch was selected for the expedition, he was employed as a chemistry lecturer in London, and was awarded six months' unpaid leave. His greatest concern, so he told Farrar, was for his son in case he was killed during the expedition—although rather than admit that he was divorced, with all the attendant social stigma of the age, he told Farrar that his wife had died, and that he was a widower. Farrar recommended that the expedition should insure Finch's life for £5000 ($19,200.00) at a cost to the committee of £75 ($288.00).

This apart, Finch was seen as an outsider. Not only had he been born in Australia but he had lived for a long time—as a result of further family entanglements—in Switzerland. He also had long hair. Now thirty-three, he had been chosen for the expedition on the strength of his alpine record (having climbed with him the previous summer, George approved the choice) and because he was one of the few climbers to have studied the difficulties caused by the lack of oxygen at high altitude. When Younghusband told Finch he had been selected, he replied: "Sir Francis, you've just sent me to heaven." But to Hinks especially he was an irritant and a prime example of the problems that climbers could create. Finch was given his medical examination on March 17, the same day as Mallory. To his astonishment, he was rejected as unfit, and the committee told him his invitation to join the expedition had been withdrawn.

The committee's decision was highly peremptory: the main objection of the doctor who examined Finch was that he appeared tired and anemic. A few days later Finch took part in an experiment at Oxford to measure his stamina at high altitudes. He was found to have an exceptional lung capacity, certainly exceeding that of the two other climbers, Harold Raeburn and a second Scotsman, Alexander Kellas, who were both in their fifties and had been selected principally because they had previously climbed in the Himalaya. But a significant faction of the committee had taken against Finch and it concluded that it was better rid of him after all.

George was appalled. His sympathy for Finch himself was mixed: he was "rather a gamble," George told Young; "he didn't look fit." What did dismay George was that in Finch he had lost his strongest—and youngest—partner. Raeburn had already confessed that he expected to go no higher than 25,000 feet and Kellas was unlikely to do any better, leaving just two, himself and Finch, for "the final part." George added that at times he felt "complete pessimism as to our chances of getting up—or of getting back with toes on our feet."

Just two weeks remained before George was due to leave. But when he heard that the committee was proposing to replace Finch with yet another middle-aged Scotsman, Bill Ling, a friend of Raeburn who was age forty-eight, he wrote to Hinks in protest. Ling, George said bluntly, was too old, and would lack the stamina for "the final push . . . we ought to give ourselves the best possible chance . . . when the critical time arrives." George went on to raise doubts that exposed the ambiguities of the expedition's aims. "I have all along regarded the party as barely strong enough for a venture of this kind with the enormous demands it is certain to make on both nerve and physique." He alluded to his predicament over Ruth and even hinted that he might resign: "You will understand that I must look after myself in this matter. I'm a married man and I can't go into it bald-headed."

George's letter, touching on issues that Hinks wished to be left undisturbed, produced a vituperative response. "I don't think that you need feel under any anxiety about your own position, because you will be under the orders of very experienced mountaineers who will take care not to call upon you for jobs that can't be done," Hinks thundered. He complained that George had been talking to Farrar, claiming that George had "imbibed" Farrar's view—"which is hardly that of anybody else"—that the main aim of the 1921 expedition was to climb Mount Everest. "We have seen enough of him at the Committee to learn that he frequently talks at random," Hinks declared.

George did not rise to Hinks's bait. Instead he wrote a witty and conciliatory letter that also proposed a solution to the crisis. To fill the last place, George recommended his fellow founder member of the Winchester Ice Club, Guy Bullock. He was "a scholar and a very good runner . . . a tough sort of fellow who never lost his head" and a man of "extraordinary stamina." He would be "a valuable man in the party, level headed and competent all around—a man in whom one would feel confidence in an emergency as one of the least likely of men to crack." For George he did indeed represent an excellent alternative to Finch. He was not as technically accomplished, and lacked Finch's flair: rather than a partnership of equals, it would be one where George led the way, knowing he could rely on Bullock's qualities of perseverance and reliability. He did his best to boost Bullock's claims, saying that he had been roaming the world in his work with the British consular service, with postings in the United States, Africa, and South America; and that he was fit, having "played football" up to six months before. His greatest advantage, however, was probably that, having just returned to Britain, he could take up to six months' leave at just a few days' notice. Farrar was troubled by George's recommendation, since Bullock was far from the top-rank climber the Alpine Club had wanted. But to the rest of the committee, Bullock was the deus ex machina solution they craved. Bullock was approached, found fit and willing, and the team was complete.

With just a week to go, George prepared to leave Ruth, their children, and the Holt once again. It was a replay of his departures during the war, when he had said goodbye to Ruth three times, and she had not known whether she would see him again. Warring within Ruth were, on the one side, her feelings of imminent loneliness and loss, and on the other her stoicism and her instinctive empathetic sense that whatever was right for George was right for both of them. They said goodbye on the morning of April 8 and by that evening George was aboard the *Sardinia* in the English Channel. He had a lonely voyage in prospect since his eight fellow expedition members had already departed or were in India already, leaving him to bring up the rear with a consignment of equipment and baggage. In his first full letter home, written as the *Sardinia* approached Malta, he told Ruth she had been as "cheerful and brave" as ever, but knew she must have been depressed when they parted. "I can't tell you how utterly hateful I found the first days on board. I longed to have you with me—but I'm no longer still depressed—and hated the thought of our separation." He pictured her at the Holt, with the afternoon sun streaming into the loggia, "doing this and that."

It is at this point in the George Mallory story that perhaps the greatest evidential mystery for biographers arrives. Simply put, where are Ruth's letters? During the three Everest expeditions she wrote to George as faithfully as ever, and he responded to her news in his replies, just as he had during the war. Yet only one of these letters has survived, the first she wrote after his last departure in March 1924. There is one clue to the possible fate of the letters, for Ruth told George during the war that whereas she thought it important to preserve his letters, she did not hold the same view of hers. But that is hardly enough to explain why all but one of her Everest letters should have vanished while all those from the war years have been preserved. David Robertson, author of the 1969 biography, who was married to George's daughter Berry, told us he considered it a mystery too. In 1951, seven years after Ruth died, he and Berry took possession of Ruth's papers; tragically, Berry died just two years later. When Robertson completed his biography, he and John Mallory—George's son—agreed to deposit all letters between George and Ruth in the library of Magdalene College, Cambridge. Robertson suggested that Ruth may not have preserved her letters to George on the grounds that she considered them "far less interesting and important than George's to her. There was no self-importance in her." We have speculated endlessly over why the letters should have gone missing but have no evidence to support any of our theories. The one saving grace is that it is sometimes possible to infer the contents of Ruth's letters from George's replies.

George viewed the five-week voyage to Calcutta as an adventure in itself. His descriptions to Ruth ranged from the details of the seating arrangements at dinner, held punctually at 7 P.M., to his own inner journey as the *Sardinia* progressed from the gray swell of the English Channel to the vastness of the Indian Ocean. George's first preoccupation was with his fellow passengers, and his initial judgment, reflecting an instinctive social disdain to which he was prone, was that where his fellow first-class passengers were concerned it would have been impossible to assemble "43 people with less intellectual life about them." He considered min-gling with the second-class passengers, but told Ruth that the ship's layout made them hard to reach. He was intrigued by a mysterious Englishman who he sus-pected had belonged to the Black and Tans, but discovered he was traveling to India on business. He took against the ship's captain but later conceded that he could be a "gay raconteur." He participated in deck games and joined a bridge school in the evening. He ran around the deck regularly and told Ruth: "I expect to arrive in India as fit as a fiddle."

At other times he retreated into his solitary mode, just as he had while stay-ing with the Bussys, snuggling with a book or his writing pad into a hidden corner in the bows, overlooking the crew's washing line. He watched for the passing mountains, noting possible climbing routes on the Rock of Gibraltar, and enjoying the sight of the Atlas Mountains of Morocco, with several fine peaks and plenty of snow. He was relieved at not feeling seasick during a storm in the eastern Mediterranean, surprised that the twelve-hour passage through the Suez Canal was so dull, and moved by the skyscapes as they steamed southwards into the gentle swell of the Indian Ocean, with giant thunderclouds building up "like a stupendous vault." When the *Sardinia* stopped in Colombo—"a place carved out of the jungle"—he sent the children some lace collars and a seed necklace he bought in the dockside market.

When George revealed his feelings to Ruth, he too seemed to have been sensi-tized by their being apart again so soon after his return from the war. "I think I have wanted you more during this voyage than at any other time when we have been separated," he told her on May 2—one day after the seventh anniversary of their engagement in 1914. Whereas during the war their letters reached each other in two or three days, this time they would take four weeks or more to arrive, although Ruth would also be able to read the reports of the expedition written by Howard-Bury and telegraphed from Darjeeling to *The Times*. George told her that he felt closer to her than ever, a feeling that had strengthened since John was born. In a curious aside, which suggested that Ruth had been prone to jealousy, he as-sured her that she need have no anxieties about any of the women passengers, for not even "the circumstances of the voyage will greatly interest me in anyone else."

Sometimes he fell into a pessimistic mood, telling Ruth that when he watched the bows of the *Sardinia* slice their way through the ocean, he had premonitions of danger. The sea was as "deeply evil" as it was attractive: "It is curious how much I have a sense of the nearness of danger." In a letter to Robert Graves he admitted he had no idea what he would do on his return from Everest. He sus-pected that he did not have the talent or dedication to make a living as writer, and wondered whether he should look for a lecturing post at a provincial university.

Ruth, he told Graves, was "bravely content to be comparatively poor for a time, but I must make some money one of these days."

⚬

The *Sardinia* docked in Calcutta on May 10. Howard-Bury had promised to send a ship's agent to oversee the unloading of the expedition equipment but he did not turn up and George had to supervise the matter himself. He made the eighteen-hour train journey north to Darjeeling, where, to his relief, he found the first letters from Ruth. Her biggest problem, he learned, was a shortage of fuel resulting from further labor disputes in the British coal mines; George did his best to reassure her and told her: "I have read all your news with enormous pleasure. Your letters do bring you much nearer. It is very nice to feel the children think of me."

The expedition members met en masse for the first time over a formal dinner staged by Lord Ronaldshay, the Governor of Bengal. Clad in his full dress regalia, he solemnly shook each of them by the hand, while the serving staff, adorned in long red coats with gold and silver braid, stood by. The dinner gave George his first opportunity to evaluate his colleagues, and he described them to Ruth in a series of brisk judgments in his ensuing letters. He had warmed to Kellas from the moment he arrived for the Governor's dinner ten minutes late and in a disheveled state, with his "giglamp" spectacles and his long parted moustache. In general George liked the surveying team: Morshead was "nice and unassuming," Wollaston "devoted and disinterested"; Heron, by contrast, was dull, and George had to overcome an instinctive dislike of Wheeler because he was Canadian. His heaviest strictures were directed at his two leaders: Howard-Bury, the high Tory, dogmatic, intolerant, and opinionated; and Raeburn, irritating, unappreciative, wrong-headed, and dictatorial. Most troubling of all was the fact that Howard-Bury and Raeburn were already finding it hard to tolerate each other and frequently clashed in their views.

And so the great caravan set off, divided into two parts. There were four Europeans to each (the ninth, Morshead, had left early to start his surveying), together with fifty mules and their muleteers, several cooks and translators, and twenty porters—described as coolies—who had been recruited in Darjeeling from the Sherpa people who came from the Everest region of Nepal. George was alert to the sights, sounds, and senses of the new landscapes, from the semijungle of Sikkim to the great Tibetan plain with its fortresses set precariously on steep, sharp mountain ridges. Through all the difficulties—the mud and rain of Sikkim, the scouring wind of Tibet, the dysentery and diarrhea, the growing antagonism between Howard-Bury and Raeburn, the cultural dissonance between the ways of

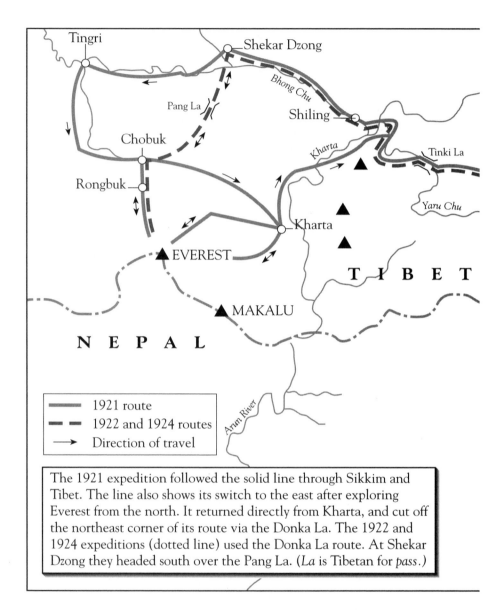

The 1921 expedition followed the solid line through Sikkim and
Tibet. The line also shows its switch to the east after exploring
Everest from the north. It returned directly from Kharta, and cut off
the northeast corner of its route via the Donka La. The 1922 and
1924 expeditions (dotted line) used the Donka La route. At Shekar
Dzong they headed south over the Pang La. (*La* is Tibetan for *pass*.)

the Europeans and their porters—George maintained his curiosity and spirit of
adventure. He peered inside the flat-roofed homes in the settlements they passed
and photographed the buildings and the people. He enjoyed the rituals of dining
as guests of the jongpens, the Tibetan community leaders. One served bowls of
dumplings accompanied by a soup and a dish of chili sauce, George eventually
discovering that he was supposed to immerse the dumplings in the soup and add a

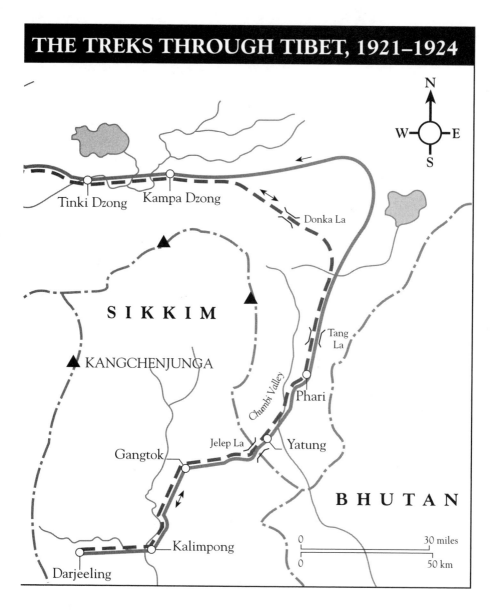

THE TREKS THROUGH TIBET, 1921–1924

Tinki Dzong Kampa Dzong

Donka La

SIKKIM

KANGCHENJUNGA

Tang
La

Chumbi Valley

Phari

Jelep La Yatung

Gangtok

BHUTAN

Kalimpong

Darjeeling

0   30 miles

0   50 km

dash of sauce. The food on the trek gradually improved: one jongpen gave them three sheep and a hundred eggs, and Howard-Bury and Bullock went out to shoot whatever local fauna they could, including some geese and a type of wild sheep.

When problems arose George dealt with them, just as he had during the war, by managing his emotions, flattening his responses to make them tolerable. "We just go drifting along," he told Ruth. He handled Howard-Bury by steering him away from sensitive topics of conversation and told Ruth that since he was a keen mountaineer and a lover of flowers, "there must be some good in him." He found Raeburn harder to deal with but, discerning that he liked to dispense advice, dutifully walked alongside him asking questions that drew on his knowledge of the Himalaya. George had the safety valve of his letters to Ruth, although he reserved his gloomier thoughts for his other correspondents, just as he had during the war. He was also establishing a construct or storyline for his experiences, visualizing the landscape ahead as the expedition approached the Yaru gorge and selecting the probable vantage point for his first full view of Everest, which he later built into his account for the expedition book. When dysentery hit the expedition, George's letter to Ruth evoked the pathos of Kellas's death: "It seemed to me a very tragic end today as none of us were with him when he died. His body is lying in a tent now and we shall bury him tomorrow or the next day in sight of the three great mountains ascended." Even so, when Raeburn was forced to withdraw through illness the following day, George was ready to take up his role as climbing leader. At first he was pessimistic, reckoning that the chances of climbing Everest were slim. But as he evaluated the forces at his disposal, with Morshead a candidate to replace the two missing climbers, he became more hopeful. He felt more confident as he selected the porters who would have to be trained for high-level load-ferrying on snow. "This begins to feel like business," he told Ruth, adding, as they ventured into the territory beyond the Younghusband map: "Don't be hopeless about the expedition; we may yet do very well."

On June 19 the expedition reached Tingri, a village set in a broad stony plain with the upper pyramid of Everest visible across a line of blue hills some forty miles to the southeast. This was to be their base for the next month, and Howard-Bury set up a camp in best military fashion, with tents, a trestle table, a canteen area, and a dark room to develop the photographs that the climbers and surveyors would be sending back. Here the team would be dividing, Wheeler and Morshead photographing and measuring the Everest approaches, Heron collecting his rock samples, Wollaston searching for insects, rodents, birds, and flowers. The climbing team—all two of it—would be heading directly for the mountain with the aim of identifying the best possible climbing route.

George and Bullock left Tingri on June 23, accompanied by a cook, a sirdar or porter leader, and sixteen porters each equipped with climbing boots, ice axes, and a set of woolen underwear. The following day, as they came near the monastery that lies on the approach to the Rongbuk Glacier, which flows down from the north face of Everest, they saw the mountain in its elemental splendor. "We paused here in sheer astonishment," George wrote. "Perhaps we had half expected to see Mount Everest at this moment. In the back of my mind were a host

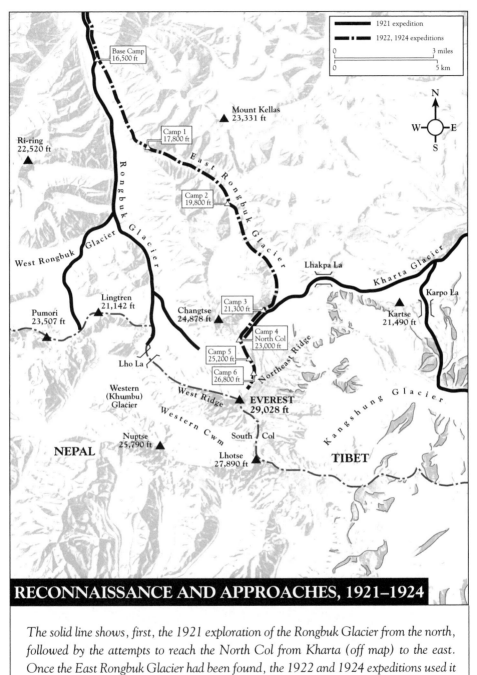

Legend:
- ▬▬▬ 1921 expedition
- ▬·▬·▬ 1922, 1924 expeditions

0 _____ 3 miles
0 _____ 5 km

Base Camp
16,500 ft

Mount Kellas
▲ 23,331 ft

Ri-ring
22,520 ft
▲

Camp 1
17,800 ft

Rongbuk Glacier

East Rongbuk Glacier

Camp 2
19,800 ft

West Rongbuk Glacier

Lhakpa La

Kharta Glacier

Karpo La

Lingtren
21,142 ft

Changtse
24,878 ft ▲

Camp 3
21,300 ft

Kartse
21,490 ft
▲

Pumori
23,507 ft
▲

Camp 4
North Col
23,000 ft

Northeast Ridge

Lho La

Camp 5
25,200 ft

Camp 6
26,800 ft

Western
(Khumbu)
Glacier

West Ridge

▲ EVEREST
29,028 ft

South Col

Kangshung Glacier

Western Cwm

NEPAL

Nuptse
25,790 ft ▲

Lhotse
27,890 ft ▲

TIBET

N
W ── ⊕ ── E
S

RECONNAISSANCE AND APPROACHES, 1921–1924

The solid line shows, first, the 1921 exploration of the Rongbuk Glacier from the north, followed by the attempts to reach the North Col from Kharta (off map) to the east. Once the East Rongbuk Glacier had been found, the 1922 and 1924 expeditions used it to approach the North Col from the north.

of questions about it clamouring for answers. But the sight of it now banished every thought. We forgot the stony wastes and regrets for other beauties. We asked no questions and made no comments, but simply looked."

The mountain, still sixteen miles away, was not a peak of the kind he knew from the Alps but a "prodigious mountain mass . . . a great bluntly pointed snow peak with a much steeper north face than people have made out." It had "the most stupendous ridges and appalling precipices that I have ever seen . . . all the talk of easy snowslopes is a myth." It had a strangely alluring air, for the face was flanked by two great ridges, the northeast and the west, which appeared like beckoning arms: "the limbs of a giant, simple, severe, and superb," was how he described them to Ruth. Between them the north face rose for 9,000 to 10,000 feet, and looked quite unassailable. "From the mountaineer's point of view so far as we have seen it no more appalling sight could be imagined."

Since tackling the north face head-on was clearly out of the question, the task for George and Bullock was to find an alternative possibility. They set up their own base camp, at a height of 16,500 feet at the foot of the Rongbuk Glacier. They placed a second camp, which they called advance base or Camp 1, two miles further up the glacier at a height of 17,800 feet beside a stream which flowed from a mound of moraine. They spent the next three weeks working their way among the great network of glaciers, the Rongbuk and its outlying branches, that flowed from the mountain's northern and western flanks. To begin with, as George acknowledged, they were suffering from the shock of encountering glaciers that were far more complex and potentially dangerous than those they knew from the Alps. They were full of bewildering fifty-foot ice pinnacles called *penitentes* and sudden pools of meltwater. It felt as if it were a maze and he was the White Rabbit: "No course seemed to lead anywhere." He and Bullock deduced that the best place to walk was along the moraine beside the glaciers but the heat of the sun reflected from the ice, together with working at this unaccustomed altitude, took its toll. At the day's end, George wrote, "it was a new sensation to find it an almost impossible exertion to drag oneself up a matter of 150 feet."

At first their prognosis for finding a route to the summit was gloomy: the closer they went to the north face, the more daunting it seemed. Then they focused on a broad ridge on the eastern side of the Rongbuk Glacier that descended northwards from Everest to an outlying peak, which they dubbed the North Peak, later known as Changtse. At around 23,000 feet there was a dip in the ridge which they called the North Col. They reckoned that if they could reach the North Col they could follow the north ridge—"a sort of rock rib," according to George—to its junction with Everest's northeast ridge. Above there, the northeast ridge was "comparatively flat and snowy," while the summit itself was "rock at a moderately easy angle." Once on the North Col, George reasoned, "I think it might go."

There was one great difficulty: the ice slope leading up from the Rongbuk Glacier to the North Col was crisscrossed with rifts and crevasses and looked both difficult and dangerous. In a search for alternatives, and to ensure they had covered every possibility, George and Bullock decided to explore the glaciers to the west of the mountain. They pushed down a tributary that they called the West Rongbuk Glacier, climbed to the crest of a ridge between two lesser peaks, Lingtren and Pumori, and surmounted a col, the Lho La, on the western edge of the main Rongbuk Glacier. They were thus the first climbers to look into a great ice valley below Everest's southwest face which they named the West or Western Cwm: "terribly cold and forbidding," George wrote, "under the shadow of Everest." They were looking into the future, for this was the route taken by the British expedition of 1953 on its way to the first ascent via the South Col and the southeast ridge. Mallory believed that the southeast ridge offered the easiest route but could see no prospect of reaching it: the 1500-foot descent to the Western Cwm was "a hopeless precipice" and the top of the adjoining Khumbu icefall, which they called the Western Glacier, was "terribly steep and broken." It was pointless prospecting any further to the south as the approaches would lie through Nepal, which was forbidden territory.

As hope alternated with disappointment, George's moods went through concomitant swings. To Ruth, he was almost ecstatic, telling her, "This is a thrilling business altogether—I can't tell you how it possesses me." He lamented that it was Bullock, not her, lying beside him in their tent: "Come close to me at least in spirit dearest—as you shall be all night." To his mother, he admitted feeling homesick. "So much still lies in front before we can turn our faces homewards . . . I don't like being separated from my roots; and if it's a long separation for me, isn't it longer for Ruth—in spite of all her energy for running the home?" He offered Farrar a pessimistic appraisal: "We have a formidable job—I've hardly the dimmest hopes of reaching the top, but of course one proceeds as though we meant to get there." He imparted his bleakest view to Rupert Thompson, a Pen y Pass friend, recalling his original doubts about the whole venture. "I sometimes think of this expedition as a fraud from beginning to end, invented by the wild enthusiasm of one man, Younghusband; puffed up by the would-be wisdom of certain pundits in the AC; and imposed upon the youthful ardour of your humble servant . . . The prospect of ascent in any direction is almost nil, and our present job is to rub our noses against the impossible in such a way as to persuade mankind that some noble heroism has failed again."

Throughout this period, George and Bullock had other duties to attend to. Chief among them was training the porters for high-level work. The traditional view held that the best way to deal with the porters was with a firm hand. There had been quarrels and disputes with them during the trek across Tibet, usually focusing on the size of loads, the length of the day's march, and rates of pay. George had to some extent inherited this view, but began to adopt a new perspective when he worked with them at close quarters, bringing his teacher's patience to bear when he and Bullock initiated them in the mysteries of climbing on ice. George cut a 100-foot stairway with his ax and brought them up on the rope. However, he wrote, "It was not a convincing spectacle, as they made their way with the ungainly movements of beginners." When one porter slipped and was held by Bullock on the rope, "It was clearly time to retire." He accorded them increased respect when he noticed one of his trainees walking beside him as they strode back along the glacier edge. "Although he was slightly built he seemed extremely strong and active, compact of muscle," and he stayed with George pace for pace.

George was taking photographs of Everest's ridges and faces, above all of potential routes. He had a keen eye for a shot but was let down by his technical shortcomings, for when he was entrusted with a plate camera he inserted the plates the wrong way around. He was mortified to learn his efforts had been in vain and spent two days retracing his steps and taking replacement shots. He felt relieved at having made good the damage, telling Ruth: "There is such triumph and satisfaction in seizing and using the fine moment."

⁂

By mid-July, Bullock and George had done all they could from the north. They remained convinced that the North Col offered the best available route but were still keen to find an approach that would avoid the hazardous ascent from the Rongbuk Glacier. As far as they could judge from the mountain's topography, they should be able to reach the col from a glacier on the far side, to the east; they also wanted to examine Everest's east face, which they had still not seen. They packed up their camp and headed north, then struck east and finally to the south. After a three-day walk they reached Kharta, a settlement beside the Arun gorge, where Howard-Bury had set up a new base of operations. It was a place of streams and vegetation, with willow trees and giant butterflies, in refreshing contrast to the chill, lifeless surrounds of the Rongbuk Glacier. "I have been half the time in ecstasy," George told Ruth after arriving. He went for a walk beside a bubbling stream and collected a bunch of wildflowers.

"The commonest were a pink geranium and a yellow potentilla and a little flower that looked for all the world like a violet but turned out from its leaf to be something quite different; and there was grass of Parnassus, which I really love, and in places a carpet of a little button flower, a brilliant pink, which I think must belong to the garlic tribe. But most of all I was delighted to find kingcups, a delicate variety rather smaller than ours at home, but somehow especially reminding me of you—you wrote of wading deeply through them in the first letter I had from you in Rome."

After four days' rest and recuperation, George and Bullock set off with a team of porters to begin their quest for a glacier that would provide an alternative route to the North Col—"the col of our desires," as George had taken to calling it. Just as on the northern side, there was a network of glaciers to choose from, and the first selected lay to the southwest of Kharta. When they set off on August 2, Everest was hidden by cloud. The next morning dawn broke to reveal the entire eastern cirque of Everest and its great neighbor Makalu rising from the basin of what they now knew to be the Kangshung Glacier. George was awestruck. "Even before the first glimmer of dawn, the white mountains were somehow touched to life by a faint blue light—a light that changed, as the day grew, to a rich yellow on Everest and then a bright grey-blue before it blazed all golden when the sun hit it, while Makalu, even more beautiful, gave us the redder shades, the flush of pink and purple shadows." At that moment, George admitted, he was for once "beaten for words." As for Everest's giant east or Kangshung face itself, a vast ice slope pitted with crevasses and threatened by avalanches, it offered no possible route: "Other men, less wise, might attempt this way if they would, but emphatically, it was not for us." (The face was climbed by an American expedition in 1982.)

The Kangshung Glacier offered no access to the North Col either. On the far side of the glacier, however, they could see a ridge: perhaps there was another glacier leading to the North Col on the other side of the ridge? They climbed to a col on the ridge, the Karpo La. Below them was indeed a glacier but because it curved out of sight they could not tell if it led to the North Col. George and a young porter named Nyima climbed to the top of the adjoining 21,490-foot peak of Kartse in the hope of obtaining a clearer view but after an arduous ascent through deep snow the clouds came down just as they reached the summit.

Back at Kharta that night George was feverish and had a severe headache, almost certainly the result of pushing himself too hard. He was also baffled, as he told Ruth. "We expected after two days march almost to be seeing our way up the mountain and to be sitting under it counting the stages towards the top instead of which the mystery has only deepened." Their best chance now seemed to rest with the Kharta Glacier, which lay due west of their camp. As George was still unwell, Bullock volunteered to explore it himself, leaving George even more frustrated, as he admitted to Ruth. Having led the way until then, he wrote, "it seemed I was to miss the climax the joy of wresting from the mountain its final secret and to hand over the responsibility of deciding the line of assault to my second in command."

Bullock set off up the Kharta Glacier on August 13. He did not uncover the final secret; but he did supply an important clue. He discovered that the Kharta Glacier led not to the North Col but to another ridge, running north-south. Could there be yet another glacier on the far side of the ridge? Bullock sent back a note to George in which he speculated whether the unseen glacier in fact ran out into the Rongbuk Valley, where they had begun their search.

By then, the same thought had occurred to George. It also fitted with a sketch map drawn by Edward Wheeler that had just been delivered to Kharta depicting a large glacier running parallel and to the east of the main Rongbuk Glacier. George and Bullock had been inclined to disregard the sketch as it contained a number of inaccuracies. But it now revealed to them an uncomfortable truth. The stream that ran into the main Rongbuk Glacier from the mound of moraine by their advance base camp consisted of meltwater from the newfound glacier, and they had missed it. This, they now realized, was the glacier—to be called the East Rongbuk Glacier—that provided the eastern route to the North Col. It was, perhaps, an understandable oversight on their part. It was far from obvious that the stream came from a glacier, as it emerged from a narrow slit in the moraine and disappeared under the ice of the main Rongbuk Glacier. They would have had to climb three banks of moraine to see anything of the glacier and even then it would have looked no different from a much smaller glacier spur nearby. Mallory nonetheless acknowledged in the subsequent expedition book, although not in his contemporary diary or his letters home, that he and Bullock had erred in not investigating it. It was a costly mistake in terms of both the expedition's resources and his separation from Ruth.

In the confident belief that they had found the key to the North Col at last, George, Bullock, Morshead, and the porter Nyima set off to climb to the Lhakpa La, the col at the western end of the Kharta Glacier, on August 18. This time their enemy was the heat, radiating from the glacier like a furnace, George wrote, "a deadly hostile power." When they reached the top, they at last saw the East Rongbuk Glacier at their feet. Although clouds prevented them from telling where it began or ended, they saw enough to realize that they could cross it to the eastern flank of the North Col. George returned to Kharta that evening with the satisfying knowledge that they had found the way onto Everest at last. He felt "as fit and strong as ever after a long day in the hills" and that night fell into "an untroubled sleep."

Even now, however, the expedition was some way from achieving its objective. Seeing the North Col was one thing; proving you could reach it was another. George was also determined to be true to the mountaineering goals of the expedition and make an attempt on the summit. "This success brings our reconnaissance to an end," he wrote. "We have found the way and we're now planning the attack." Of his fellow expedition members, all but Heron, the geologist, were willing to take part, and George felt it most likely that he, Bullock, and Morshead would form the main climbing party.

George and his colleagues had to wait another month before they could make their attempt. The monsoon weather, which they had drastically underestimated, continued to blanket the mountain in cloud. In their frustration, personal relations among the members took a turn for the worse. George and Bullock were increasingly irked by Howard-Bury, who had accused them of taking more than their fair share of food and was reducing the quantities supplied to the porters. "He has economy on the brain," George wrote; "I can't bear his meanness." He and Bullock took to buying food for the porters from their own funds and Bullock wrote home to his wife to send raisins and chocolate to help make up the deficit. To general surprise, Raeburn turned up again, having recovered from dysentery, but the other members were furious with him because he neglected to bring a sack of letters that was waiting to be delivered. George found him as tiresome as ever: "When he is not being a bore I feel moved to pity, which is not often." He and Bullock spent much of the time at an advance camp closer to Everest at 17,500 feet, in part to be ready for an attempt to reach the North Col, in part to get away from Howard-Bury. But even they fell out under the strain, suspecting each other of being lazy and greedy: "horrible confession," wrote George. Rather than allow their relationship to deteriorate still further, George insisted on talking things over with Bullock and the crisis was defused.

As September arrived, George's thoughts turned increasingly to home. He wrote to Ruth to suggest they could advance the date of their reunion if she met him at Naples or Marseilles, or Gibraltar, and they could take a holiday together. They could stay with the Bussys; or tour Provence, visiting Nîmes, Arles, Avignon, and return to Britain via Chartres and Paris; or visit Granada and Seville and sail home from Lisbon. He asked Ruth to let him know her preference by sending a telegram to Darjeeling. George made another proposal: he might bring back Nyima, the young Sherpa, to work as a servant at the Holt. He told Ruth that he had the perfect temperament—he was willing, unselfish, strong, and good-natured—and could work twice as hard as any English servant, performing a range of chores from cutting firewood and scrubbing floors to carrying packages up the hill from Godalming station. He could come for two years and they would pay him 7s. 6d. ($1.44) a week, rising to 10 shillings ($1.92), as well as fund the £30 ($115.20) round trip from India. But before Ruth could reply, George changed his mind: it was "just an idea," he said in his next letter, and he was no longer as keen on it as before.

On September 15 a batch of letters brought Ruth's latest news from home. She had dined with the Fletchers where she had read out parts of his letters. The O'Malleys had another child and David Pye had visited the Holt. So had George's parents, and his father had been "greatly impressed" by John. One of their servants had walked out, and Ruth had given another the sack. It had been a dry, hot summer, and the garden was parched. Ruth sent George new photographs of Clare, Berry, and John. George told Ruth he was delighted by the pictures: John looked "much more of a person" and Berry was "more graceful." He wanted to see the children, "dear souls," far more than Ruth might think: "I don't think I knew before how much they are part of life." He felt impelled to stay at Everest until he could make his attempt, even though "every day it delays puts off my meeting you again." He pictured himself in the Mediterranean and the "crisp foam hurrying by" as his ship speeded him to their rendezvous in Marseilles or Gibraltar, "where I shall expect to see you smiling in the sunshine on the quayside."

By mid-September the expedition was on its last legs. Its members were suffering more than they realized from having spent so long at altitude and were increasingly wearied by the effects of the monsoon. The days were becoming shorter and colder, multiplying the odds against success. But George was determined to see his mission through. On September 17, after a clearing in the weather, he attempted to reach the Lhakpa La with a team of porters carrying supplies but had to turn back because the snow was too deep. Three days later he reached the col with eleven porters, although he was dismayed to see that the slopes leading to the North Col were steeper and longer than he had thought.

On September 22 the weather improved again and the team set off at last, with George, Bullock, and Morshead assigned to the lead, as planned, Howard-Bury, Wollaston, and Wheeler in support, and only Heron and Raeburn staying behind. That night they camped on the Lhakpa La in bitter cold. In the morning, Wollaston and Morshead turned back, leaving George, Bullock, Wheeler, and ten porters to attempt to reach the North Col. They crossed the East Rongbuk Glacier and pitched another camp at 22,000 feet beneath a cliff on the slopes below the North Col. That night they were assailed by a savage wind. "Fierce squalls . . . visited our tents and shook and worried them with the disagreeable threat of tearing them away from their moorings," George wrote. "There was never a more determined and bitter enemy."

The next day, September 24, George, Bullock, Wheeler, and three remaining porters struck up the 1000-foot slope leading to the col. It was scarred by jumbled ice cliffs and pinnacles but they found a route by heading across some old avalanche debris and then striking left on a long traverse that took them to the col at 23,000 feet. They arrived, after four and a half hours of climbing, at 11:30 A.M.

They found themselves on a ledge below an ice cliff, with the snowy shoulder of the col only a short distance above. Ahead lay the broad ridge—George's "sort of rock rib"—that led to the northeast ridge and beyond that the summit. "If ever we had doubted whether the arête were accessible, it was impossible to doubt any longer."

The view to the summit apart, the most striking feature of the North Col was the wind. They had some protection in the lee of the ice cliff, even though it caught them at times and drove powder snow into their faces. "On the col beyond it was blowing a gale. And higher was a more fearful sight. The powdery fresh snow on the great face of Everest was being swept along in unbroken spindrift and the very ridge where our route lay was marked out to receive its unmitigated fury." Although George had proved they could reach the North Col, and thus opened up the way to the summit, he was not satisfied, for in theory this was the prelude to a summit attempt. Realistically, he knew that it was hopeless, for as well as the raging wind, their energies were drained, Wheeler had lost the feeling in his feet, and Bullock was exhausted. But still he felt he had to step out onto the col to judge the full force of the wind, to look towards the summit, and to take some upward steps so that he would know he had tried and had been forced to turn back. With Bullock and Wheeler, he ventured onto the col. The wind was like a hurricane in which "no man could live for an hour." The route upward was visible but as the wind screeched and roared across the ridge, it was "impossible to look too long without a shudder." After climbing a few token steps, George turned back. The 1921 Everest expedition could do no more.

"My dearest Ruth," George wrote on October 20 from Benares, midway on the train journey between Darjeeling and Bombay, where he was to board the SS *Malwa*. "I must send you a few lines to catch you before you start. I was delighted to get your note at Darjeeling and to know you are coming to meet me." Of the options George had presented, Ruth had decided to meet him at Marseilles. The *Malwa* would arrive there on November 12 and George wondered whether she would be waiting on the quayside or at the Hotel Louvre & Paix, as he had proposed. "Only 3 weeks more my dear!"

During the three-week return trek across Tibet, and then as the *Malwa* steamed homeward, George had reflected on the lessons of the expedition. He knew that the team had reached the North Col at the margins of its strength, although he believed he could have climbed a further 2000 feet or so, had there been no wind. The team had beat a difficult retreat, sheltering for a second night in the camp on the glacier basin, where George spent an hour massaging Wheeler's numbed legs and feet to ward off frostbite. They dragged themselves back up to the Lhakpa La, where the wind found them again, before they gratefully started down the final descent to Kharta. George's judgments swung from disappointment that the end had been so "tame," in that the North Col had proved the expedition's physical limits, to a surprisingly fulsome account of his own role in reaching it. "I carried the whole party on my shoulders to the end," he told Ruth. To Hinks, surprisingly, he confided more of his longings. After more than seven months away, he was "tired of traveling and travelers, far countries and uncouth people, trains and ships and shimmering mausoleums, foreign ports, dark-skinned faces and a garish sun. What I want to see is faces I know, and my own sweet home; afterwards, the solemn facades in Pall Mall, and perhaps Bloomsbury in a fog; and then an English river, cattle grazing in western meadows . . . ."

Most telling, the reality of the expedition had failed to match his dream. In a letter to Geoffrey Young, George told how he had nurtured a vision of "a few determined spirits setting forth from our perched camp on that high pass, crawling up at least to a much higher point where the summit itself would seem almost within reach, and coming down tired but not dispirited—satisfied, rather, just with the effort." But there had been a "terrible difference'" between that and "the reality as we had found it, the blown snow endlessly swept over the gray slopes—just the grim prospect, no respite and no hope." As usual, George had delivered his bleakest verdict to Young, perhaps in the hope of eliciting a sympathetic response. On November 15 Young obliged. "This is to welcome you into quiet waters, in a very sincere spirit of relief, pride and congratulation. You write, with the natural reaction after a touch with superhuman circumstances, of 'failure.' You will find this end of the world is only using the word success—success unexpected, tremendously deserved, and beyond what we hoped."

It was a reasonable judgment. George, together with Bullock, had spent three months single-mindedly searching for the best route to the summit. They had explored every glacier and climbed to every accessible col, doing so as a pair where originally there should have been four men. They had ventured into the unknown in terms of stamina and endurance, both in going so high and in remaining at altitude for so long. The strongest mark against them was they had overlooked the start of the East Rongbuk Glacier: but mountaineering is often a story of errors of judgment and missed opportunities that can be seen most clearly in retrospect. George's "colossal effort," Young told him, "forms an episode by itself on the history of mountain experience, and will only be the more appreciated the more time goes on."

⚭

While George and Young were debating his role in the expedition's achievement, so were others. Howard-Bury had been making acerbic comments about him and Bullock in his private diary. He complained that they "woke everyone

George's closest companion on the month-long trek across the Tibetan plateau in 1921, much of it undertaken on mules, was the dependable Guy Bullock, right, George's former friend at Winchester, whom he called his "stable-companion."

The eight members of the 1921 expedition. Back row, left to right, Bullock, Morshead, Wheeler, Mallory. Front row, Heron, Wollaston, Howard-Bury, Raeburn. The ninth member and original climbing leader, Alexander Kellas, died during the approach march.

The 1922 expedition, photographed by John Noel at the Everest Hotel, Darjeeling, before the trek across Tibet. Back row: Crawford, Norton, Mallory, Somervell, Morshead, Wakefield; front row: Strutt, Bruce, Finch.

The 1922 and 1924 expeditions set up base camp at 16,500 feet at the foot of the Rongbuk Glacier. In John Noel's photograph, the North Face of Everest, with the north-east ridge forming the skyline to the left of the summit, is still ten miles away.

(Above) The 1922 team members adopted different techniques for fording rivers during the trek across Tibet. Arthur Wakefield took off his boots. Howard Somervell removed his pants. George Mallory, uninhibited as ever, went all the way.

On May 21, 1922, climbing without oxygen equipment, George (left) and Norton, together with Somervell, who took the photograph, reached just below 27,000 feet on the north ridge.

George in the United States: In early 1923 George made a lecture tour of the northeastern United States and Canada, but it was a financial failure.

(Below) In October 1923, Sandy Irvine, then twenty-one, inexperienced but enthusiastic, was selected for the 1924 expedition. He was photographed while skiing at Murren in Switzerland, a month before the expedition left Britain.

George got to know Irvine, right, during the voyage to India on the SS *California* in March 1924. He found Irvine "sensible and not highly strung" and dependable "for everything except conversation."

(Below) The 1924 expedition, photographed at base camp by John Noel. Back row, left to right: Irvine, Mallory, Norton, Odell and John Macdonald, a dispatch runner for *The Times*. Front, Shebbeare, Geoffrey Bruce, Somervell, Beetham.

During the 1924 approach march, George pursued his interest in skinny-dipping, this time in a pool near Pedong in Sikkim. Two fellow swimmers, Irvine and Odell, were out of shot.

Noel Odell, pursuing his interest in geology, took this photograph of limestone formations at the entrance of the Rongbuk Valley. George (right) is pulling on his gloves while Irvine (left) is wearing his motorcycle helmet and goggles against the sun and cold. Center is Bentley Beetham.

On April 26, 1924 the climbers crossed the Pang La, a high pass thirty-five miles from Everest, where Noel Odell took this photograph. Irvine, right, and George, center in brimmed hat, lay and gazed at Everest, rising left on the horizon, with its familiar, ominous plume of cloud extending from the summit.

On June 4, Norton, photographed by Somervell, came within 1000 feet of the summit before turning back because of dehydration, exhaustion, and snow blindness.

Photographed for the last time by Noel Odell at 8:40 A.M. on June 6, 1924, George and Irvine, back to camera, wearing his oxygen equipment, prepare to depart. Shortly before 9 A.M. they left the desolate North Col for their summit attempt.

The memorial cairn to George and Irvine, together with Kellas, who died in 1921, and the seven Sherpas avalanched in 1922, was built at base camp on June 14, the day before the expedition began its long journey home.

up" when they left their tents at dawn to prepare for their departure from Tingri on June 23, adding: "They have no experience of camp life." On September 17, even more sourly, he noted that both George and Morshead "were in very bad training for an attempt on Everest"—a judgment soon belied by George's feat in leading the remnants of the expedition to the North Col. In letters to Hinks and Younghusband, he groused about George's temporary mishap with the plate camera, and called him and Bullock "foolish" for setting up an advance base in the Kharta Valley during the bad weather of early September, not knowing that they had done so partly to get away from him. He even complained about George's writing style, claiming he would have asked him to contribute to his dispatches to *The Times*, but his reports from the mountain "were so full of nonsense and often unintelligible that I thought it better not to." His one countervailing comment was to commend George's mountain judgments over those of Raeburn, who had been giving interviews in Calcutta about the climbing even though he had been away from Everest for most of the time.

To Hinks, Howard-Bury's criticisms came as manna. He told Howard-Bury that George and Bullock were like "children" in their mountaineering abilities and, grossly misrepresenting what Howard-Bury had said about the plate camera, added a damning judgment: "The failure of Bullock and Mallory to photograph anything is deplorable—they must be singularly unintelligent people not to be able to learn the elements of the thing in a day or two."

Meanwhile George was writing his own full report on the expedition: it ran to more than eighty pages and was, as he admitted to David Pye, "not a little indiscreet." It was evident that he was taking the opportunity to purge the bile he felt for the Everest committee, for he pictured them with "all the solemn divergences of opinion that must have passed between their nodding heads, the scrutiny of photographs and discussions of letters, with grave doubts coughed up in phlegmy throats as to whether the party are really 'on the right track.'" No matter how he tried to restrict himself to "pondered judgments," he told Pye, a sudden bubble of his true feelings would "out and burst."

Hinks suppressed George's report. What is known of its contents, apart from the hints to Pye, is that George described potential routes up the mountain, commented on the equipment used in 1921, and made recommendations for organizing any further attempt. Although summaries of those sections have survived, the rest has not. One of Hinks's ploys was to attribute his own views to the committee or the chairman, thereby giving them a spurious authority. This time he claimed that Younghusband, who chaired the committee, considered George's report "too long and diffuse." Instead Hinks sent committee members an "abstract" which supposedly covered George's conclusions on routes and equipment. Hinks could not resist adding a gloss of his own: "I regret more than ever the death of Kellas, who would have shown Mallory in two days how far he was negligible as a mountaineer." Although Hinks's summaries and covering letter are included in the Everest archive at the Royal Geographical Society, George's full report is nowhere to be found.

As the *Malwa* approached Marseilles, Hinks was feeling irritated on another score. The Mount Everest Committee was already laying plans for the full-scale attempt that was to follow the reconnaissance, and although Howard-Bury had suggested a period of recuperation and evaluation, with the second expedition following in 1923, Hinks at least was keen that it should proceed right away. George meanwhile had been expressing strong reservations about taking part, and Howard-Bury had warned Hinks that George would be unwilling to go before 1923. At about this time Hinks learned that George planned to take a holiday with Ruth, although he believed they were going to Spain: "His intention is to dally in Spain instead of coming straight home—helpful as usual. I am writing to try and get him to get that idea out of his mind. His ideas of responsibility want a little stirring up and strengthening."

While delivering these vitriolic judgments, Hinks not for the first time was indulging in hypocrisy, for he was also writing flattering letters to George from which it was clear, irrespective of Hinks's prejudices, that the committee wanted him to take part in the following year's attempt. On September 30 Hinks told George that he and Bullock had done "exceedingly well in all the circumstances." As for his pictures, they were "very useful"—the committee should have realized the need to give climbers "a course of instructions" in photography—and it would be a "great pity" if he were not to be a candidate for the following year.

Three days later he wrote a letter to Marseilles to welcome George home "and to congratulate you on the success achieved and to sympathise with you in the bad luck in weather which stopped your further progress." But as George approached Marseilles and his rendezvous with Ruth, his feelings against returning in 1922 became stronger, as he made clear in a letter to Avie:

> *They've had thoughts of organising an expedition for next year; but I've said it's no use going out except early in the spring, to climb before the monsoon. They can't possibly organize another show so soon, particularly as I've also said that it's barely worth while trying again, and anyway not without eight first-rate climbers. They can't get eight, certainly not soon, perhaps not even the year after. Hinks (Hon. Sec.) already wants to know whether I'll go again. When they press for an answer, I shall tell them they can get the other seven first. How they'll pore over the A. C. List and write around for opinions about the various candidates! I wouldn't go again next year, as the saying is, for all the gold in Arabia.*

CHAPTER ELEVEN

A Desperate Game

George had taken his advice to the former Cottie Sanders to heart. If you were going to spend money, make sure you did so "lavishly and without thought." The Hotel Louvre & Paix was Marseilles' most lavish and expensive hotel, with an ornate six-story frontage on the Canebière, the cosmopolitan thoroughfare, with its cafes and live orchestras, at the heart of the city. As a mark of the hotel's luxurious standards, every bedroom had its own bathroom or dressing room, sometimes both, as well as separate telephones for local and long-distance calls; Prince Edward, the Prince of Wales, was a frequent guest. It was here, after more than eight months' separation, that George and Ruth came together. It was the longest they had been apart, even longer than during his wartime service, when his first spell on the western front had been broken by his ten days of Christmas leave. Then, they had been able to exchange news within a week, instead of the six or eight weeks it had taken during the expedition. All in all, it can only have been a blissful reunion.

The rapture, for Ruth, must have been brief. Awaiting George at the hotel was a new letter from Hinks, to add to those that had been delivered to the *Malwa* at its ports of call. Couched in Hinks's diplomatic language, it contained both a rebuke and an ultimatum. After the opening courtesies, Hinks told George he was "sorry to learn that you propose delaying your return to England for a fortnight. It really is very important that we should see you as soon as possible, because though you may not be going out next year other people are."

George had underestimated Hinks and the committee, for they had already been sounding out prospective members for a return to Everest in 1922; the leader, Charles Bruce, had been lined up ever since he turned down the position in 1921. George and Ruth toured Provence as planned, visiting the Pont du Gard near Avignon. As they discussed Hinks's letters they soon realized that George had little choice but to join the 1922 expedition. Everest was in the news, bringing the cachet Young had predicted, and perhaps heralding a new career. The committee had asked him to conduct a series of lectures throughout Britain in return for 25 percent of the proceeds and it wanted him to write a substantial section of the official expedition book, an account of the mountaineering reconnaissance leading to the ascent to the North Col. (Howard-Bury was to describe the preparations and the trek across Tibet.) More important still was their sense that Everest represented unfinished business. It was George who had established the route to the North Col, and he knew he would find it unbearable if other climbers took it over and saw it through to the top. George hastily wrote to Hinks to clarify his previous letters. "I don't know precisely what I may have said in my haste from Marseilles; but please don't tell the committee if the question arises that I don't intend to go unless they do as I wish. That's not my thought. I shall have to feel that with so many chances against us we have some in our favour—but we can talk of that when we meet." George and Ruth were back at the Holt by November 25. George met Hinks in London a day or so later and within a week he was included in a list of climbers who had agreed to take part in the 1922 attempt.

The departure date was frighteningly close. George had argued that the expedition needed to start as early as possible to avoid the monsoon, which had so blighted their activities in 1921. The committee settled on May 1 as the target for arriving at the Rongbuk Glacier, which meant leaving Britain at the end of February. In just two months George was due to deliver some thirty lectures around Britain, starting with a set-piece occasion at the Queen's Hall. The Mount Everest Committee meanwhile was adding to its list of names. Howard-Bury had recommended that no one over fifty should be taken and that rule was applied to all but the leader, Bruce, with the other climbers all in their thirties and forties. The deputy leader was Lt. Col. Edward Strutt. Aged forty-eight, a future president of the Alpine Club, Strutt later acquired a reputation as an autocrat and stickler for tradition. But during the expedition he kept his colleagues amused with tales from his career as a soldier and diplomat, most notably the incident when he rescued the Emperor and Empress of Austria from a revolutionary mob and spirited them to sanctuary in Switzerland. Then there was Edward Norton, a grandson of the Golden Age alpinist Sir Alfred Wills, a keen climber with a parallel passion, as a military man who had served in India, for polo and pig-sticking—the hunting on horseback of wild boar. There were two members from the Lake District. The first was Howard Somervell, like George a Cambridge graduate, who had collected a double first in Natural Sciences. He replaced Bullock during the expedition as George's closest companion, the two men striking up a ready rapport. The second Lake District man was Arthur Wakefield, another doctor and a dedicated fell-runner. Finally, and most controversially, George Finch had been restored to the team, having passed his medical examination without providing any excuse to exclude him. He was selected both for his alpine record and because he had taken a keen interest in the problems of high-altitude climbing. Two important additions were the official doctor, Tom Longstaff, another Alpine Club elder, and John Noel, the photographer and former army officer who had made an illicit foray into Tibet in 1913. Once in India, Bruce recruited two Gurkha captains to supervise their transport arrangements, John Morris and Geoffrey Bruce, who happened to be his nephew. He also enlisted the surveyor, Morshead, who had been on the 1921 attempt, and another transport officer, Colin Crawford.

It is tempting to caricature the 1922 expedition members as relics of a bygone age of privilege, militarism, and imperialism, stranded on the wrong side of the cultural watershed of the First World War. Hinks displayed his snobbery when he calculated, with manifest approval, that the eleven members included six former soldiers and five alumni of Oxford and Cambridge universities: it was "a very strong party, of which much is expected." In fact the party's composition reflected the social basis of mountaineering at that time, for it remained principally an upper-middle and professional class pursuit, with no working-class heroes in prospect until the depression years of the late 1920s. More importantly, in contrast to 1921, it proved to be a harmonious group.

Much of the credit for that went to Bruce himself. Although he was fifty-six, and riddled with the scars of illness and battle wounds—he had retired from the army in the rank of general in 1920—Bruce was an indomitable figure of good cheer and had a sharp sense of humor. He was already renowned as the man who introduced shorts to the British army and, although he had acquired an ample pot belly, he proved as game during the long trek to Everest as his younger colleagues. He was willing to take up arms against Hinks on his team's behalf and determined to spend what it took in order to strengthen its chances. Hinks had wanted to restrict the number of climbers to six but Bruce outwitted him by including several who doubled up as doctors and then recruiting more personnel in India. Bruce held firm views about food—an army, after all, marches on its stomach—and insisted that it should be far more enticing than the abysmal fare served up in 1921. The expedition has also been cast as a ship of fools for its temerity in shipping out such luxuries as crystallized ginger, quails in truffles, and Ginger Nut biscuits, in addition to its stocks of canned ham, sausages, spaghetti, bacon, and sardines, but Bruce knew that such delicacies could work wonders for morale.

There were important improvements in equipment, some reflecting George's recommendations. In place of the raggedy collection of clothing they had taken in 1921, the climbers were equipped with woolen waistcoats, Jaeger pants, tight-woven windproof cotton smocks, and a range of footwear, including ski boots, knee-length felt boots, and Canadian moccasins. Bruce also held strong views on the expedition's porters, as they were now mostly referred to, replacing the term "coolie." He had a high regard for the capabilities of the Sherpas who would be available for hire in Darjeeling, and believed they should be carefully selected and then paid and equipped properly. He also recommended that, once at Everest, local Tibetans should be recruited for the initial load-carrying, reserving the Sherpas for the high-level work.

The most significant addition consisted of a stock of metal cylinders containing compressed oxygen, perhaps seventy or eighty in all, together with pack-frames for carrying the cylinders on the climbers' backs. By then—and again belying the supposition that the early Everest climbers were ignorant of the dangers they faced—there was a substantial body of knowledge about the difficulties of climbing at high altitude, where every step could be an ordeal and perception and reasoning can become distorted. In simple terms, the decreasing atmospheric pressure meant that the higher climbers ascended, the less oxygen they could breathe: at 29,000 feet, the height of Everest, the ratio is one-third that at ground level. The body can compensate by acclimatization, manufacturing extra red blood corpuscles to carry oxygen around the body. But there is a limit to this process, which also creates the danger of strokes and thrombosis. It is possible to climb Everest without using oxygen apparatus, and around one-tenth of all ascents have been achieved in that manner. But 29,000 feet appears close to the absolute limit of human physiology: if Everest were 1,000 feet higher, ascents without oxygen apparatus would probably have been impossible.

Primitive oxygen equipment had been used in the Himalaya before the war, but it proved ineffective. Dr. Kellas had brought oxygen equipment on the 1921 expedition, but after his death no one else in the team knew how to make it work. The British air force, anxious about the safety of its pilots, had been conducting its own research, and one of its experts, Professor Georges Dreyer of Oxford University, was providing advice to the Mount Everest Committee. Ironically it was

Dreyer who tested Finch's lung capacity with such spectacular results after he had been turned down in 1921. Dreyer's findings helped convince the Mount Everest Committee of the potential value of oxygen, and it set up a subcommittee consisting of Farrar, Somervell, Finch, and Percy Unna, an engineer and member of the Alpine Club. After Finch and Somervell subjected themselves to further tests in Dreyer's pressure chamber—Finch again performed superbly, while Somervell passed out—the committee decided to spend £400 ($1760.00) on ten oxygen sets and the accompanying cylinders. The climbers would inhale the oxygen via a mask and a tube leading from the cylinders on their backs, in theory enabling them to perform at the equivalent of 15,000 feet.

What might have appeared, to nonmountaineers, to be a sensible proposal provoked bitter controversy. George was among the critics who viewed the oxygen apparatus as an "artificial" aid which somehow cheated the mountain and demeaned the purity of the enterprise: he called it "a damnable heresy." Because the apparatus was so cumbersome too—a pack-frame loaded with three cylinders weighed thirty-two pounds—it appeared to undermine climbing's spirit of romance. "When I think of mountaineering with four cylinders of oxygen on one's back and a mask over one's face," George told David Pye, "well, it loses its charm." George believed that the body's gradual acclimatization to altitude, boosted by a deep-breathing technique he had adopted in 1921, would be just as effective.

The equipment's principal advocate was Finch, who had been appointed the expedition's oxygen officer. He argued that the cylinders were no more artificial than goggles, thermos flasks, or warm boots. But whereas the expedition members were prepared to have a civilized debate, Hinks, never one to let a controversy pass by, plunged into the fray, instigating a row that lasted long after the expedition had left for Tibet. Here was another of the mountaineers' indulgences, and one that threatened the expedition budget. He accused climbers who wanted to use oxygen of being greedy and self-indulgent, and declared that they would be much better off without it. It would be far preferable, Hinks raged, "to discover how high a man can climb without oxygen as to get to a specified point, even the highest summit in the world, in conditions so artificial that they can never become 'legitimate' mountaineering." As in 1921, Hinks's aggressive views risked polarizing the expedition. Farrar defended the equipment as no more of an "artificial aid than food" but Hinks would not let the issue go, claiming that climbers unwilling to go to 25,000 or 26,000 feet without oxygen would be "rotters."

Happily, these controversies mostly passed George by. His lectures were taking him throughout Britain, bringing enthusiastic reviews and photographs in the provincial press. The financial outcome was encouraging, for his 25 percent share netted him £400 ($1760.00), bringing far more in two months than a year's work at Charterhouse. He and Ruth were also reckoning on a share of the proceeds for his section in the official Everest book, in which he had related the story as a mystery—the quest for a route, the puzzle over access to the North Col—and how it was resolved. It represented his best narrative writing to date, striking a more accessible balance between his introspective articles for the climbing journals and the tedious recitation of events he so despised. When he read the proofs of Howard-Bury's contribution he considered them dull beyond belief. "They are worse than I expected, quite dreadfully bad," he told Ruth. Nor had Howard-Bury expressed "a word of appreciation of anyone's work or qualities."

As the conclusion of his contribution, George had looked ahead to the chances of success in 1922. He foresaw no great difficulty in reaching the northeast ridge from the North Col, but above there, reversing his original optimistic appraisal, he judged "the way is not so smooth." The first part of the ridge was "distinctly jagged by several towers" and the final summit pyramid looked steep. It was an accurate reading, for he was referring to the key obstacles on the northeast ridge, the First and Second Steps, and he wondered whether it would be possible to bypass them by traversing on to the north face. He acknowledged that the expedition would require all the luck it could get, as there were so many factors which could tell against it: a breakdown in transporting supplies, soft snow, high wind. "The highest of mountains is capable of severity, a severity so awful and so fatal that the wiser sort of men do well to think and tremble even on the threshold of their high endeavour."

Ruth saw all too little of George during January and February. His lecture tour ended in Newcastle ten days before he was due to depart and he spent his last week at the Holt in furious preparation, interrupted by a final lecture at Winchester College. Ruth can only have contemplated his impending departure with the return of a sense of dread, no matter how much he tried to minimize the risks; it would be the fifth such parting, including the three during the war, in six years. But familiarity with such emotions can help to reduce them, and there is comfort in knowing you have managed before. Ruth shared George's aims, which included his hopes for her and their children, and she was proud of what he had achieved; she was also consoled by knowing that he understood her feelings, just as she shared his. That much was clear from his first letter from the SS *Caledonia* after it sailed on March 2, in which love mingled with remorse.

"Dearest love," he asked, "is it a very bad gap now that I'm gone? I hardly like to ask for fear of suggesting loneliness to you, but with the children you'll know how to put that away. I hate the fact of your not being with me and even more the thought of my not being with you, as though I had been cruel to you; and I don't want ever to hurt you the least little bit." He again offered the intriguing aside that Ruth had nothing to fear so far as other women were concerned. "If you were to see the women folk on board, dear, even the faintest glimmering of jealous feeling would be laid to rest—I haven't even spoken to one yet." In fact, he assured her, "nothing could be less eventful than our voyage so far."

In other respects, George's letters were more relaxed than in 1921, for here was a traveler repeating a journey he had made less than twelve months before. The biggest difference was that George had the company of five of his colleagues, Somervell, Wakefield, Noel, Strutt, and Finch. He soon revised his view of Strutt, whom he had cast as a member of the old guard of the mountaineering world, for he enjoyed Strutt's fund of anecdotes: it was, George wrote, "a happy, smiling party with plenty of easy conversation." He liked talking to Noel and was impressed that the cinema film he planned to shoot could earn up to £15,000 ($66,300.00) from foreign rights. The only discordant note concerned Finch, who was proselytizing over the use of oxygen and insisted that the team attended his oxygen training classes. George was finding Finch dogmatic and fanatical, but conceded that his classes were "extremely interesting." This time, instead of rounding India to Calcutta, George and his colleagues disembarked at Bombay and traveled by train to Darjeeling, where they teamed up with the rest of the expedition. Norton was already a casualty as he had developed hemorrhoids which his colleagues blamed on a vigorous bout of pig-sticking. He soon recovered and George found him "one of the best, extraordinarily keen and active," as well as gentle and considerate. It was, he confirmed, "a very congenial party"—particularly so for "the differences between Bruce and Bury."

The expedition followed the 1921 route as far as Shekar Dzong. Once in Tibet, George was surprised "to experience a friendly feeling towards this bleak country on seeing it again." Some of his colleagues were less tolerant and each time they approached a new settlement Strutt would loudly proclaim that it was the filthiest and most miserable of any they had yet encountered. "Not that Strutt is a grouser," George added, "but he likes to ease his feelings with maledictions and I hope feels better for it." The biggest difference from 1921, when they had been two months later in the year, was the bone-chilling cold, compounded by George's old enemy, the wind. Between Phari and Kampa Dzong they were assailed by a blizzard that obliterated their tracks and converted the plateau into a frozen wasteland. When George wrote to Ruth from Kampa Dzong on April 12 he was wearing two set of underclothes, one wool and one silk, a flannel shirt, a sleeved waistcoat, a lambskin coat, and a Burberry coat, together with knickerbockers, two pairs of stockings, and sheepskin boots; and yet, he told her, his fingers were so cold he could barely write. It was all the more impressive that

George should have removed all his clothes to wade across a river, while Somervell took off his trousers and Wakefield only his boots: George was so keen to mark his achievement that he handed his camera to a colleague and asked him to take a photograph. (The picture appears to have been too shocking for some sensibilities, as it was not published until 1993.)

When the expedition reached Shiling, the location of his vision of Everest in 1921, George took great pleasure in unveiling the mountain to his colleagues. "It was more wonderful even than I remembered and all the party were delighted by it which of course appealed to my proprietary feelings." Once at Shekar Dzong the expedition diverted from the 1921 trail, striking due south instead of continuing west to Tingri. Their route took them over the Pang La, a high pass where they marveled at the panorama of the Everest range extended before them. John Noel later said that he and his colleagues felt humbled by what they saw, and wondered whether any human could possibly climb the mountain. On April 30, they reached the Rongbuk monastery, where the Lama asked them not to kill any wild animals, warned them it could be very cold, and gave them his blessing. The next day they set up base camp at the snout of the glacier, pitching their tents alongside the glacier stream, which was frozen for all but a couple of hours a day. Although Everest was still ten miles away it appeared far closer, and George told Ruth: "Everyone is duly impressed."

∽

As befitted a former general, Bruce had devised a plan for climbing Everest that resembled a military campaign. The expedition was to follow the East Rongbuk Glacier, which provided a far more direct approach than the 1921 route via the Kharta Glacier and the Lhakpa La, to the basin of ice below the North Col. After climbing to the North Col it would head up the broad north ridge to the northeast ridge, and go for the summit from there. The expedition would establish a line of camps along the route and stock them with equipment and supplies. There would be six camps in all: three along the East Rongbuk Glacier, one on the North Col at 23,000 feet, and two more at 25,000 feet and 27,000 feet. Once the camps were set up and equipped, the lead climbers would move along the line and strike for the summit from the top camp. The logistics of the approach have been compared to constructing a pyramid, building from the base until the summit climbers take off from the apex, and it set the pattern for most major Everest attempts for the next fifty years. While it sounded splendid in practice, the climbers knew—as George had already warned—that they would need a large share of luck for all the pieces to fall into place. They were also working against a deadline, for they reckoned they had a six-week weather window before the monsoon arrived. "Time," George wrote, "was likely to be a formidable enemy."

At first, all went well. Strutt left with the porters to establish the line of camps to the glacier basin below the North Col. The ascent from base camp at 16,500 feet to Camp 3 at 21,300 feet was more technical and demanding than the climbers had expected, particularly as it picked its way among the fractured ice pinnacles above Camp 2. But Strutt returned on May 9 to report that all three camps were in place. The first time George ventured up the glacier he was impressed with Strutt's organizational skills, particularly when a cook emerged from a tent at Camp 1 to hand him a mug of tea and asked him what he wanted for dinner that night. He and Somervell arrived at Camp 3 on May 12, finding the glacier basin every bit as bleak and desolate as he remembered from 1921.

The next day George, Somervell, and a porter, Dasno, set off for the North Col. The slope was icier than in 1921, and in some places they kept breaking through an ankle-deep crust of snow. They followed a zigzag course, bypassing the jumbled blue ice cliffs and crossing several crevasses that had opened up during the intervening year. They fixed a rope on the steepest sections to help protect the porters who would be laboring up the slopes with supplies, and it was not until mid-afternoon that they stood on the col. George was anxious to confirm that the ridge above the col was feasible but once he looked up it towards the northeast ridge, he wrote, "all our doubts were eased." The three men pitched a tent on the shelf below the crest of the col and returned to Camp 3.

To George's dismay, he and Somervell now spent three days in frustrating inactivity, for Bruce's carefully laid plans were going wrong. In theory, contingents of porters should have been ferrying equipment up the glacier, but the supply line had been reduced to a trickle. As planned, Bruce had hired local Tibetans to boost the load-carrying but, with the arrival of spring, many had returned to their villages to work their fields. A vigorous recruitment drive brought new Tibetans to base camp in twos and threes, women as well as men, sometimes carrying their children, ready to do a day's work for a day's pay. Up at Camp 3, meanwhile, George and Somervell read to each other from the Shakespeare collection George had taken with him to France and from a poetry anthology, Robert Bridges' *The Spirit of Man*, which he and Ruth had often read together. They discussed political and social issues, George impressing Somervell with his liberal views. "He was really concerned with social evils," Somervell later wrote. "He hated anything that savoured of hypocrisy or humbug." He added that of all the expedition members, George "was the man whom I always felt that I knew the best, and I have seldom had a better or more intimate friend."

It was not until May 16 that a large contingent of porters finally arrived at

Camp 3. By then, there had been further alterations to Bruce's plans. Originally George and Somervell, climbing without oxygen apparatus, were to make the first summit attempt, while a second attempt using the oxygen sets had been allocated to Finch and Norton. But down at base camp the use of oxygen had been undergoing urgent reappraisal. Bruce admitted he was "terrified" by the oxygen equipment: it was cumbersome and fragile and had the enormous disadvantage that once the climbers were wearing their face masks, it was impossible for them to eat or drink. To some extent Finch, the outsider, had become a convenient butt for complaints and jokes, and Strutt, who had taken against him personally, complained of the massive undertaking it would require to transport all 800–900 pounds of oxygen equipment up the East Rongbuk Glacier. In a significant shift of strategy, Bruce and Strutt decided to prioritize the first, oxygenless, attempt. This was now to be made by four climbers, with Norton and Morshead joining George and Somervell.

Finch was incensed. He had lost an experienced partner in Norton, who had been replaced by Bruce's nephew, the Gurkha officer Geoffrey Bruce, who had never before climbed on snow and ice. George was dismayed too, as the doubling in size of the summit team crucially altered the logistics of his attempt. The porters would have twice as much equipment to carry to the North Col, which meant that they would be able to establish only one further camp, at around 26,000 feet, instead of two as originally planned. George considered it "a terrible handicap" and in a letter to Ruth on the eve of his departure he admitted how far his hopes had been reduced. "We shan't get to the top," he told her. "If we reach the shoulder at 27400ft it will be better than anyone here expects." His concluding expression of endearment made clear his underlying disappointment. "The spur to do my best is you and you again—in moments of depression or lack of confidence or overwhelming fatigue I want more than anything to prove worthy of you."

On May 17 the four climbers, together with Strutt and a group of porters, carried loads of up to thirty pounds to the North Col. They descended to Camp 3 and ferried further supplies on May 19. This time the four climbers, together with nine porters, camped on the col, ready to start their summit attempt in the morning. Mallory was the first out of his tent but when he tried to rouse their porters they were all still in their sleeping bags, drained by the effort of carrying two loads to the North Col. In the end, four of the nine said they were willing to go on. When the eight men set off up the broad north ridge at 7:30 A.M. they quickly discovered that a chill wind was sweeping across the face from Tibet. They stopped to put on extra clothing—George added a silk shirt and a Shetland pullover— but suffered a further setback when the rope between George and Norton dislodged Norton's rucksack, sending his spare clothing bounding down the face.

Although the other climbers lent Norton some clothes, the odds were steadily mounting against the attempt. The climbers' extremities began to freeze when the sun disappeared behind cloud and George went ahead to prospect for a route out of the wind. He chose a line of snow in the lee of the ridge but the climbers were now handicapped by a lack of crampons, which they had left behind as the crampon straps restricted their blood supply, increasing the risk of frostbite. As a result they had to cut steps into the snow with their ice axes, further draining their energies. At around 11 A.M. they reached 25,000 feet, putting them decisively behind schedule. It had already taken them three and a half hours to climb 2000 feet, and George calculated that they would need another three hours to reach 26,000 feet and establish a camp there, allowing precious little time for the porters to return to the North Col before nightfall. He decided that the best course of action would be to pitch camp where they were: if they did not reach the summit themselves, they would at least have established a camp for the next attempt. After much searching among loose, sloping rocks they found a site for their two tents, and the porters departed for the North Col.

The four men passed an excruciating night. They were using two-man sleeping bags and George found it almost impossible to settle down with his partner Norton, who was not only six foot two in height but was in pain from a frostbitten ear. George's fingers were frostbitten too, although at the time he thought they were merely bruised. Around dawn George heard "the musical patter of fine, granular snow" on the tent. When the climbers emerged they found six inches of snow had fallen, while the temperature had fallen to 7° F. The next blow came when the rucksack containing their food tumbled down the slope below the tents. George thought it was going to follow Norton's to the foot of the face but it miraculously lodged on a ledge and Morshead volunteered to fetch it. Only at eight o'clock were they roped up and ready to press on. While George felt the familiar "stir of excitement" that comes from preparing to depart, lacing up his boots and tightening his buttons and straps, he accepted that they now had little chance of reaching the summit, privately concluding that they would do well to reach the crest of the northeast ridge.

Morshead, who was suffering from the worst frostbite, dropped out after a few steps and said he would wait at the camp. The three remaining climbers carried on up the steep, slabby ground, with the fresh snow making it hard to see where to place their feet. They were following a diagonal course towards the crest of the ridge but by midday were still some way short, George reckoning that their ascent rate had fallen to 400 feet an hour, not counting stops for rest.

In the end, the decision to turn back was no decision. It became clear that at their current rate they would still be climbing after nightfall if they were to reach the summit, and none of them were ready to take that risk. And so, George wrote, "By agreeing to this arithmetical computation, we tacitly accepted defeat." At 2:15, at a point where the angle of the slope marginally eased, they stopped for a snack of ham and cheese. They were at just under 27,000 feet, further than anyone had ever climbed, but George had no sense of achievement: he felt no desire to dwell on the view, while the summit of Everest, a pyramid rising above the slant of the face a mile or so away, was "not impressive." After fifteen minutes they started to descend, reaching Camp 5 at four o'clock, where they found Morshead ready to rope up for the return to the North Col.

It was now that near-catastrophe occurred. They lost the line of their ascent under the snow and, as they groped their way down, Morshead, who was close to exhaustion, lost his footing. As he slithered down the slope the rope dragged off Norton and Somervell in turn, the three gathering speed with nothing to stop them before they reached the glacier 5000 feet below. George was cutting steps in the lead and was below the others when Morshead slipped. At first he did not see what had happened and instead sensed, or heard, that something was wrong. Swiftly, instinctively, he drove his ice ax into the ground, twisted a coil of rope around it to make a belay, then leaned on it with the full weight of his body. "In the still moment of suspense before the matter must be put to the test," he wrote, as if describing the moment of peril from an observer's standpoint, "nothing further could be done to prevent a disaster one way or the other." He saw the rope tighten as it tugged on the ax head; the ax held. By great good fortune, the weight of the three men came on the rope singly, instead of in one combined impact. It was that, and George's instant response, the result of the tradecraft he had acquired in the Alps, which saved their lives.

It was 11:30 P.M. by the time the four men fumbled their way into the camp on the North Col. Morshead had kept sitting down in the snow, Norton urging him along by gripping him around the waist. George had resisted the temptation to glissade for part of the descent: "We were not playing with this mountain," he wrote; "it might be playing with us." They used a lantern for the final stretch but lost even that lifeline when the candle burned out. As they slid into their tents they realized, to their horror, that there was nothing to drink, as the porters had mistakenly removed the pans they needed to melt snow. Norton attempted to compensate by making improvised ice cream from a mix of strawberry jam, condensed milk, and snow. "I managed to swallow down a little before the deadly sickliness of the stuff disgusted me," George wrote. He could barely sleep that night as his body was convulsed by muscular twitching, the outcome of utter exhaustion. Only the next morning, when they descended to Camp 3, were they able to drink at last, Somervell consuming seventeen cups of tea.

When they finally reached base camp on May 22, the four men resembled a party of walking wounded returning from the front line: they were "completely and absolutely tugged out," Bruce wrote. Later, using phrases with echoes of the war, he added: "The flower of the men's condition must have gone." Morshead was in the most abject state, utterly drained and his feet already blackening from frostbite. Norton was semicrippled with frostbite, which had affected his feet as well as his ear. George's fingers were paining him and when Longstaff listened to his heart he found that it had acquired its old flutter. Only Somervell, apart from minor frostnip, seemed unscathed. The four had pushed to the limit in unpropitious conditions and had discovered that their limit was around 27,000 feet. Although they could not be accused of underestimating the immensity of the challenge, there was one factor of which they were still ignorant, although its importance was beginning to dawn on them. Dehydration had proved just as debilitating at altitude as the lack of oxygen, and later generations of climbers realized that it had to be countered by drinking as much as possible.

⸎

During their attempt, not so much biding his time as champing at the bit, Finch had been awaiting news of the outcome. He had found a third man for his oxygen attempt, Tejbir Bura, one of the Nepalese officers in the Gurkhas who had accompanied Geoffrey Bruce. On May 19—the day George and his party left for the North Col—Finch's team took up position at Camp 3. They spent the next three days adjusting and experimenting with the oxygen equipment, and tried it out when they climbed to the North Col on May 22, passing George's party as it descended "in the last stages of exhaustion," Finch wrote. In comparison their climb to the col was "like a brief Alpine ascent." They departed from the North Col on May 25 and camped that night at 25,500 feet. But the weather turned against them yet again, and they were pinned in their tents by a wind of such ferocity that it drove a stone through the canvas like a bullet. That night they were bitterly cold, but discovered that they could revive themselves by breathing oxygen from their cylinders. The next morning, having had almost nothing to eat, as their food had run out, they left at 6:30 A.M. Tejbir, who was carrying two extra oxygen cylinders, subsided to the ground when they reached 26,000 feet and although Bruce urged him on—"for the honour of your regiment"—he was compelled to turn back.

Breathing through the oxygen apparatus, Finch and Bruce continued diagonally across the face for the next four hours, picking their way over the same sloping snow-plastered slabs that George had found so treacherous. At midday they were at 27,300 feet, immediately below the great stratum of sandstone that crosses the north face known as the Yellow Band and little more than half a mile from the summit. "Everest itself was the only mountain which we could see without turning our gaze downwards," Finch wrote, and they could even make out individual stones on the patch of scree immediately below the summit. Finch felt utterly confident that they would succeed but then Bruce, whose oxygen set had developed a fault, and who was further weakened by the lack of food, collapsed. "The summit was before us," Finch wrote; "a little longer, and we should be on the top. And then—suddenly, unexpectedly, the vision was gone."

Finch and Bruce turned back and, collecting Tejbir en route, returned to Camp 3 that night—a descent of 6000 feet in five and a half hours. On May 28 they were back in base camp, where Finch calculated the arithmetic of his ascent. In comparison with George, who had averaged no more than 330 feet per hour, Finch reckoned he had ascended at up to 1000 feet an hour—an unanswerable demonstration of the merits of using oxygen equipment, Finch felt, particularly as he had been climbing with two inexperienced colleagues and in worse weather than George. It had not been an unalloyed triumph, as both Bruce and Tejbir were laid low by frostbite and exhaustion, and Finch was far more drained by his ascent than he was prepared to admit. But the implications were not lost on George as he mulled over Finch's figures. He had already told Ruth, before knowing the outcome of Finch's attempt: "I shan't feel in the least jealous of any success they may have. The whole venture of getting up with oxygen is so different from ours that the two hardly enter into competition." Now that Finch had bettered his height record by at least 300 feet, it was hard to keep his envy in check. There was a jaded note in his comments to Ruth in which he criticized Finch for demanding too much of his porters. He also complained that Finch had not taken advantage of the camp George had established at Camp 5, and that he should have done more to position his tents out of the wind.

It is at this point that the Everest expedition of 1922 could have ended. Morshead, Strutt, Norton, Longstaff, and Geoffrey Bruce were all suffering from frostbite injuries or exhaustion and had nothing left to give. George wrote to Ruth on May 26 in terms that appeared to assume that the expedition was over. "We were a *perfectly* happy party—altogether, anxiety apart, I have tremendously enjoyed it." He reckoned on reaching Darjeeling by early July, and was planning a week's sightseeing in India before traveling to Bombay for the voyage home.

On May 28 he wrote an exuberant note to Clare and Beridge: "Thank you very much for all your nice letters. I think of you too even when I am climbing mountains sometimes or lying on the side of Mount Everest. I hope you will soon be having a lovely time at the seaside. Please don't drown John. I shall be coming home not very long after you. Meanwhile I sent some hugs and kisses in advance. Your loving, Daddy." He drew some geometric patterns on the page and then, up the side, wrote: "The wind is trying to blow away my hugs and kisses." The wind evidently succeeded, for George added the further note: "This letter was blown into the stream," and to prove it, the ink of his handwriting, and in particular the geometric shapes, were smudged.

George's letter to his daughters, Clare and Beridge, written from Base Camp on May 28, 1922.

As everything in George's mountaineering career showed, he was not one to turn back readily; he preferred to push such decisions to the point where he had no realistic choice, almost as if he wanted to shun the responsibility for making them. He was also prepared to be a pragmatist, modifying his ideals if a sensible alternative presented itself. Together with Somervell, he opened up discussions with Bruce and Finch over making a third attempt—and one, drawing on the lessons of Finch's bid, that would make use of the oxygen apparatus. Bruce approved, and for several reasons. However resolute in the climbers' cause he attempted to be, he had been subjected to a bombardment of letters from both Hinks and Younghusband exhorting him to do his utmost to climb the mountain: Younghusband even wanted him to stay on until after the monsoon if the current attempts failed. Bruce also felt under pressure, if and when the expedition did give up, to retrieve as much equipment as possible from the higher camps, in particular the expensive oxygen apparatus.

It was true that the weather remained abysmal; Finch later calculated that during their month on Everest there were only two fine, settled days, and both had been preceded by heavy snowfall. What was more, the signs were that the monsoon, which they had been so desperate to beat, was arriving early. But should they abandon the expedition because of a pessimistic weather forecast? Or should they test the possibilities themselves? George was in no doubt: "To retire now if the smallest chance remained to us would be an unworthy end to the Expedition."

There was a dwindling band of climbers left to make the attempt. Morshead, Strutt, Longstaff, Norton, and Geoffrey Bruce were all preparing to go home, and Longstaff had reported that every other climber, bar Somervell, was unfit to continue. But Finch and Mallory contested Longstaff's diagnosis and persuaded Wakefield to deliver a second opinion, which was in their favor. On June 1 George told Ruth it would have been "unbearable" to miss the final attempt. His frostbitten fingers might suffer further damage, but he declared: "The game is worth a finger." He admitted that the new attempt could delay his return home: he aimed to catch a boat from Bombay on August 1, but warned Ruth not to count on that. The weather appeared to be turning against them again, which left him none too hopeful, but on one point he was resolved. In contrast to Finch's cavalier attitude towards the porters, "I'm determined we will run no risks with their lives during his next venture."

The party left base camp on June 3. George, Somervell, and Finch were to be the lead climbers, with Morris, Wakefield, and Crawford in support—the last two, George admitted, "not very pleased" at having to return to the mountain so soon. Finch had been placed in charge, as it was to be an oxygen attempt, but by the time he reached Camp 1 he felt exhausted and returned to base camp, where he succumbed to dysentery. With George as the new climbing leader, the team found Camp 3 in disarray: tents had blown open, leaving them half-full of snow, and all the stores had to be dug out. Clouds had been drifting down the glacier for most of their ascent, there had been more snow on June 5, and they wondered again whether it was worth going on. But on June 6 the sky cleared, and they decided to press on to the North Col the next day. They hoped to establish a camp at 26,000 feet on June 8 and go for the summit from there. They would start using oxygen at 25,000 feet and reckoned that the lead climbers would have four cylinders each for the summit bid.

On June 7, the weather was holding. George, Somervell, and Crawford prepared to depart for the North Col with fourteen porters, the seventeen men forming four separate ropes. But first they had another factor to consider: the risk of avalanche, following the heavy snowfall which had smothered the face on June 5. George, who noted that much of the snow seemed to have thawed, judged that the first danger area was a slope that they reached after just over two hours. The snow seemed to be adhering to the underlying ice but they subjected it to a further test by stamping out a trench and trying to push away the exposed layer with their legs. "Every test," George wrote, "gave a satisfactory result. Once this crucial place was passed, we plodded on without hesitation." In particular, they believed that their tests showed that similar danger points further up the slope were also safe. "The thought of an avalanche was dismissed from our minds," George wrote.

At 1:30 the climbers stopped to gather their breath some 600 feet below the tents on the North Col. They had just moved on again when George heard a sound like an explosion of gunpowder. "I had never before been near an avalanche of snow, but I knew the meaning of that noise as though I were accustomed to hear it every day. In a moment I observed the snow's surface broken only a few yards away to the right and instinctively moved in that direction. And then I was moving downward."

The avalanche had broken away from the lee of an ice cliff a short distance above. George managed to turn in the snow so that he was facing outward. He was held fast by the rope at his waist and, as snow poured over him, he supposed "that the matter was settled." Then he arched his back and managed to push his face and body clear. A short distance away he saw Somervell, Crawford, and a porter pulling themselves out of the snow. Below him a group of porters had just clambered to their feet. But they were pointing urgently down the slope, towards the edge of a sixty-foot ice cliff. George hurried down to find that the nine men on the other two ropes had been carried over the cliff by the avalanche. They had fallen into a crevasse and seven of the nine had been killed.

It was, of course, the end of the attempt and the end of the expedition. Several of the dead porters had relatives among the survivors, and at their request the seven men were buried where they had already been interred by the snow. A memorial cairn constructed of boulders from the glacier moraine was erected at Camp 3, and the expedition beat a sorrowful retreat. George was stricken by remorse, blaming himself for leading the party into danger. "The consequences of my mistake are so terrible," he told Ruth; "it seems almost impossible to believe that it has happened for ever and that I can do nothing to make good. There is no obligation I have so much wanted to honour as that of taking care of these men. They are children where mountain dangers are concerned, and they do so much for us; and now through my fault seven of them have been killed." Somervell's sentiments went to the heart of the matter with equal acuity. As they trailed back to Camp 3, a thought gnawed at his brain: why had only the porters, and no "Britishers," been killed? Later he wrote: "I would gladly at that moment have been lying there in the snow, if only to give those fine chaps the feeling that we had shared their loss, as we had indeed shared the risk."

∝

In the weeks and months following the disaster, there was a fevered debate over how far Mallory, and to a lesser extent Somervell and Crawford, were to blame. On July 17, the day after they reached Britain, Longstaff, Strutt, and Finch were summoned by Hinks to a meeting of the Mount Everest Committee. By then Hinks was almost incandescent over the alleged omissions and misdeeds of the climbers. Before knowing the reason, he had been enraged that half the party—these were the injured climbers—had set off for home with no word of explanation, and he had complained to one of the Alpine Club representatives on the committee at having to spend "another £2000 ($8480.00) at least to bring home your infernal climbers." After the meeting on July 17 Hinks implied that Mallory was to blame for the avalanche, claiming that the three climbers had said "nasty things" about him and that they considered his "judgement in purely Alpine matters was bad." The climbers, when they were able to speak for themselves, offered more considered views, but Strutt wrote to Mallory to say that after such heavy snowfall, "seventeen persons on the North Col was fifteen too many." Longstaff felt that Bruce had been under pressure from "the continuous urgings" from both Hinks and Younghusband, but he accused George and Somervell of an "absence of knowledge of snowcraft." Bruce, who had stayed at base camp during the attempt, wrote that once he had seen how much snow had fallen, he assumed the party would abandon their attempt and limit themselves to retrieving equipment from Camp 3.

Decisions, it is said, appear good or bad only in retrospect; at the time what matters is how you evaluate the factors at your disposal. When George went back over the events in his mind, he did not see what else he could have done. He had been aware of the avalanche risk and so had carried out tests at the first danger point in the belief that the results would apply throughout the slope. His testing method, carving out a trench and trying to push away the exposed layer of snow, was very similar to methods used today. "I knew enough about Mount Everest not to treat so formidable a mountain contemptuously," he wrote. "But it was not a desperate game, I thought, with the plans we made." The cause, he concluded, was his ignorance of snow conditions: "One generalises from too few observations." But despite carrying out their tests, "the three of us were deceived; there wasn't an inkling of danger among us."

George's pained self-analysis contained seeds of the truth. The avalanche, in technical terms, was classic windslab of medium-hard density. Windslab occurs when snow falls or is blown on to an old surface, forming a new layer that has not yet bonded with the old. The North Col avalanche was clearly windslab, rather than powder snow, as George heard the typical crack of the tension fracture when it broke away and Somervell saw this happen too. But to an important extent George and Somervell were unlucky. Having conducted their layer test, they failed to appreciate that there can be variations within the snowpack caused by differences of wind and temperature; the snowpack can also change in nature during the day.

Somervell saw snow being blown off the col and this probably drifted on the higher slopes, adding to the load on the pack. George had been encouraged to see that much of the snow had thawed, but there may have been variations in the snowpack caused by peculiarities in the melting process which are not widely understood even today. There can also be subsidiary layers within the windslab and it may have been one of these, rather than the full slab, which sheared away, making the avalanche even harder to predict. However, although avalanches can be triggered by only one or two climbers, the fact that there were seventeen men in the party certainly increased the risk. And although it may seem strange that the avalanche began above them, that can occur when the climbers' movements pull the snow away, as if they were stepping on the foot of an insecure stair carpet. It was not a deep avalanche, as George and his companions were able to extricate themselves from the debris, and the total run-out was no more than 200 feet. The seven deaths were almost certainly caused not by suffocation, but by the sixty-foot fall into the crevasse below the ice cliff. That, too, may seem unlucky: but that is the way with avalanches, where the chances of death or survival can be akin to playing roulette.

Avalanches are not solely technical events. They also result from human psychology, decision making, and the stresses that climbers face. Bruce was vulnerable to the pressure from the Mount Everest Committee, which had staked both expense and prestige on success. George had his personal goals: Finch's height record, though George denied it, was nagging at him, and he had much to gain from reaching the top. More than that, George needed to be convinced that the expedition was at an end. He could not bear the thought of giving up without being certain that all further progress was impossible, and that the obstacles they faced were as implacable as the wind which had driven them from the North Col in 1921.

Younghusband wrote generously to George after his return, invoking the climbers' dictum that those who survive to longevity owe much to sheer good fortune, and acknowledging that many others would have made the same mistake. "However much you may blame yourself, I certainly am not one to blame you, for I have done precisely the same thing myself in the Himalaya, and only the purest luck can have saved me and my party from disaster." Geoffrey Young, as always, provided further reassurance. In a letter George had recalled the death of Donald Robertson, writing of "the great sleeping ones that have but to stir in their slumber . . . Do you know that sickening feeling that one can't go back and have it undone and nothing will make good?" Young tried to put his mind at ease. "You made all the allowance for the safety of your party that your experience suggested . . . The immense percentage of 'chance,' or we may call it of the 'unknown,' present still in this hitherto unattempted region of mountaineering, turned for once against you. But to debate the 'might-have-beens,'" Young added, was "the road to madness."

At the end of his account of the accident, written for the official history of the 1922 expedition, George was far less lyrical about the prospects of a repeat attempt than after 1921. He wrote dryly of the improvements that would be required: better boots and/or crampons, lighter oxygen equipment. A future expedition would also be able to build on the experience of the previous two, and avoid their mistakes. But whereas before George had emphasized the importance of sheer determination, now the climbers would need "the keen eye for a fair opportunity and resource in grave emergency." Would George himself be a candidate for another attempt? There was more than a hint of ambivalence when he wrote of the "preceding visions" of new ascents—"visions of what is mysterious, remote, inaccessible." Now that Everest was less remote, less mysterious, did it hold the same allure?

CHAPTER TWELVE

A Sacrifice Either Way
1923–April 1924

Ruth's loyalty to George was unwavering and in July 1922, as he journeyed home from India in the aftermath of the avalanche, she came to his defense. During both the 1921 and 1922 expeditions, Hinks had been writing to her at the Holt, using this separate line of communication to pass on his complaints about the climbers, albeit in a more restrained form, and to extract information from George's letters. In 1921 he had asked her to pass on a request that George and his colleagues should desist from giving the mountains personal names—he cited Mounts Clare and Kellas—instead of the local versions already in use. In June 1922, before learning why some of the climbers had left the expedition early, he complained to her about their supposed neglect of duties: "I do not like the way in which some of these people have rushed home without attempting to do anything geographical." In July he asked Ruth if she knew when George was due home, and it was in her reply—evidently discerning the critical undercurrents—that she took up George's cause. "I think George's feeling that the accident was his fault is the result of the shock . . . He appears to have taken the greatest care all through and to have been at the time of the avalanche quite unconcious of danger." Little more than a year later Ruth's loyalty was to be put to its severest test.

During September 1922, the first month after George's return, he and Ruth settled back into family life at the Holt. They bought a car, a 1.5-liter Albert, a popular make because it was both roomy and had weatherproof aluminium bodywork. In October, they went on holiday to France, leaving the children with Vi. Clare was seven and some of her most affecting memories, recalled more than seventy-five years later, are of life at the Holt. She remembered the clusters of lupines tumbling down the bank below the loggia; games with Berry, then five, on the lawn; a terrace above the lawn with two pools that they called the tanks; and John, who was three, falling into one of them, and being hauled out by his breeches. She took her first steps as a climber by making a traverse from the loggia along the drawing room window sills and up into the branches of a copper beech tree where she swung upside down by her knees.

As for her father, she remembered him teaching her French—"he was a great admirer of the French"—and math: "He had a magic square in which the numbers added up to nine whichever way you went. I thought that was wonderful." He showed her pages from a six-volume-part work, called *A History of Everyday Things,* and both he and Ruth would tell her bedtime stories drawn from history, like the tales of the Black Prince, or from the Greek myths. She remembered him going away and coming back, and wishing he was at home for longer. "I wanted to get to know him so much, he was such an interesting person."

At about this time, through Ruth and George's charitable impulses, the family acquired a temporary extra member in the form of a teenage boy named Franz Knefel. Franz was born a Czech in 1911, had grown up in Austria, and had been abandoned by his mother as the outcome of an affair with a married man. A group of visiting Quaker schoolteachers came upon him in a children's home and brought him to England for a holiday. In 1922, through a charity named the Children's Hospitality (After-Care) Committee, they tried to find him a home. Ruth offered to help and when Franz attended a boarding school near Cirencester named Rendcomb College she invited him to stay at the Holt during his holidays. Later on, Franz's mother married her lover after his own wife had died. She tried to get Franz back but he said he wanted to stay in England and Ruth stood by him. He learned woodcarving from Ruth's relations and eventually, having adopted a new name, Franz Nevel, built up his own furniture business. Clare remembered that he had idolized her father, and that he was "infinitely kind."

During the winter, George delivered a round of Everest lectures, which took him as far afield as Dublin and Aberdeen. Despite the expedition's catastrophic end, there was an avid public response, and the lecture halls were packed. George's share of the proceeds had been increased from twenty-five to thirty percent and he was soon receiving substantial checks from the Mount Everest Committee: £75 ($318.00) in November, £225 ($954.00) in December, £100 ($424.00) in January 1923. These three alone more than matched his old schoolteacher's salary, compensating for his lack of income while he had been away. He had also agreed to conduct a lecture tour in the United States, with the first lecture to be staged in Washington at the end of January. The tour would last for two months and seemed, at first, to provide an important step to a career as a writer and lecturer. But when Hinks wrote to George in November, asking if he could stay on in the United States after the lectures to present John Noel's film of the expedition, he and Ruth were compelled to address what kind of future they wanted.

It was true that George was earning more from his exploits on Everest than he had at Charterhouse. He was topping up his income through writing articles on Everest and the Himalaya for magazines and encyclopedias, and he had been asked to contribute to the 1922 expedition book. But mountaineering hardly offered a certain future, particularly as he neared the watershed of his fortieth birthday. More important was their struggle to reconcile their conflicting aims and desires each time Everest arose. In the eight years of their marriage Ruth had said goodbye to George five times without knowing when—or even whether— he would return. During each absence Ruth had suffered agonies of separation and uncertainty and George had carried her anxieties with his. Now Ruth felt, perhaps even more strongly than George, that there had to be an end to it. They decided that once he had returned from the United States he should look for a settled job. George asked Hinks how much longer he would have to spend in the United States and how much he would be paid—an issue, he added, that was "important to me." But he told Hinks that he would need to be back in England by mid-April to start his search for a job. In the end, the Everest committee decided to postpone any film tour until the autumn, and so George's services as presenter and projectionist were not required.

Hanging over these transactions, however, were two unanswered questions. Was there to be another Everest expedition? And when would it take place? The Everest committee was in no doubt that the 1922 attempt should be followed up as swiftly as possible, and at first contemplated launching a new attempt in 1923. Bruce had warned against this on the grounds that there would not be time to recruit "the personnel," implying that few if any of the 1922 members were willing to return so soon. The committee shifted its attentions to 1924, enabling the Mallorys to put the issue to one side.

❧

Early in 1923 George sailed for New York on the White Star liner *Olympic*. His departure had been preceded by familiar financial wrangling, this time over the size of the commission required by the New York lecture agent, Lee Keedick. He had been recommended to the committee by Gerald Christy, the agent handling the British lectures. Christy's commission was 33 percent but Keedick was insisting on 45 percent, to which the committee reluctantly agreed. There was also a vigorous debate over what class of liner was suitable for a British Everest lecturer: a standard Cunard passage was available at £31 ($141.67), against £57. 10s. ($262.78) for the more luxurious *Olympic*. For once the committee consented to the more expensive option on the grounds that it would give a better public impression of Mallory when he arrived in New York.

George had hoped that Ruth would come with him on the tour: a constant theme of his letters from Everest had been his regret that she was not there to share his experiences and thus help to make them whole. Although Ruth was tempted, she decided not to go, since it would mean being away from the children for too long. George wrote to her as assiduously as ever and this time his enthusiasm and sense of excitement had returned. When the *Olympic* was hit by an Atlantic gale, he reveled in the "furious wind and lightning, and torrents of rain and great waves hitting the ship with a terrific punch." It was "wonderful how a ship of this size trembles with the shock." One morning it felt "like Tibet—and at least twenty degrees of frost." He showed his usual interest in his fellow passengers and his customary initial disdain for those from other cultures. He found it hard to understand his dinner companions—"American tourists, a man with his wife and sister"—as their vowel sounds were "completely different." What he did discern of their conversation was that it mostly concerned food. He found the husband's table manners disgusting: "He often forks things off his wife's plate."

As always, George attempted to fill every moment of his time, and he spent long hours in his cabin drafting his account of the 1922 expedition. Writing in ink, in a pair of Walker's University Expert Manuscript Books, he planned his narrative under the heading: "Various obstacles to reaching summit." Whereas the 1921 bid had been a quest, the 1922 attempt was "like a race"; and of the climbers' key attributes, physical ability and will power, the latter would assume the greater importance: "Perhaps exhaustion of the mind will precede that of the body." He provided a title and word length for each section: "Acclimatisation up to Base Camp—2000"; "Factor of exhaustion up to Camp III—1000"; and so on, arriving at a total of 17,000 words. He found it hard to write during the gales: he lapsed into "a dull mechanical way of writing" and felt guilty that he could produce no more than 2000 words a day, even though it was a rate that would put many professional authors to shame.

The *Olympic* docked in New York on January 17. George marveled at the "immense silhouettes" of the Manhattan skyline, "playing a part in a grotesque world of toy giants," and its "wonderfully gay and jolly" nightlife, "with a blaze of light from advertisements scintillating on every building." He liked the agent, Keedick—"an agreeable man"—who had installed him at the Waldorf-Astoria Hotel. But Keedick had disappointing news, as he had succeeded in arranging only a handful of lectures, claiming he was "waiting to see how it catches on." In a bid to arouse interest in the tour, Keedick had set up several newspaper interviews, and a report appeared on the front page of the *New York Times* on Sunday, January 21. It was headed "Candy Diet Helped Mountain Climbers" and focused on George's belief that lemon drops, peppermints, and chocolate had given them the most efficient shots of muscular energy at high altitude. George had delivered a cautious verdict on oxygen apparatus, pointing out that Finch had reached only 250 feet higher than he had, but concluding: "It seems to be an advantage and we will probably all use the tanks on the next trip."

George's opening lecture, in Washington on January 26, brought a promising start. The matinee audience was dull—"never a clap," George wrote, "and almost never a laugh"—but the evening was a success: "It was technically better than any lecture I've ever given," he told Ruth. He scored a hit in Philadelphia, with two audiences totaling 3000 people and enthusiastic reviews. Next in line was the Broadhurst Theater in New York, where George was due to lecture on February 4. With 1100 seats to fill, there was a lot riding on the outcome, since a triumph in New York would stimulate bookings elsewhere. That would help fund the next Everest expedition; more important for George, since he was reckoning on taking 50 percent of the profits, it would provide the financial leeway he and Ruth needed while he looked for a job. "Everything depends on this," he told her.

George took advantage of the waiting time to complete his account for the 1922 expedition book, enthusiastically writing 30,000 words instead of the 17,000 he had been asked for. He delivered his manuscript to the New York publishers, Longman's, who sent a typewritten copy to their London counterparts, Edward Arnold. He spent half a day looking into some Boswell documents at the Morgan Library and was active on the social front too, for there was a substantial gathering of friends, relatives, and acquaintances in New York, whom he listed for Ruth. There was his cousin Mrs. Wathen and her husband, George; the Oppenheimers, "she is a relative of Aunt Jessie"; Tom Pym, a friend from Cambridge; Mrs. Cobden-Sanderson, who knew the Mallorys' friend Cissie Craies; and an American climber named Henry Schwab, "who has done much in the Alps." Wathen and Schwab initiated George in the further delights and secrets of New York. Wathen demonstrated how to make sixty dollars from a morning's speculation at the Cotton Exchange; and Schwab, a future president of the

American Alpine Club, hosted a visit to "the swellest of New York clubs." He led George down to the club's former wine cellar, which—this being Prohibition time—had been emptied of its furniture and lined with lockers. To George's astonishment, one locker was opened and "a bottle of gin was produced, and handed over to a barman, who then mixed three long drinks known as Tom Collins, and I enjoyed my Tom Collins very well and we sat talking and drinking pleasantly enough until after 1.0. Quelle vie!"

The lecture at the Broadhurst, though not quite a flop, was less than a triumph. The presentation was poor, as the slide operator was late and the signal wire to George's podium was too short. No more than half the seats had been sold, although a group from the American Alpine Club, which had hosted George to dinner at the Hotel Pennsylvania four days before, did their best to enliven the audience. Reginald Poel, an actor George had known at Cambridge, assured him that his delivery could not have been better but the morning press gave the lecture scant attention. The *New York Times* carried a short report, which focused on the fact that George had swigged a shot of brandy before turning back at 27,000 feet, an angle calculated to appeal to readers contending with the privations of Prohibition. No other morning paper covered the lecture, although there was an article in that afternoon's *Tribune* which described the dramas of the 1922 expedition and praised George for his modesty and "unaffected manner of speech which made him immediately a friend of the audience." Keedick's office sent a hundred copies of the paper to prospective bookers, but the reality was that the lecture had not provided the breakthrough the tour needed.

From New York George took the train to Canada where he was due to lecture in Toronto and Montreal. He arrived in bitter cold that revived his frostbite from Everest, only to find that the Toronto date had been canceled. From Montreal he traveled to Detroit, lecturing there on February 17, then returned to New York, where Keedick had been evaluating the tour. Although George's lectures had grossed $1500 in Philadelphia and $1000 in Washington, New York had been the crucial setback. Keedick told the Mount Everest Committee that George had earned $700 less than Conan Doyle in New York and that although he was "a fine fellow and gives a good lecture . . . the American public don't seem to be interested in the subject." Keedick added that George would have fared better if he had been promoted as a star, but that had been anathema to Hinks, who had been censoring the British publicity leaflets and posters to ensure that George and Finch did not receive undue personal attention. In the interests of economy, George transferred from the Waldorf-Astoria, where the overnight rate was $8, to the Flanders on West 47th Street, which charged a modest $2.

George wrote to Ruth to convey the bleak news. He had been missing her intensely: "It is much more difficult to go without you in this country than ever it was in India. I don't know why, but I don't feel I can really be happy at all without you." Now he had to admit that "the lecture tour simply isn't coming off" and he warned her that they would be "poorer than I hoped for a bit." His letter did little to cheer Ruth, as she had been suffering difficulties of her own. Vi had been ill, leaving Ruth to cope by herself. Their car, the Albert, was plagued with problems: a burst magneto, faulty plugs, a blocked fuel supply that had stranded Ruth on a hill. George was surprisingly unsympathetic, pointing out that the car had both a handbook and a petrol strainer, and adding that he was "greatly distressed" by Ruth's "despondent tone." Just as during the war, when George had criticized her grammar, Ruth hit back vigorously, telling George she now questioned whether they should have bought the car in the first place, especially as the garage they were having built was costing far more than expected. A chastened George replied that he was sorry she was "worried about money" and told her that he had been offered $400—"about £85"—for a magazine article about the Himalaya and that he was hoping to make £250 ($1142.50) from the U.S. lecture tour. The fact remained that they would have to be "careful about money at present."

Keedick arranged only a few more lectures—at Harvard, Toledo (Ohio), Iowa City, and Hanover (New Hampshire)—even after reducing his minimum charge to $250. On March 23 George wrote to Ruth from Boston, where he had delivered his final lecture. He had relented in his judgments about Americans, concluding that he "liked them on the whole very much": they were "extraordinarily modest and humble-minded in many respects, and pathetically anxious to be thought well of by English people." But he preferred Bostonians to New Yorkers, as they were better educated and "much more like the English." He was coming home on the *Saxonia*, which was sailing from New York in eight days' time, and George suggested that instead of meeting him in the Albert at Plymouth, as they had planned, it would be better if Ruth collected him at Godalming station. "I look forward to the unsurpassable delight, the joy of getting home and being with you, dearest love."

∞

The most notable event of George's U.S. tour, at least in the public mind, concerned a four-word quote that has been ascribed to him as his answer to the question: why do you want to climb Everest? George's reply, "Because it is there," has been used to represent an existential urge, felt by all mountaineers, to achieve a goal that is both physical and spiritual. Yet some of his family and friends have rejected this interpretation, believing that George was merely providing a trite or throwaway remark to get rid of a tiresome reporter. When the remark was aired in 1953, at the time of the British first ascent of Everest, David Pye told one of his sons that it was characteristic of George's reluctance to suffer fools gladly. Some Everest researchers have argued that George may well have not even made the remark at all, and that it was a creative paraphrase by an imaginative reporter.

The evidence is against the latter theory. The quote appeared in a lengthy article that was published in the *New York Times* on Sunday, March 18, and which may have been based on one of the interviews arranged by Keedick when George first arrived in New York, perhaps combined with material from one of his lectures. After quoting George's four-word answer, the unnamed reporter followed up with a second question: "But hadn't the expedition valuable scientific results?" George replied in turn: "Yes. The first expedition made a geological survey that was very valuable, and both expeditions made observations and collected specimens, both geological and botanical." But George admitted that scientific inquiry was a by-product of or an excuse for exploration, and went on to expand on his original answer in a way which endorsed its authenticity. "Everest is the highest mountain in the world, and no man has reached its summit. Its existence is a challenge. The answer is instinctive, a part, I suppose of man's desire to conquer the universe."

The reporter commented: "This is pure romance, call it what you will, and every man recognizes its touch." He was struck by George's politeness and modesty, and the impression George gave "that he has done nothing that any earnest and industrious man might not get up and do." None of this suggests that George was trying to get rid of him. What is more, George's answers were in keeping with the content of his lectures, as revealed in a draft which David Robertson cited in his biography. "I suppose we go to Mount Everest, granted the opportunity, because—in a word—we can't help it," George had written. "Or, to state the matter rather differently, because we are mountaineers."

It is of course possible to give more elaborate answers to the perennial question: why climb? In his writing and lectures, George described the spirit of adventure, confronting and managing risk, winning admiration; even, he confessed, the desire to be proclaimed a hero. His love of the wild places was manifest, as was his delight in the inner journey that accompanies an ascent. At the same time his four-word quote was a way of asserting a fundamental truth that bounces the issue back to the questioner. Reinhold Messner, who made the greatest ascent of Everest in 1980, when he went to the summit alone and without oxygen equipment via the route the British attempted in the 1920s, echoed Mallory's remarks.

"There is no answer," he said during a subsequent interview, "I am the answer." He was what he did; and because climbers climb mountains, that is what they do and are. In other words, as George had phrased it more than sixty years before, they do it because they are mountaineers.

❧

Once back in England, George had a stroke of luck. Hinks, who knew he was looking for a job, told him about an extramural lecturing post that was on offer in Cambridge. Hinks had bumped into an official of the Local Examinations and Lectures Syndicate, the Rev. David Cranage, who had just advertised for a history lecturer to conduct classes in towns and villages outside Cambridge and to help organize the other extramural courses. It sounded ideal, especially as the lectures were run in tandem with the Workers Educational Association, founded in the early days of the labor movement to assist working people who had missed out on schooling as a result of the privilege-ridden education system. The job would thus enable George to combine his ideological beliefs with his newfound qualities as a lecturer. It would bring him close to some of his most long-standing friends in Cambridge, from Arthur Benson to David Pye, who was lecturing at the university in engineering. The pay was respectable: a salary of £350 ($1600.00) plus separate lecture fees which could add around £150 ($685.50) a year.

George sent Cranage his letter of application on April 20. He said that he had taught working men in the army and had "considerable experience of public lecturing in Great Britain and in the USA in connection with the two expeditions to Mount Everest." His references included the heads of Winchester and Charterhouse, Arthur Benson, who by then was the Master of Magdalene, and Sir Francis Younghusband. Fletcher sent a testimonial from Charterhouse which, if George ever saw it, must have left him wondering if he had misjudged Fletcher all along. Fletcher described George's "singularly attractive personality, his enthusiasm for literature and great causes, his power of getting on with and winning the regard and friendship of all with whom he works" and said that he was "intelligent, eager, generous and high principled and always growing." George Trevelyan backed George's application, predicting that he would win supporters for the adult education movement. "He is one of the finest men whom the war has left us of that generation and his sane and steady idealism would be a great asset." There were twenty-five applicants of whom five, including George, were shortlisted. All four of George's rivals had stronger formal qualifications but after the interviews on May 8 he was offered the job. He was asked to make a prompt start, as his first duties included organizing two summer schools—a "Foreigners' Vacation Course" and a "Teachers' Course in Geography."

For all their delight and relief, George and Ruth faced a monumental upheaval. They would have to sell the Holt and move to Cambridge, which also meant, for Ruth, the wrench of leaving Godalming and losing her proximity to Westbrook and her father. Worse still, it brought another separation, for there was no time to do all of this before George began his job. He moved to Cambridge at the end of June, taking lodgings in West Road. He wrote to Geoffrey Young, telling him how impressed he was with the caliber of his colleagues. "Life," he added, "has been flying for me." Soon afterwards he found the family a new home. Named Herschel House, built on Herschel Road in west Cambridge in 1888–89, it was larger than the Holt and approached Westbrook in its scale, with seven bedrooms, a fives court, and an acre of land. At £4000 ($18,280.00) for a sixty-eight-year lease it was far more expensive than the Holt but, as before, Ruth's father put up the money on condition that the lease was in Ruth's name. It needed redecorating, and George and Ruth began laying plans for the wall coverings, curtains, and carpets, with Uncle Lawrence again offering his help; but that was what they enjoyed.

The great unresolved question remained Everest. The Mount Everest Committee had been reviewing the lessons of 1922 and, having abandoned thoughts of an expedition in 1923, was laying plans for 1924. In an item of unfinished business, it agreed to pay the families of the porters killed in the avalanche compensation of 250 rupees each, around £17.50 ($80.00), plus a further £3.50 ($16.00) for any child. Longstaff delivered a paper drawing the medical conclusions from the 1922 attempt that was notable for recognizing the disastrous effects of dehydration. "Thirst is a terrible trial at great altitudes," Longstaff wrote. "The loss of body fluids by evaporation is, in my belief, a grave element in mountain sickness." He considered the vexed question of oxygen, citing statistics that appeared to confirm the benefit the oxygen equipment had brought its users, although it was impossible to quantify by precisely how much. Longstaff suspected that Finch had been far more exhausted by his attempt than he had realized because the apparatus had enabled him to drive himself beyond his true physiological limits, and he believed that Everest could be climbed without it, "given a second fine windless day."

George was keen to deliver his views, and spoke at a meeting of the Mount Everest Committee on June 14. He still leaned against using the equipment, arguing that if climbers spent four or five nights on the North Col they should acclimatize enough to reach the summit, particularly if there were two camps above the col. If there were only one camp, however, "oxygen would be an advantage." Finch remained a staunch advocate. He recommended that climbers should start using oxygen at 21,000 feet and that the expedition should stockpile cylinders at 26,500 feet, enabling the summit climbers to use it during both their ascent and their descent. He did concede—in the light of his own experience—that they would need two weeks' rest afterwards. In the end the committee hedged its bets. Although it decided to send eleven sets and ninety oxygen cylinders to Everest, it still had both practical and moral reservations about using it, and clearly preferred the climbers to make a nonoxygen ascent.

As autumn approached, so did a final decision over which climbers should be chosen for the expedition. To avoid suspicions of favoritism, the Alpine Club had formed a selection panel with twelve members including Strutt, Longstaff, General Bruce, Collie, Farrar, and George himself. The panel had decided back in May that Bruce should lead the expedition again and that Norton should be the climbing leader. It also settled on four definite candidates: Howard Somervell, Noel Odell, Bentley Beetham, and George. Somervell had proved himself in 1922; Odell was a geologist who had spent two seasons climbing with Longstaff in Norway; and Beetham, a schoolmaster, was yet another Lake District man, a friend and climbing partner of Somervell.

George was the most obvious name of all. Key panel members, such as Longstaff and Strutt, had come to a magnanimous view of the avalanche. His greatest fault was seen as his persistent forgetfulness. Bruce had noted that he was liable to forget his boots "on all occasions," and the 1922 member John Morris later wrote that he and his colleagues "took it in turns to see that none of his kit was left behind." But that was outweighed, in most members' eyes, by his priceless experience and knowledge of the mountain. Even Hinks had softened in his attitude towards him, realizing that he would be better advised to stop antagonizing so influential a figure, although George himself had by now got Hinks's measure. But George remained utterly undecided whether he should go, and in a letter to Geoffrey Young he listed the four top names besides Norton as:

SOMERVELL

ODELL

BEETHAM

SELF???

The matter came to a head at the end of October, just as George and Ruth were preparing to move to Cambridge. "Dearest One," George wrote to Ruth on October 18, "We can go into Herschel House on Monday 29th." His letter was full of plans and details of the proposed redecoration. He favored light-colored designs for the walls and amber for the doors, and wanted curtains with zigzag patterns for his study, but suggested they decide on the other rooms when she had arrived. He proposed buying some beds at a sale of furniture to be held in a tent in the garden on October 30 by the widow of the previous owner, a Cambridge don, the Rev. John Lock. He told Ruth he would arrange for removal vans to come to the Holt on October 27 and planned to join her there that weekend, ready to drive to Cambridge. The children would stay with Vi at her parents' home near Weymouth in Dorset until the move was complete.

Poor Ruth. On the very day that George wrote to her, Hinks was stepping in. Just two days before, the Mount Everest Committee had confirmed its preferred candidates for the expedition, with the four favorites those on the list George had sent to Young. George's question marks revealed the extent of his indecision, which was also witnessed by Pye, who believed that he "really did not want to go." George told Pye that he wanted to share in any success the expedition might achieve. Yet he believed that the odds were heavily against it and would have been "profoundly relieved" if it were called off. There was significant opposition from his own family, his sister Mary later saying: "We were very against him going." Even Geoffrey Young, usually so ready to provide reassurance, was opposed.

Hinks, who presumably felt that he was acting in the best interests of the expedition, realized that if George was to go, there was an obstacle to remove. Hinks knew that George had not told Cranage that he was a contender for the next Everest expedition in case it harmed his chances of getting the Cambridge job. George had told Hinks on October 16 that he doubted, in any case, whether he would be given leave of absence. On October 18 Hinks wrote to Cranage on George's behalf. He told Cranage that the expedition leader, General Bruce, was anxious that George should take part and asked him "to convey to the proper quarters the assurance that Mallory's cooperation next year is of high importance in the opinion of the Mount Everest Committee to the success of their enterprise."

For Cranage, as George later wrote, Hinks's letter came as a "bombshell." Cranage told Hinks: "You ask a difficult thing," but said he would give his request "sympathetic consideration" and promised to discuss it with his chairman. Hinks had sent a copy of his letter to George, who was equally surprised by its forceful terms and asked if Bruce really was as keen to have him as Hinks had said. Discerning that he needed to stiffen George's resolve, Hinks replied: "I think I can say that not only Bruce but all the members of the Committee are anxious that you should go. I have never heard any expression except of fear that the University might not be able to spare you."

George meanwhile was reporting some of these maneuvers to Ruth, but in a way that implied he was unlikely to take part in the expedition. In his letter about moving to Cambridge, he had added a note saying that Hinks had written to Cranage "about my going." Cranage, he added, "has not turned it down definitely. But I don't think they will hear of my going." He admitted it would be "a big sacrifice either way" and told her: "It is wretched not being able to talk to you about this, darling. You must tell me if you can't bear the idea of my going again and that will settle it anyway."

By now, it seemed, George's state of indecision was total, as he oscillated between his feelings about the expedition, which were themselves ambivalent, and his knowledge of the pain it would cause Ruth if he were to go. He confided in Hinks, telling him: "I'm having a horrible time on a tight rope." What he most wanted was that someone else, or some force majeure, should take the decision out of his hands. In her response to George's letter, Ruth had demurred, telling him that in effect he was free to go. But if Cranage and the lecture syndicate rejected Hinks's request, as George had predicted, that would put an end to the matter. He would be absolved from making the decision and he could stay with Ruth and their children, his new job, and their new home.

A day or so later, Cranage said he could go. His chairman agreed that they should not stand in George's way and he was given permission on generous terms: six months' leave on half-pay. Cranage still needed the formal approval of a full syndicate meeting on October 31, but there was little doubt that it would consent. On the same day that Cranage passed on the decision, the Mount Everest Committee wrote to George to confirm its invitation to take part. As George admitted to his father on October 25, the responsibility for the decision had been passed back to him once more. "It will therefore rest with me to make the choice. You may imagine it isn't easy, and I look for guidance as to what is right . . . . It is an awful tug to contemplate going away from here instead of settling down to make a new life here with Ruth."

So it was that George and Ruth discussed whether he should go to Everest on the very weekend when they prepared to move to Cambridge. The impulse to stay at home was all too clear, and both knew it well: his wife, his children, his new home, his new life, together with the familiar anguish both would suffer by yet another separation. But they were equally aware of the countervailing pressures. Just as in 1921, when it appeared that Bullock might find the key to the North Col, George acknowledged that it would "look rather grim to see others, without me, engaged in conquering the summit." And, as he told his father, "I have to look at it from the point of view of loyalty to the expedition and of carrying through a task begun."

Through her daughter Clare, Ruth passed on her own account of the factors that came into play that fateful weekend. "She was very uneasy about him going for the last time," Clare recalled. "She had premonitions. Financially it was very worrying. But she also felt he should finish the job. My father had made an emotional investment in the mountain. If someone else had got to the top . . . She told me it was partly because of the porters being killed. He had always felt so guilty about that and he had learned so much more about snow conditions as a result." Clare confirmed that her parents were not swayed by the patriotic connotations of the impending expedition, the notion invoked by Hinks and Collie that, since the British had made the first attempts, it was they who should see it through. It was more a matter of personal integrity, Clare said: her parents held truth and honor to be supremely important, and felt that it was right and just that her father "should go out there and save lives and finish the job." Her mother, Clare added, "was always proud of what he had done, how he had done what he thought was the best thing possible. In a very honourable sense, he had done what he thought was right."

Ruth had made her last and greatest sacrifice. Three days after the move to Herschel House, the lecture syndicate gave George its formal approval. The one remaining potential barrier was removed on November 6, when the doctor appointed by the committee passed him "fit in every respect." Two days later, George told Young: "A line to let you know I'm going out once more . . . " It would be a "big tug," George added, "with the ends of a new job gathering in my hands; and R. will feel it more this time too. I'm very happy it is decided so." He wrote to Hinks in similar terms, thanking him for his "good offices in the matter," adding: "Rather a tug altogether, but I'm very happy now it is decided."

Having done its utmost to secure his services, the committee now delivered George a grotesque financial blow. During George's discussions with Ruth, she had raised the matter of money, asking how they would manage, and so George wrote to ask Younghusband how much he was to be paid for his contributions to the two Everest books. The issue had been left unresolved since 1921, when Hinks asked George to write an account of the reconnaissance for the first book. George reminded Younghusband that he had told him a year before that he expected to be paid on the same profit-sharing basis as his lectures, and that he had written 70,000–80,000 words in time "which if it hadn't been spent that way would have been free for writing for my own purposes." Suspecting that the committee might plead poverty, George offered to refund his payments if the expeditions eventually proved to have made a financial loss.

The committee's decision again coincided most unhappily with the Mallorys' domestic affairs. On November 2, with her father acting as witness, Ruth signed the lease for Herschel House. On November 5, the committee refused George's request to be paid for his writing, on the grounds that it was "not in a position to make any payment for such contributions at the present time." It thus ignored

George's offer to repay the money if necessary; and, in any case, the implication that it was impoverished was untrue. Although the expeditions had been initially funded by overdrafts, they had always been financially secure. The first expedition had cost £4241 ($16,285.00) but donations from members of the Royal Geographical Society and Alpine Club, together with the selling of media rights, had converted that to a profit of £7845 ($30,125.00). That was used to finance the 1922 expedition which, although it cost £12,538 ($55,418.00), still showed a surplus of £2474 ($10,935.00), a sum which was used in turn to help set up the third expedition.

It was true that in early 1923 the committee was in financial trouble, much of its own making: not only had an Indian bank crashed, taking with it £700 ($31,990.00) of the expedition's funds, but the committee's cashier had absconded with another £700. The treasurer, Edward Somers-Cocks, repaid half the missing amount on condition that the cashier's offense was covered up. But in the summer the photographer, John Noel, offered to buy all photographic and film rights for £8000 ($36,560.00). The committee gratefully accepted—with the saving on photographic expenses, the offer was worth around £10,000 ($45,700.00) —and at a stroke the expedition was financially secure. What was more, the first expedition book had already virtually earned back its advance of £1000 ($4570.00), and the publishers, Edward Arnold, had paid a further £500 ($2285.00) for the rights to the second. The committee's meanness reflected its willful ignorance of life as experienced by those expedition members who had to resort to the unsavory practice called work. Hinks waited until George had confirmed that he was joining the expedition before informing him of the committee's decision, which he justified by saying that no other contributors had been paid either. He added, sanctimoniously: "The Committee, however, fully appreciated the value of your contributions."

❧

Such miserly attitudes were to have a bearing on the selection of the rest of the team. With George, Somervell, Norton, and Odell confirmed, two more climbers remained to be chosen. In order of preference, the committee had drawn up a shortlist of five: Graham, Irvine, Hazard, Culverwell, and Rusk. The most notable absentee was George Finch. Almost since his return from Everest, a dispute had been smoldering over the issue that had blighted his selection in 1921: to what extent did the committee own his experiences on Everest? Finch had worked as hard as George on the British lecture circuit, earning the committee hundreds of pounds in return for his thirty percent. Like George, he had written a section of the 1922 expedition book for which he too had not been paid, and he had allowed the committee to choose photographs from his immaculately presented set of prints and negatives. Although Finch had remarried in 1921, he was on far harder times than George, who had the benefit of Ruth's income from her father; and when he sent George £2 ($9.14) to cover some lecturing expenses, the check bounced.

The dispute became a blazing row when Finch went on holiday to Switzerland in the summer of 1923 and told the committee that he planned to deliver some Everest lectures from which he intended to keep the proceeds. To the committee, this confirmed every prejudice it held about Finch, from his long hair to his enthusiasm for oxygen equipment, Bruce going so far as to expostulate: "What an absolute swine that man is." Although the committee's lawyer warned that the climbers' contracts were probably not binding, it threatened Finch with legal action. Finch offered to postpone any independent lectures until the autumn but the committee refused to compromise and Hinks wrote to insist that Finch should abide by the letter of his contract. In the end Hinks's demand proved unenforceable. But even though Finch had devoted still more of his time to improving the oxygen equipment intended for use in 1924, the committee had long since decided to exclude him from the expedition.

In the wake of this shameful episode, the committee contrived to immerse itself in further controversy over the fifth climbing place. At the head of the shortlist was Richard Graham, a schoolmaster and yet another Lake District climber with a strong alpine record. Graham was also a Quaker and pacifist who had refused to fight during the war, remaining at his post as a teacher at Bishop's Stortford instead. The details of the episode are unclear, as the records that might flesh it out are—like other sensitive items—not to be found in the RGS archives. But at least one member of the 1924 team contested Graham's selection on the grounds that he had been a conscientious objector, even though the government preferred teachers to remain at their posts. George, who later concluded that Graham's opponent was Beetham, protested to Bruce, saying that since he, Younghusband, and Collie had approved the choice of Graham they should stand by him now. Somervell, who had returned to India after the 1922 expedition to work at a medical mission in the state of Travancore, cabled his resignation from the Alpine Club in protest at "this dirty piece of work." The row was leaked to the press but Graham, who was bitterly disappointed, withdrew from the expedition to spare it further embarrassment. His place was given to John de Vere Hazard, an alpinist and Lake District climber, who had been recommended by Morshead, the surveyor on the two previous expeditions—the two men had fought together on the Somme.

That left one climbing place to be accounted for, and it went to someone who, at twenty-one, was by far the youngest person to be selected for any of the three expeditions. In the wake of the depredation caused by the cold and exhaustion in 1922, the committee had searched for younger climbers. It had even considered excluding anyone older than thirty, while Norman Collie had argued that the ideal combination would be experienced mountaineers who would establish the route and "very hardy young climbers to finally get to the top." Only in September 1923 did one such hardy young climber come to its notice in the shape of an undergraduate then in his second year at Oxford, his name destined to be forever linked with that of George Mallory: Sandy Irvine.

Until now Irvine has largely remained a historical cypher, a bit part to George in his starring role: a muscular and athletic young man out of his depth, faithfully following in George's footsteps, going uncomplainingly to his death. He has been difficult to read because the smiling figure captured in half a dozen photographs overlay a character who was overawed by the company he found himself in. Like Ruth, he had difficulty expressing himself because, as was suspected of her, he suffered from borderline dyslexia. In fact the most recent researches have revealed a far more sensitive and responsive figure with the ideal skills and attributes to complement George, and one who shared his determination to reach the summit.

Andrew Comyn Irvine was born in Birkenhead in April 1902. By striking coincidence, he lived in Park Road South, half a mile from St. John's church and rectory, George's family home after the move from Mobberley. His father was a successful Liverpool broker and he was educated at Shrewsbury and Merton College, Oxford, where he was an accomplished sportsman. But he had to struggle with the handicap of growing up in a family where all emotion was suppressed. His father belonged to the Scottish Presbyterian Church, a sect notorious for its puritanical joylessness. When Sandy and his siblings were woken at seven each morning—he had four brothers and a sister—they were forbidden to talk to each other until a quarter to eight. His mother, Lilian, a lawyer's daughter, was a beautiful, gentle woman, and far less repressed, but remained a distant Victorian parent, content to leave her children's upbringing to nannies and maids.

All of this may have contributed to Irvine's learning difficulties. He wrote painstakingly, his grammar was awry, and he was an abysmal speller. His letters to his mother from Shrewsbury were full of mistakes, most noticeably his constant repeats of the sentiment: "I hop you are well." There were constant complaints from his Oxford tutors about his writing, and he was almost certainly admitted to Merton on the strength of his sport. He was a powerful rower who, quite unusually, was selected for the Oxford eight in his first year at the university. He rowed in two of the annual boat races against Cambridge, the greatest honor for an Oxford rower, and also played squash against Cambridge.

Sport was one medium where he could express himself; another was in practical matters, for he was studying chemistry and was a passionate engineer. He was still at school when he stripped down and rebuilt one of his parents' cars, an Essex, and he owned a Clyno motorbike. He sent the War Office a design for a synchronizer that would enable air force pilots to fire machine guns between their propeller blades, and another for a gyroscopic aircraft stabilizer. He had a sharp visual sense that emerged in his photography: he had a strong sense of composition and took some two hundred pictures during the 1924 expedition. A number depict Tibetan villagers and reveal Irvine's empathy for his subjects and their struggle to exist in such a stark environment.

Irvine was recommended to the selection committee by Noel Odell, who first met him in North Wales. Odell, who had just got married, was walking the tops of the Carnedd range with his wife when he was astonished to see a young man approaching the rounded summit of Foel Grach on a motorcycle. It was Irvine, and he asked Odell the way to Llanfairfechan, a village to the north of the range. Several years later Odell met Irvine again beside the Thames in Putney, where Irvine was training for the 1923 Oxford vs. Cambridge boat race. Odell was recruiting a team to go skiing and sledging on the island of Spitsbergen in Arctic Norway, and decided that Irvine was an ideal candidate. Irvine jumped at the chance, further impressing Odell during a training visit to Wales by leading Great Gully on Craig yr Ysfa. Irvine acquitted himself well and enjoyed every moment of the Spitsbergen trip. He and Odell returned to Britain just as the committee was drawing up its list of nominees and casting about for at least one of Collie's "hardy young climbers."

Although at twenty-one Irvine was younger than the age the committee had in mind, he had one important strength which the expedition needed since Finch had been disposed of. Irvine's mechanical aptitudes made him the ideal person to take care of the oxygen equipment. Although Odell was nominally the oxygen officer, he wanted as little to do with the equipment as possible, and so was delighted when Irvine was invited to join the expedition on October 24. Two days later Irvine made his own excitement plain when he wrote: "Subject to Medical Examination I have been finally accepted so I'm again walking on metaphorical air."

⚭

The Mallorys were reunited at Herschel House in early November. A day or so after Ruth and George moved in, Vi arrived with the children, who brought tales of eating wild raspberries and roaming in the Dorset hills with Vi's father. The house, George wrote, was "sunny and spacious" and the redecoration, with advice from Uncle Lawrence, was under way. The dining room was papered with a dark daisy Morris pattern to set against the brown varnished woodwork, while the drawing room was rendered in green. The Mallorys brought the squash court back into use and set up a tennis court on the lawn. The children were allowed to select the colors for their rooms. "I chose bright blue and scarlet," Clare re-called. "My sister chose the same. I thought she was being a copycat." Clare practiced her climbing on the ledges and window sills of Herschel House but, after she had used her skipping rope to haul Berry onto the front porch, Ruth told them they were only permitted to climb trees. "There was a wall with a rounded top between the lawn and the kitchen garden," Clare said. "We used to climb up and run along that and climb into a cherry tree."

George's life as an extramural lecturer exacted a demanding schedule. He had classes at Raunds, thirty miles away in Northamptonshire, and at Halstead, the same distance away in Essex. After a day's administrative duties he would leave Cambridge in the Albert at 4 P.M. and return to Herschel House, often after a testing drive across the misty wetlands, at 11 P.M. He attracted a loyal group of students, with as many as seventy people attending his lectures on the demo-cratic origins of the seventeenth century. Ruth, keen to spend time with him as his departure date approached, sometimes went with him, discussing his lectures as they drove, and was gratified by his students' enthusiastic response. The fam-ily spent Christmas at Westbrook and then George and Ruth went to the Peak District for a week, going out for walks in "murky murky weather," George wrote, which was "mostly wet—never really clear." In the New Year both Avie and Trafford, together with his wife Doris, came to stay at Herschel House. Trafford was working at the Air Ministry and George passed on news of his prospects to their sister Mary and her husband Ralph, whose army career had taken them to Colombo in the British colony of Ceylon. "T. looks forward without a doubt to success and promotion in the future," George wrote.

But their marriage was under strain. When he was not lecturing in the evening, George had other meetings to attend. He faced further demands on his time from the Climbers' Club, having been chosen as its chairman in February 1923, although he managed to attend only one of its four committee meetings that year. As subsequent letters between George and Ruth confirm, they went through their worst time in the autumn, while George prevaricated over his decision, and Ruth was torn between her empathy for him, wanting whatever it was he wanted for himself, and then facing yet another separation. She did her best to suppress her anxieties and perhaps did so too well, for George later praised her for having remained so cheerful. It was an ability Avie had observed during a previous expedition, when she wrote to tell George how well Ruth concealed just how "strung up and anxious" she felt. "She keeps busy but quite calmly so, over the cooking, at which she is decidedly successful," Avie wrote.

The Mallorys' finances were in an unhealthy state too. Both their accounts had gone into overdraft. It was bitterly cold in Cambridge that winter and, with the house so costly to heat, they tried to cut down on their use of coal. Ruth suffered from backache, which she blamed on the cold, and the children had streaming colds. They had not yet sold the Holt and were considering taking in lodgers or even renting out Herschel House until George returned. As George acknowledged in another of his letters, it all left its mark. They were so preoccupied with the mundane topics of life that some of the fire had gone out of their love. "We seem to have got stuck with material considerations and how often we talk of nothing but what has to be done to keep the ball rolling as though it were so much business to be transacted."

Clare's memories of her mother from that period mostly reflect an air of discontent. Ruth was keen to establish a garden to compare with those of Westbrook and the Holt. "But she hated the soil there, it had too much clay in comparison with the sandy soil of Surrey," Clare said. Ruth was discomfited by the patronizing attitudes of some of George's acquaintances, and told Clare about a dinner she had attended where the conversation turned to art. "She had been to Venice every year and knew a lot about Renaissance painters," Clare said. "She started participating quite fluently in the conversation and the hostess just changed the subject. My mother despised her for wanting to show off her own intellectual capabilities instead of drawing out her guests. She felt the hostess was really snobbish. My mother wasn't super well educated, but she did know about art." Ruth met Arthur Benson, whose comments following dinner as the Mallorys' guest at Herschel House revealed him at his worst, being simultaneously envious, supercilious, and misogynistic. Ruth was "beautiful, self-conscious, brusque and extremely inattentive," he wrote, "she believes herself to be a suggestive and humorous talker, but she is a thin and truculent performer." Benson even complained about the decor, which had "rather too calculated a simplicity."

As the departure date loomed, so did the pressure both George and Ruth felt. David Pye had wanted George to sit for the eminent portrait painter William Nicholson, the father-in-law of Robert Graves, but he could fit in only two brief sessions, far from enough. Ruth's sense of foreboding increased and this time her anxiety showed, compounded by her sense of guilt at spoiling their last time together. There is evidence that George had premonitions too. According to Eleanor Young, George asked to meet Kathleen Scott, the widow of the doomed

Antarctic explorer Captain Robert Scott, who had subsequently married Geoffrey Young's brother Hilton. George was clearly disturbed by the encounter, for as he traveled back in a taxi with the Youngs he told them he did not want to return to Everest. Geoffrey Keynes related that George had told him that the expedition would be "more like war than adventure, and that he did not believe he would return alive."

One of Clare's last memories of her father was of looking up at him and seeing an affectionate, quizzical expression on his face. George said goodbye to his children in Cambridge and traveled up to Birkenhead to stay with his parents. He was due to sail from Liverpool on the SS *California* on Friday, February 29. On February 28 he and Ruth were guests at a dinner held by the Liverpool Wayfarers' Club. Irvine, Beetham, and Hazard were there too, together with George's and Irvine's fathers. The following afternoon George and Ruth went to the docks. George was already laying plans for his return, asking Ruth to invite George Finch and his wife to Herschel House on the first weekend he was back. After George had gone on board, Ruth stood on the quayside to wave him off. There was a westerly gale brewing, and the tugboats assigned to the *California* struggled to pull the liner away. In the end Ruth stopped waving and returned to Birkenhead.

❧

"I am glad you decided to abandon waving," George told her in his first letter from the *California*. "We weren't off till 8.30 or thereabouts as the two tugs provided were hopelessly beaten by the wind. It was a wild night that first one; and yesterday in the bay was wild too, with wind and rain a plenty scudding across the waste of steel-gray white capped waters."

George and Ruth knew that they had parted with their marriage in an unhappy state. Ruth's first letter to George, the only one to have survived from all those she wrote during his three Everest expeditions, began with her usual chatty details, some describing the practical difficulties she had been experiencing. It had snowed heavily in Cambridge that weekend and the children had spent a day making snowmen in the garden. But, she told George, she had done "the one thing you told me not to and use a ton of coke straight away." Their bank manager, a Mr. Raxworthy, had just told her that her account was overdrawn by £823 ($3629.43) and George's by £112 ($493.92). Raxworthy wanted her to sell some shares but Ruth was hoping to raise £2500 ($11,025.00) from selling the Holt. She had news of the children: Clare had been "appallingly talkative" all the previous day and "nothing would stop her tongue." That morning before breakfast Ruth had found her writing out the thirteen times table. "She has determined to write out and learn all the difficult ones up to 19 times she says." There were reports from the domestic front. Nellie, their new cook, "seems very nice and cooks well"; the Cranages had invited her to dinner; her cousin Francis Wills was coming to stay. "I seem nearly as full of engagements as I was before you left. People are being most awfully kind and nice."

In her last paragraph, Ruth talked about the problems of their marriage. "I hope you are happy and having a good voyage. I am keeping quite cheerful and happy but I do miss you a lot. I think I want your companionship even more than I used to. I know I have rather often been cross and not nice and I am very sorry but the bottom reason has nearly always been because I was unhappy at getting so little of you. I know its pretty stupid to spoil the times I do have you for those when I don't. Very very much love to you my dear one. Your loving Ruth."

George too had been pondering the notes of discontent that had affected their last weeks together. Although he had not yet received Ruth's letter, he wrote to her in presciently similar terms, reflecting the mutual empathy and ability to take the other's part that underpinned their marriage. "I fear I don't make you very happy," he told her. "Life has too often been a burden to you lately and it is horrid when we don't get more time and talk together . . . Somehow or another we must contrive to manage differently; to have some first charge upon available time for our life together."

It was the start of an attempt to resolve their difficulties as far as was possible in a correspondence conducted over an ever-lengthening distance. The contents of some of Ruth's subsequent letters may be deduced from George's answers, and he was pleased when Ruth wrote in her second letter that she intended to keep busy with domestic matters and to be "enterprising and social." George meanwhile was indulging in more romantic thoughts, mixed with regret. He imagined that she, not Hazard, was sharing his cabin on the *California*, so that he could look down on her in her bunk in the morning, then go with her into the bows "in our silk dressing gowns to breathe the fresh morning air." He commented on the reasons that had impelled him to join the expedition: "Dear girl, we give up and miss a terrible lot by trying to do what is right; but we must see we don't miss too much."

On March 30, shortly before crossing into Tibet, George read Ruth's first letter at last. "Dearest one, you needn't worry that you haven't been an angel every day of your life. We went through a difficult time together in the autumn; but though we were both conscious that we saw too little of one another last term it seemed to me that we were very happy and I often thought how cheerful and pleasant you were when life was not being very agreeable. I'm quite sure we shall settle down to enjoy our home in Cambridge." When he read Ruth's second letter, he told her it was "wonderful" that she intended to "settle down and be cheerful." He predicted that his reply would reach her on May 1, the tenth anniversary of their engagement.

> *Will you think of me very specially? . . . And may it be as good a day as it was in 1914. Please thank Clare and Berry very much for their letters which I much enjoyed; and I liked the cards with flower-pictures. It will be some time yet before John can write me letters! Now farewell dearest love. I wave you many kisses and see you smiling and happy and resolved so to be even during the month of May.*
>
> *Ever your loving George*

⚛

George was in an equally positive frame of mind during the five-week trek to the Rongbuk Glacier. When the *California* detachment teamed up with their companions at Darjeeling, George had nothing but good to say of them, including those he was meeting for the first time. He liked Richard Hingston, the doctor and naturalist, who had traveled from the RAF hospital in Baghdad, "an Irishman, a quiet little man and a very keen naturalist." Edward Shebbeare, the forestry officer and an assistant to Geoffrey Bruce in overseeing the transport arrangements, was "an excellent fellow." Somervell had arrived from his medical mission in Travancore, Odell from his geological work in the Persian oil fields. "It was very nice to see S. again and Odell is one of the best." He marveled at the entrepreneurial spirit demonstrated by Noel, who—"more than ever full of stunts"—was planning to take a Citroën car into Tibet to photograph it for an advertisement. Of the other newcomers, he considered Hazard "a nice and reasonable being," Beetham "good-humoured and unselfish," Irvine "sensible and not highly strung, he'll be one to depend on, for everything except conversation."

George was especially impressed with Norton in his new role as Bruce's deputy. "[He] has got the whole organisation under his hand," he told Ruth. "He is going to be an ideal 2nd to Bruce." Norton had clearly been considering his team's bodily comforts, for he had arranged for a mess tent to be erected as soon as the expedition arrived at its overnight camps, and this time the morale-boosting delicacies included sixty cans of quail in foie gras and four cases of 1915 Montebello champagne. In a later letter, invoking a Hindi word meaning "arrangements" which had caught on among the team members, George wrote of Norton: "He knows the whole bandobast from A to Z." Although the wind, as implacable as ever, hit them on the Tibetan plateau, they did not suffer the blizzards of 1922. George's one worry, unusually, concerned his fitness, for his old ankle injury troubled him for a time and he had a stomach upset, which Hingston briefly thought could be appendicitis. Somervell prepared his surgical instruments but the tenderness passed. It was, George told Ruth, "an amazingly nice party altogether." Later he added: "I'm really enjoying myself now with a good holiday feeling . . . . "

As the great caravan trudged across the Tibetan plateau, with its seventy Sherpa porters and 300 pack animals, one topic dominated the climbers' conversations. How were they to avoid the pitfalls and mistakes that had beset them in 1922? What use were they to make of oxygen? How, in short, were they to climb the mountain? Bruce and Norton were determined to avoid the logistic logjam which, together with the weather, had been so costly in 1922. Norton had also prepared elaborate plans for advancing the supplies and equipment up the mountain, pyramid-style, as in 1922. This time, as well as hiring 150 local Tibetans to ferry loads up the East Rongbuk Glacier, they planned to form an elite cadre from the fittest Sherpas—to be known as the "Tigers"—for the most demanding high-level work. As for using oxygen apparatus, Norton, like the Mount Everest Committee, had tried to hedge his bets by planning two attempts, one with oxygen equipment, one without. But he revealed his own preferences by giving the nonoxygen team—or the "oxygen-less party," as the team members called it—the first shot.

George felt that Norton's plan was flawed, principally because it allowed for only one camp above the North Col, at 26,500 feet, which meant that both parties would be expected to go to the summit in two days. As Norton later wrote, the plan sparked an anxious debate among the climbers. Twice, at Darjeeling and Phari, the 1922 veterans, Somervell, Geoffrey Bruce, and George—George called them "the old gang"—tried to resolve the issue. Each time they failed and so, as Norton related, "we decided to continue our arguments across the endless plains of Tibet." The outcome, he admitted, was impasse.

Fate now took a hand. As George told Ruth, the health of General Bruce—a matter of concern in 1922—was in decline. He celebrated his fifty-eighth birthday during the trek with a bottle of rum donated for the occasion by his brother but a day or so later collapsed with a recurrence of malaria, combined with heart problems. Hingston, the doctor, ordered him back to Darjeeling. When George heard this on April 13 he immediately realized its import: Norton now assumed overall command of the expedition, while George stepped up to become its climbing leader.

George was hugely gratified by his promotion: "I'm bound to say I feel some little satisfaction," he told Ruth on April 14. What was more, it gave him the chance to resolve the dispute over the climbing strategy. Within twenty-four hours he drew up an alternative plan that embodied a significant new emphasis in the use of oxygen apparatus and which also reflected a shift of George's own attitude. The previous summer, when George presented his views to the Everest committee, he had sided with the antioxygen faction. Since then he had changed his mind, telling Longstaff in a letter from the *California* in March that he was "dead against" going for the top from 26,000 feet without oxygen. He also wrote to his sister Mary in Colombo, telling her: "I rather expect we shall use it, as we can carry fifty percent more oxygen than last year with same weight." In this he had almost certainly been swayed by the arguments Finch had presented. George had developed a strong sympathy for Finch, having been appalled by his treatment at the hands of Hinks and the committee over the issue of his lecture earnings, although George had only learned about this long after Finch had been dropped. As Ruth herself later revealed, it was that, plus a desire to climb with Finch again in the Alps, which led George to ask her to invite Finch and his wife to Herschel House as soon as he returned from Everest.

George's new plan devoted as much attention as Norton's to the complex logistics of equipping a series of camps up the mountain. But, unlike Norton, George believed that there should be not one but three camps above the North Col: at 25,500 feet, 26,500 feet, and 27,300 feet. Then, instead of the oxygen-less party making the first attempt, the two parties should set off simultaneously. The oxygen party would start from Camp 6 at 26,500 feet, the oxygen-less party from Camp 7 at 27,300 feet, in the hope, George wrote, that they would "presumably meet on the summit." George immodestly considered the scheme a "brainwave—no other word will describe the process by which I arrived at another plan for climbing the mountain." When he presented it to his colleagues at Tinki Dzong on April 17, it seemed to have broken the impasse. "Everyone has cordially approved," George told Ruth. "I'm much pleased about this, as you may imagine—if only for this it seems worth while to have come."

At first sight, the plan represented a compromise between the competing views over the oxygen equipment. But George was so convinced of the benefits of using it that he felt that the oxygen party had "the best chance of all of getting to the top." Having won his colleagues' approval, George conferred with Norton over who should be selected to make the attempts. Norton agreed that George and Somervell should each lead one of the two parties. When George said he wanted to lead the oxygen party himself, on the grounds that Somervell had proved his ability to climb without oxygen in 1922, Norton agreed to that too. Next, they considered the other two summit climbers. There were four or five contenders to accompany Somervell and since Norton himself was among them, he left it to

Somervell and George to decide. As for George's partner on the oxygen attempt, George felt it was "obvious" that the choice lay between the expedition's two oxygen experts. In other words, so he told Ruth on April 17, it was "either Odell or Irvine."

It was a fateful choice, and one that has been debated almost as passionately as the question of whether George and Irvine reached the summit. Seventy-five years later it still troubled some members of Irvine's family, the descendants of his brothers and sister, who privately attached blame to George for leading Irvine to his death. There have also been suggestions by Everest writers that George selected Irvine for "aesthetic" reasons, a coded reference to homosexuality: Walt Unsworth wondered, even more explicitly, whether George had formed "a romantic attachment for the handsome young undergraduate."

Irvine himself was spectacularly heterosexual. He had been having an affair with the stepmother of one of his best friends, while a second woman believed that she and Irvine were engaged. He had clearly made a strong impression on George from an early stage, for George mentioned him in several letters to Ruth from the *California*. In a letter to Mary, he said: "Irvine is a bit young and hasn't much to talk about; he was two years in the Oxford boat and knows a lot about engineering lore—one of the best." They had been exercising in the ship's gymnasium, and George told Mary that Irvine had "a magnificent body for the job, and he is a very nice fellow."

It may be that Irvine enabled George to replicate his friendships with Charterhouse pupils but those, as we have already argued, were entirely innocent or at least ingenuous. It is more likely that George saw in Irvine a reflection of his younger self, the enthusiastic, athletic undergraduate, eager for new experiences, determined to live them out. Through Irvine, George could also act out the counterpoint of his relationship with Geoffrey Young and his other senior mentors, this time with George initiating a younger partner into the ways of mountaineering.

Outweighing all of this, we feel, were the clear pragmatic reasons for choosing Irvine. He fulfilled the criteria for the ideal pairing which the Mount Everest Committee had voiced, the alliance between the maturity and wisdom of the senior mountaineers and the enthusiasm and athleticism of youth. More important still, in the light of George's conversion to oxygen, was Irvine's facility with the equipment. Although the 1924 sets were supposedly an improvement, they were still cumbersome, fragile, and leaky. Irvine said they were all "boggled" and on March 28 exclaimed in his diary: "Ye Gods! I broke one today taking it out of its packing case." But Irvine had been ceaselessly adjusting and repairing the sets, winning George's unreserved admiration for his improvements. "What was provided was full of leaks and faults and he has practically invented a new instrument using up only a few of the old parts and cutting out much that was useless and likely to cause trouble." Irvine had also been repairing the climbers' cameras and crampons, the expedition's cooking stoves, and George's bed. The only doubt over Irvine, as George conceded, concerned "to what extent his lack of mountaineering experience will be a handicap; I hope the ground will be sufficiently easy." In all other respects, the pairing seemed an ideal match, in some ways reflecting the complementary strengths of George's marriage: George the strategist and dreamer, Irvine the practical, down-to-earth partner who took care of the detail.

Norton and George announced the teams on April 21. Irvine was "awfully glad" to have been chosen as George's partner, although he admitted in his diary that he would have preferred—presumably in light of his intimate knowledge of the faults and foibles of the oxygen equipment—to be making a "non-oxygen attempt." With a due sense of diplomacy, Somervell and George selected Norton as Somervell's partner. Odell, Geoffrey Bruce, Hazard, and Beetham were all designated support climbers and reserves, consoled with the possibility, however remote, that they could make the third and fourth attempts. George described the outcome of the deliberations to Ruth in terms which expressed some lingering doubts over his switch to the oxygen camp, although it was clear which pair he believed had the best chance of reaching the summit.

> *The gasless party has the better adventure, and as it has always been my pet plan to climb the mountain gasless with two camps about the Chang La it is naturally a bit disappointing that I shall be with the other party. Still, the conquest of the mountain is the great thing, and the whole plan is mine and my part will be a sufficiently interesting one and will give me, perhaps, the best chance of all of getting to the top. It is almost unthinkable with this plan that I shan't get to the top; I can't see myself coming down defeated. And I have very good hopes that the gasless party will get up; I want all four of us to get there, and I believe it can be done. We shall be starting by moonlight if the morning is calm and should have the mountain climbed if we're lucky before the wind is dangerous.*

Most of George's doubts about oxygen were dispelled when he, Irvine, and several other climbers used the modified apparatus to climb up to the fortress at Shekar Dzong on April 24. Irvine had reduced the weight by four to five pounds, as well as making the pack-frame more comfortable to wear. "The general impression I have is that it is a perfectly manageable load," George told Ruth. "My plan is to carry as little as possible, go fast and rush the summit." He ended his letter on a note of almost triumphant optimism, setting a timetable for success and imagining how the news would reach Ruth.

Only four marches, starting tomorrow morning, to the Rongbuk Monstery! We're getting very near now. On May 3 four of us will leave the Base Camp and begin the upward trek, and on May 17, or thereabouts, we should reach the summit. I'm eager for the great events to begin . . . The telegram announcing our success if we succeed will precede this letter I suppose: but it will mention no names. How you will hope that I was one of the conquerors! And I don't think you'll be disappointed.

Ever your loving, George

CHAPTER THIRTEEN

Vanishing Hopes
May–June 1924

The expedition reached the site of its base camp at the foot of the Rongbuk Glacier on April 29. The portents were poor: a bitterly cold wind was sweeping across the glacier and snow fell for most of the day. But in the morning the skies cleared. The great bulk of Everest gleamed under a new coating of snow, while higher up the wind appeared to have blown the face clear. George was in an optimistic mood, telling Ruth that both he and the team were fit and content. "It would be difficult to say of any one of the 8 that he is likely to go further or less far than the rest. I'm glad the first blow lies with me. We're not going to be easily stopped with an organisation behind us this time." The expedition had hired 150 local porters as planned, paying them the equivalent of 1 shilling (22 cents) a day plus their food. George admitted that organizing the supply line to the sites of the upper camps was "a very complicated business." There was a great deal to manage, not only arranging the loads but also ensuring that the porters were in the right place at the right time and making allowances for their fitness and rate of acclimatization. Even so, George felt that the logistical plan had sufficient margins to ensure that "even a bad day or two won't upset our applecart."

It was not a bad day or two that upset the expedition's applecart: it was a succession of days of execrable weather, far worse than anything George had experienced in 1922, with frequent blizzards, a lacerating wind, and plummeting temperatures that on one morning reached -21.5° F. Finding a way up the East

Rongbuk Glacier in frozen boots was an enervating business, particularly as the wind had scoured the surface so that it was "hard, smooth, rounded ice, almost as hard as glass." George had an ominous feeling when he reached Camp 3 on May 5: "It was a queer sensation reviving memories of that scene, with the dud oxygen cylinders piled against the cairn which was built to commemorate the seven porters killed two years ago. The whole place had changed less than I could have believed possible."

George spent a day sheltering at Camp 3 in a tent with Somervell, Irvine, and Odell. When he produced his copy of the Bridges anthology, *The Spirit of Man*, for a poetry reading, Somervell reminded him that they had conducted a similar session there two years before. "We all agreed that 'Kubla Khan' was a good sort of poem," George wrote. "Irvine was rather poetry shy but seemed to be favorably impressed by the 'Epitaph to Gray's Elegy.' Odell was much inclined to be interested and liked the last lines of 'Prometheus Unbound.' S, who knows quite a lot of English literature had never read a poem of Emily Bronte's, and was happily introduced . . . ." The brief euphoria was soon dissipated, for that night the storm intensified. In the morning there were two inches of snow inside George's tent, while outside the spindrift was gusting into miniature whirlwinds to create a scene of utter devastation. Inevitably the weather took its toll of the porters' fitness and morale. More than fifty deserted after the first day and from then on they became harder to rouse from their tents and urge up the glacier. The porters were suffering injuries from falls and frostbite and several were snow-blind.

By May 11, the expedition was in disarray. It was far short of its target of achieving the summit on May 17 as it had not even reached the North Col: the one attempt by Odell and Hazard had ended when they turned back some 300 feet short of the col after exhausting themselves in deep snow. "It has been a very trying time with everything against us," George wrote. "The porters have seemed from the start short of acclimatisation and up against it." That night, Norton summoned all the climbers back to base camp for a crisis meeting. Norton's own fear was that the persistent bad weather presaged the early arrival of the monsoon, and that they might already be too late. On May 12 he drew up a new schedule. After a spell of rest and recuperation they would set out again on May 17, weather permitting. They would retain the original pairings—George and Irvine, Norton and Somervell—for the attempts on the summit, which they now hoped to reach on May 28 or 29—an appropriate target, as George pointed out, since it was Ascension Day.

On May 15 the entire expedition, climbers and porters alike, walked the five miles back down the valley to pay their respects to the Holy Lama at the Rongbuk monastery. The porters had been given 2 rupees (65 cents) each to make an offering, and the Lama, seated among his officials beside the altar in his court on the monastery roof, delivered "a short but impressive message," Geoffrey Bruce wrote, "encouraging the men to persevere." George did not describe the visit in his letters, suggesting that he may have viewed it as an unnecessary distraction. John Noel later remembered that during this period of enforced inactivity George "seemed ill at ease, always scheming and planning. It was obvious to me he felt this setback more acutely than any of us."

George took stock in a letter to Ruth the following day, May 16. He admitted feeling disappointed that Odell and Hazard had turned back from the North Col: "It is the power to keep the show going when you don't feel energetic that will enable us to win through if anything does." Irvine, by contrast, had "much more of the winning spirit—he has been wonderfully hard working and brilliantly skilful about the oxygen." George still felt that he and Irvine were the strongest pair, as Somervell seemed "a bit below his form of two years ago," while Norton appeared "not particularly strong." George remained concerned at Irvine's lack of alpine experience, but concluded that he would make "an ideal companion and with as stout a heart as you could wish to find." Like Norton, George was anxious about the weather, but was determined to give the attempt his best shot. "I don't forget meanwhile that there's the old monsoon to be reckoned with, and a hundred possible slips between the B. C. and the summit. I feel strong for the battle but I know every ounce of strength will be wanted."

Even now, while focusing on his imminent attempt, George was visualizing Ruth at home. He had been pleased to hear that she was hoping to sell the Holt for £2500 ($11,025.00) (the sale, at £2300 ($10,143.00), went through on April 30). He wondered whether she would be able to put people up at Herschel House during a Cambridge summer school and told her he would write to Clare and Berry. Clare kept his letter, dated May 16 1924, for the rest of her life.

> My dear Clare,
>
> I am sitting in the big green tent which we call the Mess Tent; the sun is beating on it and there is not much wind today so it is nice and warm. We are just going to have tea and I'm expecting that in a moment the mess-waiter (for an explanation of the word Mess apply to Mummy) will bring a tin of GINGER NUTS. Luckily the expedition has been well supplied with sweet biscuits though I can't say any of them are exactly sugar biscuits and my favourites are ginger nuts every time especially at high camps. This camp is 16500 ft. high, but it doesn't count as a high camp. Camp III at 21,000 is the lowest to count in that way.
>
> If I were to go outside the mess tent the first thing I should notice after our tents and the rows of wooden boxes which contain stores of all kinds would be the

ravens, very big glossy black ones—quite a number of pairs live more or less per-
manently in our camp—we also have pigeons (rock-pigeons they are called) and a
number of small birds; and today we had a visit from some burrhel, the mountain-
sheep of these parts, several of which came within 20 yards of our kitchen. And
then of course I should look at the mountain; the mountain I need hardly say is
Mount Everest; when I last looked it was smoking hard; that means to say that a
puff of cloud was streaming away from the summit; the wind always comes from
the right side of Everest as we look at him and we see the cloud trailing away on the
left, and we can tell more or less by the shape of the cloud etc how strong the wind
is. Now this morning when I got out of bed and looked at the mountain I could see
no cloud at all; and I believe there was no wind or practically none up there—
certainly there was none down here—and when we see the mountain calm in the
early morning then we think we may be able to get to the top.

Now tea has come, and with tea, for the first time since I don't know when,
CAKE, a flat warm squidgy cake with raisins in.

Shall we have a little tea party together, one day in August, with a flat warm
squidgy cake and nothing else?

Haven't you got a greedy Daddy.

> Ever your loving and sometimes
> your greedy Daddy

The expedition made its new start on May 17 as planned. George, Norton, and
Somervell arrived at Camp 3 on May 19 and the next day headed up the frozen
1000-foot slope to the North Col. They followed a series of easy-angled convex
snowfields to a wall of nearly vertical ice crowned with a chimney. Mallory led up
it, Norton wrote, "climbing carefully, neatly and in that beautiful style that was all
his own." Above the chimney they traversed the upper section of the snow basin
which had avalanched in 1922 and arrived at the familiar shelf below the crest of
the col at 2:30 P.M. Somervell had been forced to turn back through altitude sickess,
but Odell and the Sherpa Lhakpa followed them up, helping to make the route
safe for the porters by driving in stakes and installing fixed ropes on the most
difficult sections. They pitched a tent and dumped some supplies and then, after a
brief reconnaissance of the route above, set off back to Camp 3. George had an
alarming moment when he fell ten feet into a crevasse, leaving him wedged in
place by his ice ax above "a very unpleasant black hole." He was ahead of the
others, who did not hear his shouts for help, but he managed to hack his way out.
Back at Camp 3 they felt pleased with what they had achieved. They had established an important staging post and now had another four or five days in which to
build up supplies on the North Col before launching the two summit attempts.

It was not to be. The blizzards returned and the temperature plunged to a new low of -24° F. There was a further setback when four porters were marooned overnight on the North Col, and Norton, Somervell, and George set off to rescue them. The slopes were loaded with new snow but George did not hesitate, as Norton recalled. "Mallory, who on these occasions lived on his nervous energy, kept urging us on. I remember his chiding us sharply for some momentary delay and later apologizing for his impatience." There was a hair-raising moment when two of the porters slid towards the edge of an ice cliff just as Somervell reached them but they stopped in time and all four were brought down safely. Soon afterwards new storms drove the climbers back down the glacier and by May 26 there was no one higher than Camp 2.

That night, the expedition conducted a new council of war. The casualty toll made grim reading. Out of fifty-five porters—the "Tigers"—originally expected to go to the North Col and beyond, only fifteen were fit enough to do so. The climbers themselves were drained and suffering from debilitating ailments: Somervell, Irvine, and George had painful throats and hacking coughs. The supply line had all but failed, as there had been only one further carry to the North Col, and there was no oxygen equipment above Camp 3. Norton was puzzled by the inconsistent weather, no longer sure that it was an effect of the monsoon, but convinced that the monsoon would arrive within a week anyway.

After the discussion, which continued into the next day, Norton put forward yet another revised plan. They would abandon the oxygen equipment and concentrate all their energies on making two oxygen-less attempts. The climbers, he recorded, agreed nem con. There would be a change of personnel too: Geoffrey Bruce was now the strongest member of the expedition and he would take part in the first attempt. Although Norton considered that George was far from fit, he offered him the chance to partner Bruce: "He had so far borne the brunt of the hardest work, yet the energy and fire of the man were reflected in his every gesture, and none doubted his fitness to go as high as any." George accepted the offer, and then Norton asked him to decide in turn who should make the second attempt. George selected Norton and Somervell.

That evening, May 27, sitting in his tent at Camp 1, George wrote his last letter to Ruth. "Dear Girl, this has been a bad time altogether—I look back on tremendous efforts and exhaustion and dismay looking out of a tent door on to a world of snow and vanishing hopes—and yet, and yet, and yet there have been a good many thanks to set on the other side. The party has played up wonderfully." He described the ascent to the North Col as "a triumph for the old gang" and told her about his fall into the crevasse during the descent without, this time, making light of the dangers. He told her about his cough: "In the high camp it has been the devil. Even after the day's exercise I have described I couldn't sleep but was distressed with bursts of coughing fit to tear one's guts—and so headache and misery together; besides which of course it has a very bad effect on one's going on the mountain."

He described the rescue of the four porters stranded on the North Col, and told her Norton had been "very hard hit" by the episode, as he had been so anxious to avoid casualties among the porters. Norton, George added, had been "quite right to bring us down for rest. It is no good sending men up the mountain unfit. The physique of the whole party has gone down sadly. The only chance now is to get fit and go for a simpler and quicker plan." He told her how the two summit teams had been selected, but still wondered whether he would be fit enough to take part. The monsoon could still catch them out but if only the weather held, they might yet succeed: "Six days to the top from this camp!"

George told Ruth that letters had come "tumbling" into camp in the past few days, among them "yours dated from Westbrook with much about the car—I fear it has given you a lot of trouble" which included a poem from Clare, "with which I'm greatly delighted," and a letter from his mother, written "in great spirits from Aix." It was, he added, "a great joy to hear from you especially but also from anyone who will write a good letter." He could not write much more. "The candle is burning out and I must stop. Darling I wish you the best I can—that your anxiety will be at an end before you get this—with the best news, which will also be the quickest. It is 50 to 1 against but we'll have a whack yet and do ourselves proud. Great love to you, ever your loving George."

⚭

May 28 dawned without a cloud, the still air making Everest seem closer than ever in its majestic upward sweep above the Rongbuk Glacier. Somervell and Noel in particular were keen to move off, Noel to get into position to film and photograph the attempts. Despite his fears about the impending monsoon, Norton counseled caution, reckoning that the climbers would benefit from one further day's rest. George took advantage of the delay to write three more letters. He told David Pye that, although they were on the point of starting out, the "adventure seems more desperate than ever . . . You'll have good news of me from Ruth, I hope." He told his sister Mary: "I'm due to make the first dash with Geoffrey Bruce and arrive at the top 7 days hence—but we may be delayed or caught by the Monsoon or anything . . . This party has been badly knocked out but we still seem to have some guts among us I hope." He wrote to his mother too. "It will be a great adventure, if we get started before the monsoon hits us, with just a bare outside chance of success and a good many chances of a very bad time indeed. I shall take every care I can, you may be sure . . . Much love to you both."

From here, barring three notes that he sent down the mountain, there is nothing more to be heard in George's voice. But he was being observed by his colleagues, whose writings and photographs, together with the items found on his body in 1999, help form a picture of his actions and intentions in the last ten days of his life. He and Bruce arrived at Camp 3 on May 30. Irvine, who was disappointed at having lost his place in the first summit team, gave George a light rucksack that he had made from one of the oxygen packs. "Feel very fit tonight," Irvine wrote. "I wish I was in the first party instead of a bloody reserve." On May 31 George and Bruce, together with nine high-altitude porters, moved up to the North Col. Irvine and Odell, who had been assigned a support role on the North Col, cooked a supper of pea soup, tongue, and cocoa. Irvine noted in his diary that it was a "beautiful evening" and that one of George's eyes had been inflamed by the sun.

The next day, June 1, Irvine was up at 4:30 A.M. to make breakfast—a "very cold and disagreeable job," he observed. George, Bruce, and the eight porters moved off at 6 A.M. Although the day had seemed fair, once on the broad north ridge they were hit by a bitter northeast wind. George was hoping to site Camp 5 at 25,300 feet but they were still 300 feet short when four of the porters said they could go no further. The others pushed on, finally coming to a halt at 25,200 feet where they pitched two tiny tents, one a short distance above the other, on crumbling rocks on the lee side of the ridge. Bruce and the Sherpa Lobsang fetched the remaining loads and carried them up to the camp. Five of the porters returned to the North Col, leaving three to carry loads to Camp 6 the next day.

The morning brought only disappointment. The weather was still clear but when Bruce tried to rouse the porters, they said they were too tired to carry on. "Apparently the wind had taken the heart out of them," Norton wrote in his account of the attempt. Talking in Nepalese, Bruce did his best to persuade them to continue, but only one would change his mind. Without the porters to help establish a further camp at around 27,000 feet, the attempt was doomed. "After a brief consultation," Norton dryly noted, "it was decided to return to Camp Four."

That same morning, June 2, Norton and Somervell, together with six porters, had set off from the North Col on their summit attempt. They had been going for about two hours when, to their surprise, they saw George, Bruce, and their porters descending towards them. "Their story was distressingly simple," Norton wrote. After they had spent the previous day in exhausting wind, nothing "—not even Bruce's command of the language and well-known influence over these men—would induce any of the porters to go higher." Somervell added: "The only thing they could do was to come down, leaving the tents for us, and wishing us better luck with our assault on the mountain. It was a grievous disappointment, and must have been worse for them than for us."

George and Bruce reached the North Col at midday, where it was Odell's turn to be surprised. George, he said, was both "disappointed and upset" by the porters' refusal to go on. George then told Odell that he intended to make another attempt with Irvine, using the oxygen apparatus. Irvine, who had just arrived with Hazard and some porters from Camp 3, also recorded this decisive moment. "George decided that I should go down in Hazard's place and prepare apparatus for an oxygen attempt."

It is not clear precisely when George decided that his attempt with Bruce was bound to fail, or when he resolved to revert to his original plan for making an oxygen attempt with Irvine. But it was the defining moment of his life. Throughout his mountaineering career he had pushed as hard and as far as he could, refusing to give up until he was convinced beyond all possible doubt that he had no other choice. Now that the weather remained fair, and he was still on his feet, and he had a willing partner, and there was oxygen equipment at Camp 3, he could not renounce his hope of going to the summit. It offered him the supreme opportunity of being the climbing leader who climbed the highest mountain. As he had declared in New York, a climber was what he was, and this was what climbers did; and this was how they fulfilled their wildest dreams.

There was more. If he went back to Ruth with Everest unclimbed, he could face the anguish of wondering whether he should leave her and his children and their home for yet another try. He could not see how he could inflict that on her again. It was only by making another attempt now that he could be true to Ruth and all they had gone through together, and to the ideals of honesty and integrity they had expressed that were embodied in their love. It was also the only way he knew of redeeming the suffering he had caused Ruth: if he climbed Everest, the conflict at the core of their marriage, the conflict between his dreams and their love, would be reconciled.

That afternoon George descended to Camp 3 with Irvine. While Irvine busied himself with the oxygen equipment, George asked Bruce to see if he could muster enough porters to support their attempt. On the mountain, meanwhile, Norton and Somervell were pushing on. They stayed at Camp 5 that night and the following morning left at 9 A.M., having had a hard struggle to persuade their porters to keep going. At 1:30 P.M. they reached a height of 26,800 feet, pitching the tent that comprised Camp 6 on a precarious platform that they scraped out among the loose stones. Their three remaining porters returned to the North Col, leaving Norton and Somervell to contemplate an awesome panorama of peaks silhouetted against the red evening sky. Somervell felt he was witnessing "a sunset all over the world" and also had the illusion that they were camped in a field close to a wall that marked the limit of their capacities and endurance.

Still Norton was anxious about the monsoon, but on the morning of June 4, the weather held. He had been keen to make an early start but one of the thermos flasks he had filled with tea the previous night had lost its cork, emptying its contents into his sleeping bag. Norton, who knew by then the importance of not becoming dehydrated, insisted on brewing some more tea and it was not until 6:40 A.M. that they left. They now faced a choice of route. George had always favored the line he had identified in 1921, striking up to the crest of the northeast ridge and following it to the summit pyramid. Norton was worried about the two crags that appeared to block the ridge, the First and Second Step, and decided to aim for the great couloir bisecting the face like a great gash beyond the Second Step, hoping it would give easier access to the foot of the summit pyramid.

After an hour, Norton and Somervell reached the Yellow Band, the vast stratum of sandstone that crosses the north face. They found that it consisted of a series of sloping slabs and ledges where they could never be quite sure of their footholds, while the face yawned away beneath them to the Rongbuk Glacier more than 7000 feet below. The altitude was telling on them: Norton set himself the target of taking twenty steps without a pause, but could never manage more than twelve or thirteen, and they had to stop frequently to rest. By noon they were just below the top of the Yellow Band, and not far from the entrance to the couloir. The summit was looming ever closer, a triangle of white rising above the dark slopes below the crest of the northeast ridge and no more than a quarter-mile in distance and 1000 vertical feet away. On a good day in North Wales they would reckon to reach it within an hour but Somervell was at the limit of his strength. He had been in distress all morning from a painfully parched throat, aggravated by a hacking cough, and knew that he was holding Norton up. Finally he sat down on a boulder and told Norton he should go on alone.

Norton continued for another hour. The terrain was more and more treacherous, the ledges steeper and narrower and covered with powdery snow. His best hope was that the couloir would provide easier going, but he found it full of loose, waist-deep snow while the rock beyond was steeper still. He was finding it increasingly difficult to see the way, as he had removed his goggles in the mistaken belief that they were impairing his sight. In fact this was almost certainly a symptom of oxygen deficiency and he had now left himself vulnerable to snow-blindness. At 1 P.M., exhausted, already half-blind, he came to a halt. He was still some 800 to 900 feet below the summit and knew that he had run out of time to reach it and return before nightfall. As he turned back he was nevertheless convinced that there was nothing to prevent a "fresh and fit party" from reaching the summit without oxygen equipment.

Somervell had been photographing Norton as he climbed, taking a series of pictures that showed Norton, bent almost double by exhaustion, framed in the enormity of the sloping face with the snow-covered triangle of the summit tantalizingly close above. When Norton rejoined him, Somervell agreed with the decision to turn back: "We realised that it would be madness to continue, and we were somehow quite content to leave it at that, and to turn down with almost a feeling of relief that our worst trials were over."

Not quite. As dusk fell they had reached 25,000 feet when Somervell succumbed to a renewed bout of coughing. He felt something lodge in his throat and, unable to breathe or to call to Norton, began to choke to death. "I sat in the snow to die whilst [Norton] walked on, little knowing that his companion was awaiting the end a few yards behind him." In desperation, Somervell pummeled his chest and coughed up the obstruction into his mouth. It was part of the mucous membrane of his larynx, which had been damaged by frostbite. Somervell spat it out, along with some blood, and found that he could breathe again. "Though the pain was intense," he wrote, "I was a new man." They continued their descent in the dark, signalling with a torch as they approached the North Col.

That morning George and Irvine had been watching and waiting at Camp 3. Irvine had patched together two oxygen sets and Geoffrey Bruce had recruited enough porters to support a new attempt. A porter who descended from the North Col reported that Norton and Somervell had established Camp 6 at around 27,000 feet (later established at 26,800 feet) and spent the night there. "Great was the excitement in the camp," Irvine wrote. "Noel had his telephoto camera out and everyone watched unceasingly all day but not a sign." That afternoon George and Irvine decided to return to the North Col, "ready," as Irvine put it, "to fetch sick men down or make an oxygen attempt ourselves a day later." Using oxygen, they reached the col in two and a half hours. Irvine felt "surprisingly fresh" when they arrived, while Odell, who had remained skeptical about the benefits of the apparatus, observed that they seemed "well pleased" with themselves. George thought he could see tracks leading downwards some 700 feet below the summit. "I hope they've got to the top," Irvine wrote, "but by God I'd like to have a whack at it myself."

When George saw the torch signals from Norton and Somervell, he and Odell climbed to meet them some 100 feet above the North Col. They offered them some oxygen but what Norton and Somervell wanted more than anything was a drink. When they reached the col Irvine plied them with tea and soup. Their companions, Norton wrote, were "kindness itself," congratulating them on establishing a new height record on Everest—"though we ourselves felt nothing but disappointment at our failure."

Norton, who could barely see, was sharing a tent with George. That night, after they had crawled into their sleeping bags, George told him that he wanted to make one more summit attempt, using oxygen equipment. "I entirely agreed with this decision," Norton wrote, "and was full of admiration for the indomitable spirit of the man, determined, in spite of his already excessive exertions, not to admit defeat while any chance remained, and I must admit—such was his will power and nervous energy—he still seemed entirely adequate to the task." What did surprise Norton was that George intended to make the attempt with Irvine, and he argued that Odell was not only the more experienced climber, but was also fitter and better acclimatized. Irvine was in fact suffering from both a parched throat and a painfully sunburned face, and had just written in his diary that the previous night "everything on earth seemed to rub against my face and each time it was touched bits of burnt and dry skin came off which made me nearly scream with pain." George would not be deflected, telling Norton that he was taking Irvine because of the skill and initiative he had shown over the oxygen equipment, and because he had greater trust in using oxygen than Odell. Norton realized that George had made up his mind: "It was obviously no time for me to interfere."

To the climbers' delight and surprise, the weather on June 5 remained clear. Although they did not know it, they were in fact experiencing the settled period of ten days or so that often precedes the monsoon on Everest. Ironically, the blazing sun brought still more discomfort. Norton was completely blind and lay in his tent, which was shaded with sleeping bags. Despite intense pain, he crawled to the door to speak to the porters who were to support the attempt, rallying their spirits and telling them it was vital to keep going to Camp 6. Irvine, in equal distress from his sunburn, spent most of the day with Odell's assistance putting the finishing touches on two oxygen sets. That night Irvine wrote his last diary entry. "My face is perfect agony," he concluded. "Have prepared 2 oxygen apparatus for our start tomorrow morning."

George and Irvine were up early on June 6. George was wearing cotton and silk underwear, a flannel shirt from Paine's outfitters in Godalming High Street, a brown long-sleeved pullover, and a patterned woolen waistcoat that Ruth had made. Since he would be wearing the oxygen equipment on his back, he stuffed his personal items into the pockets of his windproof cotton Shackleton jacket and a pair of pouches slung around his neck. They included a pocket knife with a horn handle, a pair of nail scissors in a leather pouch, a box of Swan Vesta matches, and some spare laces and straps. He took a tube of petroleum jelly that he wrapped in a white handkerchief, and two more handkerchiefs, one colored burgundy, green, and blue, the other red, blue, and yellow, both of them monogrammed with his initials, "G. L. M." He carried several checklists of supplies, together with three recently arrived letters that he carefully wrapped in one of the handkerchiefs.

One of the letters was from his brother, Trafford, written in London on April 2, bringing news of his move with his wife and their two sons to a new house in west London. Another was from his sister Mary, and had been mailed from Colombo on April 12: George had asked her to send regular weather reports in the hope of anticipating the monsoon but, although she had news of a violent tropical storm, her letter had arrived far too late. A third, signed "Stella" and posted in London on April 2, was from Stella Cobden-Sanderson, an Englishwoman George had met in New York during his 1923 lecture tour and whom he had mentioned in his letters to Ruth. She sent gossipy news about going to the theater, a friend of the Mallorys she had dined with the previous day, and her plans to visit the south of France. George had used the envelope of her letter to note down the code numbers and pressures of five oxygen cylinders.

Odell and Hazard were up early too, preparing a breakfast of fried sardines, biscuits, chocolate, and tea. George and Irvine did not finish theirs, Odell observed, "owing to excitement or restlessness." Norton, still blind, came to the door of his tent to shake hands and offer them "a word of blessing." At 8:40 A.M. Odell took a last photograph of them. Irvine is facing away from the camera, with two silvery oxygen cylinders on his back. Both men are wearing their Shackleton jackets, breeches, and puttees. Irvine, hands in pockets, a hat pulled tightly down to protect his face, is looking towards George, who is wearing gloves, goggles, a fur-lined helmet, mitts, and a scarf, and is about to pick up his ice ax. Shortly before 9 A.M. they left with eight porters who were carrying food, bedding, and oxygen cylinders. "The party moved off in silence as we bid them adieu," Odell wrote, "and they were soon lost to view."

Climbing steadily along the line George had followed with Bruce just four days before, they reached Camp 5 in good time. George sent four of the porters back to the North Col, together with an optimistic note: "There is no wind here and things look hopeful." The next day, June 7, using oxygen for part of the way, they and the four remaining porters continued to Camp 6. After reaching the camp, George wrote two brief notes, one for John Noel, the other for Noel Odell.

Knowing that Noel would be at his camera position, a ledge he named the Eagle's Nest, George told him:

We'll probably start early tomorrow (8th) in order to have clear weather. It won't be too early to start looking for us either crossing the rock band under the pyramid or going up skyline at 8.0 P.M.

> *Yours ever, G Mallory*

The time, "8.0 P.M.," was clearly an error for 8 A.M.
To Odell, George wrote:

We're awfully sorry to have left things in such a mess—our Unna Cooker rolled down the slope at the last moment. Be sure of getting back to IV to-morrow in time to evacuate by dark, as I hope to. In the tent I must have left a compass—for the Lord's sake rescue it: we are here without. To here on 90 atmospheres for the 2 days—we'll probably go on 2 cylinders—but it's a bloody load for climbing. Perfect weather for the job!

> *Yours ever, G. Mallory*

George gave the two notes to the porters to take on their descent. When the porter Lakpa handed John Noel his note, he told Noel that the two climbers were well, and that the weather was good. To sustain them on their attempt, George had selected food that was high on sugar content: cookies, chocolate, butterscotch, Kendal mint cake, and ginger nuts, plus macaroni and sliced ham and tongue. They had a Unna cooker to heat the food and melt snow—not the Unna cooker referred to in George's note to Odell, which he had left at Camp 5—and were as well provided for as could be. The morning of June 8 was clear, and in the words of Odell, now ensconced in Camp 5 1600 feet below them, "not unduly cold." From Camp 6, George and Irvine continued on a diagonal ascent, which brought them to just below the crest of the northeast ridge at 27,760 feet, where they dumped a spent oxygen cylinder. A little further on, they faced the choice George had described to John Noel: should they veer across the face and traverse the rock band, as Norton had done? Or should they follow the crest of the northeast ridge?

By Odell's account, they chose the ridge. Odell had left Camp 5 at eight o'clock, intending to climb to Camp 6 in support of George and Irvine, using the opportunity to collect geological samples on the way. Soon after he set out banks of mist rolled across the face from the west. Odell was not unduly worried on the two climbers' behalf: although there was an occasional brief squall

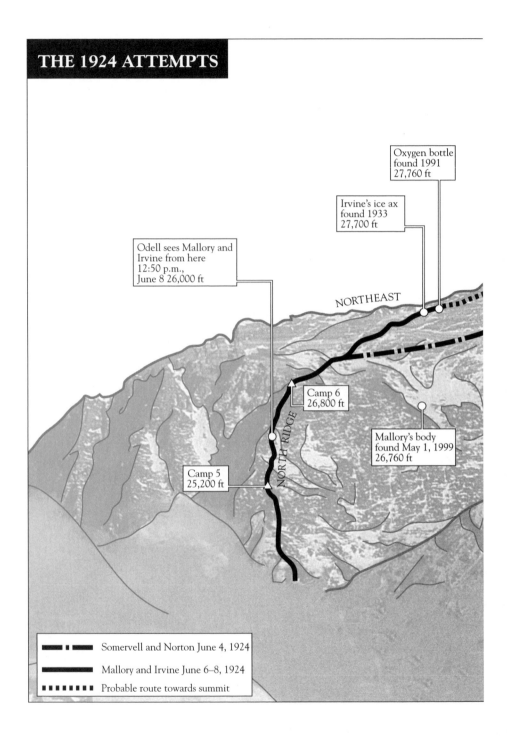

THE 1924 ATTEMPTS

Oxygen bottle
found 1991
27,760 ft

Irvine's ice ax
found 1933
27,700 ft

Odell sees Mallory and
Irvine from here
12:50 p.m.,
June 8 26,000 ft

NORTHEAST

Camp 6
26,800 ft

NORTH RIDGE

Mallory's body
found May 1, 1999
26,760 ft

Camp 5
25,200 ft

Somervell and Norton June 4, 1924

Mallory and Irvine June 6–8, 1924

Probable route towards summit

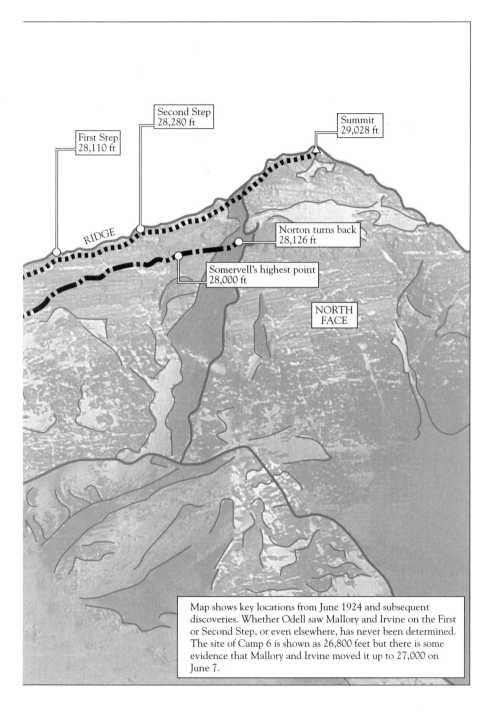

First Step
28,110 ft

Second Step
28,280 ft

Summit
29,028 ft

RIDGE

Norton turns back
28,126 ft

Somervell's highest point
28,000 ft

NORTH
FACE

Map shows key locations from June 1924 and subsequent
discoveries. Whether Odell saw Mallory and Irvine on the First
or Second Step, or even elsewhere, has never been determined.
The site of Camp 6 is shown as 26,800 feet but there is some
evidence that Mallory and Irvine moved it up to 27,000 on
June 7.

of sleet or light snow, the mist had a luminous quality that suggested it was not thick and might even remain below the level of the summit pyramid.

At 12:50 P.M., just as Odell had climbed a crag at around 26,000 feet, the mist cleared. Before him was the vision that has become part of the Mallory legend, as he and Irvine continued their seemingly unstoppable progress to the top. "The entire summit ridge and final peak of Everest were unveiled," Odell wrote in a dispatch he compiled for *The Times* a week later. "My eyes became fixed on one tiny black spot silhouetted on a small snow-crest beneath a rock-step in the ridge; the black dot moved. Another black dot became apparent and moved up the snow to join the other on the crest. The first then approached the great rock-step and shortly emerged at the top; the second did likewise. Then the whole fascinating vision vanished, enveloped in cloud once more."

Odell was in no doubt that he had seen George and Irvine, "moving expeditiously" in their bid to reach the summit. He reached Camp 6 around two o'clock, just as the snow began to fall more heavily. Inside the tent he found their sleeping bags and an assortment of spare clothes and scraps of food, together with several oxygen cylinders and spare parts. Ignoring the snowfall, Odell scrambled 200 feet up the face in the hope of seeing George and Irvine, or perhaps meeting them on their way down, but the cloud still obscured his view. By the time he returned to Camp 6 the weather had cleared, and he could see the whole of the north face, and much of the upper section of the ridge, bathed in sunshine. Of George and Irvine, there was no sign. Around 4:30 P.M., in accordance with George's note, he decided to return to the North Col. Before leaving he placed the compass he had retrieved from Camp 5 in a conspicuous place near the door of the tent, so that George would be sure to find it.

Over the next forty-eight hours the members of the 1924 Everest expedition watched and waited for news of their two colleagues. From his camera position, John Noel could only report that he had obtained no sighting of them on their supposed summit day, June 8. Norton was at Camp 3 that day where, still blind, he composed a report of his summit attempt for *The Times*, which he dictated to Geoffrey Bruce. Somervell also contributed an account that ended: "We now await news of Mallory and Irvine, who today are making another attempt, hoping that they may reinforce the feeble summit air by artificially provided oxygen, and by its means be enabled to conquer the chief difficulty of reaching the summit. May the Genie of the Steel Bottle aid them! All of us are hoping that he may, for nobody deserves the summit more than Mallory, the only one of our number who has been at it for three years."

On June 9 Hazard and Odell continued to keep watch on the upper camps from the North Col. At midday Odell could restrain himself no longer and set off with two porters to start a search. He reached Camp 5 that afternoon to find it undisturbed. The next morning, despite a savage wind, he continued alone to the tent at Camp 6. One of the poles had collapsed but otherwise it was exactly as Odell had left it two days before. He set out along the probable route George and Irvine had taken. But, "after struggling on for nearly a couple of hours looking in vain for some indication or clue," Odell accepted that he had no hope of finding them.

Before Odell left the North Col, he and Hazard had agreed on a set of signals that would enable him to convey the outcome of his search. During a lull in the wind, Odell dragged the two sleeping bags from the tent and set them out in the shape of a T. The signal meant: "No trace can be found—given up hope." At the North Col, Hazard used six blankets to set out a similar signal, this time in the form of a cross, for the anxious watchers at Camp 3. John Noel saw it first, through a telescope. Geoffrey Bruce asked what he had seen, but Noel could not bring himself to tell him and handed him the telescope. "We all looked," Noel said. "We all tried to make it different. But it was plainly a cross on the white snow."

⚭

On June 8, the day George was last seen alive, Ruth and the children were on holiday at Bacton, a seaside resort in Norfolk. On June 19 they were back at Herschel House. That afternoon in London Hinks received a coded telegram from Norton that read: "Mallory Irvine Nove Remainder Alcedo." "Nove" meant that George and Irvine had died, "Alcedo" that the others were unhurt. It thus fell to Hinks to convey the news to Ruth. He composed a telegram that was handed in at the post office at Kensington and dispatched from there to Cambridge, where it arrived at 7:30 P.M.

A short while later a delivery boy carrying the telegram called at Herschel House. Ruth cannot have been too surprised to see him, for in his letter of April 21 George had told her to expect a telegram announcing their success, although this was later than he had led her to expect. When she opened the envelope, this is what she read:

```
(0010) WL.29512/1171  40,000m  4/23  Harrow  (E0618)
```

B or C	Charges to pay	POST OFFICE	TELEGRAPHS.	No. of Telegram

Recd from

By...

If the receiver of an Inland Telegram doubts its accuracy he may have it repeated on payment of half the amount originally paid for its transmission, and if it be found that there was any inaccuracy the amount paid for repetition will be refunded. Special conditions are applicable to the repetition of Foreign Telegrams. THIS FORM MUST ACCOMPANY ANY ENQUIRY RESPECTING THIS TELEGRAM.

Sent..............M Office Stamp.
To................
By................

Prefix	Handed in at	Office of Origin and Service Instructions	Words	Received here at

A 442 7.5 KENSINGTON O 40   7.30 P ....M.

MRS MALLORY HERSCHEL HOUSE CAMBRIDGE

COMMITTEE DEEPLY REGRET RECEIVE BAD NEWS EVEREST
EXPEDITION TODAY NORTON CABLES YOUR HUSBAND AND
IRVINE KILLED LAST CLIMB REMAINDER RETURNED SAFE
PRESIDENT AND COMMITTEE OFFER YOU AND FAMILY HEARTFELT
SYMPATHY HAVE TELEGRAPHED GEORGES FATHER HINKS +

Confusion must have compounded Ruth's sense of shock, for almost simultaneously, a reporter from *The Times* arrived at Herschel House. *The Times*, which was entitled to read all Norton's dispatches as part of its contract with the expedition, had been told about the deaths too. When challenged later to explain why it had sent a reporter to Herschel House, *The Times* claimed it was anxious to ensure that Ruth heard the news before reading in the next day's newspaper.

The most immediate decision Ruth faced was when, and how, to tell the children. By then they were in bed, and she decided to postpone the moment until the morning. She left them in the care of Vi, and went for a walk with some friends. In the morning, so Clare recalled seventy-five years later, Ruth took her, Berry, and John into the bed she had shared with George. "She lay between us and told us this bad news," Clare said. "We all cried together."

Epilogue

"We leave here with heavy hearts," wrote Edward Norton in a dispatch to *The Times* from the Rongbuk base camp on June 4, as the expedition packed up to depart. Ironically the monsoon, which Norton had feared for so long, had still not arrived, and the great bulk of Everest was set against a brilliant azure sky. The camp had the air of a military casualty station, with Hingston, the doctor, assessing his charges' wounds, which included a multitude of frostbite injuries, varying stages of exhaustion, and what he diagnosed as dilated hearts. "Every one of the climbers has shot his bolt," Norton wrote.

Norton himself detected the echoes of the First World War when he wrote that he and his colleagues were at least attuned to the possibility of death. "From the first we accepted the loss of our comrades in that rational spirit which all of our generation had learned in the Great War, and there was never a tendency to a morbid harping on the irrevocable," he observed. Yet they could not but be affected by the signs of the two men's absence. Odell had known the disconcerting feeling, the premonition of a tragedy foretold, that came when he returned to Camp 6 on June 10, to find it precisely as he had left it two days before, with the men's personal belongings untouched. Now, at base camp, there were the empty tents, the vacant places at the mess table, to act as "constant reminders," Norton wrote, of what they had lost, and of how different it would all have been if Mallory and Irvine had returned victorious from the summit. The day before the expedition left base camp, Somervell and Beetham supervised the building of a pyramid-shaped cairn that bore the names of Mallory and Irvine, together with those of Kellas from 1921 and the seven Sherpas who died in the avalanche of 1922. Reinforcing the parallels with the war, it bore an uncanny resemblance to the memorials engraved with the names of the fallen that had appeared in every town and village in Britain.

Norton's perceptions presaged the sentiments being voiced in Britain. Although the attempts of 1921 and 1922 had caught the public's imagination, the 1924 expedition seemed to mark a watershed whereby the attempts on Everest acquired a new meaning. The dangers were suddenly manifest, the nature of climbing was revealed for the jousting with death it truly represented. We have argued that the first Everest expeditions had no inherent redemptive meaning, as they had acquired their own momentum before the war began. But the resonances of the 1924 expedition were undeniable. Here were gallant climbers going forward bravely, giving their utmost, dying on foreign terrain; since no bodies were found, Mallory and Irvine also stood for the most poignant of all the emblems of wartime grief and mourning, the tomb of the unknown warrior. The *Daily Graphic* expressed it most explicitly with its headlines: "Mallory and Irvine Killed in the Final Assault on the Summit—Remainder of the Gallant Expedition Returning 'All Well.'"

The Mount Everest Committee, at least in the person of Hinks, missed the point. He sent a telegram to Norton in the name of Collie, the committee's acting president, which read: "Committee warmly congratulates whole party heroic achievements published today especially appreciate consummate leadership. All deeply moved by glorious death lost climbers near summit." Hinks repeated the sentiments in a subsequent letter to Norton which talked of the "glorious memory" of Mallory and Irvine. The concept of the glorious death had been undermined by a generation of war poets, headed by Wilfred Owen, a spirit George had captured when he wrote to Ruth about the "pity" of the casualties he had witnessed. The Bishop of Chester was more sensitive to the public mood when he gave the main address at the memorial service held at St. Paul's Cathedral on October 17. He spoke of the climbers' courage and unselfishness, qualities that were displayed by the "compassionate, the brotherly and the pure in heart." He identified the element of mysticism inherent in Odell's final sighting. "The cloud clears away for a moment and you are allowed to see the two men making steadily for the summit. That is the last you see of them, and the question as to their reaching the summit is still unanswered; it will be solved some day."

Ruth, so she told Hinks, found the ceremony "very beautiful and beautifully arranged." That she should write to thank him was a gesture that exemplified her own selflessness as she attempted to come to terms with George's death. She had been inundated with letters from their friends. Mary Anne O'Malley wrote of George's unselfishness, compassion, courtesy, love of moral beauty, and his "extraordinarily delicate perception for all those things that he shaped one's own views without one knowing it." Robert Graves said that George was his "first real friend" who, with Ruth, had taught him that marriage "can after all be made a decent relationship." Edward Norton wrote of his "unfailing sound advice, his amazing ability and his bottomless acuity for work and his determination to win." Howard Somervell said that George was one of his few real friends, whom he had "loved as one of the most delightful and splendid of men." One of his Cambridge students wrote that she had felt that "his modesty had a power and sincerity which would carry him far."

For a time Ruth nurtured the fanciful belief that George might simply walk in through the front door one day. Just as George had done in moments of need, she confided her most intimate thoughts to Geoffrey Young. He was struggling with his own grief, telling her that George had been his "mountain sunlight, the light of almost passionate hope and reassurance, alone left in the twilight of my gradual surrender of the radiant life we both loved." When Ruth replied to Young, it was as if she were talking to George as she expressed her pain and how she was attempting to manage it. She did not attempt to deny her suffering, yet found consolation and a route to acceptance by invoking her love for George and the values they shared.

> *A lot of the time I feel numbed and quite unable to realise, there is only just a pain. It is no use talking of it. It has only just happened and one has to go through with it. It is not difficult for me to believe that George's spirit was ready for another life and his way of going to it was very beautiful . . . I don't think all this pain matters at all. I have always had far more than my share of joy and always shall have had. Isn't it queer how all the time what matters most is to get hold of the rightness of things. Then some sort of peace comes.*

Later, without bitterness, she referred to the assurances that George had provided and which she had come to depend on. "I know George did not mean to be killed, he meant not to be so hard that I did not a bit think he would be." She admitted to regret over the chance that had determined George's fate. "Oh Geoffrey," she wrote. "If only it hadn't happened. It so easily might not have." Young tried to persuade her not to succumb to such thoughts, and she replied: "I know exactly what you mean by not allowing oneself to dwell on might have beens. It lands one in a pond of intolerable and useless misery."

Ruth explored another issue she and George had often discussed, the nature of faith and the possibility of an afterlife.

> *I don't know if you think there is a future life I instinctively believe in. I don't feel annoyed when people don't. George didn't like I do. He said he didn't feel it mattered much for this life whether there is or not. I rather think that is the most sublime view of all but it is not mine. I don't feel in touch with George at all but I do feel that he loves me more than he ever did before and so long as I keep spiritually right he will be able to go on doing so. So most of the time I am saved from the awful dispare feeling*

that there is nothing left to live for. Then you see I also think it very possible that although this life was undoubtedly very good for George there is something better that he was ready for. So if I love him entirely I must try to be content that he should have it. I know one thing I never knew before, though I had been told, that happiness or unhappiness are very unimportant, it is the getting right with each that matters.

She wanted Young to see their children, especially Clare, who "has so much of George in her." Later she told Young that John had developed a limp in his left leg. An orthopedic surgeon had diagnosed a tubercular hip but Ruth was more optimistic. "I don't myself think that it is very serious. John is such a lovely child, so strong and healthy and well made it is impossible to think there can be very much the matter with him."

In their attempts to cope with George's death, his family had one small advantage. Since he had been on two previous expeditions, on each of which there had been accidents and near-misses, it could not have been entirely unexpected. The day after they heard the news, his father Herbert wrote to tell Hinks: "In the midst of our grief it is a real happiness to know how greatly he was appreciated. A better and more affectionate son can never have lived." His mother showed impressive resilience, writing to thank Hinks for the "care and thought" that must have lain behind the service at St. Paul's: "It was a wonderful expression of sympathy and interest." With a mother's eye, too, she perceived how much Ruth was suffering, despite her attempts at stoicism. "She reminds me of a stately lily with its head broken and hanging down."

Annie was equally perceptive in her assessment of the impact of the tragedy on the Irvine family. His parents, she wrote, were "terribly broken down. I don't think they had in the least realised how great the risk was." It was an accurate appraisal, for neither Irvine's trip to Spitsbergen, nor his training climbs in Snowdonia with Odell, had given any inkling of the scale of the enterprise, or of how far it entailed a venture into the unknown. Hinks had sent them a telegram at the same time as his to Ruth, and the news passed swiftly through the family. Irvine's father William telephoned his own father, James, in Scotland that evening. "We are broken hearted," Irvine's grandfather wrote. Like Ruth, Irvine's mother imagined that one day he might simply come back, and for years afterwards she kept a lamp burning in the porch of their home to light his way.

⚭

In the summer of 1924, Ruth and the children moved back to Westbrook, which became their home for the next fourteen years. Ruth had a bedroom with her own dressing room and a view across the gardens. The children were given rooms at the top of the house, along with Vi, faithful to the last. Across the valley the Holt was visible above the trees. Paradoxically, Ruth talked little to her children about their father, thinking to spare them her own grief. Although Ruth had left them under no illusions about what had happened to George, Clare still could not help wondering what people meant when they said he had been "lost" on Everest. Once, she dreamed that he had been found and had come back. "Of course I woke up, and was quite unhappy." Ruth used to go into the garden at Westbrook to read *The Spirit of Man* anthology, and later told Clare that one of her father's favorite poems, which was included in the anthology, was Shelley's "I Rise from Dreams of Thee."

Gradually the Mallory and Turner family lives merged. Both Ruth and her father continued to paint pottery, they and the children crowding around, as before, to see the painted bowls unpacked from their bales when they returned from being glazed and fired. The children played whist and draughts with their grandfather, a distinguished figure with his crisp white hair and beard, and they would dance to the tunes he played on his flute. Clare enjoyed walking around the garden with him, planning what flowers to grow and listening to his stories about William Morris. The children persuaded him to set up a tennis court, and they kept up the family's tradition of nudity. They ran around the lawn naked and sometimes, as John Mallory later recalled, the whole family went skinny dipping together in the River Wey: "There was no prudery in our family at all," he said.

Ruth brought up the children as free spirits, encouraging them to be adventurous like their father. "She made a conscious decision not to over protect us," recalled John. At the age of five or six, having learned to swim, John went canoeing on the Wey and cycling along the local lanes. Later Ruth taught them how to drive and how to change spark plugs and tires. They also learned to climb, both on the rocks during seaside holidays and in Snowdonia, where they stayed at Pen y Pass, and Clare and Berry took part in the ascent of a new route on Clogwyn du'r Arddu. John attended the local church school at Godalming for a time, then, like his father, went to Winchester and Magdalene College, Cambridge. Clare and Berry went to St. Mary's, a public school at Calne in Wiltshire, and to Cambridge, where Clare won a first-class degree in history and Berry studied natural sciences.

The Westbrook era came to an end when Thackeray Turner died in 1937. The house was sold, and for a year Ruth lived with a cousin. Then Ruth surprised her children by marrying her longstanding family friend, Will Arnold-Forster, whose wife Ka had died shortly before. It was to Arnold-Forster that George had first revealed his love for Ruth; and during the war Ruth wrote to George about her feelings for Will and Ka. She told George she loved Will very much "as I love flowers and trees and streams," and that he had "a delicately tuned spirit." Clare remembered that when Ruth remarried she was "glowingly happy" but sadly it did not last for long: in 1942 Ruth died of cancer. Of her three children, Berry married David Robertson, an American who was studying English at Cambridge and later became a university professor, while Berry became a doctor in New York. They had three children but Berry died of cancer in 1953. Robertson embarked on his biography of George Mallory soon afterwards. Clare married an American scientist, Glenn Millikan. They lived in California and had three sons. In a chilling replay of her mother's life, Clare's husband died in a climbing accident in Tennessee in 1947 and she brought up her children alone. In 1999 she was living in northern California. John emigrated to South Africa, where he worked as a water engineer. He married and had five children, and in 1995 his son George II climbed Everest.

⁂

Throughout all this time, the question of what had happened to George and Irvine and whether they reached the summit had been a preoccupation of the mountaineering world. In 1924, their colleagues on the expedition clearly wanted to believe that they had succeeded. Much turned on where they had been when Odell saw them for the last time through the clouds. Odell believed they had been on the Second Step, putting them at 28,280 feet and around 600 yards from the summit. Odell felt there was "a strong probability" that they had reached the top, a judgment shared by many of his Everest colleagues who could not imagine that George would have turned back with the summit within reach. Young was adamant on the point: "Difficult as it would have been for any mountaineer to turn back with the only difficulty past—to Mallory it would have been an impossibility."

For the next nine years the matter rested there. Due to a souring of diplomatic relations with Tibet, and a loss of momentum by the Mount Everest Committee, there was no further expedition until 1933. Then British climbers found an ice ax, identified as Irvine's, below the First Step on the northeast ridge. The best guess was that the ax marked the location of a fall that had killed both men. By then Odell had become less certain where he had seen them, conceding that they may have been on the First Step and not the second. Since that meant George and Irvine were behind any realistic schedule to reach the top, it all seemed to show that they had turned back short of the summit and had died near the site of the ice ax find.

The British made two further attempts to climb Everest via the North Col in 1936 and 1938, on neither occasion reaching as high as any previous attempt. After the Second World War, all further attempts by western climbers from the north were barred by the Chinese occupation of Tibet. In 1951 a British-led reconnaissance party found an alternative approach from the south through Nepal, which took them into the Western Cwm, the great ice valley that George had seen and named in 1921. In 1953, climbing via the southeast ridge that George had believed offered the best chance, a British expedition reached the summit at last. The two triumphant climbers, New Zealander Edmund Hillary and the Indian Sherpa Tenzing Norgay, were equipped with compressed oxygen, which they inhaled at double the 1920s rate, for the 1953 expedition's high-altitude physiologist had argued that the 1920s climbers who used oxygen had probably acquired only enough extra energy to enable them to carry their weighty and cumbersome oxygen sets. Once on the summit, Hillary and Tenzing looked for signs of Mallory and Irvine, but found nothing. In 1960, in the first attempt from the north since 1938, a Chinese team reached the summit via the North Col and the northeast ridge. They took three hours to climb the Second Step and a climber who removed his boots to gain a better grip lost all his toes through frostbite. The British mountaineering establishment was skeptical about the Chinese account of their ascent, which was misleading in some important respects. But the Chinese climbed the mountain from the north again in 1975, this time using a ladder to climb the Second Step and leaving a metal tripod on the summit as proof.

The Chinese ascent in 1975 was significant for another reason. At around 27,000 feet on the north face, the climber Wang Hung-boa came across a body lying on a terrace of rock. The next day he told a fellow climber that the body was that of "an English dead" but before he could be questioned further he was killed in an avalanche on the North Col. It was his news that inspired a search to locate the body, which was generally believed to be Irvine's. In 1986 a team organized by Americans David Breashears, Andrew Harvard, and Tom Holzel was defeated by wind and snow. A young German researcher, Jochem Hemmleb, took up the challenge, and his information was of vital use in steering the 1999 American team, led by Eric Simonson, to their search zone. However it was by an act of intuition that the climber Conrad Anker found George's body since he was essentially looking in the wrong place.

But did the discovery do anything more to resolve the riddle of whether George and Irvine had reached the summit? The searchers' biggest hope had been to find a camera that might just contain a preserved roll of film with the decisive evidence. Strangely, since he liked to take photographs, there was no camera with George's body, and yet the camera he had been using was not found in any of the lower camps. Descendants of Howard Somervell believed that he may have lent George a camera, and since Irvine was a keen photographer himself, that left three cameras to be accounted for, perhaps even a fourth, since Irvine wrote in his diary on June 5 that he had borrowed a movie camera—a "pocket cinema"—from John Noel.

All that was sufficient to inspire a further search for Irvine's body. The current belief was that it was still on the north face, in the location described by Wang. Hemmleb for one believed that whatever happened in the fall that killed George, Irvine had somehow survived long enough to reach the place where Wang found him, before dying of his injuries and/or exhaustion and exposure. Others were skeptical. As to whether they reached the summit, the enigma was more tantalizing than ever. Hemmleb was in a minority who argued that with the benefits of oxygen equipment George and Irvine could have succeeded, citing in his support the tally of oxygen cylinders George had marked on the envelope of the "Stella" letter and the evidence of discarded cylinders found on the northeast ridge. Yet all such theories had to overcome one massive obstacle: could George and Irvine have climbed the Second Step?

At first sight, the answer appeared to be yes. While Odell himself became less sure where he had seen George and Irvine as the years passed, other climbers who scrutinized the northeast ridge from the same location became convinced that he must have seen them on the Second Step—or perhaps even a lesser feature known as the Third Step, even nearer to the final summit pyramid. But this testimony had to be set against the accounts of climbers who had climbed the Second Step. Since the Chinese erected their ladder in 1975, no climbers following that route had tested their abilities on the toughest section of the step, a near-vertical fifteen-foot rock corner. In 1999 Conrad Anker decided to avoid the Chinese ladder and climb the corner as if coming upon it for the first time. With some difficulty he succeeded, and rated the pitch as "5.8," an American rating that was equivalent to Hard Very Severe, the highest level at which George had climbed and far above anything in Irvine's experience. Later Anker revised the grading to 5.10, putting it beyond George's known technical abilities. It would have been further out of his reach given that he and Irvine were cold, exhausted, and physically drained, and facing the psychological demands of trying to find their way on unknown terrain, made more treacherous by the snow squall that had just enveloped them.

For the time being, the question of whether George and Irvine could have succeeded ended at an impasse. On the one hand, it appeared that Odell saw them on the Second Step or even higher; on the other, George could not have climbed the Second Step, let alone the far less experienced and accomplished Irvine. So where were they when Odell saw them? The best alternative was the First Step. But the step's topography did not match Odell's description, and would also have placed George and Irvine impossibly behind schedule. This has led some theorists to reject Odell's sighting entirely, and to argue that they were following the traverse line taken by Norton and Somervell across the face. The discussion of whether they reached the summit thus ran into a set of impossible paradoxes; and until some way could be found of resolving them, the question remained poised. Most researchers believed that they had failed; most also said there was still a chance they had succeeded.

∞

The news that George's body had been found affected his family in different ways. In South Africa, John was disturbed that photographs of the body were published, but Clare was less concerned by that. As to whether he had reached the summit, Clare had a theory that was based on her parents' love for each other. She had grown up believing that George had promised to leave a photograph of Ruth on the summit. Since there was no such photograph in his pockets when his body was found, Clare was certain that he had kept his promise. Yet Ruth herself, as she told Geoffrey Young, felt it did not matter. Whether he got to the top of the mountain or did not, whether he lived or died, made no difference to her admiration for George. "It is his life that I loved and love."

Who Was Stella?

When the three letters found on George Mallory's body were examined, the identity of two of their authors was clear. One was his brother Trafford, writing from London, the other his sister Mary, then living in Colombo. But the third, who signed herself "Your affectionate Stella," remained a mystery. In the subsequent speculation among Everest researchers, two names were prominent. One was Stella Gibbons, author of the semiparodic romantic novel *Cold Comfort Farm*. The other was Stella Mellersh, a distant relative of the family on Ruth's side, and from the generation of Ruth's mother. Neither of these suggestions proved correct.

The biggest clue is to be found in the address at the head of the letter. The notepaper bore a printed address: Forum Club, 6 Grosvenor Place, Hyde Park Corner, SW1. But Stella had crossed this through and replaced it with a different address: 23 Hertford Street, W1. The 1923 British electoral register for the locality shows that two Stellas were living at 23 Hertford Street, an apartment block in Mayfair with some twenty residents. One was named Stella Hay, and she at first seemed the more interesting possibility. She lived at number 23 until 1936, changing her name several times, apparently living there at various times with a sister and possibly a husband. The other was listed as Stella Speyer, and she too used several names, for she appeared later as Stella Cobden-Sanderson, before departing from Hertford Street around the end of 1927.

George's own letters confirm that this was the Stella in question. In a letter to Ruth from New York during his lecture tour in 1923, he described how "Mrs. Cobden-Sanderson" was in a crowd of friends who attended his lecture and afterwards took him to a nearby hotel to eat ice cream. In a second New York letter to Ruth, George described having tea with her, adding that she was "Ferdy Speyer's deserted little wife and a very nice little lady she is." George's references to Stella in fact provide glimpses of a life of considerable drama. Stella, who was born in May 1886, was the daughter of the book designer and binder Thomas Cobden-Sanderson, cofounder of the celebrated Doves Bindery in Hammersmith, west London, and a key figure in the Arts and Crafts Movement. Her mother Annie was a prominent political radical and suffragette, who was given a six-month prison sentence in 1906 after being arrested at a demonstration at the House of Commons and refusing to pay the consequent £10 ($48.00) fine.

There was one connection to the Mallory family through Thackeray Turner and the Society for the Protection of Ancient Buildings, for Thomas Cobden-Sanderson was a member of the society's committee at the time when Turner was its secretary. Another was through climbing. In 1910 Stella married Ferdinand Speyer, an industrial chemist, aged twenty-four, from a wealthy banking family who were sponsors of music and the arts. Ferdy, as he was known, had been at Eton and was part of Geoffrey Winthrop Young's circle. He attended the Pen y Pass parties and appeared in a group photograph with George and Ruth in 1919. But the marriage between him and Stella was a turbulent affair. Stella had a brother, Richard, who married in 1912. Ferdy fell in love with Richard's wife, Dorothea, and on the same day in 1921 both marriages ended in divorce.

Ferdy subsequently married Dorothea, and Richard also married for a second time. But Stella never remarried. She was fond of traveling, and in 1907 and 1908 had spent nine months in the United States, where her father delivered a series of lectures on bookbinding, while her mother talked about the suffragettes. Stella acquired friends in New York, Washington, and Massachusetts and may have had additional motivation for returning to New York in early 1923, as her father had just died and her former husband Ferdy was about to remarry. Her Everest letter showed that she had clearly maintained her friendship with George, and described lunching the previous day with "Mrs. Craies," who with her daughter Cissie was another of the Mallorys' family friends. Mrs. Craies was partially deaf, and Stella described how she had to bellow into the hearing tube she used. Much later, George's daughter Clare remembered both Mrs. Craies and her daughter. Clare recalled the "trumpet hearing aid" Mrs. Craies used and described how Cissie Craies made "beautiful embroidered shawls." When Vi Meakin finally left her post as nursemaid to the Mallory family, she went to live with Cissie as her companion and helped with her embroidery.

The notepaper Stella used provides a further link with the Mallorys' climbing world. The Forum Club at Grosvenor Place was a women's club near Hyde Park Corner—the address Stella had crossed out—and shared premises with the Ladies

Alpine Club. (Both were branches of the Women's Lyceum Club.) Stella's mother Annie was a member of the Forum, and the other two often lunched there. It was probably at the Forum Club that she and Mrs. Craies had their lunch, Stella borrowing a sheet or two of its notepaper for her letter to George. Later that year, Stella became a buyer for the Peter Jones department store on Oxford Street. She remained with the company for ten years, winning praise for her aesthetic judgments and her business qualities, before going to live in the south of France. She eventually returned to live in Surrey, moving into a nursing home in Haslemere where she died in 1979, at age ninety-two. In her later years she talked of having a cache of letters from George, and there were tales that she had sold them to help pay for her upkeep, but none have ever surfaced.

The Survivors

Geoffrey Winthrop Young became a consultant to the Rockefeller Foundation in 1925 and a reader in education at London University in 1932. He carried on climbing with his artificial leg, his summits including the Matterhorn and the Zinal Rothorn, before finally giving up at the age of fifty-nine. He was president of the Alpine Club from 1941 to 1944 and was the prime mover behind the founding of the British Mountaineering Council in 1944. He died at eighty-two in 1958. Apart from his educational work, **David Pye** was an important theorist in the development of the internal combustion engine, and research director for the Royal Air Force during much of the Second World War. He became president of the Institution of Mechanical Engineers in 1952 and died, aged seventy-three, in 1960. Pye's *George Mallory*, published in 1927, remains a significant biographical work. **Mary Anne O'Malley**'s memoir of George provided much of the basis of the Pye biography. Her first novel, *Peking Picnic*, was published in 1932 under the pseudonym Ann Bridge. Like many of her books, it drew heavily on her experiences as a diplomat's wife. Her subsequent novels included *The Ginger Griffin*, *Enchanter's Nightshade*, and *Illyrian Spring*, which was also used as a handbook by visitors to Dalmatia. She died in 1974, aged eighty-six.

James **Strachey** remained a committed radical, a Fabian, campaigner for women's suffrage, and conscientious objector during the First World War. He became a Freudian psychoanalyst and with his wife, Alix, whom he married in 1920, was the first English translator of Freud's writings. He died aged eighty in 1967. **Lytton Strachey**'s pioneering *Eminent Victorians*, which redefined the nature of biography, appeared in 1918, and he wrote five further biographical studies, the most celebrated being *Queen Victoria* (1921) and *Elizabeth and Essex*

(1928). The influence of the School of Friendship and his brother's Freudian studies showed in the psychoanalytical insights he brought to his work. Although seemingly the most committed bachelor in his circle, he formed a close relationship with the painter Dora Carrington, who nursed him when he was stricken with fatal stomach cancer. He died at fifty-two in 1932. **Geoffrey Keynes**, who married in 1917, became an eminent physician and surgeon at St. Bartholomew's Hospital, London, and treated Ruth during her last illness in 1942. He was a pioneer of blood transfusion and a founder of the British Blood Transfusion Service, which almost uniquely among similar services relies on free donations of blood. He was later a writer, editor, and bibliographer, dying in 1982 at the age of ninety-five. **Maynard Keynes** was a British representative at the 1919 Versailles peace conference, although he resigned in protest at the onerous reparations and frontiers imposed on Germany. He developed the economic theories bearing his name that formed one of the cornerstones of liberal western economic policies. He played a leading role in the Bretton Wood conferences of 1944 that led to the formation of the International Monetary Fund. After marrying the ballet dancer Lydia Lopokova in 1925 he became involved in ballet and the visual arts. He died in 1946 at the age of sixty-three. **Duncan Grant** was considered one of Britain's leading artists between the wars, receiving commissions for projects such as Lincoln Cathedral and the *Queen Mary*. He continued his relationships with both men and women, and had a daughter, Angelica, by Vanessa Bell. He died at ninety-three in 1978.

Of the most significant Everest figures in George's life, **Guy Bullock**, his partner in 1921, continued his career in the diplomatic service. He was Britain's Resident Minister in Ecuador in 1938, worked in the prisoners of war department at the Foreign Office during the Second World War, and retired from his final post at Brazzaville in the then French Congo in 1947. He died aged sixty-nine in 1956. Having resolved to become a medical missionary, **Howard Somervell** spent the rest of his working life as a surgeon in India, and was an international authority on duodenal ulcers. He was an accomplished painter and later president of the Alpine Club. He died aged eighty-five in 1975. **George Finch** continued to work as a chemistry researcher, lecturer and consultant. He gave up climbing after three fellow members of a climbing party were killed in the Alps in 1931 and took up sailing instead. He was a president of the Alpine Club and died at eighty-two in 1970. **Edward Norton** remained a professional soldier, serving in India and rising to become acting military-governor of Hong Kong. He died aged seventy in 1954. **Noel Odell** remained a geologist for his working life, first as a consultant, then as a visiting professor at universities around the world. He completed his academic career as an honorary professor at

Clare College, Cambridge. In 1936 he climbed Nanda Devi, the highest mountain climbed to that date, and took part in the unsuccessful Everest attempt of 1938. He died in 1987 at the age of ninety-six.

George's parents, **Herbert** and **Annie**, moved from Birkenhead to Dodleston, near Chester, where Herbert was the rector. When Herbert retired, he and Annie lived in a hotel in Chester, where he continued to work as an honorary canon at Chester Cathedral. Later he and Annie moved into lodgings. Herbert died in 1943, Annie in 1946. Both George's sisters lived well into old age, **Mary** dying at ninety-eight, **Avie** at 101. George's brother, **Trafford,** rose through the Royal Air Force, taking command of one of the two main fighter groups during the Battle of Britain in 1940, then heading the RAF's Fighter Command. In November 1944 he was on his way to a new posting in the Far East when his plane crashed in the French Alps and he and his wife Doris were killed. Like his brother George, he is commemorated at St. Wilfrid's church in Mobberley.

Climbing Grades

In 1897, O. G. Jones devised a system of classifications by which climbers could judge the standard of a route against their own level of personal attainment. There were four classifications, or grades, in all: easy, moderate, difficult, and exceptionally severe. Later the list expanded to seven: Easy, Moderate, Difficult, Very Difficult, Severe, Very Severe, and Extremely Severe. The last grade was used alongside Exceptionally Severe for a time, then replaced it, and was later shortened to Extreme. There were also differentiations within each grade such as "Hard Very Severe," usually rendered by abbreviations such as "HVS." As rock climbing standards advanced, the original classifications were themselves downgraded: routes first described as Exceptionally Severe were relegated to anywhere from Very Difficult to Very Severe. The modern Extreme grade acquired its own numerical subdivisions, running from E1 to E9 or even higher. The fact remains that although George Mallory was not the leading technical climber of his day, he was among a group of pioneers pushing climbing to new and more demanding standards.

Bibliography and Sources

Abraham, Ashley. *Rock climbing in Skye*. Longmans, 1908.

Abraham, George. *British Mountain Climbs*. Mills and Boon, 1909.

———. *The Complete Mountaineer*. Methuen, 1907.

———. *Modern Mountaineering*. Methuen, 1933.

Abraham, George, and Ashley Abraham. *Rock Climbing in North Wales*. G. P. Abraham, 1906.

Anker, Conrad, and David Roberts. *The Lost Explorer*. Simon and Schuster, 1999.

Breashears, David, and Audrey Salkeld. *Last Climb*. National Geographic, 1999.

Bridge, Ann. *Facts and Fictions*. Chatto & Windus, 1968.

———. *Peking Picnic*. Triad Granada, 1932.

———. *Portrait of My Mother*. Chatto & Windus, 1955.

Bruce, C. G. et al. *The Assault on Mount Everest 1922*. Edward Arnold, 1923.

Carr, Herbert. *The Irvine Diaries*. Gastons-West Col Publications, 1979.

———. *The Mountains of Snowdonia*. Bodley Head, 1925.

Clark, Ronald, and Edward Pyatt. *Mountaineering in Britain*. Phoenix House, 1957.

Cleare, John. *Mountains*. Macmillan, 1975.

Coates, Nigel. *Godalming: A Pictorial History*. Phillimore.

Finch, George I. *The Making of a Mountaineer*. Arrowsmith, 1924.

Firstbrook, Peter. *Lost on Everest*. BBC, 1999.

Fletcher, Frank. *After Many Days*. Hale, 1937.

Franklin, Colin. *The Private Presses*. Studio Vista, 1969.

French, Patrick. *Younghusband*. Flamingo, 1994.

Garnett, Angelica. *Deceived with Kindness*. Pimlico, 1984.

Gillman, Peter, ed. *Everest: The Best Writing and Pictures*. Little, Brown, 1993.

Graves, Robert. *Goodbye to All That*. Cape, 1929.

Green, Dudley. *Mallory of Everest*. Faust, 1990.

Hale, Keith, ed. *Friends and Apostles: The Correspondence of Rupert Brooke and James Strachey 1905–1914*. Yale University Press, 1998.

Hankinson, Alan. *Geoffrey Winthrop Young*. Hodder and Stoughton, 1995.

Haskett, Smith, W. P. *Climbing in the British Isles*. Volume 1, England. Longmans, Green, 1894.

Hassall, Christopher. *Rupert Brooke: A Biography*. Faber and Faber, 1972.

———. *Edward Marsh*. Longmans, Green, 1959.

Hemmleb, Jochen, Larry Johnson, and Eric Simonson. *Ghosts of Everest*. The Mountaineers Books, 1999.

Holroyd, Michael. *Lytton Strachey*. Vintage, 1995.

Holroyd, Michael, ed. *Lytton Strachey by Himself*. Vintage, 1971.

Holzel, Tom, and Audrey Salkeld. *The Mystery of Mallory and Irvine*. Pimlico, 1999.

Houston, Charles. *Going Higher*. The Mountaineers, 1998.

Howard-Bury, George. *Mountains of Heaven*. Hodder and Stoughton, 1990.

Howard-Bury, Charles, and George Mallory. *Everest Reconnaissance*. Hodder and Stoughton, 1922.

Irving, R. L. G. *A History of British Mountaineering*. Batsford, 1955.

———. *The Romance of Mountaineering*. Dent, 1935.

———. *Ten Great Mountains*. Dent, 1940.

Janaway, John. *Godalming: A Short History*. Ammonite Books.

Jones, Nigel. *Rupert Brooke*. Richard Cohen Books, 1999.

Jones, O. G. *Rock Climbing in the English Lake District*. G. P. Abraham, 1900.

Keegan, John. *The First World War*. Hutchinson, 1998.

Keynes, Geoffrey. *The Gates of Memory*. Clarendon Press, 1981.

Mallory, George. *Boswell the Biographer*. Smith, Elder, 1912.

Marsh, Edward. *A Number of People*. Heinemann, 1939.

Masters, Brian. *The Life of E. F. Benson*. Chatto & Windus, 1991.

McLewin, Will. *In Monte Viso's Horizon*. Ernest Press, 1991.

Mobberley Preservation Society. *Mobberley Reflections*. 1981.

Mobberley Women's Institute. *A History of Mobberley Village*. John Sherratt and Son, 1952.

Morris, John. *Hired to Kill*. Hart-Davis, 1960.

Murray, W. H. *The Story of Everest*. Dutton, 1953.

Neate, Jill. *Mountaineering Literature*. Cicerone Press, 1978.

Noel, John. *Through Tibet to Everest*. Hodder and Stoughton, 1989.

Norton, Edward et al. *The Fight for Everest: 1924*. Edward Arnold, 1925.

Pimlott, Ben. *Hugh Dalton*. Macmillan, 1985.

Pyatt, Edward, and Wilfrid Noyce. *British Crags and Climbers*. Dennis Dobson, 1952.

Pye, David. *George Leigh Mallory*. Oxford University Press, 1927.

Reynolds, Kev. *Mountains of Europe*. Oxford University Press, 1990.

Robertson, David. *George Mallory*. Faber and Faber, 1969.

————. *Mallory's Climbs before Everest*. Monograph, 1986.

Roche, Paul. *With Duncan Grant in Southern Turkey*. Honeyglen, 1982.

Sabben-Clare, James. *Winchester College*. P. and G. Wells, 1981.

Salkeld, Audrey, and John Boyle. *Climbing Mount Everest: The Bibliography*. Sixways, 1993.

Shone, Richard. *The Art of Bloomsbury*. Tate Gallery, 1999.

————. *Bloomsbury Portraits*. Phaidon, 1993.

Skidelsky, Robert. *Maynard Keynes—Volume 1, 1883–1920*. Macmillan, 1983.

Smith, J. R. *Everest, the Man and the Mountain*. Whittles, 1999.

Smythe, F. S. *Camp Six*. Hodder and Stoughton, 1937.

Somervell, T. Howard. *After Everest*. Hodder and Stoughton, 1936.

Spalding, Frances. *The Bloomsbury Group*. National Portrait Gallery, 1997.

————. *Roger Fry: Art and Life*. Granada, 1980.

————. *Duncan Grant: A Biography*. Pimlico, 1998.

Strouse, Norman. *C-S, the Master Craftsman*. Adagio Press, 1969.

Tidcombe, Marianne. *The Bookbindings of T. J. Cobden-Sanderson*. British Library, 1984.

————. *The Doves Bindery*. British Library, 1991.

Unsworth, Walt. *Everest*. The Mountaineers, 2000.

————. *Encyclopaedia of Mountaineering*. Hodder and Stoughton, 1992.

————. *Hold the Heights*. Hodder and Stoughton, 1993.

West, John. *High Time: The History of High-altitude Physiology and Medicine*. Oxford University Press, 1995.

Woolaston, A. F. R. *Letters and Diaries*. Cambridge University Press, 1933.

Young, Geoffrey Winthrop, ed. *Mountaincraft*. Methuen, 1920.

————. *Mountains with a Difference*. Eyre and Spottiswoode, 1951.

————. *On High Hills*. Methuen, 1927.

Young, Geoffrey Winthrop, Geoffrey Sutton, and Wilfrid Noyce. *Snowdon Biography*. Dent, 1957.

Younghusband, Francis. *The Epic of Mount Everest*. Edward Arnold, 1926.

————. *Everest the Challenge*. Nelson, 1936.

The principal journals we used were the *Alpine Journal*, the *Climbers' Club Journal and Bulletin*, and the *Scottish Mountaineering Club Journal*, all of them primary sources of invaluable information. George Mallory wrote four articles for these journals before Everest. "The Mountaineer as Artist" (CCJ 13, March 1914); "Mont Blanc from the Col du Géant by the Eastern Buttress of Mont Maudit" (AJ 32, September 1918); "Our 1919 Journey" (AJ 33, November 1920); "Geoffrey Winthrop Young on Mountain Craft" (CCJ 14, December 1920). Two more of his articles appeared during the Everest years: "Mount Everest: The Reconnaissance" (AJ 34, May 1922, also in *Geographical Journal* 59, February 1922) and "The Second Mount Everest Expedition (AJ 34, November 1922, also in GJ 60, December 1922). These journals also contain articles about climbs with Mallory in Britain and the Alps by Karl Blodig, R. L. G. Irving, Bill McLean, Harold Porter, David Pye, Harry Tyndale, and Geoffrey Winthrop Young. The *Alpine Journal* contains articles about the three Everest expeditions by Guy Bullock, Percy Farrar, George Finch, Richard Hingston, Arthur Hinks, Charles Howard-Bury, John Noel, Edward Norton, Noel Odell, and Percy Unna.

We drew on a range of guidebooks in various editions. Apart from those listed in the bibliography, we particularly used: the Climbers' Club guidebooks for North Wales; the Fell and Rock Climbing Club guidebooks for the Lake District; and the Scottish Mountaineering Club guides to Skye and the Islands of Scotland. For the Alps, we used the two definitive sets: *GMH Guide Vallot—La Chaine de Mont Blanc* (Devies, Henry, and Lagarde) in three volumes; and the SMC *Guide des Alpes Valaisannes* (Kurz) in four volumes. We also used the Conway and Coolidge *Climbers' Guides to the Pennine Alps* (two volumes, 1890 and 1891) and *To the Bernese Oberland* (four volumes, 1902 and 1904).

We used the following libraries and archives. (Where libraries and other collections have granted us specific permission to quote from documents, we have listed them again and expressed our thanks in the Acknowledgements section.)

The Alpine Club, for minutes of the Mount Everest Committee and other papers, a copy of Geoffrey Young's Pen y Pass diary, its collection of contemporary newspaper reports on mountaineering events, its picture library, and of course for its unrivaled collection of mountaineering books and journals. The library at the Royal Geographical Society, for the papers and records referring to the work of the members and officials of the Mount Everest Committee in organizing and managing the three 1920s expeditions and their aftermath, including letters by George Mallory, and for its photographic library. The British Library, for its books and for its files of letters by Duncan Grant, James Strachey, Lytton Strachey, Maynard Keynes, and George Mallory, and the files pertaining to the work of the Alpine Club secretary, T. S. Blakeney. Cambridge University Library for files relating to Mallory's work for the Examination and Lectures Syndicate and for Charles Sayle's diary. The library at Magdalene College, Cambridge, which holds letters written between George and Ruth Mallory from 1914 to 1919; Mallory's letters to Ruth from 1921 to 1924, and one written by Ruth; and letters and other documents concerning Mallory's time at the college.

The Internet was an invaluable source for reports on the 1999 U.S. expedition and the continuing debate over whether George Mallory and Sandy Irvine reached the summit: see, especially, *mountainzone.com, everestnews.com,* and, for the views of Tom Holzel, *velocitypress.20m.com* or *tholzel@aol.com.* Jochen Hemmleb can be contacted via Hoffmann & Campe, Harvestehuder Weg 42, 20149 Hamburg, Germany.

We conducted local research at Godalming library and museum, Godalming, Surrey; the Surrey county archives in Guildford; the Cheshire county archives at Chester; Birkenhead public library; Chesterfield public library; Altrincham library, which contains Stephen Murray's manuscript *Mobberley Records* (1946–48); the Trafford Metropolitan Borough local studies center at Sale; the Gwynedd County Archives at Caernarvon for the Climbers' Club archive. We gratefully acknowledge the help provided by the staff at all of these libraries.

Finally and most importantly, the descendants and relatives of George and Ruth Mallory provided invaluable information drawing on personal reminiscences and on written and documented accounts of family history.

Photo Credits

S1: Section 1 (between pages 64 and 65)
S2: Section 2 (between pages 128 and 129)
S3: Section 3 (between pages 192 and 193)
t: top   b: bottom   l: left   r: right

Mollie and Sally Dalglish: S1 1, 3t, 4b, 5b, 6t
Angela Gresham-Cooke: S1 2t, 2b
Stella Longridge: S1 3b
Salkeld Collection: S1 4t, S2 1, S3 5t, 7t
Clare Millikan and family: S1 5t, S2 1, 3t, 4t, 4b, 6br, 7
Geoffrey Winthrop Young/Alpine Club: S1 6b, 7b
R. G. Chew/Marcia Newbolt: S1 7t
National Portrait Gallery, London: S1 8tl
Michael Holroyd: S1 8tr
Henrietta Garnett/Tate Gallery: S1 8b
Paul Morgan: S2 3b
Marianne Nevel: S2 5t, 6bl
David Robertson/H. E. L. Porter: S2 5b
Peter Gillman: S2 8t, 8b
Royal Geographical Society: S3 1t (photo by A. F. R. Wollaston), 1b (photo by A. F. R. Wollaston), 2b (photo by John Noel), 3t (photo by George Mallory), 3b (photo by Howard Somervell), 6t (photo by Bentley Beetham)
Alpine Club: S3 4t
Julie Summers: S3 4b
John Noel Photographic Collection: S3 2t, 5b, 8b
Noel Odell/Peter Odell: S3 6b, 8t
Somervell Collection: S3 7b

Index

THE MOUNTAINEERS, founded in 1906, is a nonprofit outdoor activity and conservation club, whose mission is "to explore, study, preserve, and enjoy the natural beauty of the outdoors . . . . " Based in Seattle, Washington, the club is now the third-largest such organization in the United States, with 15,000 members and five branches throughout Washington State.

The Mountaineers sponsors both classes and year-round outdoor activities in the Pacific Northwest, which include hiking, mountain climbing, ski-touring, snowshoeing, bicycling, camping, kayaking and canoeing, nature study, sailing, and adventure travel. The club's conservation division supports environmental causes through educational activities, sponsoring legislation, and presenting informational programs. All club activities are led by skilled, experienced volunteers, who are dedicated to promoting safe and responsible enjoyment and preservation of the outdoors.

If you would like to participate in these organized outdoor activities or the club's programs, consider a membership in The Mountaineers. For information and an application, write or call The Mountaineers, Club Headquarters, 300 Third Avenue West, Seattle, WA 98119; 206-284-6310.

The Mountaineers Books, an active, nonprofit publishing program of the club, produces guidebooks, instructional texts, historical works, natural history guides, and works on environmental conservation. All books produced by The Mountaineers Books fulfill the club's mission.

Send or call for our catalog of more than 450 outdoor titles:

The Mountaineers Books
1001 SW Klickitat Way, Suite 201
Seattle, WA 98134
800-553-4453
mbooks@mountaineers.org
www.mountaineersbooks.org